The purpose of this book is to show how reason can unite people with one another through the sharing of life's universal or intrinsic values. The work sets forth values and perspectives that cross over all ethnic, racial, cultural and religious boundary lines.

The Christian views set forth reflect the background and commitment of the authors but do not imply the sort of doctrinal rigidity that would alienate others. Rather, their ecumenical hope is that all world religions, peoples, and seekers might find new strength and unity in an intelligent, informed affirmation of God's loving Care.

To Dr. Nibley
with the respect and
best wishes of

Dale Hazelett

Dec. 1990

# Benevolent Living

# Books by Dean Turner

*Lonely God, Lonely Man*

*The Autonomous Man*

*Krinkle Nose*

*The Einstein Myth and the Ives Papers* (co-editor)

*Classroom in Crisis:*
  *Parents' Rights in the Schools* (co-author)

*Commitment to Care*

*Escape from God: The Use of Religion and*
  *Philosophy to Evade Responsibility*

# Benevolent Living

*Tracing the Roots of Motivation to God*

### Richard Hazelett

### Dean Turner

With a Foreword and Postscript by
### Charles Hartshorne

Hope Publishing House
Southern California Ecumenical Council
Pasadena
1990

Hope Publishing House
—a program unit of the
Southern California Ecumenical Council
696 South Madison Avenue
P.O. Box 60008
Pasadena, California 91116, U.S.A.
  Fax orders to: 818-792-2121
  Telephone Visa or MasterCard
    orders to: 800-326-2671

The Acknowledgments section of this volume contains copyright and trademark notices from publishers
and others granting permission to reprint material
herein. For legal purposes, the Acknowledgments
section constitutes a continuation of this page.

Printed in the United States of America

*Library of Congress Cataloging in Publication Data*

Hazelett, Richard

Benevolent living: tracing the roots of motivation
to God/ by Richard Hazelett and Dean Turner;
foreword and postscript by Charles Hartshorne.
xvi + 432 p. 23 cm.
Bibliography: p.
Includes index.

ISBN 0-932727-32-8 (alk. paper) : $19.95. —

BJ47 .H36 1990
241—dc20                                          89-11197
                                                    CIP

The paper of this book will not turn yellow or
disintegrate. It is printed on acid-free (alkaline-
buffered) paper that should last for centuries. ∞

In memory of
GABRIELLE FISCHER

May we presume to say that, at thy birth,
New joy was sprung in heaven, as well as on the earth?

*John Dryden*, "Ode"

Give me truths:
For I am weary of the surfaces,
and die of inanition.

Ralph Waldo Emerson, "Blight"

Military alliances, balances of power, leagues of nations, all in turn failed, leaving the only path to be by way of the crucible of war. The utter destructiveness of war now blocks out this alternative. We have had our last chance. If we will not devise some greater and more equitable system, our Armageddon will be at our door. The problem basically is theological and involves a spiritual recrudescence, an improvement of human character that will synchronize with our almost matchless advances in science, art, literature and all material and cultural developments of the past two thousand years. It must be of the spirit if we are to save the flesh.

*General Douglas MacArthur*

# Contents

ELLIPSES in quotations have been omitted in the interest of ease in reading. Assurance is given that meanings have not been altered by selective quotation.

The reader may assume that the block quotations are all congenial to the authors' point of view.

Sexist language has been altered in some translated quotations. Yet, for the sake of smooth reading, masculine pronouns are often used herein to refer to God. Such usage should not be construed as attributing gender to God.

# Foreword
## by Charles Hartshorne

IN THE LITERATURE of philosophy known to me, there is nothing much like this book. It is by two authors, neither of whose names, I think, will be familiar to very many of those who ought to read it.

One of the authors, Hazelett, is an engineer (clearly successful and distinguished as such) whose life-long avocation has been philosophy. The other, Turner, holds the Ph.D. degree and is the author of publications in the philosophy of religion, morality, and science. He is well known in his teaching field, which is philosophy of education. That I know both of them is simply because I had them as students in classes of mine twenty-five years ago. They were mature, articulate, obviously and keenly interested students, such as one does not forget. They have kept in touch with me since that time. They have now produced a remarkable work. It is, among other things, a critique — sharp, hard-hitting, well documented, and indeed one might truly say learned — of some of the chief tendencies in recent academic philosophy.

The book is an eloquent defense of belief in God, primarily as a practical necessity for human living on a high ethical level. "Religion is the morale in morality" is one of their numerous quotations. Broadly speaking, the central thesis is one that any number of liberal philosophers of religion have espoused, especially since Kant's second *Critique.* But it is here vigorously supported in a great variety of ways. The point is not that atheists cannot in some cases live by high ideals, but that not only are these ideals inherited from theistic religions but they also make more rational sense and have stronger survival power when given appropriate theistic formulation. Peirce, Whitehead, Bergson took this position, and I began to take it before I knew any of these writers.

Hazelett and Turner are not fundamentalists, and they claim no infallibility, but they give powerful expression to the proposition that secular humanism, meaning atheistic humanism, is a danger to the good life. They cite a charge that the vast genocide in Cambodia and Laos was largely planned by disciples of Sartre. I do think it is high time for us all to begin to realize that the misdeeds of fanatic believers in some human message about God (for instance the Koran) — the terrible religious wars, inquisitions, crusades —are in the process of being equalled and surpassed by the non-believers in God. A frightful quotation from Stalin is one example. If religion failed, secular humanism is, so far, an at least equally dismal non-success. Perhaps the real hope must now be, as Whitehead said it was, in a nobler conception of God. Religious tyrants believed in tyrant ideas of deity; it does not follow that a cosmic tyrant rigidly controlling all for their own good is the most appropriate way to conceive the One who should be worshipped —meaning by worship complete devotion, such as is implied in the commandment to love God with all one's being. It is not genuinely possible to do this with the classical concept of an unmoved mover moving all other things. Free beings, such as we are, cannot want to be wholly determined by any other entity, no matter what name is given this entity. Moreover, to love unreservedly one who is totally unmoved by our or any creature's weal or woe is a monstrous psychological absurdity. Rabbi Abraham Heschel said it before any Christian: "God is the most [and best] moved mover."

Hazelett and Turner compliment me on my practice of looking for truth in *every* great philosopher, not just in my special favorites. I can return the compliment. They outdo me in this practice in many cases. I have underestimated the relevance of a number of writers including Pierre Duhem, Fr. Jaki and Brand Blanshard (one of whose major contentions I claim to have refuted). I have done better in acknowledging the positive values in Jonathan Edwards' praise of natural and true virtue and beauty in reality, but here they have gone still further. Whitehead, and to some extent Peirce, tried to find definite truths in each great philosopher. I adopt this systematically. In this light I see: the inseparability of freedom and chance as admitted by Epicurus and (less clearly) by Aristotle; Plato's "self-motion" of the psychical, and doctrine of World Soul as knowing and caring for its bodily members; Aristotle's five ontological modal laws; Leibniz's discovery of spiritual atomism; Hegel's doctrines that metaphysical truth is a unity of contraries and that subjectivity overlaps objectivity. My way of connecting supreme freedom, knowledge, and love in every creature is in a formal sense an extension of the medieval doctrine of "transcendentals" and "categories," the latter applying to all creatures and the former to God and creatures. Some Renaissance thinkers anticipated this extension, for example Campanella. The entire history of philosophy, as Hegel claimed, can be made into an argument for metaphysical truth. The extent to which this can now be done seems extremely inadequately known to deconstructionalists, whose vague insinuations about the history of philosophy I find less impressive than do some of my colleagues, one of them in my department (Louis Mackey, who gives a useful account of the relevance of the new fashion in France to theology).

The reader will perhaps not be surprised if I say that my enthusiasm for this book, though strong, is not unqualified. I accept the authors' gracious invitation to express some of my critical reflections on their ideas in the Postscript. Nonetheless, this book deserves attention by all those concerned intellectually with ethics or philosophy of religion, no matter what their convictions, provided they accept the principle proposed by Popper, that to be rational is to be *open* to criticism by others. None of us is divinely endowed with infallible wisdom or able to make an infallible choice as to which, if any, of the traditionally revered religious documents (Bible, Old or New Testament, Koran, Bhagavad-Gita) is to be relied upon to furnish literally true answers to ethical or religious questions. This book is almost an encyclopedia of considerations relevant to ethics or religion in this nonfundamentalist sense. In this

book there is Utilitarian, Christian, and theistic bias, but it is completely acknowledged as such. With extraordinary fairness and patience the authors set forth at least many of the considerations relevant to their position, whether pro or con. If one of them, Hazelett,
is an outsider, or amateur in academic philosophy, both of them
really do what many academics just claim to do. By their definite
commitments and arguments, they really expose themselves to
criticism. They take voices from many quarters into account. They
show magnificently what lesser known thinkers can do to force in-
siders to live up to their pretensions as seekers of the truth as collectively pursued. Their voices, too, should be heard.

A distinctive feature of the work is the use of newspaper cartoons
to give humorous illustrations for ethical or religious points. Thus,
to illustrate the relativity of situational evaluations, a member of
a group of vultures enjoying a bloated rhino carcass says to another,
"These are the best of times." To illustrate the absurdity of nationalism as a substitute for religion, one is shown two stone tablets
and a huge pile of similar tablets, with the caption: "These [the two
tablets] are the Commandments, and those over there [the pile] are
the government guidelines that go with them."

Finally, the book has the most careful and many-sided analysis
of happiness that I can recall reading. Who, I wonder, can be so
wise, or so foolish, as to feel no need to learn more on this subject?

*The University of Texas at Austin* *

---

* *A volume of the Library of Living Philosophers in honor of Hartshorne is to be
published by Open Court Publishing Co. in 1991.* —R.H.

# Benevolent Living

Tracing the Roots of Motivation to God

# 1

# *The Motivation of Righteous Conduct*

We are warned not to waste our time, but we are brought up to waste our lives.

*Eric Hoffer*

IN OUR TIME, knowledge has become so extensive and complex that most people are too intimidated to think for themselves. Only on narrow technical or day-to-day matters do most people feel free to form their own judgments. Many scholars suppose that, in the face of so much new knowledge, common folk cannot hope to acquire much deep understanding. An elitism is widely practiced and accepted in various disciplines. Some of the cognoscenti feel that students are wasting their time unless they specialize in a single area, implying that the effort to gain independent understanding through original thinking is just not practical. "Just leave it to us, trust us," they say in effect.[1] This is not an attitude that welcomes cultural pluralism or new ideas, nor does it welcome re-analysis of old ideas or sources of knowledge.

The basic concern of ethics is to determine with the aid of reason the kind of life one should live. By ethical principles, a person can choose to further the ends of action that are defined as good or right or wise, as well as reasonable.[2] Yet ethics should not place life in a straitjacket of casuistry. Ethics has been looked to as a justification for constructive action. What it should do is to provide motivation for widespread benevolent behavior. Though sound principles are simple, the proofs of them are not simple.

Should ethical knowledge have some foundation beyond that of prevailing authority? Is ethics a suitable field in which to debate the status quo? Is it possible that independent thought can be stimulated in traditional fields such as ethics? Or is there a point beyond which it is futile to proceed? This book develops auspicious answers to these questions. The discipline of ethics should ideally be a part of science, and science properly examines and questions its own foundations and premises whenever reason requires. Understandably, most people do not readily expose their dearly held beliefs to disinterested, threatening dissection.

The word "ethics" is apt to call to mind ancient prohibitions and duties. Many people in our permissive times view ethics as merely a series of tiresome negative imperatives or outworn limitations on freedom. For a good part of the populace in the Western world, it is enough to subscribe to a nonracist, nonsexist, non-chauvinist policy and promote no-smoking laws, no nuclear weapons, and peace at any price. Thereby other moral matters may be conveniently left to whim and chance if a person so wishes, and many do.

In ancient Greece, Socrates philosophized that "The unexamined life is not worth living."[3] However, a tragic fact is that the examined life has often proven not worth living either. Many headstrong seekers after truth have come to regret their zeal, for their study of philosophy has led to a swamp wherein dreams fade and ambitions are lost. Students are apt to conclude that no one has adequately answered the philosopher-skeptics who question and devalue the guideposts and ideals which, in the past, have provided the direction for living. The strength to resist temptation becomes lost, along with the sense of what is required to keep a society functioning. The lapses of philosophers then become the lapses of multitudes.

Historically, philosophy has had a constructive side. Philosophers are the itinerant workers of the intellectual world. Philosophical modes of thought were used as the foundations of modern astronomy, physics, and chemistry. These disciplines became separated from philosophy only after several centuries during which they were known under the name of natural philosophy. More lately, some philosophers have explored the philosophical presuppositions of the founders of modern natural science. Some are persuaded that the foundations of ethics are inextricably linked with tenets of traditional world religions. Others are persuaded of just the opposite, that ethics properly rests only on non-religious philosophy.

Religious beliefs usually rest upon a basis of unquestioned authority — for instance, the authority assigned to historical events too remote to be questioned cogently. In the West, there have always been atheists and agnostics, even in the high Middle Ages, though doubters did not then much publicize their doubts. The flowering of natural science brought into question basic tenets of Christianity, Judaism, and Islam. In some eighteenth century intellectual circles it became fashionable to attack theistic religion. Scottish philosopher David Hume provided a classic attack, as had Sophist philosophers in ancient Greece. Modern philosophers have called into serious question the authority of scriptures and churches. Most philosophers now want nothing to do with religion except to attack it. One professor even claims that any attempt to justify or reform any of the Judeo-Christian religious tradition is "an exercise in polishing the brass on the Titanic."[4]

When one element of an authoritarian structure of belief is eliminated or badly eroded, as has happened in consequence of advances in natural science, the shock renders the whole structure fragile. Religious organizations may try to save themselves by imposing even more authority. This move impresses some but not others. In a near vacuum of ethical ideals, moral and ethical relativism thrives. Ethical relativism is the increasingly popular position that values have no objective existence. From this error, it follows that one system of morals or rules is as good as another and that there is no rational way to choose among them.

It is easy to show that ethical relativism is irrational, for as soon as one affirms it, self-contradiction results. For example, a person who follows a path of total tolerance is by necessity intolerant of at least one thing, namely, intolerance.[5] Hence, moral relativism cannot be consistently stated. The moral relativist lacks effective means to question the ethics of a Hitler or a Stalin or even to express indignation. This is an important fact of which college students are likely to be left unaware.

Meanwhile, religious professionals have shunned philosophy for lack of the patience or boldness to pursue or innovate. Consequently, the religious needs of people who respect religion but who like to think for themselves are not met by either philosophers or clergy. In frustration, a lay person may well muse that religion and philosophy are both too important to be left to the respective professions as presently constituted.

While many of the skeptical are not aware of it, they actually live by the popular philosophy of humanism, according to which human beings and their needs are the central fact and ultimate meaning of life. In present usage, humanism as a philosophy entails atheism. Humanism puts forth its own answers to the problems of ethics. For the last two centuries humanists have thought that the attainment of general freedom from want, together with education, would elicit benevolent behavior and do it without the help of religious ideas. Humanists contend that the morals associated with Christianity and Judaism do not depend on these theistic faiths, or for that matter on any kind of theism.

Is this true? Skeptical questioning directed to the skeptics may be overdue. To answer the humanists and others, it is necessary to go back to the very foundations of knowledge and ask how we can justifiably claim that we know anything at all. Here we shall find that the logical concept of coherence is already widely acknowledged as a formal criterion of basic scientific knowledge.

Coherence means the non-contradiction and mutual support of presumed truths in logic and in epistemology, which is the theory of knowledge. Next we shall find, perhaps surprisingly, that a form of theism, and even belief in a hereafter in a meaningful sense, can be supported through the coherence theory of truth. Truth is the quality of an opinion or judgment about reality — how it corresponds to reality. But in new fields, the problem is to know what the reality is, the reality with which our stated truth is to correspond. In this sense, coherence will turn out to be the criterion of knowledge, even the criterion of pioneering scientific knowledge.

The criterion of coherence will be found useful in determining the foundations of ethical knowledge and in determining that Western theism is essential to the highest ethical development of persons. At some points, this determination will be through the process of eliminating incoherent views. As an example of such an incoherent claim, consider this: If a person is thoroughly pessimistic about the value of life but nevertheless denies the reality of motivation implicit in seeking and pronouncing any truth about life and says so, then in this very expression of pessimism one is caught in a logically incoherent situation. One can't coherently say, "Life is not worth living" — and then go on living.

As we shall see, a person can't believe thoroughly that "All valuable experience will ultimately amount to nothing," and then go on trying to realize value, for that amounts to committing a kind of contradiction between words and performance. Such pessimisms are incoherent because they cannot be coherently stated. In such a statement, one implicitly affirms what one verbally denies, in the very acts of speaking or writing. More often than not, this sawing off of the limb upon which one sits passes unnoticed. We shall find much use for the testing of theories by the method of coherence.

The essence of anxiety can always be stated as incoherence in some sense, whether intellectual, social, or moral. Intellectual incoherence is incurred, for instance, in the acceptance of astrology by those with even the slightest education, in the face of the total lack of scientific evidence of its validity. Criminal activity exemplifies social incoherence or alienation. It is the opposite of cooperation with others, even though the criminal relies upon that cooperation in many ways. Inner moral incoherence is exemplified by many contemporary psychiatrists who say that there is properly no such thing as guilt, yet who become indignant should they become victims of stealing or of insults.

The opposite of the state of doubt that arises from incorrect judgment is the security of settled conviction. The opposite of the experience of alienation is a sense of solidarity with one's neighbors. The opposite of the suppressed feeling of guilt that comes from denying its existence is inner peace. Psychologically, the absence of incoherence or conflict constitutes by itself a pleasure that is most often overlooked. It is a subtle, pervasive satisfaction that, in its gentle persistence, is far more important than is generally realized. Indeed, the feeling of inner coherence magnifies every other pleasure.

Leo Tolstoy, Imperial Russian count, novelist, and reformer, appreciated the centrality of ethics. In his little book *On Life*, he spells out with stark clarity the earliest-encountered problem of life in society.[6] For him as for us, life without the desire for happiness is hardly imaginable. A person who feels no desire for happiness is hardly alive. Tolstoy exposits that at the beginning of life, one is conscious only of oneself. For newborn infants, other beings are not yet objects apart from the infants' own existence. Even when they eventually learn from observation that others are alive, too, the life of other beings may still be seen mainly as an aspect of their own existence, which alone seems important and real. If they desire good for others, it is in order that the happiness of other beings may augment the happiness of their own lives.

Gradually, Tolstoy continues, children perceive that their own happiness depends upon other beings. And when they observe these other beings, they see that they, too, are directly conscious only of their own lives and happiness. Hopefully, such a narrow view of the thoughts of others is quickly outgrown. If it is not, those subjects are bound to attribute or project their own restricted view to others.

That is, the victims of such a self-centered view may calculate that not merely one being, or ten beings, but all the innumerable beings in the world consider their own personal happiness to be the most important thing in the world. Such people believe that their own personal happiness, which alone has shed meaning on life, is not to be easily won. Indeed, all other beings, on this perverse view, will attempt to wrest away the means of one's happiness. These fearful victims, being bound to live in society, are likely to devise ill-considered ways to deal with this egocentric predicament. Some may decide to gain power over others. At a semi-civilized level, this might be done, in Tolstoy's words, "by means of one's wealth, power, honor, glory, flattery, deceit," in order "to compel other beings to live, not for themselves," but for the power seeker — that is, to force all beings to love, not themselves, but the power seeker alone.

Even if a person is so fortunately placed in life as to be able to enforce this compulsion upon others, as Count Tolstoy was, one finally learns that such power cannot be enough. The longer one lives, the more one becomes conscious of the need for some other meaning and purpose.

Certainly, civilized morality in children grows slowly and haltingly, as the Swiss psychologist Jean Piaget has shown.[7] How does one escape this inherent conflict of the one and the many in society? From the most ancient times, as Tolstoy notes, people have sought a happiness that should not be canceled by mutual conflict or by suffering and death. According to Lao-tzu, life is essentially the path of peacefulness and lowliness. According to Confucius, life is the diffusion of that light which, for the happiness of humanity, descended upon them from Heaven. According to Moses, life is that which God breathed into human nostrils in order that the race, by fulfilling His law, might flourish. According to Jesus of Nazareth, life is love for God and for neighbor.

These definitions have one thing in common: they replace the unattainable and spurious self-centered search for happiness with an aspiration that is not self-centered. Upon only one condition can a human being's apparently conflicting desires be resolved, namely, the condition that all creatures should live in large measure for the good of others, in a continual mutual service toward each other —the service of each to all and hence of all to each. Only then can each and every person be loved by all, and only then can each person among their number receive the happiness that is desired.

If one admits this as a fact, Tolstoy muses, then one's previous activity directed toward egocentric happiness

> will be replaced by another activity directed to the attainment of the greatest possible happiness for one's self and the whole world. Your enjoyments will be superfluous and painful, as they now are, only when you seize them for yourself. The force of one's life is transferred into toils and sufferings for the happiness of others, and these sufferings and toils become one's own happiness for one's self. Love is the only reasonable activity of humankind. The animal personality inclines to happiness; reason demonstrates to humankind the delusiveness of self-centered happiness, and leaves but one path. Activity along this path is love. And lo, like a key made for this lock alone, one finds in one's own soul a feeling which gives that very happiness which one's reason indicates as the only possible one.

Tolstoy continues:

> Who among living people does not know that blissful sensation — even if but once experienced, and most frequently of all in the earliest childhood, before the soul is yet choked up with that lie which stifles the life in us — that blessed feeling of emotion, during which one desires to love everybody, both those nearby — father, and mother, and brothers, and wicked people, and one's enemies, and one's dog, and one's horse,

and a blade of grass. One thing only is desired, that it should
be well with everybody, that all should be happy. Still more,
one desires to act so that it may be well with all, to give oneself
and one's whole life to making others comfortable and happy.
And this, and this alone, is that love in which lies the humane
life.

Tolstoy's analysis reveals the starting point of an ethical life. We
are born with innate needs for life in society but not with a technique that will enable us to fulfill them. Along this line, the British
journalist Anthony Clutton-Brock has written, "We can eat without
learning to eat; we can make love, even, without learning to make
love; but when it comes to turning the mind outward and away
from itself, then it is the mind itself that has to learn, has to realize
and discover its external interests by means of a technique pain-
fully acquired."[8]
One comes to know that egoism fragments the world and
fragments the person, hence is self-defeating. To pursue happiness,
individuals must be as sensitive to the needs and rights of other
persons as to their own. Moreover, they must be resolutely dedicated
to acting responsibly to help fulfill the needs and rights of others
as well as their own.[9]
Yet if one leaves the matter there, subtle but serious inconsistencies remain. An ethics only of creaturely love entails a nullifying
circularity, resulting finally in meaninglessness. Such problems
usually are buried at a subconscious level. This very concealment
has rendered ethical progress a slow affair.
An episode in the history of eighteenth-century America is
instructive as to the effect of worldview or philosophy of life upon
morals. Jonathan Edwards is mainly remembered as a fire-and-
brimstone preacher, yet he was the most influential American
philosopher up to the twentieth century. His great impact on the
religious and moral life of America is now forgotten. As minister
of the Congregational church in Northampton, Massachusetts, about
the year 1740, he managed for a time to influence religious belief
in the Connecticut River Valley. Edwards' biographer Perry Miller
recounts

the transformations: young people forsaking frolicking, impure
language, and lewd songs; reform in dress and avoidance of
taverns; beaux and fine ladies become serious and mortified;
throughout New England the Bible in esteem, the Lord's day

observed, differences reconciled and faults confessed; old grudges and long-continued breaches made up in entire amity. In Northampton, party spirit so far ceased that town meetings were no longer disfigured by unchristian heats, and, almost too amazing to relate, they came to an agreement about the common lands! The divine power had supported many hearts under great trials, the death of children and extreme pain of body; and finally, proof beyond all proof, under its influence some "have, in such a calm, bright and joyful frame of mind, been carried through the valley of the shadow of death."[10]

The illumination and the euphoria did not last. Edwards' congregation effectively exiled him from Northampton, doubtless for his excessive zeal in some directions. His death in 1758 resulted from his volunteering to be the first person in Princeton to try the freshly discovered smallpox vaccine. The batch was too potent for his frail health and he died of smallpox before he was able to assume the duties as president of what is now Princeton University. Edwards' work, despite its historical impact, is now rarely referred to, even as history.

Yet his achievement suggests that there are ways to motivate benevolent conduct that have not received all the attention they deserve. Historically, the basic theistic worldview has endured for four to five millennia and has motivated its adherents to build several civilizations spanning the globe. In cultural history, religion without philosophy has proven more constructive in the eliciting of moral behavior than has philosophy without religion. Albert Schweitzer, the eminent German-French medical missionary, musician, theologian and philosopher, notes in one of his masterful metaphors: "While religious moralists with one mighty word can get down to the waters flowing far below the surface, philosophical ethics often dig out nothing but a slight hollow in which a puddle forms."[11]

However inconvenient this fact may seem to many, it is backed up by the work of careful historians of culture. An open-minded person will take this into account and perhaps be induced to learn why it is so.

There is a further awkward historical fact. Monotheism, that is, religion of only one God, quite evidently shared the parentage of a child — natural science. This is contrary to what is now generally taught. This link of religion and science evolved so early and so subtly that it is scarcely evident, either to scholars or to lay people.

Another awkward fact is the cogency of the argument for God's existence that stems from the manifold and pervasive evidences of design in the universe and its laws. It is widely supposed that this argument is dead, but it is not. The last sixty years have seen a quiet development of it, at more than one level of discourse.

Can it be that ethics is ready to be called as much a part of science as it is of philosophy and religion? Can religion itself partake of science? We shall see that ethics can partake of the long-standing moral power of theistic — that is, monotheistic — religion while at the same time honoring every requirement of philosophy and scientific method. Essentially, there should be no conflict. Central elements of traditional theistic religion and ethics can be demonstrated together as a kind of knowledge. Some of the demonstrated truths are not themselves ethical truths but support a philosophy or worldview that enables ethical precepts to be perceived as valid and useful — even attractive and compelling.

The competing philosophy of humanism in its various forms has largely supplanted such sources of motivation. Some inconvenient facts about humanism will be brought forth herein. The authors hope that humanist readers will not close their minds until they have understood what is offered in its place.

At bottom, this is a book of philosophy — that is, philosophy in the sense of proto-science. It presents a system of thought that relies only on knowledge which in principle is available to everyone who cares to look for it. Can a philosophical endeavor arrive at that unadorned theism which is a common denominator of the Judaic, Christian, and Islamic traditions and apparently also of the primeval Chinese theistic tradition a thousand years before Confucius? Can it support the higher ethics found in these traditions? Yes, that is the conclusion toward which we shall tend. But is philosophy sufficient to support the detailed theology of any of these traditions? The authors are Christians, but they do not attempt in this book to use the methods of reason to support the further reaches of faith. Yet, we certainly believe more than we presume to have proved. No denial of the validity of general evangelical beliefs is intended herein. There are many good books that expound them. The purpose of this work is more limited and modest, yet more ambitious, namely, to show the unsuspected power of a solely philosophical, proto-scientific approach to religion and ethics. We believe that this approach can strengthen the basis of ecumenical endeavors and make them reach farther than ever.

The Hungarian-American scholar Thomas Molnar observes, "The Western world has so completely evacuated any unifying myth and energizing belief from its mental structure that it has lost the faculty of understanding psychological-religious motivations, whether among allies or enemies."[12] If some readers remain unconvinced by the answers herein, they should at any rate gain insight into the psychological motivations inherent in Western theistic ethics.

The authors find that ethics, with the worldview upon which it must rest, is a winding stair and not a single idea. For one to most fully understand ethics requires the mastery of concepts imbedded in philosophy, psychology, and religion. On contemplating coolly the several concepts involved, one marvels that nearly all humans actually do achieve a degree of ethical competence. With persistence and clear thinking, the authors believe that one may reach the end of the winding stair and thereby enter into a secure inner peace that is otherwise unavailable to critical minds.

**FRANK and ERNEST**®              by Bob Thaves              January 21, 1982

I'D LIKE TO DO IT ALL OVER AGAIN, KNOWING THE THINGS I SHOULD KNOW NOW.

THAVES

Ethics is a positive venture capable of bringing order and joy into life, whereby life is lived and viewed in such a way as to make sense. Schweitzer writes:

> The enthusiasm which comes from thought has the same relation to that which is produced by mere random feeling as the wind which sweeps the heights has to that which eddies about between the hills. If we venture once more to seek help from the light of reason, we shall no longer keep ourselves down at the level of a generation which has ceased to be capable of enthusiasm, but shall rise to the deep and noble passion inspired by great and sublime ideals.[13]

The preliminary strategy of this book is that of an engineer or artisan who first looks at the world and sees what works and what doesn't. The further strategy is more of the nature of science, that is, the explanation of why one system works while others do not. The matter of explanation leads back to an unseen reality, a theistic reality. Although the science arrived at is not strictly natural science, the method used in theology and ethics turns out to be similar to that which has been successful in the established sciences.[14]

A work of the present scope presents a broad target to critics. Some will object to the neglect of many well-known figures in ethics, religion, and the philosophy of science. However, the breaking of new ground entails that much of the old be passed by. Readers are advised to be wary of philosophers who shoot from the hip. Philosophers are notoriously rough on one another. This comes about in part from the humanly impossible task of comprehending all of the many possible positions in the field. For most seekers, philosophy has been a Great Dismal Swamp. For such reasons, lay input into the deliberations of philosophers has been lacking, specifically the restraint and pruning that lay oversight would bring to bear. While the key knowledge-claims herein are not widely accepted among secular scholars and, to many, may not seem spontaneously probable, the reader is asked to weigh the possible alternative positions before settling on a conclusion.

It would be pleasant to console a professor emeritus of ethics at Boston University who has been heard to grumble that the numerous books on ethics that are stolen from the university library should, if they taught their readers effectively, be returned to the library through the freshly reconstructed free will of the thieves. He laments, however, that this simply does not happen. The authors' fond hope is that any thief of the present work might return it to the owner after reading it.

> Our youth continue to float on clouds of anxiety
> and meaninglessness; our priests still remain
> encapsulated within institutions whose death knell
> sounds daily; our prophets invoke values and
> judgments that fail to inspire and ignite; and our
> rulers try to downplay our decadence with patriotic
> rhetorics of self-congratulation and self-celebration.
>
> *Cornel West*

# 2

## Socialism as a Motivating Force

Building socialism is [an] arduous job, as there is
no successful experience ready at hand.
*Hu Yaobang, late General Secretary of the Party*
*People's Republic of China*

The great modern sin consists in taking advantage
for personal ends of the trust which the complexity
of the modern social order makes it necessary for
men to repose in one another; it consists in doing
to others something other than you profess to be
doing to them.
*Arthur Lovejoy, 1908*

FRIEDRICH HAYEK, Austrian-British economist,
philosopher, and Nobel laureate, well notes that it is almost self-
evident that "freedom is the matrix required for the growth of moral
values." He maintains that "It is only where the individual has
choice, and its inherent responsibility, that he has occasion to affirm
existing values, to contribute to their further growth, and to earn
moral merit. Obedience has moral value only where it is a matter
of choice and not of coercion." Hence, Hayek goes on, it should
not be a surprise that "Free societies not only have generally been
law-abiding societies, but also in modern times have been the source
of all the great humanitarian movements aiming at active help to
the weak, the ill, and the oppressed. Unfree societies, on the other
hand, have as regularly developed a disrespect for law, a callous
attitude toward suffering, and even sympathy for the malefactor."[1]
Freedom in the sense of freedom from domineering in familial,
societal, business, and political arrangements, if not quite a universal
prerequisite of ethical behavior, is the condition requisite to most

of it. William James indicates the importance of a high degree of freedom, not only for economic functioning, but for the development of personal powers of all kinds. He speaks in the language of his time:

> Man's chief difference from the brutes lies in the exuberant excess of his subjective propensities — his pre-eminence over them simply and solely in the number and in the fantastic and unnecessary character of his wants, physical, moral, aesthetic, and intellectual. Had his whole life not been a quest for the superfluous, he would never have established himself as inexpugnably as he has done in the necessary [aspects of life]. And from the consciousness of this he should draw the lesson that his wants are to be trusted; that even when their gratification seems farthest off, the uneasiness they occasion is still the best guide of his life, and will lead him to issues entirely beyond his present powers of reckoning. Prune down his extravagance, sober him, and you undo him.[2]

One may infer that freedom — that is, an open society — is the proper, even the "natural" or ideal condition of humankind. However, the observations of Hayek and James do not imply that, if only the dictators and oligarchs of the world would grant freedom to their people, everything would suddenly be peaceful and productive. The world is not so simple. Freedom merely to pursue one's shifting whims within broad limits may be either bad or good. At times it may be a means to the finding of new and better ways to serve one's fellows, but at other times, it is quite the opposite.

Nevertheless, a political movement that makes no appeal to freedom cannot hope to succeed. But what is freedom? For the nineteenth-century British philosopher John Stuart Mill, freedom is the power to do as one wills without coercion or constraint by others, and limited only by the right of others to similar exercise.[3] Yet dreams and aspirations are apt to be thwarted by tyrannical rulers, as well as by some heads of families, so that genuinely free actions do not result, even if one feels free. The American longshoreman-philosopher Eric Hoffer deepens the concept by writing, "Freedom means freedom from forces and circumstances which would turn man into a thing, which would impose on a person the passivity and predictability of matter."[4]

That is what dictatorships or totalitarian rule do. But neither the definitions of Hoffer nor of Mill suggest that freedom at the human level entails something positive — not only freedom from restriction but something more. For there is no bondage like that of liberty misused. The Russian novelist Aleksandr Solzhenitsyn comments:

> In early democracies, as in American democracy at the time of its birth, all individual rights were granted on the ground that man is God's creature. That is, freedom was given to the individual conditionally, in the assumption of his constant religious responsibility. Such was the heritage of the preceding one thousand years. Two hundred or even fifty years ago, it would have seemed quite impossible, in America, that an individual be granted boundless freedom with no purpose, simply for the satisfaction of his whims. Subsequently, however, all such limitations were eroded everywhere in the West; a total emancipation occurred from the moral heritage of Christian centuries with their great reserves of mercy and sacrifice. The West has finally achieved the rights of man, and even to excess, but man's sense of responsibility to God and society has grown dimmer and dimmer.[5]

In order to avoid the hobbling confusions arising from the infinite possibilities for action, one needs a discipline that lends structure to life. This fact will be explored at length but, for now, we may note only that socialism has supplied such a discipline for many. State socialism, in the minds of multitudes of people, has taken the place of traditional religion as the foundation of meaning in life and as the criterion of what is good. In it, the means of production and distribution of goods and services are owned by the state. The discipline of socialism denies the freedom of persons to start or conduct businesses, to organize production, or to sell or to buy except as consumers. Such restrictions have been thought to be a small price to pay for the benefits anticipated under socialism, among which are anticipated the joy of working every day to benefit others in a system that is to assure that result. Socialist hopes have always included the building of democratic societies of material plenty and happiness. The cry of economic justice through such government intervention is that of the Marxian maxim, "From each according to his ability, to each according to his needs." The enthusiast believes that security and love will quickly come to reign and that the mad pursuit of wealth will then die away. To this end, many countries have adopted state socialism in a democratic political framework. Even the nations with greatest economic freedom now are socialistic in a substantial portion of their economies.

As an extreme but pervasively influential form of state socialism, Marxism emphasizes the value of labor and advocates "the dictatorship of the proletariat." Additionally, it is a recondite philosophy called dialectical materialism.[6] Modern Communism takes the form of Marxism-Leninism as professed officially by the leaders of the Soviet Union. Modern Marxists talk less about class struggle than did Karl Marx and insist that Marxism is a form of humanism — that is, of secular or atheistic humanism. Humanism in this sense is not to be confused with either humanitarianism or the historic humanistic devotion to literature, philosophy, history, art, and political theory. Nearly all American Unitarian churches, some Quaker groups, and the leadership of some of the older American Protestant churches have embraced humanism. It generally dominates secular colleges of liberal arts.

By the mid-nineteenth century, Francis Hutcheson, Cesare Beccaria and especially Jeremy Bentham had already taught much of the world that they should act to further "the greatest happiness of the greatest number." When Karl Marx pointed out that the great majority of people were working, laboring people, the logical way to fulfill the program of Bentham was to help the proletariat. Abraham Lincoln, though no Marxist, seems to have said, agreeably, "The Lord prefers poor people, He made so many of them."

Marxists hold that the human being is the supreme being for humans. In place of the God of Western theism, they elevate the collective human mind. Following in spirit the nineteenth-century German philosopher Ludwig Feuerbach, they suggest ironically that "An honest God is the noblest work of man." Marxists also agree with the nineteenth-century British mathematician W. K. Clifford who enjoins parents to keep their children from the priest, lest he make them into enemies of the human race. Clifford trumpets his own profession of humanist faith in a ringing passage, in the language of that day: "The dim and shadowy outlines of the superhuman deity fade slowly away from before us; and as the mist of his presence floats aside, we perceive with greater and greater clearness the shape of a yet grander and nobler figure — of Him who made all Gods and shall unmake them. From the dim dawn of history, and from the inmost depth of every soul, the face of our father Man looks out upon us with the fire of eternal youth in his eyes, and says, 'Before Jehovah was, I am!' "[7]

Marxist-Leninist political-military rulers have often identified theists as psychotics or criminals who take mirages for reality and who fail to submit themselves to the common will.[8] The intention of Marxists and other state socialists is to suppress egoism and avarice while honoring what they take to be the requirements of scientific method. In this way, they intend to bring about a state of general happiness. On its face, it is a grand and noble endeavor. Few will deny that the promotion of general human well-being must be a large result of any viable ethics. Yet when state socialists falter in achieving their material goals, they find that they must be content merely to attempt to ameliorate the social causes of unhappiness.

According to a recent official Chinese statement, echoing Marx and Lenin, "Ethics are a reflection of the economic base of a society, not an abstract concept divorced from history."[9] For Lenin (and his followers), "Morality is what serves to destroy the old exploiting society and to unite all the working people around the proletariat, which is building up a new, a communist society. Communist morality is that which serves this struggle and unites the working people against all exploitation." All other power centers are to be shut down. Even the right to gather in private associations is to be denied. "Bourgeois morality" with its religiously based commandments is rejected. According to Marx and Lenin, acted-out envy, inter-class violence, lying, and the dissolving of family ties are all permissible if the great end is served thereby. For Lenin, all this was not mere theory. Lenin's terroristic bloodletting of 1918-20 was carried out against entire classes and occupational groups without regard for any rule of law, custom, or honor. Neither personal guilt nor responsibility was weighed.[10] This pattern has been generally imitated in the early phases of other Communist regimes.

In fact, some Communist rulers have more or less quietly decided that Marx and Lenin were wrong in their contempt for "bourgeois morality" and that some of the bourgeois values are needed to make their people productive or even happy at their work. In 1961, the Communist Party of the Soviet Union promulgated "the moral code of the builder of Communism." It contains phrases like "devotion to the Communist cause," "conscientious labor," "one for all and all for one," "honesty and truthfulness, moral purity, modesty, unpretentiousness, mutual respect in the family," etc.

The question nags: Does such a code motivate? Heretofore, Soviet leaders have regarded positive motivation as consisting simply of the direction of attention to external and societal goals collectively. Social good, not individual good, has been the theoretical basis of Marxist moral values. Economic relations heretofore have constituted a kind of mystic unity of all. Little attention has been paid to individual feelings of satisfaction. Persons have been considered real only in their social aspect. The good and the valuable have been sought directly in their externalized forms, notably in the state-socialist structure itself. Under the military force inherent in Leninism, whatever has not been obviously and directly supportive of this end has been scarcely tolerated.[11] The motivational problem with which Marxists must concern themselves appears to be in part a consequence of the denial in the writings of Marx of any ethic of personal responsibility, despite his various indignations.

Regardless of the early hopes and joyous camaraderie, state socialism has failed abyssmally, not only in economic results but in the motivations underlying the results. Specifically, state socialism renders genuinely satisfying daily work next to impossible, and people generally only go through the motions of work. The reasons will shortly be discussed, but the bad results are underlined by the fact that the biggest experimenters with state socialism — the Soviet Union and China — after many decades of failed efforts to make it work, have recently been partly abandoning it for more freedom of enterprise. It seems that some Communists in power have been made to see, at least at times, that "The economic crime is not to make a profit," as a prominent democratic socialist has put the matter.[12] At this writing, Gorbachev's policies of *glasnost* and *perestroika* have attempted far-reaching reforms in the Soviet Union, in which they have been outdone by their eastern European satellite countries. Of course, as one might well expect, the reformers are meeting with serious resistance on the part of the old Communist Party stalwarts and bureaucrats, who have vested interests in keeping intact the old Marxist-Leninist dictatorships. Yet, we should be most encouraged by the fact that in Poland, Hungary, Czechoslovakia, Bulgaria, and in the German "Democratic Republic," the Communists have so terribly failed that, at long last, they have allowed free elections or seem about to at press time, whereby their old powers are mostly melting away. In Czechoslovakia, East Germany, and Romania, the Communist governments have been put out of business by fed-up citizens. Incredibly, these drastic collapses of Communist power have occurred in only one year. The hated Berlin Wall has been torn down by the people.[13]

In China, socialism has spectacularly failed to make an economically better life possible. The comparisons to the progress made by the free Chinese in Taiwan and Hong Kong prove profoundly embarrassing to all state socialists. For a recent few years, the Chinese equivalent of *perestroika* brought, in its relative freedoms of market and enterprise, increasing prosperity to the land, as well as much-needed foreign currency. Notwithstanding this, the Communist government has announced that these retreats from socialism are being rolled back. At this writing, the rulers have shut down more than three million new private businesses and free rural collectives. The prospect of economic ruin does not trouble socialistic true believers who have become drunk with their vast powers to push people around.

Nor apparently do other kinds of ruin trouble them. At least a thousand young unarmed Chinese students in Tiananmen Square, Beijing, laid down their lives in what was to have been a peaceful attempt to moderate the brutal state-socialist so-called "People's Republic." Countless bystanders were shot, and thousands of dissidents are said to be in prison. Over a million Tibetan natives have been murdered by the Chinese soldiers and police because of their resistance to the rape and occupation of their country. Thousands of others have been tortured. The Chinese Communist regime continues to support the infamous Khmer Rouge, which murdered at least a million of its fellow Cambodians in 1975.

That state socialism tends to tyranny should surprise no one since the appearance, decades ago, of the little book, *The Road to Serfdom*. In it, Hayek shows how economic freedom has generally been prerequisite to freedom of other kinds.[14]

With all its obvious flaws, why has Marxism spread and endured? The main reason, of course, is that it has been pushed onto people by brutal force of arms. Another reason revolves around the failure of traditional religions to hold the allegiance of reflective modern people and provide them with meaning and purpose. In this vacuum, these newer movements confer the sense of moral superiority enjoyed by communicants of almost any faith. Marxism should have a special significance for Christians and Jews, for it is a reminder and denouncement of the fact that they have not lived up to the ideals of their faiths.[15] "In an era without faith," writes David Satter, "Communism has emerged as a powerful anti-faith. It cannot be defeated militarily and its adherents cannot be bribed into giving it up. It can be defeated in only one way: by being confronted with an idea that is better."[16] The lesson of Communism is that any philosophy that affords even some apparent temporary significance to one's life is better than no philosophy.[17]

Marxism provides a superficially consistent view of history and allows a person to feel that life has meaning in a "self-sacrificing devotion to a Collective Humanity" — that is, in serving "a Leviathan embodying the collective power and corporate interests of the Human Race."[18] Arnold Toynbee, the British historian who writes these words, also muses that Communism has "the merit of being a leaf taken from the book of Christianity — a leaf torn out and misread."[19]

Underlining this insight, many Marxist leaders in their youth came under Christian influence. Karl Marx was born into a well-to-do German Jewish family. His father, a lawyer, was forced to become a Lutheran in order to keep his job at the higher court of appeals. Marx, for a period of his youth, seems to have been a serious Christian.[20] Josef Stalin was trained in a Russian Orthodox seminary. Much of the leadership of Third World Communism was recruited from the Christian mission schools established in the nineteenth century — for example, Chou En-lai and Oliver Tambo.

These mission schools imparted to their students a dedication to make a better world. They caught the vision of progress stemming from the Enlightenment of the eighteenth century. The Marxists promised them programs for speeding up the forces of history to remove a hypocritical ruling class and to establish in its place the kingdom of humanity. In like manner, "liberation theology" is now sweeping through Latin America. It is in some cases a clothing of Marxism in a Biblical dress, with little emphasis on theism.[21] While this secular semi-religious approach to reform is unfortunately one-sided, its flourishing could easily have been predicted by any responsible Christian who was fully aware of the evil excesses of free enterprise in Latin America. We have been personally acquainted with priests whose devotion to reform has been essentially disconnected from its original Christian motivation of revolution by peaceful methods.

It is easy to criticize the writings and the results of Marxism and socialism, and many have done so from various standpoints.[22] But simple laisser-faire free enterprise has also failed. There is evidence that laisser-faire free enterprise always fails morally when unguided by sound religious and moral principles. Some recent examples, right at home, may be mentioned. When free-world bankers lend hundreds of billions of our savings to far-away ruling thieves on the hope of higher interest payments than the home folks can bear, the result is neither economically nor morally respectable. More recently, American savings and loan bankers have wasted or stolen hundreds of billions entrusted to them, with the connivance of a depressing array of accomplices, some of them in Congress.[23] When owners of American casual labor camps gouge the unfortunate, as the conservative *Wall Street Journal* reports, the results are malodorous.[24] It is easy to see that freedom of enterprise through the free market does not itself solve the general ethical problem. As for distribution, Winston Churchill truly states that capitalism (i.e., free enterprise or the free market system) is ruthlessly unequal in its distribution of blessings, while Communism is ruthlessly equal in its distribution of miseries.

Can one say that the free market system is itself an occasion for unethical behavior? The ethically concerned economist Kenneth Boulding is correct in finding some ground for this suspicion:

> Market behavior and market institutions — that is, commercial life — frequently leads to the development of a type of personality which mistakes the abstractions of commerce for the realities of existence, and hence loses much of the richness of full human relationship. The exchange relationship is by its very nature abstract, and indeed it owes its success to its very power of being abstract. When we make a purchase from a store clerk we do not enter into a full personal relationship with that person. Even the relationship of employee to employer, though it is richer and more complex than that of simple commodity exchange, is still exchange, and still falls far short of the richness and complexity, say of the marital relationship. And this is as it should be: the worker-employer relationship

is not the same as the child-parent relationship, and any attempt to make it so will create frustration and resentment on both sides. There must be economy in human relationship if *large* fabrics of society are to exist at all, because if we are to have relationships with *many* people these relationships must be limited and abstract rather than full. There is danger, however, in a predominantly commercial society, that people will take economic behavior as the measure of all things and will confine their relationships to those which can be conducted on the level of the commercial abstraction. To do this is to lose almost all the richness and purpose in human life. He who has never loved, has never felt the call of a heroic ethic — to give and not to count the cost, to labor and not to ask for any reward — has lived far below the peak levels of human experience. Economic man dwells in Limbo — he is not good enough for Heaven or bad enough for Hell. On the whole he escapes the deadly sins (how much better, for instance, is the commercial vulgarity of Coca Cola than the heroic diabolism of Hitler), but misses also the Great Virtue, and in that he is less than Man.[25]

The free-market system stands in need of ethical principles to restrain and guide it. It can never be the source of such principles.[26] To suppose that one is fulfilling the requirements of morality merely by obeying the signals of the marketplace is to pursue a fatally simplistic ethic. If such narrowness were general, it would bring the free system down. Indeed, the free system, so far as it still exists, is presently in danger for this reason.

With such strictures, why has capitalism flourished? Before discussing that, some defining is needed. Capitalism is better named the free-market system, which it is in theory. The theory is largely the practice of Western countries. The new name is better if only because socialism, too, requires capital — i.e., savings and land — with which to function; hence capital is not a distinguishing element. The scholar Jean-François Revel explains that capitalism "is a fusion or juxtaposition of a myriad of individual behavioral fragments that have come down to us from the dawn of time, that are unified only in our minds, and that we have finally assembled into a general, erratic and imperfect concept."[27] Hayek adds: "We have never designed our economic system. We were not intelligent enough for that."

The free market, present in most countries, enables participants to perform, as exchanges, what other participants signal that they wish to have done. It does this with a maximal variety of interaction. That is its purpose, whether by design or not. The market is essentially an information-transmitting device that works through continual repricing together with exchange of money. The more complex the politico-economic system, the more information is needed for the making of sound economic decisions and, aside from the market, the harder such information is to come by. The problem inherent in intense centralization at even a town level, let alone in a nation, may be likened to the loss of information that occurs in our phone messages as they become condensed and garbled when funneled through third, fourth and fifth parties. Also, in centralization there is a greater chance of immovable blockages resulting from unintentional hangups. In view of the fundamental human limitations on the amount of information that even a governing group can gather and evalute, no governing group of a complex national politico-economic system can replace the market without causing unacceptable waste. Idealistic motives cannot change this fact. We live in what the Austrian-British philosopher Sir Karl Popper has called abstract societies, distinct from the former small face-to-face societies. The transition made a degree of specialization possible that went far beyond what any one person can comprehend. Hayek elaborates: "This extensive social division of labour, based on widely dispersed information, has been made possible entirely by the use of those impersonal signals which emerge from the market process and tell people what to do in order to adapt their activities to events of which they have no direct knowledge." Abstract rules of conduct, rather than perceived common ends, necessarily govern our large-scale economic life. To operate this economic order we must obey "inherited traditional rules" that "we never deliberately made, and the obedience to which builds more complex orders than we can understand." Hayek's elaboration of this insight enables us to listen anew to the old saying: "Fools rush in where angels fear to tread."

A manufacturer does not produce shirts merely upon knowing that Smith needs some. He produces them upon knowing that dozens of wholesalers will buy certain quantities at various prices because they, or rather the retailers they serve, know in turn that thousands of consumers, whom the manufacturer does not know, want to buy them.[28] In a free setting, buyers and sellers, borrowers and lenders, transact with each other because they both expect to benefit thereby. So far as informed buyers and borrowers have good motives, the results of the market and the use of money are apt to be good. If they have bad motives, the results are apt to be bad. If the free economic game is worth the while, it is because the motives of most of the participants are both good and informed, or at least not bad. The less this is true, the more justification there will be for government to step in, whether clumsily or not.

The eighteenth-century moral philosopher Adam Smith did not consider the existence of the motive of profit-seeking as either good or bad. He correctly took it to be a human characteristic that, as Irving Kristol has it, is in itself no more moral or immoral than is the sexual instinct. The free market economy potentially permits all people to better their condition, even though all participants seek only their own particular good.[29] Of course, profit-seeking operations can be immoral, since profit is often gained unjustly without one's contributing any net value. Yet a system that in fact enables the general populace to better their condition — yes, to profit — is indeed morally justifiable. If that betterment is actually occurring, to allow such a system to die would be immoral.

The free-market economy greatly improves the chances of all persons to have their economic wants satisfied, but there is a price. A regime of economic freedom entails that there will be competition, and therefore some people will gain in comparison with others. Socialism and Communism eliminate the free market and thereby the discomforts of competition. As Hayek makes clear, economic competition is a game of discovery, a game which brings to light previously unknowable abilities of persons to provide what people want, at prices as low as that of any ready competitor. The free market leads to "the use of more skill and knowledge than any other known procedure." The profits made by skilled and knowledgeable entrepreneurs enable them to make further productive use of their abilities. The justice of competition lies in the rules of the game and not in the results, for the results cannot be known in advance. No valid rules, aside from those of the market, have been discovered that determine the quantities of just returns. Sheer good fortune will help to enrich some, giving rise to envy. Severely handicapped starters and drastic losers in the game should be assisted, privately or publicly, but no quantitatively valid rules for doing so have been discovered. Hayek discusses the non-rational and hence never-settled results of governmental distortions of earnings, whereby government yields to the wishes of the various economic special interest groups in a never-ending melee of shouts and legal scribblings.

Where many critics go wrong is in supposing that, since the market behaves in a regular way, some single thinking being or small group must be directing it. Extending this mistaken line of thought, the critics suppose that the inequities which result from the play of a free market are not only predicticable but are the result of the will of this supposed shadowy figure behind the scenes. Hayek shows that this is not so. Moreover, he challenges the coherence of the ideal of "social justice," by which term is meant the situation that "society," according to enlightened conscience, ought to bring about through society's agent, the government — usually meaning the national government. Hayek in his great, ripened work shows that, if such a mistaken conception were to become fully realized, the result would be the destruction of the very values distinguishing the open society — the values that brought our civilization to a point where we could afford to consider the implementation of anything like "social justice."[30]

Modern production under any system demands a high degree of motivation and an almost infinite capacity for painstaking care and attention to detail. The scholar Elizabeth Hoyt states, "Just as we tend to underestimate or overlook some of the values of other peoples, so critics of our productive system tend to underestimate the imagination and courage, the ability to organize, to integrate, and to keep track of detail, that are required to build and operate a productive enterprise. They tend to assume that any well-intentioned group can do it, without the rewards of profit or of power, and under conditions of extreme restriction and control. That is the theory of Communism everywhere."[31]

Albert Schweitzer contends that individuals should possess wealth and capital, provided that they make use of it in responsible stewardship:

> One man serves society by carrying on a business in which a number of employees earn their living; another by giving away his wealth in order to help his fellows. Between these

two extreme kinds of service, let each decide according to the
responsibility which he finds determined for him by the circumstances of his life. The one thing that matters is that each
shall value what he possesses as a means to action. Whether
this is accomplished by his keeping and increasing his wealth,
or by surrender of it, matters little. Wealth must reach the
community in the most varied ways, if it is to be of the greatest
benefit to all.[32]

State-socialist intellectuals usually do not talk much about the need
for self-sacrifice. They prefer to talk about everyone's acquiring
material plenty. But everyone must at times sacrifice, and not only
in behalf of family or neighbors. Schweitzer states, "Society cannot exist without sacrifice." The devotion of ethical individuals acting
freely will see to it that "as many sacrifices as possible are voluntary, and that the individuals who are most severely hit are relieved
of their burden" by other individuals. "This is the doctrine of self-
sacrifice." Schweitzer goes on to say that an ethic that would attempt
to solve social problems through coerced redistribution of burden
does not utilize the individual ethics of those coerced; hence, it can
only decree that society advance "at the price of the freedom and
prosperity of individuals and groups. This is the doctrine of being
sacrificed by others."[33]

Socialists might reply that, even as mere followers, they would
not feel coerced by the decrees of a trusted central authority. If the
central authority were to know all that it needed to know to make
good decisions, well and good. But we have seen that they cannot,
and this fact largely explains the failures of state socialism. As the
American economist Henry C. Simon told his students: "I don't
object to socialism as a description of heaven."[34]

The British economist Sir Dennis H. Robertson defines the
economist's task regarding the market with uncommon clarity. In
his Columbia University speech, "What Does the Economist
Economize?" he concludes that *love* is the thing to be economized,
which is to say apportioned carefully — even by economists in a free
society:

There exists in every human breast an inevitable state of tension
between the aggressive and acquisitive instincts and the instincts of benevolence and self-sacrifice. It is for the preacher,

lay or clerical, to inculcate the duty of subordinating the former to the latter. It is the humbler, and often the invidious, role of the economist to help, so far as he can, in reducing the preacher's task to manageable dimensions. It is his function to emit a warning bark if he sees courses of action being advocated or pursued which will increase unnecessarily the inevitable tension between self-interest and public duty; and to wag his tail in approval of courses of action which will tend to keep the tension low and tolerable.

All good luck to the newspaper editor who, in a time of heavy unemployment, tells the man who has got a job that he must not obstruct the reduction of costs by playing it out [i.e., featherbedding]. All good luck to the broadcaster who tells the steady-going professional family that at such a time they must cast their cherished virtue of thrift to the winds and spend freely in the public interest. But I am afraid these devoted preachers will have a hard and thankless task. It is the business of the economist to do what he can to save them from being set [this task].

What does the economist economize? " 'Tis love, 'tis love," said the Duchess, "that makes the world go round." "Somebody said," whispered Alice, "that it's done by everybody minding their own business." "Ah well," replied the Duchess, "it means much the same thing." Not perhaps quite so nearly the same thing as Alice's [Victorian] contemporaries thought. But if we economists mind our own business, and do that business well, we can, I believe, contribute mightily to the economizing, that is to the full but thrifty utilization, of that scarce resource Love — which *we* know, just as well as anybody else, to be the most precious thing in the world.[35]

We have seen that the rewards of a system of free enterprise are to some extent a matter of chance. Can the fortunate and the able legitimately permit themselves comforts that enable them better to serve others? Can some degree of self-indulgence be consistent with love for others? Of course, we all need some recreation (i.e., re-creation), but with some, there is no end to the selfish accumulation of luxuries and the consumption of expensive services, often overdone to the point of harmful selfishness. It is easier to err on the side of being selfish than on the side of giving.[36]

A related matter is self-aggrandizement in the reach for power, wealth, or prestige. Even socialistic regimes permit their leaders and functionaries a measure of it. Some may think self-aggrandizement wrong, and indeed it is all too often unhealthily motivated and corrupt. The nineteenth-century American religious leader Joseph Smith responds that self-aggrandizement is a correct principle on condition that the ambitious person grant priority to elevating and benefiting others. "If you will elevate others, the very work itself will exalt you. Upon no other plan can a man justly and permanently aggrandize himself."[37] The words of Jesus of Nazareth speak to a similar point: "Love thy neighbor *as thyself*."

What of the failure of the free system to solve the repeated economic crises of unemployment in the last century? Moralists should not duck this problem. Unemployment is not only a financial blow: it strikes at the family and all its values, such as the education of children. Hard times wipe out job security and effectively wipe out instances of worker ownership, forcing worker-owners to sell their stock shares and forcing some worker-owners to lay off other worker-owners. Consequently, the entire political and economic social structure in which mass unemployment occurs is called into question. Indeed, this occurred widely in America during the Great Depression of the 1930s.[38] Entrepreneurs live in fear of changes resulting from the business cycle. Free enterprise is a system of profit and *loss*. Yet, promising ways to achieve general and reasonable employment security within a free society are now available, even though such methods are not currently in academic circulation. To render the conservative spirit viable, one must be a little adventurous.[39]

Absentee ownership or control occurs to some extent in almost any large system. Under state socialism, the control of factories or fields by the local employees is a myth, if only because direction from the economy is always necessary in any system. Since the market is ruled out, this control must reside in the monolithic socialist state. Absentee owners or managers in either system too readily ignore the duty of proper stewardship over people, tools, and resources. To be out of sight is likely to be out of mind. Too often, the only concern of an absent owner or manager is profit or status, and the faster the better. To take only one example of harm caused thereby, the need for time to develop inventions and manufacturing processes is likely to be neglected, to the detriment of all. Yet absentee ownership is implicit in the very structure of the stock and capital market, where such remote control, at least under current conditions, is a necessary evil, though that control is not so remote as in socialist economies. We have seen an advertisement of the brokerage firm of E. F. Hutton, proclaiming in big print: "People invest for one reason: to make money." What a wonderful propaganda piece for socialism! Fortunately, the claim is not fully true. Yet many investors use the stock market like the gaming tables of Las Vegas, with no thought of an owner's duty of stewardship.[40] As Churchill stated, "capitalism" or the free-market system is a very bad system. But it is, he insisted, the least bad system that has been developed to date.

Churchill evidently meant this judgment against state socialism to apply only to the economies of large scale where, as we have seen, abstract relationships must prevail everywhere beyond narrow confines. Indeed, the necessities of large economies — the economies of nations and of the world — are what this chapter has been about. None of this is an argument for the extreme individualism that ignores neighborly helpfulness or ignores the kind of cooperation that sprang from, say, the ruggedly situated villages of Scandinavia. Socialism can have another, more viable meaning, namely, that of micro-socialism or communitarianism occurring on a small scale, without coercion from a nation-state. Dedicated groups, usually sharing a religious commitment, can and do successfully operate their own more or less socialist communities. One reads of the Boimondau watch-case factory in southern France. The Hutterites live in such a manner. Just because the American Pilgrims couldn't make socialism work doesn't mean that it can't work in communes of similar size in which the members are self-selected with their eyes open. Such ventures may of course be regarded as a kind of extended family. As in families, there is the possibility of warmth and caring in community relationships. Communes may be suitable for some but not for others. The protracted labor of writing this book could hardly have been permitted in a commune. Be that as it may, communes that relate as a unit to the larger market economy outside can still enjoy the plentifulness that outside markets make possible.[41]

What about a theocracy? Zion, Illinois, was a theocracy, so far as that is possible within a sovereign state. In a theocracy, political and religious power are in the same hands. In large societies on this earth, even theocracies must fail. There are numerous reasons why they must fail. Even the church is not the kingdom of God, as those who serve on church boards should know. The fact is that, here on earth, where we human beings are most often highly imperfect, it is impossible for any government to bring about by force a perfect harmony and unity in the production and distribution of goods. Another reason is simply the fact that "Power tends to corrupt," and we all know what absolute power does. This side of heaven there will always be those who will try to thrive on corruption.

There are a few more facts that must be faced by all politicians and economists if we are to achieve a more humane society, free from the excesses and evils of either state socialism or laisser-faire free enterprise. These facts are, first: Money and profits have no intrinsic value; they have simply extrinsic value, which means that they can be used as instruments for accomplishing either good or bad ends. Money is wherewithal. All of us have numerous intrinsic life needs, the fulfillment of which are legitimate proximate ends. Yet it is certain that these ends cannot be fulfilled without means, and money is often that means. Money and profits can be pursued selfishly, hoarded selfishly, and used selfishly. Yet the same money and profits can be pursued and used to further the fulfillment of all of our needs for better health, better education, more fruitful and happy methods of self-expression, etc.

People who relate with money as though it has intrinsic value are axiologically sick. People who preoccupy themselves with the accumulation of money as an end in itself, irrespective of a devotion to using it as a means to accomplish benevolent ends, are sick in their souls. In this sense, the "love" of money indeed can be the root of much evil. But people are equally as unrealistic who indiscriminately condemn the pursuit of money or profit as an intrinsic evil. We have known some self-righteous ascetics who are guilty of this while living off of other people's money.

Poverty is not an intrinsic value, and prosperity is not an intrinsic evil. Both poverty and prosperity always have and always will tempt people to many evils. Prosperity is power for good or ill. Prosperity is not good of itself and at best can only furnish a foundation for a satisfactory life. The bulk of the Chinese in China are poor though not desperately so, since they appear to be at least as happy as people in the affluent West. Yet desperate poverty occurs, there and elsewhere, and no one can defend the results. Whether prosperity is well used depends on the ethics of the prosperous persons. When people produce more than they consume, some of the surplus goes into the hands of the producers. In any case, the wealth, the capital, then exists. Someone should control it or use it. The monolithic, half-blind and deaf State has proved to be a bad steward. Therefore, *persons* should control wealth. Admittedly, people must learn to cope with prosperity. To do so well is a matter of personally ingrained ethics and worldview. The free-market system — the open society — is the arrangement that affords trust to persons to do what is right.

If no one has money, who is in a position to help the poor? If no one accumulates wherewithal with which to help the economically helpless, then who can give them a helping hand? Without money, who can pull them out of their starvation by paying for their food? Who can relieve them of their sickness by paying their medical expenses? And who can lift them out of their grime? The government can't do these things without the wherewithal of the people. The government is not the real source of transfer payments, contrary to uncritical popular belief. "Go and sell what thou hast, and give it to the poor." How can people sell what they have if they have never acquired anything to sell?

The State is insatiable and must be checked, a fact well known to the American Founding Fathers. This fact holds under any economic philosophy. An all-encompassing, economically monolithic state amounts to one gigantic corporation with everything run from the center. Such a state inevitably bogs down with a stifling and dehumanizing bureaucracy. It is an overwhelming fact that in any monolithic state none of the intrinsic values that make for the good life can ever possibly be forced by any amount of power. Unselfish love cannot be forced. Unselfish joy cannot be forced. Integrity cannot be forced. Good health cannot be forced. A sense of security or well-being cannot be forced. By now, the human race should have given up hope that any monolithic form of government, devoid of separate balancing powers, can ever do justice to the needs of its people.

State socialism and the endeavor for economic justice through the intervention of big government initially presents a splendid, inspiring vista. State socialism may motivate a society for a time, until the mass of people thoroughly experience its hollowness. The subtlety of ethical motivation in economic activity is not so easily probed as socialists have thought.[42] The cure for the ethical ills of the free-market system lies in applied ethics rather than in coercion. The cure lies in giving and sacrificing, both personally and through voluntary associations, not in tearing down that which makes plentifulness possible. Without living ethics, there are no solutions. Even the motivations for the improvement of political and economic structures can arise only from personally internalized ethics. Socialist motivation will be discussed in a broader, humanist context late in Chapter 14.

A more realistic combination of the open society, together with the limited national-governmental intervention permitted by the United States Constitution interpreted in its original intent, should progressively improve the economic lot of humankind. This is the hope of the authors.[43] Adam Smith's "invisible hand," which guides self-interest to unintended public good, is an amazing device, as some economists are now rediscovering. Yet as Boulding, Robertson, and Schweitzer have shown, the market does not prevent all disarray and even adds some of its own. Although the play of the free market system minimizes the need for sacrifices and philanthropy, the market cannot eliminate such need.

Radical utopian reformers muse with Omar Khayyám: "Ah Love! could thou and I with Fate conspire to grasp this sorry Scheme of Things entire, would not we shatter it to bits — and then re-mould it nearer to the Heart's Desire!"[44] This has been the Communist way. The inherent limitations of human knowledge that we have explored will forever bar creation of a large politico-economic utopia. Human freedom and the operation of political economy inevitably place limitations on the power of righteously motivated people to create the good life for all human beings. Wise social reformers will strive not to overturn the social order but rather to continually adjust and strengthen a reasonable legal climate that guarantees protection of the individual citizen from excesses committed by free enterprise and which guarantees the freedom of the individual to pursue his or her own self-fulfillment while freely contributing in his or her own way to the fulfillment of others, to their education, and to science.

The sacrifice of some private interest for the public good is a theme of Christianity and Judaism and indeed of the responsible elements of other faiths. The love thereby enjoined upon each person entails an inward-springing willingness to at times ignore the signals of the market — that is, to sacrifice part of one's wealth and to find joy in doing so. Whatever one may think of religious faiths that enjoin sacrifices, the question for now is whether these faiths comprise some motivating elements of wisdom or truth. If they did not, freedom would present intractable problems for the flourishing of constructive motivation. If they do comprise such truths, what are the truths and how can one come to know and appreciate them as such? Before turning directly to such questions, we shall take a side trip in the next chapter through some illuminating history of science.

> The prevailing belief in "social justice" is at present probably the gravest threat to most other values of a free civilization. Not only the most cherished beliefs but also the most revered moral leaders — sometimes saintly figures whose unselfishness is beyond question — may become grave dangers to the values which the same people regard as unshakable. Against this threat we can protect ourselves only by subjecting even our dearest dreams of a better world to ruthless rational dissection.
>
> *Friedrich Hayek*

> Modern capitalism is a curse — not because some men have capital, but because some men have not. A modern city can be a nightmare — not because its houses belong to those who own them, but because they do not belong to those who live in them. This is the real case against modern capitalism; and it is also the case against modern collectivism, or socialism, which is its child.
>
> *G. K. Chesterton*

> The key feature of Communist propaganda has been the depiction of people who are more productive as mere exploiters of others.
>
> *Thomas Sowell*

# 3

## The Cradle of Science

The view of reality in modern paganism is
equivalent to a thorough disdain for explanation
itself, whose place is taken by mere description.

*Pierre Duhem*

THEISM AND SCIENCE are often thought to be anti-
thetical. Debates between religion and science have flourished for
two centuries and more. The nineteenth-century historian and college president Andrew Dickson White, author of *A History of the
Warfare of Science with Theology in Christendom*, recounts many interesting reports of the narrow-mindedness of clergy.[1] One often
hears the opinion that theism has nothing to contribute to scientific work. In influential quarters, it is likely to be regarded as the
enemy of science and reason. How do such perceptions bear up
in historical perspective?

Interestingly enough, the further one goes back in time, the more
evident it becomes that, in its foundations, physical science has been
nurtured by Western religion. Theists have been prominent in
science since the Renaissance. As late as 1948, seventy per cent of
American scientists claimed to be theists, and a majority of these
were actively affiliated with religious groups.[2]

Many of the more creative physicists of our century such as Planck, Poincaré, Schrödinger, and A. H. Compton have retained enough humility and sense of ultimate mystery to warn their colleagues of the inherent limitations of physical science. They have pointed out that physical science never can be used to negate the basic assumption of freedom of the human will.[3] Of course, there have been agnostics — notably the English biologist Charles Darwin in the nineteenth century. Yet that century also produced James Clerk Maxwell, who devoted his Sundays to theological studies throughout his life.[4] At roughly the same time, there were such Christian believers as Ampère, Faraday, Joule, Helmholtz, Oersted, and Kelvin — to name only the more prominent.

Going back to the pivotal seventeenth and sixteenth centuries, we find such devout Christians as Robert Boyle, Tycho Brahe, Leonardo da Vinci, and Copernicus.[5] The pre-eminent Isaac Newton is said to have spent more of his energies on theology than on physics. Johannes Kepler, who systematized the planetary orbits, also developed the theory of lenses and invented the multi-wheeled counter which we use as the odometer in motor vehicles. He exclaimed, "O God, I think Thy thoughts after Thee." Galileo Galilei, the most central figure in the development of physics, was well versed in theology and remained loyal to the Christian faith despite his famous censure by the Vatican, an episode that was an almost trivial detail in the broad picture.[6]

What of the time before these men lived? During the last two centuries the opinion has prevailed that no scientific activity worthy of note took place in medieval Europe. One prominent historian of science called the Middle Ages "a mid-day slumber."[7] Indeed, historians are apt to mark the end of the medieval period by the rise of such figures as Leonardo da Vinci and Copernicus in the late fifteenth century. To grant this opinion its due, it must be admitted notably that the medieval Church pronounced, at the Council of Tours in 1163, that, since every man's body was the image of Christ's body, dissecting a man was equivalent to dissecting God — a reverential stance that stalled the progress of anatomy and surgery for several centuries.[8]

Is it really credible that for five centuries scientific progress had been arrested? A case for an alternative hypothesis has been posited, as early as 1904 by the French physicist Pierre Duhem, who made contributions to physical chemistry and thermodynamics.[9] He argued that for physics to be fully understood, its historical roots had to be known. He began writing on the topic of history of science, expecting to move quickly from the ancient Greeks straight to Galileo. Like his colleagues, he assumed that the medieval universities, preoccupied with theology, were unlikely to have accomplished any creative work in science.

Duhem's thoroughness led him into the pursuit and discovery of countless unknown manuscripts, mostly in Latin, lying untouched for centuries in scattered libraries. He spent twelve years of heroic effort on innumerable arcane, dusty manuscripts, many of which were written in obscure styles of handwriting that varied with the era and the location. By then it was clear to him that large segments of scientific history were missing in the accounts of his contemporaries.[10]

Working without secretaries or graduate assistants, without copying machine or typewriter, he nevertheless produced a gigantic ten-volume work, *Le système du monde: Histoire des doctrines cosmologiques de Platon à Copernic* (The System of the World: Cosmological Doctrines from Plato to Copernicus).[11] Among other things, it established that Jean Buridan, a professor of philosophy at the Sorbonne, was teaching around 1330 the theory that later became known as Newton's first law of motion, which states that physical objects upon which no force acts will be influenced by their inertia to continue in their existing state of motion or of rest. Centuries before Newton, we find Buridan writing:

> God made the heavens move with motions identical to the ones with which they still move. He impressed on them various *impeti* [sic] in virtue of which they continue to move with uniform velocity. As these *impeti* do not in fact encounter any resistance which would oppose them, they are never destroyed or diminished.[12]

Buridan consciously contradicted Aristotle's theory that continuous forceful contact between mover and moved is necessary to maintain motion, even in the case of projectiles. His insights were not lost, for even without the aid of printing, his theories and other contemporary work percolated through Europe. Galileo knew of Buridan.[13]

Buridan challenged Aristotelian theory further, for he claimed that "the motions of the heavens are subject to the same laws as motions of things on earth. There is a single mechanics by which all created things are governed, the orb of the sun as well as the top driven by a child."[14] Aristotle had claimed that different laws control the heavens and the earth. Unfortunately, Buridan's views were expressed in language and formulas unfamiliar to modern physicists and engineers; this may account for their long eclipse until Duhem rediscovered them. In any case, modern science did not burst suddenly into being with the "modern" era or Renaissance. Duhem notes appreciatively:

> The science of mechanics and physics, of which modern times are so rightfully proud, derives in an uninterrupted sequence of hardly visible improvements from doctrines professed in medieval schools. The pretended intellectual revolutions were all too often but slow and long-prepared evolutions. The so-called renaissances were often but unjust and sterile reactions. Respect for tradition is an essential condition of scientific progress. The graceful flight of the butterfly with glistening wings makes one forget the slow and painful crawling of the humble and somber caterpillar.[15]

Duhem declares, "Science does not know of spontaneous generation."[16] His work points up the gradual and continuous evolution of the physical science of mechanics as well as "the astonishing coherence of science as it has existed for the past four hundred years."[17] Yet Duhem's view has remained that of a minority.[18]

In academic communities the history of science is now apt to be regarded, not as one of gradual evolution, but as a series of radical "revolutions" — a Darwinian crushing of one idea by the fresh discovery of another. This view of the history of science as a series of intellectual jumps is favored by Alexandre Koyré and Thomas Kuhn. The Italian Renaissance has been taken as an instance of such a quantum leap. But Duhem cogently disputed the view that the Renaissance with its truly spectacular scientific advances arose simply out of the long-buried literary and artistic remains of ancient Greece and Rome. This thesis greatly qualifies the opinion of the popular historian Will Durant who said that "The Renaissance ended the thousand-year rule of the Oriental mind in Europe."

Is there reason, with Duhem, to cast doubt on the reality of this "great liberation"?[19] More grounds for doubt are afforded by the fact that the ancient literary remains were never entirely buried but were carefully preserved primarily in monasteries and quietly revived by the time of Buridan. While no one can deny the scientific impetus contributed by Greek philosophy and science, we begin to see that the historians' neglect of the science of the Middle Ages has led to a distorted view of that period. Even the literary, graphic, and musical achievements of the Middle Ages became widely recognized only a few decades ago.

The sheer arduousness of Duhem's work in the face of formidable barriers is evidence that the Middle Ages were a neglected period. So says Duhem's contemporary champion, Stanley L. Jaki, a Hungarian-American Benedictine priest and Templeton Prize recipient, who notes some causes of this skewing of the history of science. He suggests that the belittling of the scholarly accomplishments of the Middle Ages is owing to the Protestant religious reformers of the sixteenth century as well as to those leaders of the eighteenth-century Enlightenment who were hostile to the idea of a revealed religion that was not based on reason. Furthermore, Jaki suggests that these eighteenth-century scholars had little use for religion as revealed in alleged historical events rather than in reason.

In France the Enlightenment took a decidely anti-theistic turn, leading to the excesses of the French Revolution. The governing members of the Third Republic in the late nineteenth century regarded themselves as the heirs of that revolution and undertook an increasingly systematic and virulent campaign to free France from all clericalism and to deprive French Catholicism of all intellectual and social respectability. Accordingly, the French government forbade Catholic universities from calling themselves universities, and their degrees were no longer recognized by the state. By 1905 most religious orders had been suppressed and expelled from schools and hospitals, and all French education, including elementary and secondary schools, was in state control.

Duhem, who died in 1916, was systematically relegated to minor provincial positions by the French educational establishment, largely due to his long-standing disagreement with a bellwether of French scientists, P. E. Marcelin Berthelot, an excellent experimental chemist who had blocked the qualified Paul Tannery from a chair for the history of science because of his Catholicism. Not only was Duhem also a devout Catholic, but he had a cheerful lack of tact in intellectual encounters.[20]

Such background helps to explain the fate of Duhem's *Système du monde*. Even under the conditions of World War I, the famed scientific publisher A. Hermann managed to print the early volumes. Jaki, who is a physicist, historian and philosopher, calls Duhem's massive work "easily the most original, creative, and potentially epoch-making achievement for the interpretation of Western cultural history." Koyré, though an adversary, wrote of the first six volumes that the work was incredibly rich in data and in texts that could not be found anywhere else in print. The first five of the ten volumes were published by 1917. The publication of the crucial latter five volumes was to be purposefully delayed 37 to 42 years, and completion was not achieved until 1959. The early volumes had sold out by the mid-1930s, so we may suppose that the publisher did not take a loss on the project; nevertheless, the new director of the Hermann publishing firm stalled for thirty years against the persistent efforts of Duhem's daughter Hélène. Her perseverance was maintained despite broken commitments, postponed deadlines, and even a forfeited grant. She finally learned of the determined covert opposition of influential French academics, but the final five volumes appeared only after the eminent French physicist Louis de Broglie in 1954 threatened to sue the delinquent publishing director — who died two days later.[21]

To return to the content of Duhem's work, *Why* did science as a self-sustaining enterprise get its start only in the Christian Middle Ages? Why did science suffer a stillbirth in all ancient cultures? Why did this happen despite brilliant technological achievements in several of these cultures? Except for classical Greece, these cultures were nearly devoid of a true search for scientific law. Systematic searching is what the word "science" means, classically and properly. Science is not technology. Technology is largely the application of already discovered scientific law to the meeting of human needs.

Following Duhem and Jaki, the answer to these questions has more than one facet. *First*, we may note that the successful search for scientific law generally requires prodigious efforts. The labors and the many blind-alley pursuits of Kepler and of Michael Faraday are well documented in their own writings. The labors of Galileo, Newton, Maxwell and others are evident in their voluminous scientific writings, though the inevitable wrong turnings are generally omitted. Why would people go to such time and trouble to learn things of no apparent practical value — certainly of no cash value —

unless they thought that there was such a thing as a universally valid law of nature to look for? Indeed, how does the very idea of the existence of such laws arise?

Theism — that is, monotheism — is one facilitating condition. In the biblical book of Deuteronomy, God commands, "Thou shalt have no other gods before me. For I the Lord your God am a jealous God." In another passage, in Malachi, God says, "I change not." The importance of theism for science is seen when other religious cultures are considered. Most Westerners, nurtured in a theistic heritage, do not spontaneously empathize with those whose heritage does not include belief in God who alone created the universe, sustains it and makes it intelligible. For if there be several gods, as in ancient Greek polytheistic religion, then each event in the world would depend on the particular god who was attending to whatever matter was at hand. Moreover, as the texts of Homer and Hesiod make clear, a pagan would have to reckon with the all-too-human and varying moods of the Greek gods and their Roman counterparts. To take such polytheism seriously is to bar oneself from discovering the very idea of universal physical law.

Yet in its passion for reason and order, the late classical Greek world produced the geometer Euclid, the astronomers Anaxagoras, Aristarchus, Hipparchus and Ptolemy, as well as the versatile Archimedes — all of them in the second and third centuries B.C. Nor should we forget Plato and Aristotle (fourth century B.C.) for their contributions to logic and for their explorations of the great questions of epistemology and cosmology. In order to be scientists, all these thinkers had in some sense to put aside the theory of nature that was inherent in polytheism. Should we suppose that these exceptional thinkers were influenced by suggestions of monotheism such as we find in Plato and earlier in the philosopher Xenophanes of the sixth century B.C.? It is tempting to think that they were, but the extent of such influence is not known.[22]

However, the scientific enterprise was already somewhat under way by the late sixth century B.C. in Ionia (western Asia Minor), among the philosophers of Miletus, namely Thales, Anaximander, and Anaximenes. The point is not whether their naive proto-scientific and proto-cosmological speculations were correct, but rather that these Milesians rejected myth and fable as explanation, supposing rather that natural events occur according to law in a world that is somehow a unitary system.

Whose law? So far as we know, no one's; the laws were taken to be just there, embedded in the system of nature and knowable by the seeker. However, this does not imply that these ancient Greeks had a materialistic view of nature as opposed to spiritual; at that early date, the distinction had not been formulated clearly enough to be denied.[23]

Among the Milesians, science seems not to have got past the stage of talking and writing; the labor of the investigation of nature by experiment was lacking. Millenia later, in medieval Europe, further thought would push aside the mutually contradictory theories of the early Greeks. Nevertheless, overly simple speculation was where it all had to start. With the clear precedent of the Milesian philosophers, we must accord to ancient Greece the title of father of science, even though theism may not have been involved. In any case, the scientific thought-patterns that these Greek scientists developed did not finally find any broad or continuing support in their own culture. Even Archimedes, the greatest engineer of antiquity, refused to write a handbook of engineering. It would of course have involved his physics.[24] Perhaps in ancient Greek culture it would have been déclassé to dwell upon such servile, useful matters. The authentic Christian spirit is quite the opposite in its willingness to serve — to do what needs to be done without worrying about one's appearance of dignity. To the extent that science might be expected to be useful, as it has proven to be, this Christian spirit has furnished a motive for the development of science.

What of the Islamic world with its brilliant, intellectual civilization up to the time of the Crusades? Indeed, Moorish Spain was a great school of ancient thought for the West. Why didn't a successful search for scientific law develop in the Moslem world? After all, Islam is theistic — more plainly monotheistic, some would claim, than Christianity. The Islamic failure to improve much upon the science they inherited appears to stem from the fundamentalist view, widespread even now, that the assertion of natural law implicit in science blasphemously constrains an omnipotent God or Allah. Unconstrained by any kind of law, Allah is presumed to have power to vitiate any scientific law at will.[25] Obviously, a law must by definition persist with some reliability in order to be a law. Hence, a dilemma has been presented to those Moslems who pursued philosophy or who might have pursued science.

There is a *second* reason why science as an ongoing activity flourished within Christendom, which helps make it the cradle of science. If the one God is to be taken as the Father Almighty, the Maker of Heaven and Earth, of all things visible and invisible, then evidently He created more than bare nature and nature's laws; He created our very selves, too. In assuming this common Parenthood, there arises the intriguing thought that all of us as God's children have been created in such a way that we can learn some of the singular laws that a rational God has put into place. This supposition was and is properly the heart of the metaphysic of *scientific realism*, wherein the world is taken as existing independently of our minds, as well as being sufficiently intelligible to meet our needs.[26] All that is demanded of seekers is that they have the faith and persistence to search and to think. The American philosopher Charles Sanders Peirce points out, "Every scientific explanation of a natural phenomenon is a hypothesis that there is something in nature to which the human reason is analogous; and that it really is so all the successes of science in its applications to human convenience are witnesses." Peirce declares further that "Every single truth of science is due to the affinity of the human soul to the soul of the universe, imperfect as that affinity no doubt is."[27]

Galileo was explicit about *il lume naturale*, which is man's inward power or light to know what is real: "Taking one's understanding *intensively*, in so far as this term denotes understanding some propositions perfectly, I say that the human intellect does understand some of them perfectly, and thus in these it has as much absolute certainty as Nature itself has."[28] Indeed, Galileo "was overwhelmed by the clarity of the great book of Nature read with the eyes of reason."[29] Similarly, in an early letter, Kepler reveals the mainspring of his own life's work. He expresses the hope that his writing would

> have everywhere among reasonable people fully the effect that the belief in the creation of the world be fortified, that the thought of the Creator be recognized in its nature, and that the Creator's inexhaustible wisdom shine forth daily more brightly. Then people will at least measure the power of his mind on the true scale, and will realize that God, who founded everything in the world according to the norm of quantity, also has endowed them with a mind which can comprehend these norms.[30]

If the cosmos is God's creation, then it speaks to us of Him. What about the Chinese peoples in all of this? Science did not arise among them, despite the outstanding inventiveness of the Chinese that first led to the compass, cast iron, rockets, block printing, movable type (it wasn't Gutenberg!), paper, the rudder, sails for tacking into the wind, canal locks, suspension bridges, natural gas drilling to

4800 feet, the decimal system, negative numbers, smallpox vaccina-
tions, wheelbarrows, water wheels, foot-stirrups, tuned bells, the
tempered musical scale, porcelain, parachutes, chess, etc. Most of
these inventions were made before the fall of Rome, some of them
before Christ.[31] However, there have been anticipations of natural
science. Chu Hsi in the twelfth century A.D. found oyster shell
fossils on high mountains and argued that there must have been
at some time a vast uplift of land from under the sea. This correct
speculation, like others, was not followed by any sustained resolve
by other scholars to investigate or to teach. Jaki lists examples of
despair and of rejection by the Chinese of their own thinkers, as
well as of the European thinkers, while science was flowering in
Europe.

Why was science stillborn in China? No one who knows the
Chinese will suppose that it was for lack of native ability. The trouble
appears to have been an accident of religious history. China long
ago took the "will of Heaven" — impersonal, silent, voiceless — to
be the mysterious and inscrutable force behind all happenings and
that, so far as people can know, "Everything produces itself and
does not depend on anything else."

Not since about the second millenium B.C. has Chinese culture
embraced monotheism. Even the biochemist and historian of science
Joseph Needham, an avowed Marxist, states in his multi-volume
work *Science and Civilisation in China* that it was the absence of theism
in Chinese culture that prevented the ascendancy of science there.
He writes: "It was not that there was no order in Nature for the
Chinese, but rather that it was not an order ordained by a rational
personal being, and hence there was no conviction that rational
personal beings would be able to spell out in their lesser earthly
languages the divine code of laws which he [God] had decreed
aforetime."[32]

By contrast, Christianity supplied to Europe what Chinese religion
lacked, namely, the *conviction* that humanity can understand reality,
thanks to the identity of the source of our own being with the source
of scientific law. In addition, monotheism implies a *single* source
of law. The result is that the laws which we discover are truly laws —
reliable, self-consistent, and universal in time and place. Incidentally, the Ionian philosophers of Miletus had no concept of creation;
for them, the cosmos was uncreated and eternal, as for the Chinese.

Among Jaki's magnificent books is *The Road of Science and the Ways
to God*,[33] which is important for its incisive and usually cogent critique

of the systems of modern philosophy. What spectacular devastation Jaki wreaks upon them! With a broad brush, he criticizes them from the standpoint of the realist natural scientific philosophy that is the backbone of modern natural science.

As a system, moderate scientific realism is opposed to subjectivist or anti-realist (or some "idealist") philosophies such as those of David Hume, Immanuel Kant, Georg W. F. Hegel, and their many intellectual heirs. Moderate scientific realism is opposed to Hume insofar as he denies causality which, in the words of a certain Pennsylvania Dutchman, was well announced: "Dere iss t'ings vot does t'ings." Scientific realism is also basically opposed to phenomenalism — a philosophy that implies roughly that, so far as you *can* see something, it may well be regarded as not existent.[34] Scientific realism is likewise opposed to positivism, which implies that if you *can't* see something, it doesn't exist. Taken to the extreme, positivism would exclude natural laws themselves, as well as the consciousness of those people who discover and use them.

Certainly, these facile characterizations do not do justice to the many genuine insights of modern philosophers within these movements. Nevertheless, as systems they are incompatible with that activity which is natural science. In many minds, this is reason enough to regard them as fatally flawed. Still, the study of the systems themselves has value in revealing how to cut down the ever vigorous weeds of error and to gain important secondary elements of truth.

Also, moderate scientific realism and process philosophy, while not in all respects incompatible, do not always support each other. As derived in this century from the philosophers Alfred North Whitehead and Charles Hartshorne, process philosophy implies that nearly everything is in flux, that there is no strict continuing self-identity of things or persons, and that everything affects everything else except when it doesn't. The latter position is not helpful in classical science. But criticism should be tempered. It would be less glib to say that process philosophy provides a conceptual framework in which wide relational interaction can be conceived to occur. Hence, it affords needed scope for important concepts in psychology, gravitation, quantum mechanics, and theology.[35]

The matter of causality just mentioned brings up a third way to show why Christianity may justly be called the cradle of science. Most ancients appear to have taken seriously the idea of cyclic time, the view that what happens now has happened before and will happen again, and again, and again, with never-ending repetitions — even identical repetitions. At the end of each such cosmic cycle there would be a so-called Great Year during which everything would start over again to repeat itself. Belief in these inexorably influential cosmic cycles swept ancient India and is found in Mesopotamian, Hindu, Buddhist, Jain, and Persian literature, as well as to a significant extent in that of Greece and Rome.[36]

Arnold Toynbee helps us to understand what this "wheel of fate" meant to the ancients. In erroneously supposing its truth, they deduced that we human beings are all

> the perpetual victims of an everlasting cosmic practical joke, which condemns us to endure our sufferings and to overcome our difficulties and to purify ourselves of our sins — only to know in advance that the automatic and inevitable lapse of a certain meaningless measure of Time cannot fail to stultify all our human exertions by reproducing the same situation again and again *ad infinitum*, just as though we had never exerted ourselves at all.

Where the idea of eternally recurring cosmic cycles was taken seriously, science could not arise. The *first* reason, adumbrated above, is that a belief in eternal cycles condemns budding scientists to evaluate their prospective tasks in the belief that this "automatic and inevitable lapse of a certain meaningless measure of Time" renders all their exertions trivial, not only their exertions during this cosmic cycle but also their identical exertions in all the past cycles and in the next one and in the next, and so on forever as these cycles recur upon themselves in a blind circularity.[37] Commenting on the mental lull which overcomes humans when their sense of the unique value and flow of time is weakened, Jaki calls the doctrine of eternal recurrence the "chief nemesis of the scientific enterprise in all ancient cultures."

The early leaders of the Christian church, notably Origen in the third century, rejected the idea of eternally recurring cycles and of the Great Year marking the beginning of each new cycle. Origen reasons that, if eternal returns were real, then Adam and Eve would again re-enact what they did, and Moses would again lead six hundred thousand out of Egypt. Jesus would again be incarnated, born, betrayed, crucified, and resurrected, only to be with His Father forever after, again and again. Origen believes that the unique, once-occurring historical events bore a cosmic meaning that is of a higher level than that of a colossal practical joke. Hence, he holds that such events could have happened only once, never to recur. For Origen, as for Christianity, the Creation was an absolute beginning which implied a linear direction of history, a Creation followed by a unique, progressive flow of time and a definite meaning for each moment.[38]

The philosophy of eternal recurrence ultimately was suppressed in Western civilization. Christendom, by rejecting blind irrational fate as a universal cause, supplied strength to the liberating belief in the linearity of time, which belief became an essential presupposition of modern science. In this way also, the Christian faith nurtured the Greek idea of scientific laws. Such laws specify the efficient causes of events to be those events immediately preceding, rather than some inscrutable repetitive Fate. Science progresses through consideration of identifiable antecedent causes, not occult ones.

A *second* scientifically relevant problem with the myth of eternal return is its implict denial of Creation and hence of any Creator distinct from the physical universe. If there was no Creation, then God was simply one part of primeval and eternal nature. In a different way, the recently discredited steady-state theory of the universe carried a similar implication, namely, that the universe of itself is necessary, eternal, and unchanging, with no need of a Creator.[39] Either way, the denial of Creation weakens, as we have seen, an important motive to do science. The notoriously refractory philosophical problem of the basis for scientific induction seems soluble only in theism.[40]

Finally, we may note a *third* reason why the myth of eternal return, rejected by Christendom, proves inimical to the activity of scientific discovery. Consider the popular song *Que será será,* "Whatever will be will be." Since songwriters do not indulge in empty tautologies, this song entails fatalism — i.e., merely another of the many ways to avoid responsibility, and an insidious way it is. One of the authors remembers from long ago being profoundly troubled by this song. For fatalism, when accepted consistently, undermines any reason for exerting oneself at all, whether to do science, or to philosophize about fatalism, or to do anything at all that is not directly pleasurable.[41]

An objector may reply that some materialists among scientists do find scientific activity directly pleasurable and hence pursue it without benefit of theism. This is true, but they inevitably make use of the presuppositions provided long ago by theism that are by now part of the background of science.

No one supposes that Origen or Augustine foresaw the prodigious development of science as a consequence of rejecting the idea of time as cyclical process. Nevertheless, in Duhem's words, "The Fathers of the Church cleared the terrain for modern science."[42] However, the idea of eternal returns is still with us, if only through Friedrich Nietzsche and Karl Marx's collaborator Friedrich Engels.[43] It is also part of astrology, which once more flourishes all around.[44]

The eighteenth-century English historian Edward Gibbon summed up his multi-volume *History of the Decline and Fall of the Roman Empire*, saying, "I have described the triumph of Barbarism and Religion." Here Gibbon was referring to Christianity. In response, Toynbee in considering that same period writes: " 'The triumph of Barbarism and Religion' was not the plot of the play, but only an epilogue." The mortal blow, he implies, was delivered hundreds of years earlier, culminating in the Peloponnesian Wars, and "the hand that dealt it was the victim's own." In other words, the civilization "had decayed from inherent defects of its own before Christianity arose."[45]

Some have thought Toynbee's thesis to be overdrawn in this case.[46] However, in light of the history considered in this chapter, one should not dismiss it, either. We may well attend to the remark of Lord Bolingbroke: "History is philosophy teaching by examples."[47]

Occasionally, educated people or professional historians have heard a little of Duhem's work in the history of science. Yet it is still unusual to find anyone who appreciates the role of the Christian religion in the development of science. Jaki cites several examples of the calculated ignoring or distorting of Duhem's significant work.[48] This will surprise no one who has experienced the contempt for theistic religion that now prevails in secular academic life. Jaki justly charges the intellectual establishment with the " 'scholarly' lie that science and Christianity are irreconcilable" and that "Christianity had to be discredited so that science could arise."[49]

The fact remains that the spirit of physical science is most congenial to Christianity, which encouraged and fostered it. It should henceforth be an odd procedure for a scientist or philosopher of science to demean the theistically derived presuppositions of science, especially since one of those presuppositions is the rationality — that is, the consistency and intelligibility — of all that exists. The conviction of the existence of a loving, powerful God as sole Creator and wholly rational personal Planner, Builder, and Maintainer of the universe made it possible for science to flourish as it has. As to Judaism, one does find in their late scriptures a move in this direction, when God is addressed, "Thou hast ordered all things by measure and number and weight" — a passage that is often quoted by thinkers of the Middle Ages.[50]

If ancient Greece is to be called the progenitor of science, Christianity has both a logical and historical right to be called the cradle of science. Jaki writes, the Christian certitude about the rationality of nature, about the human ability to investigate its laws, "owes its vigor to the concreteness by which Christ radiated the features of God." For God created in "that fulness of rationality which is love."[51]

Today it appears that every organized religion, even Roman Catholicism that nursed science in its childhood, is neglecting the lesson to be drawn from the history of science, namely, the understanding of why Christianity made science as an ongoing activity possible some seven centuries ago.

Having seen something of this complex history, we now need to ask: Can ethics without some sort of theistic foundation be an intellectually coherent field? Can such ethics be expected to elicit behavior that is socially and personally productive? To these questions we shall shortly turn. But first, we must consider the validity of what is called natural theology.

God is seen not with the eyes but with the mind.
*Augustine*

# 4

## Evolution or Creation?

The scientist John Haldane once suggested to Monsignor Ronald Knox that in a universe containing millions of planets it was inevitable that life should appear by chance on one of them. "Sir," said Knox, "if Scotland Yard found a body in your Saratoga trunk, would you tell them, 'There are millions of trunks in the world—surely one of them must contain a body'? I think they still would want to know who put it there."

*John J. McAleer*

AN ATHEIST FRIEND has in his library a book entitled, on its spine, *What God Hath Revealed to the Human Race.* But on opening it, one finds only five hundred pages of blank paper. We may admire his cleverness but still reject the implication of this "book."

In most secular colleges, the discipline of philosophy has become stridently anti-religious. Many academicians make no pretense of their contempt toward any who do not embrace atheism. At Boston University, a student mentioned theism seriously to a bright young logic instructor. The young teacher turned contemptuously on his heel and disappeared down the hall without a word.

Natural theology is properly knowledge of a Supreme Being that is obtained without resort to mystical experience or revelation. It is the kind of knowledge of God which is, in principle, directly accessible to all inquirers. Those who hold to the sufficiency of authoritarian and traditional religious knowledge should not despise natural theology; rather they should take it as a valuable ally, protecting their revealed religion from the accusation of resting only on faith or on someone's private experience. "A skeleton cannot walk, but you cannot walk without a skeleton." Natural theology functions as the skeleton.

In the Bible, the argument from the design of the universe for the existence of God is put simply in the Psalms: "The heavens declare the glory of God, and the firmament proclaims His handiwork." Or again, by implications: "I will praise thee, for I am fearfully and wonderfully made; marvelous are thy works."[1]

The earliest sustained argument based on nature for God's existence was made by Plato, in *The Laws*.[2] Of those who have contributed since, the thirteenth-century theologian Thomas Aquinas and the eighteenth-century theologian William Paley stand out. Paley is remembered for suggesting the Creator's special intervention in directly creating each of the myriad species of plants and animals in all their needful details that enable them to survive and flourish.[3] Such intervention, widely known as creationism, is one kind of *teleology*, which in turn is the more inclusive doctrine that natural happenings somehow are informed by purpose or a goal.

Simple biological evolution is the theory that all life evolved in a tree-like branching of physically related descent, that all life is physically descended from a few primitive micro-organisms or even from only one, developing through the generations from lower forms to more complex forms. These later, complex forms are commonly held to be of higher quality than the simpler predecessors, with human beings at the top of the hierarchy. Charles Darwin did not originate the theory of simple biological evolution, his grandfather Erasmus Darwin did.

Micro-evolution within species is an undeniable fact. Countless inheritable micro-variations in plants and animals have been observed. Darwin found evidence of micro-evolution in the plumage of finches in the Galápagos Islands. Moreover, animal and plant breeders select such inheritable micro-changes continually. As further evidence of simple evolution, biologists cite the similarities of organization and of function found among many creatures. They point to a human embryo, how it remarkably resembles the embryos of other creatures at early stages, that gill slits are found in the human embryo at one stage, a fact suggesting that land and marine life have a common ancestry.

Further, the same biochemical building blocks are used in all life. In *Origins*, a widely read, jolting, big book, the agnostic Robert

Shapiro, a professor of chemistry and an expert on the genetic effects of environmental chemicals, expresses his misgivings about evolutionary theories in general. Yet he tells us, "In every known organism, heredity is preserved in nucleic acids, proteins are made in ribosomes, the same set of amino acids is used to construct proteins, energy is stored in ATP [adenosinetriphosphate], and an almost identical genetic code is employed."[4] The greater the apparent difference of a creature or organism from humans, the greater also is the number of differences in the otherwise similar amino-acid sequences of its enzymes known as cytochrome C, as well as in other series of molecules.

**FRANK and ERNEST®**     by Bob Thaves     February 23, 1983

ONE GOOD THING ABOUT CREATIONISM ---- IT CERTAINLY MAKES ME FEEL A LOT LESS GUILTY!

Informed creationists acknowledge these facts but deny that they necessarily support any theory of evolution. They assume that God had reasons for repeating or adapting these patterns so consistently among organisms in the manner we find.

Charles Darwin added to the simple theory of evolution a mechanism that would put the course of otherwise simple evolution on auto-pilot as it were. His ideas were that (1) the inheritable variations to be found among species have occurred in nature entirely randomly and mechanistically and, further, that (2) the natural selection of these random inheritable variations could explain, in a mechanistic fashion, many of the physical adaptations of animals and plants to their environments. In this way, the evolving of higher forms would have mimicked purpose that might not have been there. The webbed feet of ducks, the protective coloring of moths, the hollowed bones of birds, the appropriateness of plants as food, as well as countless other happy accommodations, are cited as arguments for Darwin's theory, even as they are cited by creationists as evidence for individual divine creation of species.

Darwin argued that minute inherited, purely random variations or mutations are exploited in constructive ways by the ongoing natural selection of the variations as they interact with the given environment — physical and social. That is, some inherited variations contribute to the probability that a possessor of one of them will survive and leave progeny with the same new characteristic, while less suitable inherited variations do the opposite. For instance, the moths of Britain underwent a darkening of color while the smoke of modern industry darkened the trees upon which they rested. Darwin did not claim to have proved that life has a common descent in the manner he suggested. He did suggest that for one so to believe explains some otherwise puzzling facts. The Darwinian theory gained support from the work of Gregor Mendel, who presented a mechanistic pattern for genetic inheritance; his work pointed to a physical basis for it. That physical basis has since been discovered and is even now being revealed by biochemists in greater and greater detail.

In brief, Darwin and his successors have argued that evolution not only occurred but that it occurred as a result of natural, scientifically intelligible processes that had no need of divine interventions to achieve the results we find. Darwin's theory enables biologists to connect facts about different species into patterns of hereditary causes of structure that are scientifically intriguing in their economy and apparent clarity. To some who seek to know why we encounter the evils that we do in life, the impersonal process of Darwinian evolution allows scope for evils to occur since, on such a view, God need not be blamed as directly willing evils. Even theistic biologists point out that the alternative of presuming that God is in control of whatever happens in nature may, if invoked too readily, cut the nerve of motivation for doing natural science. Recourse to theistic explanation, no matter how valid and warranted it may become at some end-point of explanation, goes beyond the reach of natural science — a prospect likely to make scientists giddy.

Most biologists believe that even the very origin of life can be explained on mechanistic principles without divine intervention. They may be hard put to counter the arguments against a popular theory of this kind in *The Mystery of Life's Origin*, by Charles Thaxton, Walter Bradley, and Roger Olsen.[5] The book in much of its detailed argumentation can be understood only by chemists. Yet these authors carefully contend that the "prebiotic conditions" that some alleged to be essential to the evolution of primitive life from inert matter never existed. For example, there seems to be no good evidence for the early existence of a reducing atmosphere containing hydrogen compounds, which would have had to hover over the earth at the time when evolution is supposed to have gotten under way. There seems to be no good evidence for the alleged "prebiotic soup." There is no evidence for the common, dishonestly spread notion that life has been created in the laboratory. There is no evidence for the dogma that the basic building blocks of life (the incredibly intricate molecules of self-replicating proteins, nucleosides, nucleotides, ribonucleic acids and nucleic acids) all could have come into an intercoordinated functional relationship, together in a cooperative unison, merely by chance.

Many biologists know, as most laymen do not, that Darwinism has so far proved unable to explain a number of significant facts that it is commonly invoked to explain in schoolbooks and lay publications. There is an awkward, undeniable fact of paleontology, which is the study of the history of fossils embedded in sedimentary rocks. According to this cumulative record of the history of the earth, entirely new species have arisen suddenly, being separated by wide gaps of form and function from the previously existing species. The existence of these gaps is attested also by facts of molecular chemistry and by the novel, controversial system of taxonomic classification afforded by "cladistics." The Australian M.D. and scientist Michael Denton elaborates on these and many related problems in his readable book *Evolution: A Theory in Crisis*.[6] But Darwin's own observations led him to insist that only minute variations in individuals take place and that all of the larger changes in species are the cumulated result of these micro-mutations.

The trouble here is that, most usually, the fossil record contains no sign of the alleged intermediate species, which would have had to arise quickly and be quickly superseded in order for the gap to be filled in the geologic time frame that was available. The gap between almost any two orders or families is genetically so great that no number of random mutations of genes, occurring over however protracted a period of time, could have more than a zero probability of ever bridging it by mere chemical accidents as Darwinian theory demands. Though heated debate continues, there seems to be no more chance of this happening than there is of a 747 luxury airliner evolving accidentally out of a 737, or out of a DC-10. The conclusion applies *a fortiori* to the gaps between classes and phyla of creatures.

The brilliant little book *Darwin Retried*, by the distinguished and versatile lawyer Norman Macbeth, is a learned and impartial work of dissent with prestigious recommendations. Of special interest is Macbeth's summary of the failure of breeders to prove evolution in the laboratory. Many biologists hoped that, by bringing about thousands of artificially induced mutations in the genes of *Drosophila* flies, breeders could do in the laboratory what it had taken millions of years for nature to accomplish by random chemical changes. Macbeth shows that all of the breeding experiments aimed at creating new species have proven to be in vain. Inevitably, just as the breeders were hoping that the next generation would be a new species, the next generation on the contrary either never occurred at all because the flies became infertile, or else the next generation, after vast numbers of micro-changes, simply reverted back to the fly as it was before any mutations in it were brought about. In studying these facts Macbeth concluded, along with many breeders, that there is no evidence that micro-changes ever succeed in bringing about macro-effects.[7] That is, if many hundreds of mutations were induced in a given species, it still could produce no new species.

The current estimate of beneficial or positive mutations is that they occur at the rate of about once in three thousand to ten thousand times; the rest are neutral or negative in effect. Then how could the many needed and supposedly random variations to define a new adaptation all happen at once and lead to anything but non-functional, abortive creatures? Even with constructive mutations, would not the poison apparatus of a snake in its complexity be worse than useless until enough constructive mutations had occurred to enable the snake to poison its prey? Darwin himself felt dumbfounded in trying to account for the complexity of the human eye.[8]

Again, there is the unique and improbable defense mechanism of the bombardier beetle that dwells upon chalk formations. When danger threatens, it ejects and mixes *two* fluids, each consisting of *two* chemicals, into its rear-directed, "flame-throwing" combustion chamber where, to the discomfiture of the aggressor, they literally explode and liberate noticeable heat and odor of combustion. All four chemicals are necessary and would be useless if only three of them were present. The combustion chamber is made of heat-resisting material, without which the operation would backfire and so be most uncomfortable for the beetle. The end result is wonderful enough, but think of the countless little disasters entailed in the alleged accidental sortings of the component features required to bridge this evolutionary gap — that is, if it had to occur by Darwin's random micro-mutations. Was it only randomness followed by life-and-death selection that enabled this very ingeniously designed mechanism to come into being? One is inclined to say, in sympathy with those allegedly gradually evolving beetles, "Ouch!"[9]

Such objections are not new, nor are these examples knockdown arguments. Darwin was more aware than most of his successors of the strength of opposing views. Yet the objections to Darwinism deserve more public attention, and more play in elementary text-books, than they have been receiving.

The late respected geneticist Richard Goldschmidt entirely gave up trying to account for the development of new species in terms of micro-evolutionary changes cumulating into macro-changes. Then, in his desire to save evolution, Goldschmidt invented the hypothesis of the so-called "hopeful monster." That is, he proposed that new species were brought into existence suddenly by radical "saltations" — by systemic mutations all at once. The epitome of an instance of this theory would be this: a reptile laid an egg, and a bird was hatched from the egg. The theory is more a statement of the underlying paradox than a scientific theory. On Goldschmidt's assumption of blind, random mutations, no resolution has appeared or seems likely.[10]

Of course, there would be no problem of accounting for a bird hatching out of a reptile's egg if we assume that God extensively and radically manipulated the genes in the egg in a way unaccomplishable by random chemical events occurring in nature on their own. With this latitude, the Goldschmidt hypothesis becomes a kind of theistic evolution. Another hypothesis is that of Niles Eldridge and Stephen Jay Gould, who suggest more temperately that radical evolution producing new species occurred in each case within small groups, not all of a sudden but in short steps and in a short time, geologically speaking. Surface plausibility is increased by assuming this slower pace, but any mechanism for this transformation to take place under blind chance remains as unknown, and conceptually almost as difficult, as with Goldschmidt's "hopeful monster" theory. Yet, an adaptation of the Eldredge-Gould theory is open to theistic evolutionists, too, since they believe that positive genetic mutations productive of new and stronger species are generally, though not necessarily always, brought about by the influence of God, whether by intervention on the scene or more subtly. The American botanist Asa Gray suggested this much in 1880 under the clear term "mediate creation." Lately, the label "deistic evolution" has been used.[11]

**FRANK and ERNEST®** by Bob Thaves                          October 27, 1983

The broadest problem with atheistic evolution, or the theories of Goldschmidt, Eldridge and Gould as they stated them, is that the theories place an unreasonable burden upon blind chance in the creation of the forms of life we know. The alleged sufficiency of totally random variation in bringing forth a basis of complexity for the natural selection of viable life is called into question when we consider countless groups of complex phenomena. To take an example, consider the unlearned behavior of a pair of wrens rapidly building a nest out of random materials and possessing no instructions. Again, to examine the fine structure of the reticular formation of the mammalian brain "makes one humble," to cite the Scheibels, the first systematic investigators.[12] Beyond this there is the unimaginable complexity (prima facie evidence of intelligent design) within and between the 14 billion ($14 \times 10^9$) nerve cells in the human body. Each has numerous contact projections or dendrites. Nerve cells are only one class of cell within the human body. There are said to be a total of about 10 quadrillion ($10^{16}$) animal cells of something like two hundred thousand different kinds.[13]

Michael Denton depicts the overwhelming, awesome presence of intelligent design in the submicroscopic levels of the world in which all creatures exist and function. He says:

> The intuitive feeling that pure chance could never have achieved the degree of complexity and ingenuity so ubiquitous

in nature has been a continuing source of scepticism ever since the publication of the *Origin [of Species]*; and throughout the past century there has always existed a significant minority of first-rate biologists who have never been able to bring themselves to accept the validity of Darwinian claims. Perhaps in no other area of modern biology is the challenge posed by the extreme complexity and ingenuity of biological adaptations more apparent than in the fascinating new molecular world of the cell. To grasp the reality of life as it has been revealed by molecular biology, we must magnify a cell a thousand million times until it is twenty kilometres in diameter and resembles a giant airship large enough to cover a great city like London or New York. What we would then see would be an object of unparalled complexity and adaptive design. On the surface of the cell we would see millions of openings, like the port holes of a vast space ship, opening and closing to allow a continual stream of materials to flow in and out. If we were to enter one of these openings we would find ourselves in a world of supreme technology and bewildering complexity. Is it really credible that random processes could have constructed a reality, the smallest element of which — a functional protein or gene — is complex beyond our own creative capacities, a reality which is the very antithesis of chance, which excels in every sense anything produced by the intelligence of man?[14]

All these facts and more allow one to doubt not only the usefulness of the atheistic emphasis on blind chance, but also its sufficiency as a creative device.[15] We may turn now to another kind of evidence of divine design, namely, the seeming design of the physical universe as a theater for the flourishing of life. We find many arrangements of the inorganic world which, taken all together, are amazingly commodious to life. The scientist J. E. Lovelock has gathered much of the evidence for this into his book *The Ages of Gaia*. The title derives from the Greek goddess of the earth whom Lovelock tends to reify into a metaphorical aid to understanding. He presents the thesis that life functions in some important biological ways as if it were all one organism making continual adjustments as though by an invisible hand for the good of the whole. There are benefits to be derived from the study of Lovelock's data, even though the idea of one single organism borders on a pantheism that could undermine the reality of individual creatures with their freedom of choice and responsibility.[16]

One's amazement over the auspicious plan of the universe increases when one considers the seemingly overwhelming probability that lethal combinations of chemical and physical factors would have made the development of life impossible without a plan, one with specific physical constants studded into the plan. Without a plan, disastrous astronomical and geological conditions inevitably would have taken place, making the creation or progress of life impossible. The emergence of life, it seems, was not an accident. Still, the philosopher Holmes Rolston III, a Christian theist, happily characterizes original life as an "accident waiting to happen."[17]

> The fallacy of any age lies mainly in what it takes
> for granted.
>
> *Dallas Irvine*

# 5

## *Universal Design*

Anything as well ordered and perfectly created as
is our earth and universe must have a Maker, a
Master Designer. Anything so orderly, so perfect,
so precisely balanced, so majestic as this creation
can only be the product of a Divine Idea. There
must be a Maker; there can be no other way.
*Wernher von Braun*, rocket engineer

BESIDES DARWIN, the most renowned antagonist
of natural theology has been the eighteenth-century Scottish
philosopher David Hume.[1] Hume's arguments have been exploited
to great effect in the twentieth century by Bertrand Russell. Many
in academia maintain that Hume destroyed the argument for God's
existence from universal design. Hume and Darwin have in common the resort to the negative concept of blind chance as an explanation of the world and its happenings without having to rely
on God for such explanation. In brief, Hume's treatment amounts
to abstract conjecture containing fatal flaws.

A simplified and general rebuttal to Hume must suffice here. The
crux of Hume's argument is that ultimately nothing can be explained,
that ultimately there is no reason for anything — a state of affairs
that he was never able to give any reason for, or to explain. Followers
of Hume argue that there is no reason why there must be a reason
for things. How convenient for them! They set themselves up in
a position of privileged intellectual immunity, where those who
believe in God have to explain everything, while they have to explain

nothing. Theists have to give good reasons for their belief, but objectors do not have to give good reasons for their denial nor even explain how the world came to exist just by happenstance — i.e., for no reason.

**FRANK and ERNEST®** by Bob Thaves                          August 31, 1988

No one can give a logical reason to argue that ultimately there is no logical reason. Nor can anyone give a rationale for the assumption that reality ultimately is devoid of a rationale. Similarly, there can be no abiding value in the assumption that there can be no abiding value. Nor does it make sense to argue that reality ultimately does not make sense.

Atheists hold that the existence of the universe is a bald accident, i.e., that it is devoid of reason, purpose, and ideals because God does not exist to inform it with reason, purpose, and ideals. The laws of nature are pegged on nothing but blind chance, which means that they are there for no reason or purpose whatever. Since they are there for no reason, there is no reason why they should continue to be there tomorrow, and no reason why they should ever have been there in the first place. The sun always rises in the east, but it is the laws of nature that make this happen, and since the laws of nature are in the world for no reason, then there can be no reason why the sun should not rise tomorrow in the west instead of the east, or indeed why it should continue to exist at all.

According to atheism, the laws of nature are meaningless accidents, and we are the accidental beneficiaries of these same meaningless events occurring as the sun rises every morning. Scientifically inclined atheists hold that the original reality was a gigantesque glob of hydrogen atoms in existence for no reason and made up of lifeless, absolutely unfeeling, unreasoning, care-less, purposeless, and meaningless inert particles. As aeons of time passed, these inert particles of dead matter somehow accidentally produced *persons.* The existence of the earth, and our life on it, are ultimately grounded in nothing but blind chance.

But if anything can exist, then so can God exist. *How anything at all could exist is a stunning mystery.* The atheistic argument that everything is reducible to chance is not an argument against God. If anything can just "chance" to exist, then so can God. Atheists claim that the existence of the universe needs no explanation. If that is the case, then neither does God's existence need any explanation.

Scientific laws are unified and mutually ordered to a superb degree of perfection. We have discovered hundreds of laws of nature that we have formulated in very precise language so that all scientists and engineers affirm their truth in predicting how nature will operate. Moreover, these laws operate uniformly and consistently throughout all known space, and they transcend all of the known changes in time as far back into the past as our scientific knowledge of nature goes. That is, the same laws that are operating in the universe in 1990 were also operating in 1980, 1970, 1960, and so on. If nothing but blind chance accounts for reality, then why don't the laws of nature sometimes "just chance" to change?

All of the sciences are predicated on invariance in the operation of nature's laws. "Lawful" means constant. Invariance means uninterrupted constancy. To derive invariance from chance is to work with incompatible categories. If a single one of these laws failed to operate invariantly, then the whole system would come tumbling down.

None of the laws of nature work in opposition to each other but function in a stunningly delicate order of coordinated inter-dependence, without which the sciences would be inconceivable. Clearly, this proves that the universe is a Rational System evincing the presence of reason and purpose informing the structure of the cosmos. For how could all this order be there without there being one single purpose?

Why do all electrons *always* have a negative charge as long as they exist? If nothing is involved but blind chance, then why don't at least some electrons, at least some of the time, alter their charge? That is, why don't the laws governing the existence and behavior of electrons at least now and then just chance to change?

To find a reason why electrons exist in the world, and to find a purpose that is served by God maintaining their presence in the world, one has only to ask, What would happen in the world if all of the electrons in it suddenly vanished? Without electrons, there could be no opposite charges for the protons; consequently there would be only repulsion with no attraction, hence no normal matter could exist. It would be impossible for our biological organisms and the physical objects around us to exist at all.

When something exists, its existence makes sense only if it has a rationale. When something happens, its happening makes sense only if it has a coherent rationale. A rationale consists of two elements: (*a*) a constructive reason or purpose, and (*b*) a cause. For example: There is a piece of chalk here on the desk. The chalk does not "just happen" to exist, and it is not here in this room just *de trop*. We are able to make sense out of the chalk because it was created for a constructive reason, to serve a constructive purpose, to fulfill a real life *need*. If we could find no reason for it to exist, no purpose served by its existence, and no real need fulfilled by its being here, then its being here would seem *un*reasonable, purposeless, and needless, and hence unintelligible or absurd. *Un*reason, purposelessness, and needlessness constitute the very essence of unintelligibility or absurdity.

For the existence of anything to make sense, it must be *for* something. Any action makes sense only when it is for something. Otherwise, the action would be blind, devoid of a rationale, and could make no sense at all. For the existence of the universe to make sense, it must be informed with a coherent rationale.

Physicists and chemists tell us that the existence of the universe (and all physical objects within it) is sustained by atomic energy or action. Take all of the atomic energy or activity out of a physical object and nothing remains. In modern physics, the ultimate concept is *action*. Potential energy means potential action. Where there is no action there is no manifestation of energy whatever.

According to atheism, all of this atomic activity is strictly *im*personal: i.e., it is totally devoid of a rationale and is categorically blind. Consequently, the existence of the universe is inherently unintelligible or absurd because it ultimately is devoid of reason, purpose, or ideals. The word often used by atheists to describe the existence of the universe is "absurd" — witness the recent French existentialists Albert Camus and Jean-Paul Sartre, as well as Bertrand Russell and others.

It would be absurd for people to use reason to make sense out of their study of the structure of the universe unless that universe were in fact structured on the basis of reason. There can be no *reason* to assume that we can find truths intelligible to reason in the structure of reality unless the world is ultimately informed with reason. It is a contradiction in terms to assume that we can find a rationale for the universe being structured the way it is unless it is in fact informed with a rationale. To make sense of the laws of nature, we have to view the laws of nature as the expression of God's reason and purpose in the world, which is to guarantee a dominance of order over disorder, beauty over ugliness, and unity over disunity sufficient to make possible the existence of living beings with identity, sanity, and integrity.

Ethan Allen — soldier, scholar, and a founder of Vermont — agrees by saying, "That wisdom, order and design should be the production of nonentity, or of chaos [and] confusion, is too absurd to deserve a serious confutation, for it supposeth that chaos or confusion could produce the effects of power, wisdom and goodness; such absurdities as these we must assent to, or subscribe to the doctrine of a self-existent and providential being."[2]

One of the most influential atheists is the late Jacques Monod of France, a biologist noted especially for his book *Chance and Necessity*. According to Monod, here paraphrased, if we look far enough back into the history of the universe, we find a time when there was a state of

(a) Universal lifelessness (since there were no planets in existence with physical and chemical conditions on them conducive to the origin and sustenance of life).

(b) Universal purposelessness (since purpose is the intention of some living being to do something, and there were no living beings).

(c) Universal meaninglessness (since meaning does not float around in space but exists only in the mind of some living being who reads meaning into what is happening in its life).

(d) Universal *un*reason (since reason is found only in the mind of some living being, and there was no living being).

(e) Universal care-lessness or lovelessness (since caring and loving are acts performed by a living being).

(f) Universal valuelessness (since there was nobody to whom or for whom anything could have any value).[3]

Monod simply assumes *ad arbitrium* that God does not exist. He takes God's nonexistence for granted as a fact without offering any reasons. He argues in his book's final chapter, "The Kingdom and the Darkness," that any intellectually and emotionally honest person must *despair* and look upon reality ultimately as a great abyss before which no one can or should hope. He further insists that we must accept the darkness and live in it, rather than entertain the "lie" that somewhere above the dark clouds hovering over man there is an abiding light.

The British-American philosopher Alfred North Whitehead muses, "Scientists animated by the purpose of proving that they are purposeless constitute an interesting subject for study."[4]

Monod's philosophy violates a fundamental principle of scientific method, namely, that an effect cannot be derived from a cause or causes that have nothing in common with the effect. Monod merely assumes that absolute lifelessness "somehow" produces life, while in fact this assumption is totally unwarranted. If the primordial forces of the universe are by definition absolutely lifeless, then they contain nothing within themselves that can be conducive to the origin and sustenance of life. Like the old cliché that says that you cannot get blood from a turnip, we look in vain for any blood in Monod's turnip. If the forces of nature are by definition absolutely impersonal in nature, then there is no conceivable way they could ever "accidentally" give birth to *persons.*

There is no possible way to derive personal effects from causes that are impersonal. A person is a free spirit who can choose, imagine, think, reason, love, will, care, and create. If anyone can believe that absolutely impersonal forces can blindly produce persons, then indeed that person can believe anything whatever. The assumption that this "somehow" just happens is simply gratuitous. The appeal to the word "somehow" is neither scientific nor logical; it explains nothing. The theist could use the same device by saying that "somehow" God just exists and creates worlds.

Monod's philosophy is unscientific. All of the evidence at hand indicates that every finite living being of which we have any definite knowledge (in the present or past) was created by some prior life, though not necessarily earthly life. Life produces life, and only life produces life. The assumption that life ultimately is produced by non-life rests on not one smidgeon of known fact. All the evidence indicates that purpose is always generated by prior purpose, that meaning is always generated out of prior meaning, and that reason is always generated out of prior reason. The assumption that care is generated by forces that are absolutely care-less is categorically a contradiction in terms. On the contrary, it is love that creates love, perpetuates love, enriches love. The idea that love is generated accidentally by blind lovelessness is contrary to logic and to known facts.

The origin of life out of absolute lifelessness is logically impossible, and it is empirically inconceivable. Nothing is accomplished, or established, by the blind atheist dogma that this is just the way it happens. There is, in actual fact, no evidence on record of any living organism ever having originated out of a lifeless state. Monod inadvertently admits that purpose can be derived only from bigger and more comprehensive purpose. Not realizing its implications against his basic philosophy, he tells us plainly in *Chance and Necessity* that "it is only as a part of a more comprehensive project that each individual project, whatever it may be, has any meaning" (p. 14). This observation is true, and one can only wonder why Monod is willing to betray it so flagrantly in his philosophy of human purpose (or purposelessness!) in the universe. Moreover, he admits outright that we have no knowledge whatever of any life that did not originate out of prior life (p. 142). His assumption that life originates out of nothing but dead particles is an article of atheist faith, grounded in no demonstrable factuality.

Atheism literally does not make sense, because it bogs down in paralogisms. That is, it appeals to what it denies, for it appeals to reason ultimately to denigrate reason. Atheism tries to make it seem valuable to believe that ultimately there is nothing of intrinsic value. We may wonder what can possibly be gained, either intellectually or morally, by assuming that reality ultimately is devoid of a rationale. To make sense, we must affirm that there is a Cosmic Scheme of Things, that our lives are grounded in some permanent reason, purpose, and love.

The modern case for the existence of God in natural theology rests finally in the necessity to affirm His existence for the sake of general intelligibility or understandability. It is simply unintelligible to presuppose that reality ultimately is unintelligible. Yet that is what atheists are driven to hold. J. B. S. Haldane, an atheist, cites as the main characteristic of the universe its "inexhaustible queerness," as he calls it — implying that all of the diverse handiwork of the universe came into being without a handiworker, that life came out of lifelessness, and that the universe's order came out of a primordial disorder.[5]

Often the expectations of pioneering scientists are confirmed. Yet, on fundamental matters, surprises, which are a kind of "queerness," are more characteristic of scientific progress. For example, it was a surprise to find that the earth is round, that motion of itself is not retarded, that the earth goes round the sun, that atoms are divisible and almost empty, that the continents were originally one mass — indeed, that a creature exists (a human being) who can comprehend many of the inexhaustible fruits of creation. The American philosopher Charles Hartshorne states, "Science predicts everything better, we could almost say, than its own future."[6] That is, we are always discovering surprising new ways to comprehend what, without God, would be an incomprehensible, impenetrably mysterious, and extremely complex world.

Of course, there is more to God, and more to understanding His universe, than can be comprehended by pure reason. Father Stanley Jaki suggests that the Judeo-Christian belief in God as the absolute and free Creator entails the idea that His creative rationality takes the form of free, singular *choices*. Hence, God's choices cannot be known to us without observation of the divine handiwork in its inexhaustible singularities — both the handiwork that we directly sense and that which we infer through the mind. The grand handiwork has the unmistakable mark of being *voluntary* in its creation.

Nevertheless, Jaki observes that all this "queerness" of the universe does not seem such to a theist. Loren Eiseley, a theistic anthropologist, titled a book of his, not the "queer" universe, but rather *The Unexpected Universe*. For the theist, the many odd, unique features of the universe express not queerness, but rather attest to the power and the personal decisions of a rational Creator possessed of an overarching free *Will*. While the origin of species presents one problem, a deeper one is that of the origin of finite being itself, that is, the context in which species could appear at all. Admittedly, the theory of the creation of the universe out of God's own being does not fall within the domain of explanation of natural science. Even so, why should it be considered anti-scientific mystery-mongering to invoke the idea of God the Creator? We have seen how the doctrine of Creation coheres with the motivation to do natural science. Yes, the process of Creation remains a mystery, "the deepest, though most luminous" of mysteries.[7]

The theories of creation, evolution and their ramified forms have become a political educational issue, as well as an academic one. The evidences in various directions are manifold and complex. We cannot attempt further analysis here but must plead for humility and open-mindedness in both directions. Fortunately, no position need be taken here as to the correctness of any of them. Our sole concern is to show how we may see the universe and ourselves as in some sense the result of a divine plan, no matter what theory of biological origins may ultimately be found correct. Of course, the creationist theory is compatible with this concern. But so are all the various evolutionary theories, so long as blind chance does not usurp the place of God's will, rationally understood.

A significant contribution to understanding was made by the English philosopher-theologian F. R. Tennant, whose *Philosophical Theology* appeared in 1930 and has not had the large audience that it deserves.[8] Elaborating on the idea of "The forcibleness of Nature's suggestion that she is the outcome of intelligent design," Tennant argues that this forcibleness cannot be traced to the many individual cases of biological adaptation such as those previously cited. Rather, the forcibleness of the appeal of natural theology consists in "the conspiration of innumerable causes to produce, by their united and reciprocal action, a general order of Nature." For why should the manifold stuff of the universe arrange and adapt itself to form "an intelligible and organic whole"? If this benign result be regarded as "due to an intelligent Creator designing the world to be a theatre for rational life, mystery is minimised, and a possible and sufficient reason is assigned."

This is what Tennant calls the "wider teleological argument" for the existence of God. Teleologists who take Darwinian evolution seriously have had to shift their search for the evidence of purpose "from special design in the products" of evolution to "directivity in the process," and to the presence of "plan in the primary collocations." As a result, the wider teleological argument is an argument to discover the cosmic *telos* — that is, the completion or fulfillment of a cosmos as the result of an aim or will.[9]

Natural theology in our time receives a further boost from a student of Tennant, Peter Bertocci, who discusses the relative probabilities of two kinds of explanation. The first is that the evolutionary creativity operates by randomness or chance. The second is that the creativity is that of God's overall design. Bertocci invites us to consider an analogy. Say that the likelihood of humankind's appearance in the universe is, in terms of probability, as though we had drawn the five best trumps from a deck of cards. Imagine those trumps to be the capacities to think, know, feel, see, and hear, all existing in a setting where they can be used to good effect.

The thing to be explained by the wider teleological argument, Bertocci points out, is "not simply my holding the best five trumps," but the existence in the first place of the deck of cards which allows trumps to be drawn in this particular way. The deck of cards, according to Bertocci, "is so made that my having five trumps is one of the possibilities, and when I am in a universe in which I am holding trumps, the most reasonable hypothesis is that my trumps are not [merely] chance happenings produced by a universe which by [Darwinian] hypothesis had no trumps."[10]

Thus, the truly probing questions about the origin of life are these: What sort of universe is it in which such an evolutionary process of biological adaptation can occur? What prior cause can account for the proximate causes of organic adaptation?[11] What is the subtle framework of order and promise that must have been latent in even the primeval hydrogen?[12]

We may dismiss farfetched suggestions of a natural selection of universes and attend to Tennant when he suggests, "Presumably the world is comparable with a single throw of dice. And common sense is not foolish in suspecting the dice to have been loaded."

If we are to conclude that the world, and ourselves as part of it, derives from God, then we must also face the poignant question, Whence come so many evils?

This is Hume's question, too. For as Tennant says, "The wind is not tempered to the shorn lamb, the fieriest trials often overtake those who least need torments to inspire fear, to evoke repentance, or to perfect patience." The problem of evil in what is presumed to be God's world is, for most people, the largest problem that a theistic worldview must face. The essence of Tennant's perceptive reply to the question is:

> There cannot be moral goodness in a creature such as man without the possibility of his sinning. Without freedom to choose the evil, or the lower good, a man might be a well-behaved puppet or a sentient automaton, but not a moral agent. Were our conduct determined like the movements of the machinery of a clock, our world might manifest a pre-established harmony and fulfill the purpose of a clock-maker. A world from which the possibility of moral evil was excluded would be other than a moral order. It is idle, then, to wistfully contemplate the happiness which the world might have known had its creator made us capable only of what is right.

Is God, who foreknew the possibility of moral evil, therefore indirectly responsible for it? Tennant ventures: "He permits, so to say, the evil in order that there may be the good." Yet we cannot hold God responsible for "the actual emergence of man's moral evil; our sin is not God's act but the product of our volition, or evolved freedom." In some different world, moral evil *might* not have come to exist. Yet in our world, the basic human motivations to evil are inevitable consequences of the process through which humans came to be human. The possibility of our doing evil is balanced by the good that we can effect through the same freedom that enables us to do evil.

What of natural or physical evils such as earthquake, avalanche, disease, famine? Water on one hand is good; it quenches our thirst, cleanses us, and supports the myriad chemical reactions that sustain life. Fish live in it. Yet it is the very same physical properties of water that have the capacity to drown us. Tennant replies:

> A world which is to be a moral order must be a physical order characterised by law or regularity. Law-abidingness is an essential condition of the world being a theatre of moral life. Without such regularity in physical phenomena there could be no probability to guide us: no prediction, no prudence, no accumulation of ordered experience, no pursuit of premeditated ends, no formation of habit, no possibility of character or of culture. Our intellectual faculties could not have developed.

> The reign of law is a condition of the forthcomingness of the highest good, in spite of the fact that [lawfulness] is not an unmixed good but a source of suffering. We cannot have the advantage of a determinate order of things without its necessary disadvantages. The disadvantages, [such as] particular ills, need not be regarded, however, as directly willed by God. That is to say, they are not desired as such, or in themselves, but are only willed because the moral order, which is willed absolutely or antecedently by God, cannot be had without them.

"Now to will a moral order," Tennant continues, "also involves adoption of what we necessarily must call a determinate world-plan." However, this "rules out once and for all any other possible goals and methods. All determination is negation." If two consequences have both followed from some decisive event during creation, we cannot have the one without the other, though the one may be pleasing or beneficial to humans while the other may be painful or, in its immediate effects, hurtful. The proposition "that there could be a determinate evolutionary world of unalloyed comfort, yet adapted by its law-abidingness to the developement of rationality and morality, is a proposition the burden of proving which must be allotted to the opponent of theism. In so far as experience in this world enables us to judge, such proof seems impossible." In similar fashion, Tennant is also able to vindicate divine goodness amid physical evils:

> To save mankind from the painful consequences which flow from a determinate world-order, such as the earthquake and the pestilence, would involve renunciation of a world-order, and therefore of a moral order, and the substitution of a chaos of incalculable miracle. The general suspension of painful events, requisite on the vast scale presupposed in the elimination of physical ills, would abolish order and convert a cosmos into an unintelligible chaos in which anything might succeed upon anything. Physical evil, then, must necessarily be. And the goodness of God is vindicated if there be no reason to believe that the world-process involves more misery than Nature's uniformity entails.[13]

But each person as moral agent is said by some to be at odds with the cosmos — specifically, at odds with Nature taken as "red in tooth and claw." The inference is that each person as having a moral constitution must be a kind of excrescence on Nature. The English biologist T. H. Huxley in his famous 1893 *Romanes Lecture* suggests as much when he describes the world we live in as no "school of virtue." This is partly true, but we have just seen that there is another side. Even for Huxley, the world of Nature is "instrumental to the emergence, maintenance, and progressiveness, of morality."[14]

Huxley has another charge to press. With the Orphics, Platonists, Catharists, and Albigenses of long ago, he holds that the material world provokes base appetites against true good. In this way, Nature is held to be the cause of "original sin" and is "diabolically provocative" of man's diverse immoralities. Tennant replies:

> This also is true: but again it presents but one aspect of the facts. For, apart from man's bodily appetites and impulses it is inconceivable that ethical principles should gain purchase

on him. Hunger and sex are the bedrock of human morality; and the self-determination which human morality presupposes is hardly possible without the conflict between moral reason and non-moral impulse. Morality cannot be made without raw material. In providing this raw material Nature is instrumental to man's acquisition of the moral status. Morality thus has its roots in Nature.

That is, if the human is in a sense Nature's child, "Nature is the wonderful mother of such a child. Any account of her which ignores the fact of her maternity is scientifically partial and philosophically insignificant."[15]

Would "the best of all possible worlds" be one in which all problems had been solved, in which no effort, moral or otherwise, need be exerted? This state of affairs would be Nirvana, the cessation of both desire and striving. Tennant's insights show us that, whatever the best possible world may be, it is not a state of static perfection. The truly best possible theater for our free will is a world in which God is doing the best that can be done for the realization of valuable experience.

But could not the world have been better now if humans had previously used their freedom of choice to make better decisions? Certainly! Yet the human freedom to make mistakes is necessarily part of a plan that enables us to generate value. The case is thus made for viewing the universe, despite some appearances to the contrary, as the product of a design for happiness and as intended to be enjoyed by all. Yet if that is its purpose, one still is left wondering why God could not somehow have created the universe without the continual occurrence of so many crushing evils that appear to have no redeeming value. Must some evils always be viewed as resulting from the will of God, or is an alternative view available?

The Devil has figured prominently in the theology of Christianity, Judaism, Islam, Zoroastrianism, and many other cultures. Is it reasonable to suppose that the explanation of the existence of evil lies with the Devil? Before attempting an answer, two quite different concepts of the power of darkness must be distinguished. First, there is the "generic Devil" — the alleged primordial being who is eternally coexistent with God and independent like Him. Many religionists, philosophers, and common folk in history have believed that ultimately the struggle for good is pitted against principalities and powers that are intrinsically and irrevocably evil. Each of the incompatible cosmic powers is always struggling against the other.

Such an eternally existent Devil represents a kind of polytheism similar to that held by the ancient Greeks, at least the early ones. Such a view seems to have been held explicitly in ancient Mesopotamia and the early Christian Manicheans.[16] Certainly, polytheism or belief in a primordial Devil affords no basis for natural science, since any happening of any kind can be attributed to the whim of some all-too-human deity. If there is to be something external to God that is primordial, and primordial apart from His primordial nature, then there would be a schizophrenic universe, even scientifically schizophrenic, a state of affairs we do not in fact find. Any such system implies ultimately a theomachy or cosmic diabolism of unnecessary, hopelessly destructive conflict or evil. Whoever holds such a belief has forfeited not only hope and knowledge but, in consistency, any motive to philosophize about the matter. There can be no possible rationale for belief in a primordial evil being opposed to the rational and the good.

One cannot speak broadly and realistically to the subject of evil and bypass the second concept, that of the non-primordial Satan of the Old and New Testaments. Satan or Lucifer was an angel who rebelled in heaven and was expelled therefrom. He is not primordial or eternal; his partial reign of evil-doing is to come to an end. In the eyes of many religious people, the evil on the earth may largely be blamed on this concept of the Devil. Many people, students among them, ask the question of whether the existence of the biblical Satan should be interpreted allegorically or as a literally existing evil spirit in the world who touches us, invades and possesses our minds and tempts us to sin, or who attempts to manipulate us into committing evil acts.

Satan may be interpreted as the ultimate symbol of humankind's free choice. Satan taken as an allegory symbolizes the fact that we have to choose between good and evil, and that all people have the capacity to be their own Satan, their own Devil. When we do something diabolical, we use our freedom of choice to knowingly and deliberately commit an evil act. Then it may be said that we *are* Satan, that this is what diabolism is. Satan can be taken as a symbol of diabolism, of that diabolism found in human beings. Human evils may be traced to human freedom and to essential limitations in God's power.

Whether one relates theoretically with the idea of Satan either as an allegory or as a literal being, in either case it is irresponsible to try to escape from responsibility for committing one's own evil acts by attributing their cause to Satan. Unfortunately, the presumed power of Satan is used by many as an excuse to escape from any personal responsibility for the evil acts which they have freely chosen to commit. If the Devil were literally an evil spirit in our presence, but suddenly he died, any of us could still continue to do all of the evil things without him that we have ever done with him, simply by exercising our free will irresponsibly to continue to commit evil acts. To try to account for moral evil in the world by isolating it from the factor of our freedom of volition is to take the force out of the entire enterprise of ethics.

There are several allusions to the Devil, or Satan or Lucifer, in the Hebrew scriptures and many in the New Testament, including some to Beelezebub. We are warned to beware of Satan's snares and cunning, to shun and fight Satan by walking with our hand in God's hand. Even those who accept such literal views of the Devil's existence can nonetheless with total commitment oppose and stand up to any and every form of manifest evil that appears. After all, true religion must be concerned with striving to overcome real evil. To reify evil into an entity that we can neither apprehend with our senses nor cope with in any other manner is at best problematical. Again, we can get nowhere towards improving life unless we assume responsibility to subdue evil and do good.

What is one to make of Jesus' allusions to Satan? Should an inquiring person take the idea of Satan literally because of these? In His life both as a student and as a teacher, Jesus clearly possessed vast creative genius. As a life mentor, Jesus taught in some ways explicitly and in other ways implicitly. In His implicit teaching, and in reporting His own history, He employed metaphors, similes, parables, allegories, and hyperboles. He sometimes used gigantesquely exaggerated figures of speech in order to stimulate reflective thinking or to make a ringing and memorable point. For example, He talked about the "mote" in one's eye, and "everlasting hellfire." Our loving father would not literally burn any of His children forever. To insist that Jesus always intended, or wanted, to be taken literally is to overlook His creative, imaginative, and subtle use of reflective intelligence and language in making His points. Moreover, Jesus obviously possessed a uniquely great sense of humor. Sometimes He used sardonicisms and puns with irony, which means that we would completely miss His points if we interpreted every word He said with a nonreflective and unimaginative literalness. Jesus surely also realized that sometimes He had to confine His language to that which His simple listeners, uneducated and immured in custom and tradition, could understand.[17]

One must not confound Satan-worshipers with Christians, or other theists, who believe in the Devil as an angel in heaven who exercised his freedom to reject his responsibilities and turn against God. Albeit, anyone who has encountered Satan-worshipers in our country has probably discovered that pledging allegiance to the literal existence of the Devil has in no way helped these persons to become constructively caring or responsible individuals. Rather to the contrary, belief in and worship of a literal Satan has tended to lead their growing numbers into moral escapism, self-deception, and the commission of hideously sadistic acts against their fellow human beings and the other animal creatures.

There was in Jesus' time a widespread belief that the existing order of the natural world would end with the general intervention of God and the crushing of evil as personified by Satan. This belief was a ground for hope that evil would not continue to be a crushing burden through future generations. Has any hope taken the place of this hope, in the skeptical eyes of the modern world?

We have a resource that was hardly available to the ancients. We have begun to see, as the ancients could not, how very many of our own earthly problems can be ameliorated by our assuming the responsibility to take constructive action on our own, with the help of God which we must constantly seek and pray for. The human race has already proved that many physical evils can be controlled through the cooperation of science with medicine, engineering, and the useful arts generally. In the more developed nations, material needs are increasingly well met, even excessively so, and it may be said that we now have the "furniture" of the land of heart's desire. Modern housing affords comfort and security from exposure to the elements and intruders. Travel is incomparably safer and faster and cheaper than in earlier times. Low-cost instant communication now reaches to the world's remote corners. The varieties of productive and interesting ways to live have expanded enormously. Agricultural knowledge and mechanization enable more control of hunger and malnutrition, and our health is preservable in ways far exceeding those even of our parents. The astounding progress of medical technology is alone enough to suggest that the twentieth century isn't all bad. It is possible to suppose that God abetted and foresaw our general pattern of material progress and the ground for hope implicit therein.

What of moral evils? Are they likewise to be overcome? Can we dare to hope for a comparable moral improvement, whatever the fate of Satan? This book posits a hopeful answer to that question without supposing that moral evil will be entirely eliminated while human free will remains.

We do not know what it is to run a universe, but it does appear that, even if a "best possible world" be conceivable, God did *not* make any such world for our generation or any previous generations in recorded history. Yet, the possibility is here suggested that God made and continues to support the best universal design for happiness as it will appear in the light of eternity, and that this world leaves to us creatures the need to control or eliminate the evils we encounter. The gradual course of human learning must catch up with the evils first. We might suppose that, basically, "the universe is unfolding as it should." In this view, the fullest glory of God's creation may become evident only during the unwinding of incomprehensible stretches of future time, compared to which the entire life and education of the human race up to now is but a moment.[18]

**FRANK and ERNEST®**      by Bob Thaves      November 10, 1986

In view of the many evidences of divine design, among which is our own freedom of will,[19] the theory of divine design is, to say the least, logically coherent and has explanatory value. On what evidential basis can anyone say that it isn't true? Since we cannot experience the remote future during our earthly lifetimes, we certainly cannot come to know that the hope of conquering most evils, as part of God's plan, is false.

This brings up the question of what it means to prove a theory that purports to be scientific. The interesting and widely useful conclusion of the Austrian philosopher of science Sir Karl Popper is that the exposure of theories to a conceivably *possible* falsification by experience of facts is of the essence of scientific method. Such facts might arise, for instance, from a chemical experiment designed to test a deduction from a hypothesis, in which some conceivable result would render the theory false. When a theory under evaluation cannot conceivably be falsified by some definite experimental outcome, then it will not be establishable as a natural law, according to Popper's criterion.

Can the theory of the existence of the supremely powerful and good Creator God be conceivably falsified? That is, can any imaginable single fact prove that a loving, caring God does not exist? No, because this chapter has just explained away the force of the seeming counter-examples. We must say no because, as just explained, no experience that we might have on earth could falsify the theory, and no instance of experienced evil could prove that there is no actual benign God. It is always possible to subsume facts of evil under one of the explanations that have been presented herein.

Does this mean, then, that the statement: "God exists and He acts in the world" is not a scientific statement? The skeptic may press the case by asking: What kind of science is it that frames its theories in such a way that anything which looks like counter-evidence can be explained away? Is the statement that God exists any more of a scientific statement than the statement: "There lives somewhere a Devil with horns and a pointed tail"?

Both statements have in common the condition that neither is conceivably subject to being falsified by any fact that someone might discover — that is, not unless someone were to make an inventory of the entire universe and conclude that neither God nor the Devil were to be found. According to Popper's criterion of conceivably possible falsifiability, we cannot conclude from the design argument that God exists. Such theories may be true or they may be false but, as a matter of science, how can we know?

The answer is, Easily. The denial of the actuality of a God who cares would leave us with the only other seriously considered hypothesis, which by many is stated as fact, namely, that some lifeless, material force accidentally created a universal order with life in it. That hypothesis has, by comparison, been shown to be infinitely improbable — actually inconceivable. Hence, the argument against God's design is a *reductio ad absurdum*.

Obviously, if by default of any other conceivable explanation a theory is shown to be true, then it is unfalsifiable simply because it *is* true.

Popper allows that, even in physics, some statements which are not conceivably falsifiable do have scientific use and so become part of the web of truth.[20] Thus, he did not intend conceivable falsifiability to be the one universal criterion of what is true. The lack of coherent alternatives should allow reasonable people to accept, by default, the design argument for God's existence. The design argument gains cogence by its coherence with other arguments to be presented. For the present, we may conclude that the non-falsifiability of God's existence per Popper's criterion is not to count against His existence as inferred from the design argument.

In considering the problem for the design argument that is presented by the experience of pain — that its existence is indicative of ultimate randomness and disorder — the American theologian Philip Yancey invites philosophers to overcome their neglect of what he calls "the problem of pleasure":

> Why is sex fun? Some animals simply split in two when they want to reproduce. Why is eating fun? Plants and the lower animals manage to obtain their quota of nutrients without the luxury of taste buds. Why can't we? Why are there colors in the world? Some people get along fine without the ability to detect color. Why complicate vision for all the rest of us? Where did pleasure come from? Don't atheists and secular humanists have an obligation to explain the origin of pleasure in a world of randomness and meaninglessness?[21]

Good questions. The reader should tentatively entertain the idea that God did design the universe as a theater for the pursuit of happiness in which the human race is likely, in the long run, to find every reason to thank Him. In this view, God built into the world and into us the power to use our free wills to create a supremely high amount of good, if all things at all times be considered together.

The poetic body of the Book of Job, notably Chapter 40, is most reasonably read as implying that God has done, is doing, and will do all that is possible to make the superiority of our world over other conceivable worlds finally obvious — mysterious though some of God's ways must forever be. We may ignore the problematic prose prologue and epilogue of Job.[22]

One objection inevitably arises to the design argument. It is the fact that we all must die. Is not death the ultimate evil? The theory of biological evolution entails death as necessary in sexual creatures, for death makes room for new life and for descendants more nearly perfect due to evolution itself. If there had been no descendants, there could have been no process of evolution leading up to the human race in its present state. There is a growing number of biologists these days who do not accept evolution as a comprehensive theory; for them, this response to the objection of death is insufficient. Given the inevitability of death, is it realistic to speak of our world as being superior to other conceivable worlds? Is it sensible to think of our world as the best possible world for the purposes God created it to serve for us at this time? An affirmative answer can be given to the last question only by those who believe that there is an afterlife and, more generally, who believe that the earth is as good a place as possible for human beings to experience those conditions that enable us to begin to *learn how to care.*

This means that if God could have created a better world for us to start in, then His loving, caring nature would have obligated its creation. Perhaps it is only in some such sense that we human beings, with our limited time horizons, dare to think of this universe as the best possible.

The idea of an afterlife is anathema in the secular academic world. Later, an entirely new case will be made that persons can survive the grave. If valid, then the conditions and qualities of personal caring can conceivably come to be improved upon.[23]

# 6

## The Two Levels of Ethical Motivation

A little philosophy inclineth man's mind to
atheism, but depth in philosophy bringeth men's
minds about to religion.

*Francis Bacon*

ABRAHAM LINCOLN was a voracious reader of
serious books, and the anecdotal lore told of him suggests his
philosophical mind. It is said that once while Lincoln was riding
on a "mud-wagon coach" on the old washboard roads made of split
halves of trees, he opined to his fellow passenger, Colonel Baker,
that all people are motivated by selfishness in doing good or evil.
Baker was challenging his position

> when they were passing over a corduroy bridge that spanned
> a slough. As they crossed this bridge, they espied an old razor-
> backed sow on the bank of the slough, making a terrible noise
> because her pigs had got into the slough and were unable to
> get out, and in danger of drowning. As the old coach began
> to climb the hillside, Mr. Lincoln called out: "Driver, can't you
> stop just a moment?" Mr. Lincoln jumped out, ran back to the
> slough and began to lift the little pigs out of the mud and water
> and place them on the bank. When he returned, Colonel Baker

remarked: "Now, Abe, where does selfishness come on in this little episode?" "Why, bless your soul, Ed, that was the very essence of selfishness. I would have had no peace of mind all day had I gone on and left that suffering old sow worrying over those pigs. I did it to get peace of mind, don't you see?"[1]

Was Lincoln straining the use of the word "selfish" here? If not, wouldn't we need some other word to express the difference between the two principles of action alleged to be at work at the same time, namely, benevolence and "selfishness"?

The most central work of Jonathan Edwards is a little unfinished book called *The Nature of True Virtue*. It elaborates Edwards' main ethical insights and shows why Edwards is to be regarded as a towering figure whose thought can help to rescue ethics from its present moribund state. The eighteenth-century Anglican bishop Joseph Butler in his published sermons was pivotal in the history of ethical philosophy. Edwards in his book seems to have known about Butler's thought and improved on it.[2]

Both Butler and Edwards argue that there is not necessarily any "vulgar antithesis" between the pursuit of one's own interest and that of others, even when one is considering a single set of acts. A person attending to the needs of others may experience the inner satisfactions of sympathy or self-congratulation. Happiness-pursuit or "simple self-love" overlaps benevolence or happiness-promotion; hence, those who seek their own happiness can simultaneously seek the happiness of others. These objectives can dovetail.

One can *enjoy* buying or making things for the enjoyment of one's family, and one can *enjoy* feeding snowbound birds. One's happiness-pursuit on one hand, and one's benevolence or happiness-promotion on the other, are both pursued in order to gratify an inclination. Thus they may be called common goods. Whatever it may be that a person loves, that thing is gratifying and pleasurable whether it is one's own happiness or the happiness of others. And if this is all that opponents mean by self-love, "no wonder they suppose," says Edwards, "that all love may be resolved into self-love. For it is undoubtedly true that whatever a man loves, his love may be resolved into loving what he loves." This neutral, pre-ethical sense of self-love, which Edwards calls simple self-love, may be assumed (for the time being) to be implicit in all motivation whether self-centered or benevolent:

> If nothing could be either pleasing or displeasing, agreeable or disagreeable to a man, then he could incline to nothing, and will nothing. But if he is capable of having inclination, will and choice, then what he inclines to and chooses is grateful [i.e., gratifying] to him, whatever that be, whether it be his own private good, the good of his neighbours, or the glory of God. And so far as it is grateful or pleasing to him, so far it is a part of his pleasure, good, or happiness.[3]

The conclusion to be drawn from this is that happiness-pursuit is a love of one's own proper, single, and separate good or experience of value which arises necessarily from the nature of a perceiving, willing being. This happiness-pursuit is essential to the possibility of ethical behavior or of any other intentional, voluntary behavior. As such, it is not, strictly speaking, an ethical matter but rather the pre-ethical basis for motivation to do either good or evil. The universality of happiness-pursuit is the large fact in which the very possibility of ethics is grounded. More is to be said of this later.

Happiness-pursuit is also a principle that defines the role of a second principle, namely, that of benevolence, for it unites a person's interest with that of someone else. It causes the good of another to be the person's own good "and makes that to become delight which otherwise cannot." Simple self-love or happiness-*pursuit*, arises from one's own being, even though from self-love there arises also a principle that unites one person to another. It is through the second principle, that of benevolence or happiness-*promotion*, that the good of another being does in a sense become one's own. This second sort of self-love — this benevolence or "compounded self-love" (as Edwards sometimes calls benevolence) is not entirely separate from love of God, but "enters into its nature."[4]

Edwards' greatest ethical insight is the distinction between levels of morality that look alike. *"True virtue"* needs to be sharply distinguished from the lower level, *natural morality*, which is marked by two common traits. People are usually so constituted as to need love and also to feel guilt on occasion. Edwards calls this trait "natural affection," which is the opposite of psychopathic or sociopathic personality. The second common trait of natural morality, called by Edwards "natural conscience," is a sense of fairness or justice that develops naturally in groups of people who regard themselves as having equal rights among themselves.

# CALVIN and HOBBES

by Bill Watterson

April 9, 1989

Edwards' view of natural morality is similar to Adam Smith's concept of the "ideal impartial spectator," the voice within the breast of any man of "real constancy and firmness, the wise and just man."[5] Natural morality is much like the Golden Rule. Confucius stated it in negative form: What you do not like when done to yourself, do not do to others. The validity of this rule is acknowledged within all authentic religions and is thus a part of the conscience of civilized mankind from antiquity on. Lincoln expresses a corollary: "As I would not be a slave, so would I not be a master."

In the positive form of the Golden Rule, people are to do unto others as they would be done by, with due allowance for differences in situations, tastes, and abilities. Although you may love avocados and wish that your hostess would serve them, you would not serve them to someone known not to like them.[6]

The acceptance of the Golden Rule does not necessarily depend on its connections with revealed religion, for there exists a universal and natural recognition of its validity. The breaking of the Golden Rule entails the incoherence of breaking a more abstract rule, namely, the rule that one's actions in their moral aspect be capable of being *universalized*. This democratic idea is actualized when, for instance, the question is asked in rebuke of a litterbug: "What would the world be like if everybody did that?"

The American ethical philosopher Frank Chapman Sharp points out that ordinary persons do not call conduct right or wrong unless they suppose themselves to be viewing it from an impersonal standpoint. This means that they suppose, negatively, that their attitudes are not determined by their egoistic interests or by any purely personal relations to the parties concerned.

Further, in cases of approval, ordinary persons will suppose that the act is one that they would approve of anyone's performing under the same conditions. Thus "wrong does not become innocent or right merely because the act took place a hundred years ago instead of this morning," nor because one did not happen to see it oneself, nor because one has never happened to be in that position, nor because someone involved happens to be an acquaintance, a member of one's family, or oneself.[7]

Paraphrasing Edwards, to do to others that which we would be angry for their doing to us, and to hate persons for doing to us that which we would incline to and insist on doing to them if we were exactly in the same situation, is to disagree with ourselves and contradict ourselves.[8]

This "inclination to agree with ourselves" is another description of "natural conscience" or fairness in Edwards' view: "That uneasiness now mentioned, consists very much of that inward trouble men have from reflections of conscience; and when they are free from this uneasiness, and are conscious that they have done toward others the same which they should have expected from others in the same case, then they have what is called peace of conscience, with respect to these actions."[9]

Edwards' idea of "natural conscience" is similar to a view developed by the contemporary American philosopher John Rawls, who notes that those free individuals who do not have authority over one another will naturally reach an understanding, a "mutual acknowledgement of principles" about what is *fair*. This acknowledgment amounts to a tacit social contract which will spontaneously produce certain practices.[10] Thus, one generally has the liberty to walk the streets of one's home town, for normally in walking the streets, no infraction of the Golden Rule occurs. But none of us has the right to enter the houses of others without permission, since our common understanding denies that right to others.

For Rawls the idea of justice is at bottom the idea of *fairness*. To perfect this idea, he qualifies his first ethical principle by a second, namely, that the arranging of inequalities or privileges is to be regarded as arbitrary and unjustified unless it is reasonable to expect that the inequalities "will work out for everyone's advantage." For example, by common rule, police chiefs have the power to command their patrolmen and detectives, rather than the reverse. This inequality and privilege is not a practice based on an arbitrary, unjustifiable inequality if it works out to (substantially) everyone's advantage, as does this practice.

Rawls' second principle also requires that the position of police chief be equally open to all who are qualified by requirements such as skill, literacy, and knowledge of criminal laws.[11]

We are exploring a kind of *social consistency* among people who regard each other as equals. Principles such as those advanced by Rawls, if consistently applied through time, become part of the conscience of the members of a society. Thus it comes about that persons the world over agree on certain fundamentals of human behavior — for instance, the general tacit understanding that a person does not break into queues. This rule defines a stable way of relating to one's neighbors, and infractions of it will irritate people who have internalized this rule. Power-minded, narcissistic persons who consider themselves above *hoi polloi* or the masses will ignore their ire.

In contrast to natural morality and its scope of motivation, Edwards finds a more comprehensive and spiritual morality of benevolence — an attitude of "general good will" which he calls the "true virtue" of benevolence toward "intelligent being in general" or "the universal system of existence." These phrases denote all intelligent persons, with God at the head. True virtue for Edwards consists chiefly in love of God.

By contrast to this higher morality of general benevolence, "natural" morality tends to practical results that are less exalted, less effective, and less joyous. Natural morality does have some effectiveness, but "true virtue," while including natural morality, broadens and purifies it. Natural morality and true virtue must go together if they are to answer the inner need for *coherence* in knowledge, life and thought.

In the chart "Circles of Ethical Concern," *Circle A* is the innermost of a system of explanatory spreading circles that are here added to Edwards' treatment. To understand why "true virtue" is so important, we need to examine the whole gamut of moral disposition. Circle A is restricted to mere selfishness — that is, self-love which is turned inward and is merely private. Though this "is exceedingly useful and necessary," as are the natural appetites of hunger and thirst, "nobody will assert that these have the nature of true virtue." However, those whose scope is thus restricted will find it in their private interest to appear altruistic, that is, to give at least lip service to principles of meekness, peaceableness, benevolence, charity, generosity, justice, and the social virtues in general.

In *Circle B*, which includes Circle A, reciprocity or measured mutual service enters. Edwards declares that "the natural consequence of a private self-love" is that people "should love those who are of their party and who are warmly engaged" on their side, promoting their interest. Suppose that these cohorts are members of the same trade association, cartel, or labor union. There is no more "true virtue" in a person thus "loving" friends merely from narrow self-interest or happiness-pursuit than there is in self-love or narrow happiness-pursuit itself, the principle from which such "love" proceeds.

A French litterateur has said, "Appreciation is a fine sense of gratitude for favors yet to be received." When people are so imprudent as to neglect the granting even of this kind of appreciation,

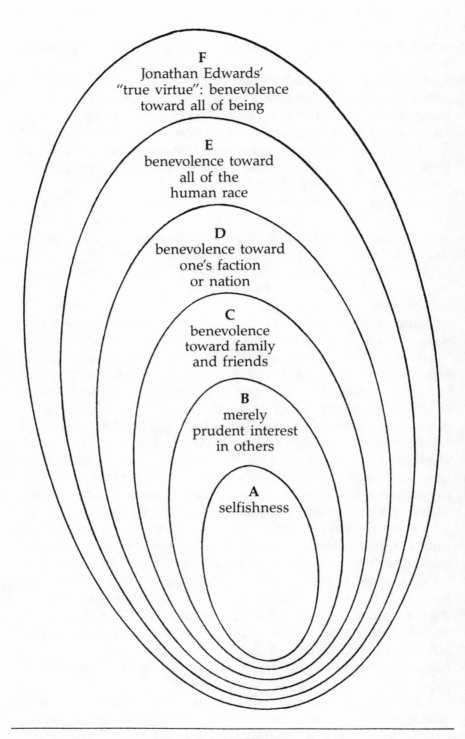

**F**
Jonathan Edwards'
"true virtue": benevolence
toward all of being

**E**
benevolence toward
all of the
human race

**D**
benevolence toward
one's faction
or nation

**C**
benevolence
toward family
and friends

**B**
merely
prudent interest
in others

**A**
selfishness

*Circles of ethical concern*

we see through them at once and call them selfish — i.e., disposed to pursue their own inward pleasure just for the pleasure itself. Similarly, our human disposition to hate those who hate us or to resent injuries done us, arises from narrow self-love in the same manner as loving those who love us and being thankful for kindness shown to us.

Merely prudent self-love "is not itself true virtue, but is the source of all the wickedness that is in the world," Edwards posits. Yet even narrow self-love or prudence often restrains one from acts of "true wickedness" — e.g., you restrain yourself from striking the person who insults you, for the person might strike back, or sue you. From tribal Africa the earthy saying has been reported: "One who defecates in the road will meet with flies on returning."

The prudent avoidance implied in these examples does more, for it sets one on the task of seeking true virtue, Edwards says, so far as one may learn thereby the rudiments of relating to others in ways that others find advantageous. These principles of natural morality have the same effect in that "they tend [in] several ways to restrain vice, and prevent many acts of wickedness. So natural affection, love of our party, or of particular friends tends to keep us from acts of injustice towards these persons." Instinctive pity saves us from much cruelty. But this does not mean that the principles of natural morality are of the nature of true virtue.

Circle C includes Circles A and B. Most frequently, natural morality is exercised with regard to one's family, especially between parents and children. The question in natural morality is "What's in it for me or my in-group, given our natures as creatures possessed of natural sympathy?" Though Edwards does not count morality thus restricted to be true virtue, he does allow that "Many times men, from natural gratitude, do really, with a sort of benevolence, love those who love them." This becomes more than mere reciprocity. Edwards writes, "The constitution of the world" makes families "to be united in interest, and accordingly to act as one, in innumerable affairs, with a communion in each other's affections, desires, cares, friendships, enmities, and pursuits."[12]

Yet our minds are large enough to take in more, in ever widening, inclusive circles. In Circle D we note the kind of morality of faction or patriotism that, while more comprehensive than Circle C, still includes less than the morality which is Edwards' main concern. This mediate morality has to do with benevolence extending beyond narrow self-interest and beyond family ties to encompass factions such as labor unions as well as one's nation.

> When private affections extend themselves to a considerable number, we are ready to look upon them as truly virtuous, and accordingly to applaud them highly. Thus it is with respect to a man's love of a large party, or a country. For though his private system contains but a *small part* even of the world of mankind, yet being a considerable number, they — through the contracted limits of his mind and the narrowness of his views —are ready to engross his sight, and to seem as if they were *all*. Hence, among the Romans, love of their country was the highest virtue, though this affection of theirs, so much extolled, was employed as it were for the destruction of the rest of mankind. The larger the number is, to which that private affection extends, the more apt men are to mistake it for true virtue, because then the private system appears to have more of the image of the universal.

If anyone is disposed to a benevolence that extends "only to some particular persons or private system" — that is, one that includes no more than Circle D — then such limited private benevolence is not subordinated to benevolence to "intelligent being in general." Therefore, to Edwards, even the scope of this circle does not qualify as true virtue. Circle E includes in its scope the entire human race — still short of the true virtue of Circle F.

In treating of pity, Edwards makes distinctions that help us understand the significance of the widening circles, for he distinguishes between the two faces of human pity. The kind of pity that arises from a particular instinctive feeling is natural to humankind "when they see others in great distress. But I think it evident," Edwards continues,

> that it is not of the nature of true virtue. It is the nature of true benevolence to desire and rejoice in the prosperity and pleasure of its object, and in some proportion to its degree of prevalence. But persons may greatly pity those that are in extreme pain, whose positive pleasure they may still be very indifferent about. In this case, a man may be much moved and affected with uneasiness, who yet would be affected with no sensible joy in seeing signs of the same person's enjoyment of very high degrees of pleasure.[13]

Edwards observes that there are men who have such a grudge against some others "that they would be far from uneasy at their very death, nay, would even be glad of it. And when this is the case, it is manifest that their heart is void of benevolence toward such persons, and under the power of malevolence. Yet at the same time," Edwards continues, "they are capable of pitying even these very persons, if they should see them under a degree of misery very much disproportioned to their ill will." This merely natural sort of pity is the only kind that operates in Circle A and is what the German philosopher Max Scheler calls "emotional infection."[14]

In Circle C and in larger circles of moral concerns, one can find a reason to *exert one's will* to feel pity or to cultivate and magnify the natural, instinctive feeling of pity. Consequently there exists

> a truly virtuous pity, or a compassion [for] others under afflic-
> tion or misery, [arising] from general benevolence. [This] pure
> benevolence would be sufficient to excite pity [for] another in
> calamity, [even] if there were no particular instinct or any other
> principle determining the mind thereto. It is easy to see how
> benevolence, which seeks another's good, should cause us to
> desire his deliverance from evil. And this is a source of pity
> far more extensive than the other. It excites compassion in cases
> that are overlooked by natural instinct; and even in those cases
> to which instinct extends, it mixes its influence with the natural
> principle, and guides and regulates its operations. And when
> this is the case, the pity which is exercised may be called a
> virtuous compassion.[15]

If friends should come tell you in grief that their beloved child has just died, you would feel natural pity at the very least. Beyond that, you exert your will to sympathize with them. When you have left their presence, you continue each time you remember them to imagine their grief. You *will* to remember it, in order that you can anticipate their needs and help them bear this burden. If the bereavement had occurred at a distance and you had heard of it indirectly, you would do the same.

Extending one's interest into Circle C, you contribute local volunteer work or money to charitable organizations such as the Red Cross. Although the natural pity for sufferers that you have experienced in the past may linger, you do not need to experience natural pity at the time of willing these decisions. These willed commitments extend the effect of your pity and do it through intelligently guided benevolence. If you are a theist, your motives will be largely religious, partaking therefore of Edwards' true virtue —*Circle F.*

If, contrary to fact, pure benevolence toward every "intelligent being" were the source of natural pity, then doubtless, as Edwards holds, natural pity "would operate to as great a degree in congratulation in cases of others' great prosperity, as in compassion towards them in great misery." But as we have seen, this does not happen. Hence, "These things may convince us that natural pity is of a nature very different from true virtue, and not arising from a disposition of heart to general benevolence, but is owing to a particular instinct which the Creator has implanted, chiefly for the preservation of mankind."

Why are some inferior affections prematurely accounted truly virtuous? One reason is that "there are affections of the same names which are truly virtuous" — like pity. A similar distinction may be made of gratitude. If you feed a dog, the dog will fight for you, not necessarily because you are a superior person but because you provide the food. That is natural gratitude.

Yet there is also "a virtuous gratitude," or a gratitude that arises not only from the satisfaction of one's private wants, but that arises also from "a superior principle of disinterested general benevolence." If a dog were to have a touch of it (and evidently some do), the dog would fight for your neighbor on occasion, whether the prospect of food be there or not. When we receive kindness from someone we already love, from someone who knows our altruistic concerns and has acted to further them, "we are more disposed to gratitude, and disposed to greater degrees of it, than when the mind is destitute of any such friendly prepossession." Edwards adds, "When the superior principle of virtuous love has a governing hand, and regulates the affair, it may be called a virtuous gratitude."

> When natural affections have their operations mixed with the influence of virtuous benevolence and are directed and determined thereby, they may be called virtuous. There may be a virtuous love of parents to children, and between other near relatives; a virtuous love of our town, or country, or nation. Yea, and a virtuous love between the sexes, as there may be the influence of virtue mingled with instinct; and virtue may govern with regard to the particular manner of its operation, and may guide it to such ends as are agreeable to the great purposes of true virtue.

Approbation or appreciation that is based merely on natural morality is, as Edwards tells us,

> the more readily mistaken for a truly virtuous approbation, because by the wise constitution of the great Governor of the world, when [natural] conscience is well informed and thoroughly awakened, it agrees with Him fully and exactly as to the object approved, though not as to the ground and reason of approving. It approves all virtue and condemns all vice. It approves true virtue and indeed approves nothing that is against it, or that falls short of it. Natural conscience is implanted in all mankind, to be as it were in God's stead, as an internal judge or rule, whereby to distinguish right and wrong.[16]

Yet, as Edwards notes, these inferior principles of natural conscience "are like fire in a house, which we say is a good servant, but a bad master: very useful while kept in its place, but if left to take possession of the whole house, soon brings all to destruction."[17] A person having a "well informed and thoroughly awakened" natural conscience would agree, for instance, that taking mind-altering drugs is not a good pastime. The question is, can people motivate themselves not to take drugs? Can they even motivate themselves to become "well informed and thoroughly awakened" on the matter? Obviously, many do not. The American theologians Waldo Beach and H. Richard Niebuhr observe correctly that the natural moralities of narrow, private self-interest and natural conscientiousness

> keep the world in a kind of disordered order. Yet this relative goodness of natural morality is, from the point of view of true virtue, a more than relative badness. It is the kind of "goodness" which, in Augustine's simile, characterizes a robber band; there must be some loyalty and justice in the band if it is to survive for even a little while so that it can rob.[18]

*Circle E* includes in its scope benevolence toward the entire human race. Many people, lacking knowledge of God, now take the scope of Circle E to be sufficient. Some animal concerns may be included in this circle. Edwards does not address humanism in his book, but he would have said that concern for all of humanity, though laudable, still falls short of true virtue for much the same reasons that the scope of Circle D does. The reasons why these circles fall short constitute the reasons for writing most of this book and will not be clear until later.

**FRANK and ERNEST®**     by Bob Thaves        October 11, 1985

" TRUSTWORTHY, LOYAL, HELPFUL, FRIENDLY, COURTEOUS, KIND, OBEDIENT, CHEERFUL, THRIFTY AND BRAVE"? ALL AT ONCE?

Edwards asks, How do so many people manage to deceive themselves?

> The reason why men are so ready to take these private affections for true virtue is the narrowness of their views; and above all, that they are so ready to leave the divine Being out of their view and to neglect Him in their thoughts as though He did not properly belong to the system of real existence, but was a kind of shadowy, imaginary being. And though most men allow that there is a God, yet in their ordinary view of things, His being is not apt to come into account and to have the influence and effect of a real existence, as it is with other beings which they see and are conversant with by their external senses. It is not natural to them to view the Deity as part of the system and as the head of it.[19]

Here we are landed into *Circle F*, the one comprehensive circle of moral concern, including as it does, "benevolence toward all of intelligent being." True virtue is sometimes found in the making of decisions in which there can be no satisfaction from natural morality. Victor Hugo's hero of *Les Misérables*, Jean Valjean, turned himself over to the police after years of singularly productive achievement, in order to free a lowly man who had been unjustly detained — a man who could not have had any effect on Valjean otherwise. Such an act goes beyond the natural basis for justice as fairness and constitutes "a virtuous love of justice." It is the view that every living, personal being, even the least, should enjoy "such a share of benevolence as is proportioned to its dignity."

A subtle contrast appears in the fact that a well-informed but merely natural conscience, "will *approve* of true virtue, and will disapprove and condemn the want of it, and opposition to it; and yet without seeing the true beauty of it." On the positive side, Edwards tells us that he has observed that

> in pure love to others, i.e. love not arising from [merely private] self-love, there is a union of the heart with others: a kind of enlargement of the mind, whereby it so extends itself as to take others into a man's self; and therefore it implies a disposition to feel, to desire, and to act as though others were one with ourselves.[20]

Edwards observes that a truly virtuous person appreciates true virtue in another person: "When any one under the influence of general benevolence sees another being possessed of the like general benevolence," this attaches one's heart to the other and draws forth greater love of the other. The reason is, insofar as the other — the beloved — has benevolence for the same object, one's being becomes "enlarged." One then is less lonesome in the pursuit of ideals than before. One's strivings are affirmed in the pleasure of enlarged acquaintance.

When the object sought is the good of "Being in general," multiple sources of difficulty are removed. Whoever "truly and sincerely seeks the good of others must approve of and love" whoever joins in seeking that good, for that is the activity in which "true moral or spiritual beauty primarily consists." To receive love and kindness may be a reason for reciprocating that love, but that reason is merely natural. Whatever "spiritual beauty" of *general* benevolence a person may possess would be the "primary objective foundation" of one's love for that person, so far as that love is truly virtuous. "It is impossible," says Edwards, "that any one should truly *relish* this beauty, consisting in general benevolence, who has not that temper."

> Genuine virtue prevents that increase of the habits of pride and sensuality which tend to diminish the exercises of the useful and necessary principles of nature. And a principle of

general benevolence softens and sweetens the mind, makes it more susceptible of the proper influence of the gentler natural instincts, directs every one into its proper channel, determines the exercise to the proper manner and measure, and guides all to the best purposes.[21]

Theologians Niebuhr and Beach pithily express Edwards' vision of attainable earthly good:

The gift of true virtue — love to God and universal benevolence — makes apparent to man the self-interestedness and partiality of his natural ethics. Edwards discerns, under the illumination of revelation, that there is something profoundly contradictory to the human spirit in this relative morality; it is the morality of *fallen* man who feels that he ought not be as he is, that something is required of him which exceeds his present ability, namely, to be just and loyal in a truly universal sense with complete disinterestedness.

The ethics of universal good will seeks the good of all beings in their interrelationship; it desires justice in the universal community; it is free from concern for the self. This is the ethics of the love of God, of delight and joy in him as the source of all existence; it is the ethics of the love of all being as united in God and by him. This ethics of universal benevolence transforms all particular loves, as when sex love, parental love, and patriotism are transformed by universal loyalty.

Those who are so called to universal citizenship become the pioneers of a new humanity. This was history as Edwards saw it, fundamentally the story of redemption from self-love to the love of all being, from self-glorification to the glorification of God, from the provincialism of town, nation, and humanity to citizenship in universal society, from the love of profit to the love of God.[22]

Let us pause to take stock. What historical evidence is there of the superiority of Circle F, the scope of moral concern that goes beyond the visible world, as contrasted with lesser circles? More specifically, has there been any real difference between the morals of Christian (or other theistic believers) and those of nonbelievers?

Edwards answers yes, and so does his biographer as quoted earlier regarding the Great Awakening centered at Northampton. The French statesman and author Alexis de Tocqueville answers yes as to America of the early nineteenth century, in which he sojourned and found a ubiquitous and sincere religiosity.[23] The English moral philosopher T. E. Jessop also answers yes in his little book *The Christian Morality*. With the coming of Christianity to the Roman Empire, Jessop tells us, there began moral change that ultimately became immense. True, Christian influence has always been "uneven, zig-zag, incomplete" because of shallow conversions, backsliding, as well as because of crude, vigorous, resisting human willfulness and even some problematical creeds. Moreover, every generation must be converted anew. Jessop quotes the younger Pliny of Rome, a pagan writing around A.D. 100, with examples of the "tender sensibility" that some pagans possessed, "which Christianity was to enlarge and multiply." Yet Jessop finds the bitterness of Juvenal truer to the coarse and cruel generality of Rome.

One may merely mention the well patronized "bloody agony of the amphitheatre." Even the Stoic philosophy holds the prevention of suffering not to be a matter of moral concern. The Greeks were "less cruel and were not coarse, but their refinement, judged morally, resulted in their being able to throw a veil of grace and gaiety over their vices, which romped in public and in private to everybody's expectation," including sexual looseness generally. Jessop continues:

> The distinctive features of that hard and licentious paganism remained until the Church became a social and political power. Thereafter, the face of society began to show a change, and never since has anything like such cruelty and vice been, for any length of time, a prominent and accepted part of the mood and habits of any large society within Christendom. True, under the changed face there have been many unchanged hearts, but these have usually had to trim their conduct to the changed structures and standards.

Under early Christianity, there was a rise in the social evaluation of children, especially of girls, who more often had been exposed to infanticide. "The ending of it is one of the miracles of Mediterranean history." Jessop tells us:

Little pockets of men and women separated themselves radically from their environment when they took marriage as a sacra-
ment and dedicated their infants to God in baptism, and when
husbands accepted for themselves the fidelity which their
neighbours, often with the cruellest sanctions of law, imposed
on their wives. The pockets grew and multiplied, slowly
spreading the new notion of the sanctity of the entire family.

In the West, Jessop goes on, it is Christianity that has made *men*
see that sexual discretion is "not a freak but a virtue." That is, it
has made some of them see it. Jessop points out the novelty of the
Christian virtue of humility that in antiquity was "more than
condemned; it was despised." Its ranking as a virtue in "proud
Europe" is a wholly Christian achievement. "An ample and tenacious
forgiveness is undoubtedly a Christian characteristic," for the New
Testament emphatically calls us to it. Yet again, the philanthropy
that "jumps across the world" has sprung pointedly from Christian conscience during the last two or three centuries. Jessop concludes that no good explanation has yet been offered for the
"historical fact that European society underwent a very large change
after Christianity became dominant in it, except the historical fact
that it was Christianity that became dominant in it."[24]

Jessop's contention is strengthened by the British-American
historian Christopher Dawson, who writes eloquently and con-
vincingly of the historical connection between Christianity and the
rise of Western civilization. In Dawson's view, nearly all of the history
written in the past two hundred years contains more or less subtle
anti-theistic biases, and he tries to set the record straight in many
matters.[25] Dawson has written of the pivotal role of Christianity in
the renewal of civilization starting after the Roman collapse.[26]
Thomas Molnar notes that "what we call corruption is to be found
in the ancient structure of most societies," in the developing countries and elsewhere. The developing countries, unlike Judeo-
Christendom on the whole, still have the ancient structure.[27]

No one living in the West would deny that we are in a time of
decadence, with Roman vices reappearing. One may wonder
whether the anti-theistic government of France around the turn of
the century was ultimately responsible for the initial defeat of France
in World War II, in contrast to the French military performance in
World War I. For it takes a generation or so to reap what is sown.
The early training of future leaders, who are normally older persons

when they reach power, is determinative. It appears that the same process is now having its effect in English-speaking lands. Though some might find fault with Christian or Judaic religious knowledge so far as its basis is solely that of blind faith, no sensible person should reproach these faiths themselves for such decadence, since the decadence has become worse after the decline of theistic religious belief.

Psychological measurements of religious commitment, of happiness, and of morality are notoriously problematic, if only because definitions and sensitivities vary. Such tasks have been likened to "measuring a cloud with a rubber band, in a shifting wind." Yet, surveys in the Western world generally yield positive correlations between happiness and monotheistic faith. Perhaps the most interesting survey is that of George Gallup Jr. He found that 68 percent of the "highly spiritually committed" in America reported that they were "very happy" and that 63 percent were "very satisfied" with the way things were going in their lives. By contrast, of the populace with "very low spiritual commitment," only 30 percent reported that they were "very happy" and only 36 percent were "very satisfied." The highly spiritually committed subjects also placed greater importance on family life, were more tolerant of persons of different races and religions, were far more involved in charitable activities and were vitally concerned about the betterment of society.[28]

One need not rely exclusively on statistics but can observe those believers and nonbelievers personally known to one. Even when all other facts be the same in two settings — the theistic and the atheistic — the bare fact of theistic belief does make a difference. The fact has been widely ignored, in part because intellectually defensible explanations have been slow in coming.

Is there anyone who will do for our time what Edwards and Finney did for theirs?

But enough of background; it is time to turn to the principal arguments of this book.

> The reason why all mankind do not find happiness, when they are so anxious for it, is that they are seeking *it*. If they would seek the glory of God, and the good of the universe as their supreme end, *it* would pursue them.
>
> *Charles Finney*

Man, if totally without religion, faces apparent
infinite absurdities in life. As a result, he refuses to
think out what his situation really is, or falls into
cynicism, despair, or rebellion against what cannot
in the end be altered or escaped. Without reason in
religion, man is evading life in the proper human
form, which is that of the thinking animal whose
job is to think whatever he *can* think, and not to
stop at some arbitrary point, falling back into the
pre-human stage of unexamined impulse. There
should be reason in religion, and the true religion,
whatever it be, must constitute the most perfect
reason man can attain.

*Charles Hartshorne*

# 7

## Self-Consistency

I desire so to conduct the affairs of this administration that if at the end, when I come to lay down
the reins of power, I have lost every other friend on
earth, I shall at least have one friend left, and that
friend shall be down inside me.

*Abraham Lincoln*

SUPPOSE you were somehow convinced that you would never achieve any consistency or unity among your life's purposes and activities. In such a case, you would be unable to hope for any reasoned decisions or setting of priorities among disparate values. Of course, biological life, superficially satisfying, can go forward even when you are unconcerned about consistency, but your life would move on a fragmented, non-rational, animal level. Without the presumption that there can be one comprehensive goal or task for life, ethics as an orderly discipline would be impossible for you.

If one does have an overall goal, one can be self-consistent when true to it. Self-consistency is related to conscience. Can conscience be a reliable guide? Of course, the consciences of well-functioning persons the world over agree on some fundamentals of preferred human behavior. In this sense, conscience can indeed be a helpful guide. Without our consciences, how would we go about the business of living? Nearly all of our decisions must be made prompt-ly, without indulging in time-consuming calculations, just as we

who have sound hind-brains or cerebellums walk without considering each step and the adjustment of the many muscles involved.

Still, counter-examples are not hard to find. Charles Darwin relays
the account of one Dr. Landor, a magistrate in West Australia whose
native worker on his farm, after losing one of his wives to disease,
came and announced to Landor that

> "He was going to a distant tribe to spear a woman, to satisfy
> his sense of duty to his wife. I told him that if he did so, I would
> send him to prison for life. He remained about the farm for
> some months, but got exceedingly thin, and complained that
> he could not rest or eat, that his wife's spirit was haunting him,
> because he had not taken a life for hers. I was inexorable, and
> assured him that nothing should save him if he did."

Nevertheless, Darwin tells us, "the man disappeared for more
than a year, and then returned in high condition; and his other wife
told Dr. Landor that her husband had taken the life of a woman
belonging to a distant tribe; but it was impossible to obtain legal
evidence of the act."[1]

The fact is that "conscience" can itself be educated. But by what
standard? The answer to this question entails the whole basis of
ethics. The notion of conscience hardly advances our search for a
foundation for ethics, inasmuch as the shaping of conscience itself
largely depends upon the ethics of one's society.

Conscience and self-consistency are closely bound together. Self-
consistency is in part a virtue and in part an obstacle. Consider
dedication to creative work, which is most often carried out as a
series of initially untidy attempts and approximations, even as this
book has been. Creativity is impeded by fear of inconsistency in
the "horizontal" sense — that is, fear of improving one's early efforts
and thus refraining from improving them because the initial efforts
would be invalidated.

The earlier efforts are properly viewed as scaffolding for the
developing structure. The final result will embody a self-consistency
of content and of function — a "vertical" self-consistency. Such a
high-order consistency is realizable only through tolerating secondary, temporal "inconsistencies" or apparent waste along the way.[2]

Self-consistency may also be a handicap when it is merely an
unthinking, agreeable conformity to the values of others. The

psychologist Henry Winthrop puts it: "The well-integrated personality" is apt to be considered as one "whose personal attitudes are a better reflection of the prevailing attitudes of a group or community of which he is a part, than are the attitudes of any other person in that group or community."[3]

On the contrary, the meaningful self-consistency we shall consider is usually thought of as a positive attribute of character. For instance, Douglas S. Freeman, the biographer of George Washington, writes of the basic feature of an integrated personality as that whose "response to a specified stimulus may be predicted with measurable accuracy."[4] The Bible declares God to be the great "I change not." These words express a desirable horizontal consistency of dispositions; whereas in contrast, "A double-minded man is unstable in all his ways"[5] — both horizontally through time and vertically in structure of personality and values at a given moment.

Yet horizontal consistency, through time, can be overdone. In his fine essay "Self-Reliance," Ralph Waldo Emerson writes, "A foolish consistency is the hobgoblin of little minds, adored by little statesmen and philosophers and divines." He recommends that, whatever variety of actions one performs, they should each be honest and natural to one at the time. For inasmuch as they emanate from one will,

> the actions will be harmonious, however unlike they seem. These varieties are lost sight of when seen at a little distance, at a little height of thought. One tendency unites them all. The voyage of the best [sailing] ship is a zigzag line of a hundred tacks. This is only a microscopic criticism. See the line from a sufficient distance, and it straightens itself to the average tendency. Your genuine action will explain itself, and will explain your other genuine actions. Your conformity explains nothing. If I can be great enough now to do right and scorn eyes, I must have done so much right before me as to defend me now. Be it how it will, do right now.[6]

These words of Emerson are often quoted or misquoted to justify all manner of inconsistency. But clearly, Emerson is not attacking consistency that is oriented around fundamental values and great ends. In time experience widens: one grows up and puts away childish things. Old habits continually bring one into situations for which no existing habit is appropriate. To live is continually to adjust one's habits.

The American psychologist Prescott Lecky in his valuable little book *Self-Consistency* insists that most problems of behavior are due to inappropriate values that have become a fixed part of a person's life style, ideas and attitudes. The felt need for self-consistency — even a premature one — clarifies much human behavior (and even some behavior of dogs). Another American psychologist, Frederick C. Thorne, elaborates on Lecky's thoughts: "The first necessity for a scientific psychology is the conviction that behavior is meaningful and that each life story has its separate characteristic plot. To discover that plot is to understand the organism's behavior and to see in its adjustment to the environing world the dramatic unfolding of its own purposive achievement."[7]

Few manage to weave a life story that consists of a definite, persisting purpose. Yet, in Bertrand Russell's view, "Continuity of purpose is one of the most essential ingredients of happiness in the long run."[8] By contrast, purposeless activity can be a form of pain, and Feodor Dostoyevsky describes for us the torment of being required to carry stones pointlessly from one place to another and then back again.[9]

Purposes may conflict: a person may be torn between two loyalties or principles and so may be compared to "two souls struggling for undivided reign." To the American philosopher John Lavely, the concept or form of person is "a matrix of a single basic desire, a desire for coherence." But, he continues, coherence can "just as well be spoken of as a desire for wholeness, order, harmony, or integration."[10] According to Lecky's analysis, a personality is to be defined as

> an organization of values which are felt to be consistent with one another. Behavior expresses the effort to maintain the integrity and unity of the organization. All of an individual's values are organized into a single system the preservation of whose integrity is essential. The nucleus of the system around which the rest of the system revolves is the individual's valuation of himself. Any value entering the system which is inconsistent with the individual's valuation of himself cannot be assimilated; it meets with resistance and is likely, unless a general reorganization occurs, to be rejected. This resistance

is a natural phenomenon; it is essential to the maintenance of individuality.

Lecky finds that the chief problem in clinical psychology

> is not merely to change the attitude of the patient to some special detail of experience, but to revise his old philosophy and develop a new general outlook. If a value is assimilated into the organization or expelled from it, the process is not one of addition or subtraction, but rather of general revision and reorganization. If a person conceives himself to be a poor speller, the misspelling of a certain proportion of the words which he uses becomes for him a moral issue. He misspells words for the same reason that he refuses to be a thief. That is, he must endeavor to behave in a manner consistent with his conception of himself. A study of the spelling behavior of these students shows that each individual seems to have a definite standard of poor spelling which he unconsciously endeavors to maintain.

"Strange to say," Lecky continues, "the spelling of foreign languages seems to be impaired very little if at all."[11] He draws parallel conclusions about those many people who are poor at mathematics or who have social or behavioral problems. He contends that, unlike any one instinct or emotion, the striving for unity is more or less constant through time. On this basis, we can understand neurotic and psychotic phenomena "in terms of dynamic disorganization resulting from the final failure of the individual to function in [a] unified manner."[12]

Likewise, we can analyze the feeling of obligation in general as what Lavely calls "the feeling that I ought to make my actions coherent with my ideals." This presupposes a desire for a unified, self-consistent life. "I ought to act in accord with my beliefs *if I want a unified life*. If there is discord between my ideals and what I did, remorse or regret result."[13] If Lecky is right, people do desire a unified life and so ought to act in accordance with their ideals, whether those be noble or otherwise. There is a sense in which a person's very identity is constituted by self-consistency of attitudes, preferences, and habits.[14] While the drive for self-consistency does not explain all behavior, the point here is that inner self-consistency *feels* good, especially when compared with the unease of its opposite. One is at peace with oneself. In the words of the American psychologist Guy Alan Tawney:

> Consistency is the fundamental demand of the mental life, a demand backed up by some of the strongest and most insistent emotions, a demand which aims at the continuity and self-maintenance of the activity in which the life of the mind consists. As an actual experience, consistency is an immediate relation felt as satisfaction, ease and peace of mind. It is not intoxicating, but as a pleasure it is vastly superior to any intoxication, because it draws no refuse of pain in its wake and because it is an index to all goods and to the avoidance of all ills.[15]

Certainly, internal self-consistency is a pleasure that is gentle, pervasive and, above all, persistent. It is not a fast-growing plant; to mature, it requires cultivation and practice, together with a mindset that favors it. Over a period of time, self-consistency may be called a kind of happiness, perhaps the most important kind, for it provides a gentle and reliable continuity of satisfaction. Moreover, other kinds of happiness depend on self-consistent performance. Consistency, when it becomes systematic, acquires the quality that earlier we called *coherence* or a "sticking together."

How does a person acquire coherence? How are one's time, energy, and resources to be apportioned among myriad possible tasks, persons, projects, and hobbies in any coherent fashion? Without some overall goal or value or criterion, there is no reasonable way to settle conflicts or to achieve self-consistency in action. To satisfy the requirements of thought, one's ultimate value should afford a self-consistency and inner strength so satisfying and nearly complete that one willingly adheres to the value through all hardship. Where are we to look for any such abiding, reliable master goal or value?

The prophets of theism each put forth a unified ethical goal, namely, that of devoting all effort to satisfying the will or the precepts of Ahura-Mazda, Jehovah, God, or Allah. Under some interpretations, the deity is thereby to be pleased with the contribution of the nation or of each individual. Why doesn't a person join a religious organization and carry out the will of God according to that particular faith? People need to suppose that there really exists some basis for general coherence and that the basis is known at least to the keepers of religious mysteries.

Immediately the question arises: In view of the great number of theistic and secular faiths with their conflicting complex dogmas, precepts, and scriptures — each of which is accepted by its communicants as emanating from unquestionable authority — how is a person to choose a suitable group? Often the irrelevant or even subtly pernicious affirmations that some churches require of their communicants seem to warrant the response that the U.S. Patent Office wrote to Hazelett's father, C. William Hazelett, when he sought a patent: "All your claims are rejected on the ground of their multiplicity."

Inner coherence not only feels good, it lends power to its possessor. Energies that had been spent in maneuvering among inner conflicts are now spent in productive activity and the enjoyment of one's powers.

What goes into the making of such a man as Jonathan Edwards? The American historian Richard L. Bushman points out that most men conceal their anxieties. They compromise their internal conflicts rather than reconcile them. Yet as Bushman writes, with Edwards mainly in mind,

> an unusual integrity in the great man compels him to harmonize the warring elements. From his anguished quest for peace comes a new personal identity and with it a magnificent release of energy and determination. The combination of a compelling new identity and individual magnetism galvanizes others, and the great man, often without calculation, finds himself at the head of a movement.[16]

Despite the problems associated with existing religions, we may suspect that Jews and Christians, and Moslems, too, have got hold of some large but slippery truths and that their prophets have pointed toward the truth, whatever excrescences may have accumulated. The argument to be developed in favor of theism hinges on the question of *coherence* taken in different senses: (1) as a psychological concept, (2) as a social concept, and (3) as a general criterion of knowledge of commonsense items, of natural science, of ethics, and of God.

If love and care, including God's Care, mean anything, it is concern for the happiness of those loved. Hence we may suppose tentatively that God, in creating the universe, wished His creatures to be happy. In 1731 the English thinker John Gay pithily expressed old insights which infer the goodness of God from observing His works, claiming that He could have no other design in creating humankind than their happiness. Therefore, Gay reasoned, God not only wills their happiness, but also the means of their happiness. Moreover, Gay continued, God wishes that a person's own behavior, so far as it may contribute to the happiness of humankind, should contribute to His plan. Gay drew this conclusion:

> Here then we are got one step farther, or to a new criterion — not to a new criterion of virtue immediately, but to a criterion of the will of God. For it is an answer to the enquiry, How shall I know what the will of God in this particular is? Thus the will of God is the immediate criterion of virtue, and the happiness of mankind the criterion of the will of God; and therefore the happiness of mankind may be said to be the criterion of virtue, but once removed.[17]

Later, it will be shown that the promotion of the general happiness of creatures is, *when taken by itself*, an incoherent goal. Writing about the Latter-day Saint or Mormon communion, historian Sterling M. McMurrin describes their theological conviction that

> The vocation of man is found in the primary experience of moral struggle and that the God whom they worship participates in that struggle, suffers when they suffer, fails in their failures, grieves for their sins, and rejoices in their triumphs. They are made to believe that they are, as the Apostle said, "fellow laborers together with God," for God has not created evil for some more ultimate purpose, nor the conditions from which it comes, nor does he permit it when he might destroy it.[18]

We may consider the solution offered by Charles Hartshorne:

> The problem is solved if the general welfare of men is, as a whole, effectively enjoyed by a single subject in a single satisfy-

ing experience. Such a subject could not be less than divine. But the divine is here posited as a beneficiary or recipient of created values. Granted this view, a man's ultimate purpose can at last be intelligibly stated. Old phrases can be used, but with a new singleness of meaning. The purpose is to serve and glorify God, that is, literally to contribute some value to the divine life which it otherwise would not have. Altruism toward God would include and embrace and unify all altruism.[19]

Here a difficulty must be faced. Before taking seriously the possibility of this collecting of our joy into God's consciousness, we need to consider how we may know of the alleged sensitive and continuous power of God to know the joys and sorrows of each of us, whereby God can participate in them. Even some of those who accept the design argument for God's creation of the universe

**FRANK and ERNEST®**          by Bob Thaves          July 22, 1982

will doubt this pervasive, indwelling power that would be part of His universal *immanence* in the sense of His knowledge of everything that is happening.[20]

What is the role of Scripture in this investigation? Neither in natural theology nor in the present book is Scripture used as proof. In natural theology, statements should in principle be verifiable by all. It is interesting to note that the power of God to know our feelings is assumed throughout the Bible. There, one finds many indications of God's pleasure and displeasure at human acts. Genesis 6 tells us that God was sorry to have created human beings.

In Psalm 69 God is said to be pleased by praise. Proverbs 16 says the Lord protects those in whom God is pleased. Paul the Apostle is specific: "They who are carnal cannot please God." "Without faith, it is impossible to please God." "We speak not as pleasing man, but God." Again, "You have learned how you ought to walk to please God." "Do not grieve the Holy Spirit of God."[21] Plenty of divine wrath is recorded.

The view of God as acting in a living, knowing relation to the events of cosmic and human history is pervasive in the Bible, which presents God as continually interested, even passionate, about the behavior of His creatures. In short, God in the Bible loves, hates, and cares, in response to what individual creatures believe and do. Thus the Bible may be said to corroborate the conclusion that Edgar Sheffield Brightman, Alfred North Whitehead, Arthur Lovejoy, Charles Hartshorne, Dean Turner and others, have reached through their reason.

These passages contradict the many theologians, even the most prominent of them, who have insisted that God neither needs us nor is influenced by us. Suppose that a person says, "I can be equally happy and serene and joyous regardless of how men and women suffer around me." Are we to admire this attitude even when it is attributed to God? It resembles nothing so much as the traditional old Oriental despot.

How can one be freely motivated by contemplating the value that could be contributed to another if that other is so constituted as to be unable to receive value from any source? Was Jesus talking only about Aristotle's notion of a divine "unmoved mover" when He enjoined us to be perfect, even as our heavenly Father is perfect? Is perfection defined only statically? To some of us, these challenging questions answer themselves.[22]

Where did the doctrine of the absolute independence of God come from? The idea appears in Plato[23] and finds expression, too, in Aristotle who claims, "The independent man neither needs useful people nor people to cheer him, nor society; his own society is enough for him. This is most plain in the case of a god. The perfection of God is in being superior to thinking of aught besides himself." The reason, Aristotle continues, "is that, with us, welfare involves a something beyond us, but the deity is his own well-being. The unmoved mover [God] is himself unmoved." As religious knowledge, Aristotle's speculation may be an improvement over the free-wheeling gods of Olympus as conceived by earlier Greek writers.[24]

It was Philo Judaeus, a Hellenic Jew living at the time of Jesus, who effectively founded classical theism. He stated, "The Deity is not benefited by anyone. He is sufficient for himself. He is always acting, not acted upon. The great cause of all things does not exist in time, but he is superior to both time and place."[25]

With Augustine in the early fifth century A.D., the existence of creatures "is a good which could in no way profit God."[26] Augustine asks: "Who is so foolish as to suppose that the things offered to God are needed by Him for some uses of his own?" From his evident mistranslation of Psalm 16, Augustine concludes: "We must believe, then, that God has no need of man's righteousness and that whatever right worship is paid to God profits not Him, but man. For no man would say he did a benefit to a fountain by drinking, or to the light by seeing."[27]

All these views influenced Thomas Aquinas in the thirteenth century. Since Augustine and Aquinas lived before the Reformation, their views have been influential in both Protestant and Roman Catholic seminaries.[28]

Is our pleasing of God physically conceivable? Scientifically oriented persons may object that, even after supposing that God has planned and sustained the universe with our future good in mind, how is one to suppose that God, however conceived, receives any information about us that arrives in time to be of any interest either to Him or to us? The universe is so vast that it takes billions of years for light traveling at 186,283 miles a second to cross any appreciable portion of it. Light and radio waves are widely regarded by scientists as the fastest mode of distant causation or signal transmission.

In some difficult but rewarding writing for diligent laymen, the French physicist Bernard d'Espagnat develops the implications of the quantum-mechanical theorem of John S. Bell and some recent, apparently decisive experiments that test the Bell theorem. Under certain conditions, a truly simultaneous, instantaneous correlated effect occurs, namely, the correspondence of spin direction of subatomic particles. The experimental results imply that far-separated pairs of once-adjacent particles influence each other's spin direction from a distance. On the surface, it looks like communication directly between the particles, but this is evidently not the case. The experiments seem to settle a long-standing trilemma in quantum-mechanical theory and incidentally to do it in a way that

Einstein had opposed as embracing "spooky action at a distance."[29] D'Espagnat concludes that the evidence points to a universal spatial "nonseparability" or "nonlocality." That is, all objects in space are to be considered as subject to physical influences by each other, and the influences are instantaneous. This conclusion is supported by the independent arguments of the American physicist Henry P. Stapp. The influences bridge distance without need for a time interval such as required by light waves or other classical physical effects. According to the theory of quantum mechanics, even enormous distance is not to impede the influence of any object upon any other.

An analogy or perhaps an example is that of our own consciousness, which is not localized at any one place in the brain. In any case, it has been known for decades that a succession of electrons that had been presumed to go serially and singly through either one of two adjacent pinholes will accumulate their traces upon a screen in the form of a wave interference pattern. Within the confines of classical physics, this could not occur unless *each* electron had gone through *both* pinholes. In some sense, it must have happened so.

For d'Espagnat, all this entails a kind of universal "holism." He discusses the need for something like theism in the context of physics, though the theism in his writing is not necessarily of the personalistic kind but follows more after that of Spinoza.[30] The question arises, Was Isaac Newton right in considering space as "the sensorium of God"?[31] Such a view is consistent with the traditional view of God as acting everywhere through His own laws. Such a God can plausibly know instantaneously whatever is happening anywhere.

On this broad view, the known limitations on the speed of conventional signals may be regarded as irrelevant for God's knowledge. D'Espagnat calls his moderate realism a "theory of veiled reality." His overall quest may be said to have the same goal as that of rational theists, but it starts from the opposite end of the problem.

Of course, the idea of God's knowing our ongoing joys and sorrows — the idea of His being in this sense omnipresent or immanent — lacks an indisputable basis in current physics. So do consciousness, joy, and feelings in general. So does the concept of the Creation itself or any other explanation of beginnings. No one item of this list is physically either more or less conceivable than another. So much the worse for the universality of our standard contemporary physics. The object here has been to show that God's ongoing knowledge of the universe is conceivable in the sense that it cannot be disproved by physical considerations.

From another point of view, the question of God's communications need not have been asked. A Creator God is not dependent on physics; rather, physics is dependent on Him. God as omnipresent has no need of light or radio waves to receive messages. If the atheist is uncomfortable with such thoughts, then let him or her explain how the intelligible world order that makes a science of physics possible could ever have originated and been sustained without God.[32]

Many people have testified to direct experience of God. Most of us are not that privileged, at least not in these times, when we are so busy with countless mundane matters. We have been preoccupied like children opening their Christmas toys. Aside from intriguing inferences appealing to quantum mechanics, the authors suggest that some of the experiences that are labeled mystic may be closely related to the unanalyzed but joyous sense of inner coherence that results from acknowledging God's continuing care.[33] Be that as it may, we shall shortly find that the concept of coherence has much to do with our method of attaining truth.

> Religion is the key of history. We cannot understand the inner form of a society unless we understand its religion. We cannot understand its cultural achievements unless we understand the religious beliefs that lie behind them. In all ages the first creative works of a culture are due to a religious inspiration and dedicated to a religious end. The temples of the gods are the most enduring works of man. Religion stands at the threshold of all the great literature of the world. Philosophy is its offspring and is a child which constantly returns to its parent.
>
> Moments of vital fusion between a living religion and a living culture are the creative events in history, in comparison with which all the external achievements in the political and economic orders are transitory and insignificant.
>
> *Christopher Dawson*

# 8

## Ethics and the Cosmos

Purity of heart is to will one thing.

*Søren Kierkegaard*

Benevolent people are apt to be happier than selfish people, even when they are atheists. The late-nineteenth-century English ethical philosopher Henry Sidgwick describes the plight of those who lack even natural morality:

> It seems scarcely extravagant to say that, amid all the profuse waste of the means of happiness which men commit, there is no imprudence more flagrant than that of Selfishness in the ordinary sense of the term — that excessive concentration of attention on the individual's own happiness which renders it impossible for him to feel any strong interest in the pleasures and pains of others. The perpetual prominence of self that hence results tends to deprive all enjoyments of their keenness and zest, and produce rapid satiety and ennui: the selfish man misses the sense of elevation and enlargement given by wide interests; he misses the more secure and serene satisfaction that attends continually on activities directed toward ends more stable in prospect than an individual's happiness can be; he misses the peculiar rich sweetness, depending upon a sort

of complex reverberation of sympathy, which is always found in services rendered to those whom we love and who are grateful. He is made to feel in a thousand ways, according to the degree of refinement which his nature has attained, the discord between the rhythms of his own life and of that larger life of which his own is but an insignificant fraction.[1]

It is said that "Happiness is like jam. You can't spread it without getting a little on yourself." The psychologist Bernard Rimland conducted a startlingly simple experiment. He asked each of his students to make a list of the ten people they knew best, classifying these people as being either happy or not. In doubtful cases, the student could choose a substitute or withhold judgment. Then Rimland asked the students to classify their subjects as selfish or unselfish, having defined selfishness as "a stable tendency to devote one's time and resources to one's own interests and welfare — an unwillingness to inconvenience oneself for others."

The results indicated that the happy people in vast majority were grouped as unselfish and the unhappy people as selfish. About four-fifths of those classified fell into one of these two combinations, and only one-fifth into either of the other two possible ones. Rimland confesses: "While I was not a devil before collecting these data and while I am certainly not an angel today, these findings have unquestionably affected my Devil-to-Angel ratio."[2]

The computer scientist Douglas R. Hofstader presents a lengthy argument to show that isolated individuals who seek economic gain are each likely to gain more through a cooperative, helpful spirit than through the spirit most of them in fact displayed in an experiment he conducted. In the experiment, the majority tried to take crafty, secret advantage of the presumed cooperation of others, entailing that all ended up with nothing.[3]

A person's benevolent actions have, in and of themselves, no more worth to the beneficiaries when they occur under influence of belief in God than when they do not. Yet, observation suggests that theists are generally happier than atheists or agnostics while performing the same beneficent acts. We can verify the greater happiness of theists without consulting either Scripture or behavioral science, but we may recall the words of Jesus: "My yoke is easy and my burden is light."[4]

How might we analyze the motivations here? Serious theists are more likely to perform benevolent actions again and again and with increasing efficiency, because the reasons for their enjoyment go beyond mere natural sympathy. Experiencing joy and beauty themselves, they cultivate a sensitivity that enables them to bring about more joy in others. In a word, their benevolent actions are more generative of similar actions than the benevolent actions of the atheist. Moreover, the theists' own joys are not to be ignored in any overall reckoning of the joy that we together present to God.

Edwards says, "A benevolent propensity of heart is exercised, not only in seeking to promote the happiness of the being towards whom it is exercised, but also in rejoicing in his happiness."[5] Edwards continues by suggesting that no beings can be happy without communicating their happiness. The happiness of society, including that of God, "consists in the mutual communication of each other's happiness." It doesn't satisfy only to learn of the happiness of others without also communicating one's own.[6] A nineteenth-century disciple of Edwards, Charles Grandison Finney, elaborates a similar conception of benevolence:

> Benevolence enjoys everybody's good things, while selfishness is too envious at the good things of others even to enjoy its own. There is a divine economy in benevolence. Each benevolent soul not only enjoys his own good things, but also enjoys the good things of all others so far as he knows their happiness. He drinks at the river of God's pleasure. He not only rejoices in doing good to others, but also in beholding their enjoyment of good things. He joys in God's joy, and in the joy of saints. He also rejoices in the good things of all sentient existences. He is happy in beholding the pleasure of the beasts of the field, the fowls of the air, and the fishes of the sea. He sympathizes with all joy and all suffering known to him.[7]

As discussed earlier, the two levels of morality have been distinguished by Edwards. Those who function on the higher level, which is "benevolence to Being in general," may well be said to be in a state of *grace*, if one may so rehabilitate an old word that is here useful in a variant meaning. This level is to be contrasted with "natural morality." Given that one level is higher in moral quality than the other, for what reason is it higher?

The first reason, taking the example of Christianity, is simply to say that real Christians acquire their moral character in part by imitating Jesus. Again, moral traits in God may be inferred directly from His design of the universe and its laws. Finney builds his arguments partly upon what we experience of God's care, and partly upon analogy with the more care-ful conduct of men and women influenced by Jesus. Finney tells us:

> Benevolence is a compound word that properly signifies good willing, or choosing the happiness of others. This is God's state of mind. All his moral attributes are only so many modifications of benevolence. An individual who is converted is in this respect like God; the balance of his mind, his prevailing choice, is benevolent. He sincerely seeks the good of others, for its own sake. He chooses to do good because he rejoices in the happiness of others, and desires their happiness for its own sake.[8]

Another reason why one of Edwards' moral levels is in fact higher than the other has to do with the possibility of the *conservation of values*, notably through prospective experience of life hereafter. Observation suggests that such a belief can markedly improve personal functioning and happiness. Only the worldview of theism provides a basis for seeing life beyond the grave as plausible, while atheism does not.

A third reason why Edwards' "true virtue" level of morality is especially effective is wrapped up in the other reasons. If God merely created the universe and started it up, only to become a *Deus absconditus*, then our love of Him could be only formal. Why is it important that we find, if we can, reason to love a God who is currently active and who is affected by us?

The answer is that we can thereby pursue a unified task, a single purpose, namely, the unending task of pleasing God. "Goal" is not quite the right word for this task, since the pleasing of God is to be an ongoing, endless activity, never becoming a matter of completed attainment. In that respect, pleasing God is not different from the task of pleasing another human being, for neither effort is to culminate in an attainment of static, lasting bliss.

Edwards says, "We ought to make God our supreme good. In whatever way we do this, if it be chiefly in showing kindness to our neighbors, yet if this be done chiefly from love of God, then herein we make God our highest end."[9] Finney puts the matter:

"Multitudes of professed Christians seem to have no conception that *benevolence constitutes true religion* [and] that nothing else does." When the whole of morality is taken as a commitment to the highest good of God and the universe of beings, then "moral law, moral government, moral obligation, virtue, and the whole subject of morals and religion are the perfection of simplicity."[10]

Why should theists be happier in pursuing their ethical tasks than atheists? Simply because theists are able to arrange their lives around one unitary cause that includes and *coheres* all other desirable goals and tasks and causes, with the minimum of conflict. We serve God when we serve each other. We serve God, too, when we prepare ourselves to serve others.

In contrast to theists, those persons who try to arrange their lives around what Edwards calls a "private system" cannot practically achieve this self-consistency and coherence and maintain it over a period of time. If for a while they seem to, they still lack as their own possession the joyous knowledge of a God who perceives all earthly happiness and sorrow as His own.

If one person's idea of value conflicts with that of another person, the result is apt to be a mutual experience of disvalue. This unproductivity occurs in marriage, the workplace, the driving of automobiles, as well as in international relations. Yet, when people hold to the promotion of the same ultimate value, namely that of augmenting God's joy, the result is a shared joy in pursuing what is essentially the same goal. Because of this, we are entitled to imagine a workable universal society, in which private goals are voluntarily narrowed in number and are bent into as much conformity as may be needful to cohere with the master goal or task. Even fully socialist experiments, with no individual ownership of property, have succeeded for a time in a setting of theistic belief.

It must be admitted that to pursue any noble-seeming goal whatsoever affords more satisfaction, at least for a time, than having no goal at all. The infamous German National Socialist or Nazi movement had the slogan for its youth: "Strength through joy." It was strongly motivating for some years. Yet, all turned to bitter irony in the collapse of 1945. The American philosopher Durant Drake eloquently observes:

> To throw oneself wholeheartedly into the game, to play one's part for all it is worth, transforms what may be taken as an

irksome duty into a glorious opportunity. The happy man is the loyal man, the man who has taken sides, who has enrolled himself definitely in the service of some ideal and tastes the zest of battle. He has something to live for, and something lasting. He has put his heart into a cause that [as he believes] the limitations and accidents of life cannot take from him; he has laid up his treasure where moth and rust doth not corrupt or thieves break through and steal.

Drake continues with a sense of history, but with a needful caution:

Any cause, any ambition, any great endeavor that can stir the blood, and give life a direction, purpose, and continuity of achievement, has the power to rescue life from ennui, from emptiness, and give it positive worth. But most ambitions pall in time, and many a cause that has taken a man's best energies has come to seem mistaken with the years. There is only one great campaign which is so eternal, so surely necessary, so clear in its summons to all men, that the heart can rest in it as in something great enough to ennoble a whole life. That is the age-long war against evil, the unending summons to better human life, the service of God. Once a man learns this deepest of joys, nothing can take it from him; whatever his limitations, however narrow his sphere, there will not fail to be a right way, a brave way, a beautiful way to live. There is comradeship in it; in this common service of God we stand shoulder to shoulder with the saints and heroes of all races and times, with all, of whatever land or tongue, who are striving to push forward the line, to make good prevail and banish evil. In this devotion to ideal good a man is no longer an individual, he is a part of the great tide that is resistlessly making toward the better world of the future, the Kingdom of God. The great Power in the world that makes for righteousness is back of him, and in him; in no loyal moment is he alone.

The pleasures of life are a limitless source of delight, but they must not usurp the chief place in a man's thought. His first concern must be to keep true, to play the game; he must seek first the Kingdom of God and His righteousness, if he would have these other things added unto him. He must lose his life — his worldly interests, his dependence upon ease and luxury, his personal success — if he would truly find it. In a hundred such phrases from the Great Teacher's lips one finds the secret. Blessed is the man whose *delight* is in the law of the Lord.[11]

We may suppose that theists are happier because they have a sense of *global coherence* — the knowledge of a cause that is definite, all-embracing, supreme, and compelling. The object of one's supreme devotion, one's *summum bonum*, has unity and permanence, but it has more. The love of God can be pursued or adhered to in all circumstances without violating one's sense of self-consistency and without dampening a hope of prospective social coherence. In this way, personal goals become simplified and purified; they are voluntarily adjusted to conform to the all-embracing shared cause. The individual comes into possession of an overall purpose that unifies beliefs, ideals, motives, plans, thoughts, and actions. It is a purpose which takes into account the facts of existence and which tends to bind the human family and other creatures into a community of peaceful and productive interaction.

The theist has a vision of life as lived within a coherent universal scheme of things. The theist has the secure knowledge of the love of God and of our pleasant duty to love Him in return. This duty is expressed mainly through loving our neighbors and others. Hartshorne writes, "All these values, including the joy of serving them, would be viewed as contributory to one achievement, the enrichment of the divine life."[12]

One can then know the kind of experience described by Augustine, according to which "Man's life is blessed as well as tranquil when all his actions are in harmony with reason and truth."[13] Only then can there be harmonious connection of a person's motives with the world around him.

In effect, several modes of coherence are involved: the non-contradiction of all facts, the coherence of scientific laws, coherent knowledge of reality, inner or psychological self-consistency, and the realized or hoped-for coherence of wills in society. A theist who has discovered these forms of coherence rejoices in the joy of God and neighbor. In this way, the theist experiences glimpses of a Universal Web of Love. This web is not completed; indeed, it will never be complete. In it, each service is to be seen as a continuance of strands of service that extend from the prophets and spiritual leaders of the past to their followers, relayed from one to another. At length, the strands of service in the Universal Web of Love reach us and go through our hands to those who will follow. That is, by our own services, we strengthen others to be more useful and pleasant to yet others, on into the indefinite future.

A person who perceives and cherishes the Universal Web of Love acquires the conviction that the spreading of the knowledge of God will forge an ever wider and stronger Web of Love through mutual service. The Web of Love is the universal nexus for the social coherence of principle, thought, will, and action.

**PEANUTS®**                 by Charles Schulz              October 19, 1970

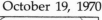

At their best, the principal religions of the world have held some vision of the Universal Web of Love. Each strand of the web may be thought of as bearing impulses both of service and of pleasure. One's service to another may be said to travel in one direction, but the service causes responding reverberations of pleasure, and so of further service, and of still further pleasure. Through the Web of Love, all of this radiates in all directions in Sidgwick's "complex reverberation of sympathy." Mutual services affirm the lasting meanings and render the pleasant reverberations self-sustaining and therefore joyous. With use, the strands multiply and intertwine into cables.

This is what civilization is about. Australian social scientist Alexander Sutherland suggests that civilization is a matter of the ability of people to constitute a "hearty consolidation" of great numbers. He points out that it is "incomprehensible to a savage, how hundreds of millions of people can dwell together without fighting, knit in hundreds of useful co-operations and forming cities of myriad dwellings."[14]

Discoverers, inventors, productive statespersons and business-persons have the pervasive and persistent satisfaction of knowing that their work has almost endlessly fruitful ramifications. Most of the rest of us know something of such satisfaction through creative interactions with family and friends, and through our work.

The "complex reverberation of sympathy" can be regarded as going beyond earthly beings. Hartshorne writes:

> We enjoy God's enjoyment of ourselves. This enjoyment-of-being-enjoyed is the essential factor in all our enjoyment. Nor is this a paradox. We experience every day how much we enjoy being enjoyed by other human beings. How much more is the value of living due to the secret, yet ever-present sense of being given, with all our joy and sorrow, to God! For, other men being also similarly given to God, whatever joy we impart to them we also impart to deity. And only God can adequately enjoy our joy at all times, and forever thereafter through the divine memory, which alone never loses what it has once possessed.[15]

There are counterforces that dampen otherwise pleasant rever-berations, as when we have done something for someone who not only didn't appreciate the service but who used the advantage so gained to bedevil others. Thoughts of service misdirected into mean-inglessness, hatred, or incoherence dampen those reverberations that would otherwise reinforce each other in joy. In a seamless Universal Web of Love, these lapses will be banished by construc-tive philosophy — the philosophy of Cosmic Care — whereby we shall all serve God as He serves us. In this vision of the future, the pleasant reverberations throughout the web are not dampened but cumulate into joy and into "the peace that passeth understanding."

A man in an engineering firm once told his partner-brother jocularly, during a period of intense activity: "You're working so that people like me can have fun. Otherwise, what good is your work?" Similarly, John Maynard Keynes has suggested that the merry people of tomorrow "are absolutely indispensable to provide a *raison d'être* for the grave of to-day."[16] These men could see the humor in their own remarks. However, a prominent but uneconomic American economist recently declared that people who do not wish to work should not be required to do so, suggesting that they be supported at public expense.

Why should we begrudge them our largesse? Because they are not weaving the Web of Love. Their sloth, their lack of sincere involvement, their failure to serve mutually, detracts from our own joy of work since their cut of the economic pie is, by their own will, unearned and hence not in the service of God. They fray or break the Web of Love, leaving others to patch it up. In such matters, knaves most often miscalculate the motives and the sense of righteousness of people who know how to enjoy their own service to others. Lucy in the cartoons of Charles Schulz complains, "Nobody understands us crabby people." On the other hand, crooks and knaves may not understand indignation.[17] We should be concerned with motivation generally, including the motivation of parasites, knaves, and crooks.

The Jewish Talmud says that "Our tears go to God." It is not only our joy that is to be seen as going to God but our sorrow, too.[18] If this were not so, God would not be the Caring God that we know. God has to pay a price for being God. The day God ceases to suffer, He will indeed be dead. To suppose with Aristotle, Augustine, and Thomas Aquinas that God is absolutely self-fulfilled and happy is bound to magnify, at least in some minds, the ideal of self-centered hedonism. To be truly moral, a person has to be prepared to suffer for the sake of God's joy.

The Russian philosopher Nicolas Berdyaev calls this willingness to suffer "the mystery of the Cross."[19] Yet this is not so painful for Christians as it sounds — or for that matter for Jews or modernist Moslems. Finney declares:

> The benevolent soul sympathizes with all joy and suffering known to him; nor is his sympathy with the sufferings of others a feeling of unmingled pain. It is a privilege to sympathize in the woes of others. He would not be without this sympathy. It so accords with his sense of propriety and fitness, that, mingled with the painful emotion, there is a sweet feeling of self-approbation; so that a benevolent sympathy with the woes of others is by no means inconsistent with happiness. God has this sympathy. There is, indeed, a mysterious and an exquisite luxury in sharing the woes of others. Where this result of love is not manifested, there love itself is not.[20]

A cross-light is shed upon several religious truths by consideration of new sects that make simpler demands upon their adherents than do Christianity or Judaism. A large proportion of Buddhists direct their devotions to the risen Amitabha Buddha. To recite once a week this buddha's name — O-mi-t'o Fo — is said to be sufficient to assure the reciter a place in the Western Paradise after death. This practice is surely a disincentive to ethical behavior as usually understood.

The Hare Krishna sect has been well known to Western urban dwellers through their colorful dress and bizarre baldness. From them we may learn of a practical value in belief in an afterlife, plus the value of a common allegiance to one over-arching entity, but we do not thereby learn much of how the One God of Nature and of life views our lives, or how thoughtful people can achieve a coherence that permeates their lives and loves.

We have arrived at the heaviest challenge. To see the world as pleasant simply in connection with belief in a loving, receptive God may be instrumentally valuable, but does this prove anything about Him or the divine nature? How is our discussion of God's receptivity to human joy any different from vulgar *pragmatism* — that is, believing something merely because it is expedient to do so, or because it feels good to believe? The answer to this important challenge is the subject of the following chapter.

> The religious worldview which seeks to com-
> prehend itself in thought becomes philosophical, as
> is the case among the Chinese and the Hindus. On
> the other hand a philosophical worldview, if it is
> really profound, assumes a religious character.
>                                         *Albert Schweitzer*

# 9

## Coherence, Truth, and Reality

Philosophy ought to imitate the successful sciences
in its methods, so far as to proceed only from
tangible premises which can be subjected to
careful scrutiny, and to trust rather to the multitude
and variety of its arguments than to the con-
clusiveness of any one. Its reasoning should not
form a chain which is no stronger than its weakest
link, but a cable whose fibers may be ever so
slender, provided they are sufficiently numerous
and intimately connected.

*Charles Sanders Peirce*

HAVING THE CONVICTION of the existence of
a caring God, anyone can pursue a goal or task that is widely and
deeply rewarding. It feels good, yes, but in comparison with the
opposite presumption, it feels good so deeply and reliably that God's
existence can be known through a strategy beyond the argument
from universal design. Before one comes to know God, one may
experience occasions of inner conflict so intense as to put one in
danger of losing any motivation to act and think rationally, whether
about theism, atheism, or anything else. But when God is
discovered, one then for the first time is able to make real sense
out of the existence of the world and the life in it.

Self-consistent theists pursue a task or cause that entails inner
peace and provides the motive for social cooperation. They see that
if people generally were to hold to the promotion of the same
ultimate value — that of adding to God's joy — a remarkable
coherence would result. Destructive conflict may still swirl around
believers, but they can now see the possibility of general improve-

ment. Because of their own experience of increased coherence, both internal and social, believers avoid hopeless grief and waste. As they become more altruistic, occasions for conflict and deceit lessen. They may find this experience so satisfying that it serves to enlarge their will to think and act rationally. The vision of a world in peaceful interaction comes into focus.

The one coherent basic view of the world — the theistic view — embraces not only commonsense knowledge but scientific truth as well. The one coherent worldview embraces living beings and their motivation. It embraces society and the physical world as a setting for the realization of one's hopes and ideals. It is a total worldview capable of solving practical contradictions that otherwise are ubiquitous and insoluble.

We have described this worldview as that of One God at the center, who created the world for the free realization of value, both for Himself and for His creatures. Only in accepting the existence of the One God who sustains the world, who knows the creatures' joys and sorrows — all of them — who cares and loves, and to whose joy or sorrow each of us contributes, is one able to view the world as fully rational and livable — as hundreds of millions of believers can testify, whatever be their differences.

The academic world now knows answers to about every sort of question except why anyone should strive for anything in the first place. At this point of growing lassitude, all goes askew. For the consistent atheist, life is "a tale told by an idiot, full of sound and fury, signifying nothing." Any position that purports to be global and comprehensive must accord to motivation a commanding place in the scheme of things, as well as a just place to the metaphysics and worldview that makes rational motivation conceivable.

People who deny the theistic worldview thereby undercut in principle their own motivational foundations and thereby commit a kind of non-simultaneous contradiction. That is, they push away the ladder of assumptions upon which their forebears climbed. Such a procedure is unscientific, if not absurd. Scientists may refine the early concepts of a science as it develops, but they cannot devour the very foundations that the science must continue to accept, lest they find themselves in the same company as those who deny that the earth rotates.[1]

What good reasons are there to suppose that our benevolence toward God can indeed be a genuine communication? We have already considered whether physics presents a description of the universe which is compatible with believing that God knows our joys and sorrows. Though mystery remains, we found no sufficient reason for denying such a belief but rather substantial plausibility for it. We have learned something of the divine care implicit in the general operation of the universe. But can we, on independent intellectual grounds, justify the belief that God knows our joys and

Jack Tippit                                    December 1960

*"It's designed to prepare children for today's complex world. No matter how they put it together, it doesn't come out right."*

sorrows and is affected by them? Does God's care truly extend to such ultimate and detailed sensitivity? We indeed have the intellectual basis for this belief because it is only in this direction that comprehensive coherence and integration can be found, whether in philosophizing about common sense, natural science, ethics or theology.

In the first place, comprehensive coherence is the theory of knowledge — the criterion or test — that is finally relied upon in all of science. Without our knowledge of an omnipresent God who has knowledge of our affairs, we have no pursuit that can render unified and coherent the motivations, enthusiasms, and actions of our lives, or even of our scientific pursuits.

Among the motivations rendered coherent by contributing to the happiness of God is the motivation behind the very pursuit of knowledge and truth. Without an affirmation of God, the search for knowledge becomes incoherent, and the search cannot be rationally motivated. Without God, there simply is no basis on which to keep all interests, beliefs, values, attitudes, and actions logically and emotionally related to one another. "The commonest stupidity," writes Nietzsche, "is to forget what one is doing." By contrast, theists do know what they are doing. So do some atheists, in part, but they do not find a task that can be consistently pursued in all circumstances.

Does the coherence have to be centered in the theistic goal of contributing to the happiness of God? We can arrive at an affirmative answer by a process of elimination. Then we shall be left with a world order in the care of the One God who loves and is genuinely present to His creatures. A denial of the possibility of a comprehensive and coherent goal for one's life in this world is disastrous, not only morally but intellectually. We have found reason to suppose that God has arranged things so that He knows of our personal joys and sorrows in order to enjoy the fruits of His own creation — that is, to enjoy our happiness. This entails the possibility of a comprehensive and coherent goal. No worldview that is less ambitious achieves such a completion.

The final validation of theism by the coherence criterion or test of truth concerns the matter of *motivation*. Not only philosophy but also science has mostly slighted motivation. Natural scientists generally leave motivation out of account in their work, for the good reason that it may be a biasing contaminant. In most contexts, this is correct procedure, since a scientist who strongly desires a certain experimental result may arrive at a result biased through faulty observation or unconscious manipulation.

Yet there are proper exceptions. We have already seen that the human motivation to do science follows directly from belief in a sole Creator God and that it is scientifically fruitful to assume that the Creator was motivated to create our singular universe with its *persisting* universal laws. Thus we have a cosmic motivation that is itself coherent, orderly, and essentially unchanging. In keeping with this, we concluded that God as the Creator was motivated to create us in such a fashion that we could understand His laws. Finally, we discussed the human motive to render knowledge and life's activities coherent and integrated, including the motive to philosophize about God.

Taken together, the coherence of our knowledge of the world system as a whole is spectacularly increased by the assumption of theism. Moreover, this fact of increased coherence is further evidence for theism. Despite the appearance of circularity, the coherence theory of knowledge and test of truth is the instrument whereby the circle of knowledge is expanded. A true theory will accommodate every relevant fact without contradiction.

The method of coherence that has just been used to validate theism must itself be validated. One test of the truth of any proposed scientific law is its consistency or non-contradiction with the accepted body of scientific knowledge. An alternate test is to determine whether the proposed law is consistent with the body of such knowledge when reinterpreted in the light of the new law. Scientific truth must be consistent, and consistency is one test of the truth of statements. However, is it a sufficient test of truth for the present purpose?

To answer this question, it is needful to turn to epistemology, which is the study of the foundations of knowledge, wherein we consider how we know whatever we do know. The method of arriving at truth in this book is not different in principle from that which has been used in the development of physical science at its cutting edge. It is not essentially different from the primary method we use in arriving at our everyday commonsense knowledge such as our knowledge of our surroundings and of the reality of other people.

We use the method of coherence continually in everyday life. For example, most of us do not know the details of the steering mechanism of an automobile, yet in learning to drive, we find that our turning the steering wheel clockwise always directs a moving auto to the right. Because the same maneuver always has the same result, we become secure in the knowledge that the auto is built so as to achieve that result. At other times we may respond to a situation by saying, "Something doesn't fit." That is, we surmise that the report is false because it doesn't cohere with our previous knowledge.

If a witness in a courtroom gives one account of certain events and another witness gives a different account of the same events, the inconsistency reveals that at least one account must be mistaken. However, if three or more witnesses give identical accounts, such consistency increases the likelihood that the witnesses are correct. This sort of evidence was used in the empirical design argument for God's existence, already presented.

Peirce points out that all those who are interested in science, "are animated by a cheerful hope that the processes of investigation, if only pushed far enough, will give one certain solution to each question to which they apply it." For example, one man, Ole Römer, pioneered the investigation of the velocity of light by noting the time of the eclipses of Jupiter's moons while Jupiter changed its distance from us. Another, H. L. Fizeau, corroborated Römer by timing a round trip of a reflected light beam over a measured course (nowadays it might be a radar beam). Still another, J. Clerk Maxwell, corroborated the result by the initially improbable method of calculation from the electromagnetic characteristics of adventurously presumed self-propagating light waves. "They may at first obtain different results," Peirce writes, but,

> as each perfects his method and his processes, the results are found to move steadily together toward a destined centre. So with all scientific research. Different minds may set out with the most antagonistic views, but the progress of the investigation carries them by a force outside of themselves to one and the same conclusion. This activity of thought by which we are carried, not where we wish, but to a fore-ordained goal, is like the operation of destiny. No modification of the point of view taken, no selection of other facts for study, no natural bent of mind even, can enable a man to escape the predestinate opinion. This great hope is embodied in the conception of truth and reality. The opinion which is fated to be ultimately agreed to by all who investigate, is what we mean by the truth, and the object represented in this opinion is real.[2]

While experiments that employ one method may establish a good case for some definite value of the velocity of light, the concurrence and mutual support of the results of a number of widely different methods — that is, their coherence — can increase the presumption to a point of justifiable certitude. One is then entitled to believe that the result converged upon is *true* and that it *corresponds* to the otherwise dimly or dubiously known *reality*. On the other hand, inconsistency beyond the limits of the error attributable to problems of measurement spoils such certitude. Moreover, a verified consistency extends its force to other results in physics, astronomy, and chemistry.

In the above example, Römer's result corroborated the Newtonian assumption of the constancy of the period of revolution of Jupiter's moons. Römer assumed this constancy in his calculation of the speed of light in its trip from Jupiter to Earth. The observed constancy was not quite complete. Römer surmised correctly that the variation in the observed time of eclipse of the moons was due to the variation of the distance over which the light had to travel as Earth and Jupiter diverged from and converged toward each other in their respective orbits, thereby explaining the discrepancy. Thus, Römer's observations and all the others corroborate Newtonian dynamics, which precisely relate speed, acceleration, orbits and trajectories by means of the concepts of force, gravity, mass, and inertia. The result of this sort of mutual confirmation is an ever-extending network of coherent relationships of knowledge.

The seventeenth-century German astronomer and mathematician Johannes Kepler candidly explains at length how he pursued his painstaking thinking about planetary orbits through trial and error. In Kepler's case, the data were already at hand in the form of the accurate observations of his mentor Tycho Brahe. Holding as Kepler did to the faith that the universe is fundamentally a harmonious, rational, mathematically ordered structure, he devised hypotheses and laboriously tested them by making corresponding calculations of planetary positions. Inconsistency with Tycho's observations was the measure of error. When a hypothesis was found to be in error, as each but the last hypothesis was, Kepler tried again with a new hypothesis formed in the light of the previous failure. In this way, after many years of intense labor, Kepler arrived at a theory of elliptical planetary orbits that was coherent and which is perhaps the most graphically beautiful fruit of faith in universal law.[3]

In a broadly similar way, Michael Faraday, the early nineteenth-century English electromagnetic genius, tested his countless hypotheses by adventurous experiments.[4] More sweeping than the conceptual structure either of Kepler or of Faraday was that of Kepler's contemporary, Galileo, who discerned the far-reaching coherence to be achieved through a proper concept of motion in time. This became the bedrock of physics and made Newton's work possible. Galileo employed Euclidean geometry, and he identified time as universal and as uniformly passing in only one direction. The synthesis enables the results of countless dynamic observations to coalesce into simple theories of elegant coherence and simplicity.[5] In the classical theories of motion as elaborated by Newton, we have consistency and something more: the laws tend to imply each other in a process of reciprocal confirmation. One can start from a selection of less than half of them and derive the rest in either direction. In such cases we may speak of coherence, not merely of consistency.

At the point of forward thrust of scientific theory, an investigator may have no guide other than the consistency that eventuates into *coherence,* since there is no other way to determine whether the theory adequately represents or *corresponds* to generally accepted reality. For instance, consider the early nineteenth-century English chemist John Dalton who is credited with the modern atomic theory of matter which postulates dozens of kinds of elemental, permanent atoms, each being interchangeable with the countless atoms of the same kind.[6] But Dalton never saw an atom, and individual atoms were never in any sense visible in the nineteenth century. This fact kept the Austrian physicist Ernst Mach from affirming their existence. He would ask an incautious student, "Oh, have you seen one?" What made scientists almost universally insist with Dalton on the existence of atoms and ignore Mach was that the atomic theory already had enabled chemists to bring intelligible order into a vast array of observations and predictions. With shorthand notations to keep track of the various kinds and ratios of elemental atoms, chemists could state the composition of thousands of compounds and anticipate the existence of thousands more. The results could then be manipulated in the form of equations to predict and record chemical reactions in general. So again, it is not a matter merely of consistency but of coherence.

A few randomly chosen specific facts in such a system of knowledge imply countless others. That is, they do not merely succeed in avoiding contradiction among observed facts, but they also serve to hold the system of scientific laws together. Without the method of coherence — meaning finally coherence among *concepts* — the atomic theory could not have been confirmed during the time when Mach was active. The believers were right, for recent verifications and even photographic "portraits" of atoms have removed any lingering doubt.

In most ordinary matters, truth is taken to be that which *corresponds* to that portion of reality already known with reasonable certainty. Consider a fact: the sun is shining. The statement is true. Why? Because you already know what it is for the sun to be shining, and you look and see that indeed it is shining. There is no end of things that we all know and express about the world and which we have no occasion to doubt. We know that we each have a body. We recognize many people and objects on sight or sound. We know the geography of our neighborhood. We have a command of our own language.

Each of us knows an immense number of practically indubitable facts that can be verified by looking or asking. In this way we ascertain the correspondence between statement and reality. Thus, our test of the truth of the statement of a new situation is that of seeing whether our verbal judgment about it *corresponds* to that base of already presumed reality — that is, refers adequately or "co-responds" to it.

This kind of correspondence is the most readily comprehended criterion of truth. You see a cardinal on a branch and say so. You already know what a cardinal is and what one looks like, and your perception corresponds to what you know and what you say, so you have no real doubt.[7] Generally, we expect that statements and beliefs, as well as perceptions, must *correspond* to reality in order to be true.

Only in special circumstances is there any reason to entertain doubts about such matters. In the matter of the cardinal, distance could be one cause of doubt, though the doubt is readily removed by a closer approach or by use of a field glass. Is then the criterion or test of truth basically the *correspondence* of a hypothesis to the real object of that hypothesis? There are situations in which this will not do, because the reality is not known independently of our hypothesis about it.

Consider the time when we were tiny children, back before we can remember. Evidently we all failed to believe in the existence or identity of persons or of any of the above-mentioned common things. There was even a time when each of us failed to suppose that there was an outside reality that we could know. Very early, emerging from the state of booming, buzzing, confusion, each of us had to form the concept of a permanent object itself — that is, of something real and substantial.

The patient work of the Swiss psychologist Jean Piaget enabled him to infer that this concept enters a child's head at the age of a year, more or less. Though the development of the concept of a permanent object occurs in stages, a pivotal occasion is the child's seeking of a known object such as a ball temporarily hidden by a fold in the bedspread. The concept of a permanent object evidently arose in each of our minds through its enabling us to coherently organize a vast array of visual and tactile impressions that were previously just there, uninterpreted. Piaget substantiated these facts in a philosophically important book of genetic epistemology, *The Construction of Reality in the Child.*[8]

A child's suspicion that a ball might not be a permanent object is dispelled by finding the ball after it has been hidden. We once all were scientists in our own way. That is, we were working at the cutting edge of our own knowledge, selecting truths by the test of *coherence,* since there were no sufficient prior concepts in our minds to *correspond* to. By the method of coherence, we arrived at hypotheses that would organize our sense-impressions under the headings of various concepts. Only after an enormous input of sensory data did we acquire enough sense of enduring *reality* to test the *correspondence* of our momentary judgments of fact or reality against our experience.

We see that, in the temporal, genetic order of knowing, the correspondence test of knowledge or truth comes into play *after* the test of coherence has started the knowledge process. Our growth in knowledge is a matter of the slow development of systems of sense-data (i.e., percepts) and concepts that cohere. New coherences develop, replacing earlier erroneous or less complete coherences or fixations which are now seen as inadequate. We achieve concepts of a reality and substantiality that we finally all have rather agreed upon, at least so far as the presumed reality is palpable or observable. This agreement adds a social dimension to our privately perceived coherence. The task is never completed. We continue to build our knowledge and to discard old concepts; thereby we continue to approach, but never reach, a comprehensive knowledge of reality.

Decisions and revisions of history, especially history reaching back a lifetime or more, must be made on the basis of the coherence of the reports. A historian rejects those reports that do not cohere with documented facts in other accounts. In dealing with the history of previous centuries and of people long since departed, there is of course no currently experienceable reality to which one's account can correspond. The late American philosopher Brand Blanshard once asked us to consider the truth of the judgment: "Burr killed Hamilton in a duel." Blanshard says,

> If this belief about Hamilton is true, then a thousand references in newspapers, magazines, and books, and almost endless facts about the fortunes of Hamilton's family, about the later life of Burr, and about American constitutional history, fall into place in a consistent picture. If it is false, then the most credible journalists, historians and statesmen, generation after generation, may be so deluded about events that happen before the eyes of a nation that no single historical fact is any longer above suspicion. If evidence of this weight is to be rejected, then in consistency we must go on to reject almost every hint that takes us beyond immediate perception. And intellectually speaking, that would pull our house about our heads. What really tests the judgement is the extent of our accepted world that is implicated with it and would be carried down if it fell. And that is the test of coherence.[9]

Detectives, including literary detectives, rely on the coherence test of truth. So do those who test for truth in any system of logic or mathematics. In these fields, investigators have established a system upon axioms, definitions, and "primitive ideas" whose validity depends upon the internal and mutual consistency of the structures resulting from their application.

A criticism of the coherence criterion or test of truth is the claim that the diabolic German Nazi movement was a coherent system. Perhaps it was, in the weak sense that any movement that lasts for a time must have some conceptual coherence to enable a relative social coherence to form. However, the grotesquely untrue elements of faith demanded by the Nazi party — elements that were not consistent with the real order of things — marked the way to the Nazi downfall in 1945.

The most frequent objection to coherence as the criterion of truth is that a system can cohere and yet be false. For instance, a novelist can invent and describe a whole world of characters and circumstances that cohere. Or two detectives or two scientists may hold differing theories that cannot both be true, though they be self-consistent and explain the same phenomena.[10]

But this objection rests on a misunderstanding. The criterion of coherence is to be taken as requiring consistency of a theory with every fact. There is to be no arbitrary segregation of an island of data as in a fanciful work of fiction.[11] Blanshard urges that coherence is the criterion that is used when our hypotheses are under pressure.[12] It is by applying the criterion of coherence to our data, he teaches, that we achieve "systematic vision."

Blanshard is surely correct here, and the history of science bears witness to it. The *correspondence* theory of knowledge has value where it ties a *previously identified reality* to our new concepts. Systematic *coherence* as it is used in science is the corroboration — a mutual support — among elements of a complex vision, excluding nothing actual. This is the criterion for the selection of new concepts on which to base our affirmations, both in science and in common sense. Blanshard and the American philosopher Nicholas Rescher hammer out in enlightening dialogue the matter of coherent beliefs that correspond with reality.[13]

In other words, if we take science seriously, we must affirm a *reality* to which our statements correspond. This is scientific realism. We should affirm further that the world of physical laws and physical facts exists consistently and coherently by its nature. This is part of the ethos of science. If this were not true, the physical sciences would not be possible. Precisely this metaphysical realism, inhering as it does in Judaism and Christianity, helps to explain why science grew and flourished in Christendom.[14]

However, it would be unrealistic to argue that the whole of reality (physical and spiritual) is coherent in every sense. It goes without saying that much incoherency of belief and purpose is found in the behavior of creatures. For example, people may have incoherencies within their own thinking, as well as emotional conflicts and incompatibility between what they espouse in theory and what they act upon in practice. Also, there are conflicts between creatures when their wills clash or when they inflict suffering and needless destruction upon one another.

Einstein maintained that "Existence should have a completely harmonious structure."[15] Likewise, Blanshard considered the whole of reality as absolutely coherent (i.e., everything implies everything else, within a universal unity). Both of these thinkers held to strict determinism and thus had to deny that any creature can have any degree of freedom of volition or choice. We shall see later that this denial is itself incoherent — an example of incoherence in the sense of contradiction among ideas. A rational solution to the problem of experienced incoherence can be found only in the assumption that God has a perfectly coherent reason for allowing room in the world for the possibility that some incoherencies can transpire. Without freedom of volition and choice, any intelligible philosophy of ethics would be impossible.

Our knowledge must correspond with reality in order to be genuine. Indeed, this is what is most commonly meant by knowledge. Yet our very conception that there is independent reality outside ourselves is itself reached through the method of coherence, as we have seen in the discussion of our knowledge acquired in babyhood. Coherence is then our deepest test of truth, notably where new areas are being explored. Here, our information about reality lacks that richness of interpreted sensory content that has resulted from many previous applications of the method of coherence. Yet, where our past experiences are concerned — and that is nearly everywhere — verification comes more readily simply by correspondence of new data with the old knowledge.

The method of coherence stands in some contrast to other theories of how science is said to progress. Too narrow an idea of the nature of science has blocked for many the path here being tread. The word science means two distinct things. Most familiarly, it is the existing body of already achieved and verified scientific law; this is the science ordinarily taught in school and featured in our encyclopedias. But science is also an exploratory activity of discovery and understanding. Investigators must understand the shape of this activity if they would add to basic knowledge. Scientific discoveries are not deduced from indubitable foundations but rather grow from "the vague and confused to the articulate and precise."[16] The Austrian philosopher Otto Neurath notes: "We are like sailors who must rebuild their ship on the open sea, never able to dismantle it in dry-dock and to reconstruct it there out of the best materials."[17]

Hence, there is good reason to challenge the popular myth about science that originated with Francis Bacon, namely, that scientific discovery "is a kind of distillation from innumerable factual observations altogether devoid of theoretical bias."[18] This is admittedly correct insofar as "We must begin with experience, since otherwise there is no problem; and return to experience, since otherwise no solution is made good; and proceed on the analogy of experience, since otherwise there is failure of that continuity and resemblance in which explanation consists."[19]

Yet, as the South African-American philosopher Errol E. Harris shows, many examples can be presented from several fields to refute the Baconian view historically and logically. His very helpful study *Hypothesis and Perception: The Roots of Scientific Method* maintains that fruitful scientific endeavor consists of an interplay of observation and adventurous speculation — of facts on one hand and ideas on the other. This position, known as the hypothetico-deductive method, mediates between two extreme positions. The first is extreme empiricism or exclusive reliance on ordinary fact as for instance with Bacon, or even on supposedly simple sense impressions. The second extreme is that of pure rationalism or *a priori* reasoning — i.e., thought which lacks grounding in sense experience.[20]

Harris is not the first to express the view that a combination of these approaches is necessary,[21] but he develops the idea thoroughly and in the context of the coherence test of truth. Harris notes that "Observational data acquire significance only in the light of the theory by means of which they are interpreted." For instance, when Copernicus in the sixteenth century presented a new theory of the observed motions of the sun and planets, the appeal of his system did not rest on any new observations — there weren't any — but rather on the "unity, consistency and coherence" of the theory as opposed to the ancient, earth-centered system of Ptolemy. Indeed, Ptolemy's system of epicycles fitted the observations as well as Copernicus' theory of circular planetary orbits, since both theories, antedating Kepler, then required the addition of secondary *ad hoc* hypotheses in order to fit the facts.

Harris observes, as he did in regard to Copernicus' theory, that Kepler's theory, too,

> was not inspired by new empirical discoveries; it was the pure result of thinking in accordance with the intellectual demands of a conceptual system. It was not a generalization from observed facts but the development of the implication of a theoretical schema so that the observed data could be intelligibly, consistently and coherently interpreted by its means. It

was only if the right question were asked that the observations could be seen as an answer to it. The method of discovery, therefore, is one of construction, but a construction which is in some sense "deduced" from the facts, while at the same time the facts are "deduced" by applying the hypotheses to the observations. Conflicts and contradictions in the course of this process reveal errors, which must be corrected by mutual adjustment of the elements, and the conclusion is considered adequate only when a complete system has been evolved in which all the contributory factors and elements fit harmoniously together.[22]

Newton's encompassing, interlocking edifice of the laws of motion and gravitation has been well called "the system of systems." His experimental work on gravity and motion was minimal and was occasioned simply by his needs for precision and for demonstration. He did measure the acceleration of the motion of objects affected by gravity, and he demonstrated centripetal force in relation to absolute space by means of his rotating bucket filled with water. From his theoretical work, we can see most clearly that scientific speculations "are the fruits of an organizing activity on the part of the discoverer, combining and integrating the partial developments of an earlier conceptual system that his predecessors have made in their search for consistency and comprehensiveness."[23] Newton's theory of gravitation is the paradigm of the application of the coherence test of truth among both old and new concepts in arriving at a new valid, overarching concept.

Because the coherence test of truth operates so conspicuously in the method of natural science, it was worth examining closely in order to suggest its proper role in theology, too, where we have seen it function in a manner not fundamentally different from the way it does in the other sciences. Yet the methods of science broadly speaking should not seem strange, for science turns out to be common sense that has been refined and rendered precise. Common sense is "the product of the same urge to coherent understanding which gives rise to science."[24]

Both Harris and the English medical scientist Peter Medawar have clarified for modern readers the notorious philosophical "problem of induction" as being wrongly put and hence a non-problem. Hume, though lacking in understanding of true scientific method, had done a service to epistemology through his *reductio ad absurdum* of this Baconian theory of scientific discovery, which is the supposition that theory emanates of itself from the enumeration of random bare facts. Hume showed the futility of supposing that a mere random accumulation of facts, presumed to be all mutually isolated, permits one to make predictions of future happenings. Hence, this brand of Baconian empiricism, so far as it is a competitor of the coherence theory of knowledge, can be laid to rest.[25]

Like Jesus of Nazareth, like Augustine and other thinkers, Jonathan Edwards was concerned about human happiness. Yet, like them, he refused to take human happiness as the *ultimate* goal to be directly and consciously pursued without reference to some yet more universal endeavor. Edwards was aware of his contemporary eighteenth-century challengers who held that "our fellow-creatures, and not God, seem to be the most proper objects of our benevolence." But we have seen how the world and our place in it become intelligible and coherent when we acknowledge God the Father as the partaker and conserver of all joy and sorrow: "Inasmuch as ye have done it to the least of these my brethren, ye have done it unto me."[26]

An objector may ask: Is it not unscientific to resort to God as the direct explanation of anything? Does not such a move commit the sin of blocking the path of scientific inquiry by arbitrarily stopping the inquiry and pleading the intervention of God when an investigation might uncover further natural, impersonal causes?[27] Indeed, the objector can point out that the ancients were mistaken when they tied every facet of their cosmologies directly to the will of some personal deity. Is it not significant that the achievements of Galileo, Newton and others, did away with such explanations in natural science?

But at some point in the inquiry into the ultimate nature of things, the methods of natural science must fail, and then we shall have to acknowledge that, beyond some impassable boundary of knowledge, there is God acting. We do not possess ultimate explanations in physics, but if we ever thought we did, we would face the fact that no purely physically *ultimate* explanation could explain itself, as was mentioned earlier.

Of course, the supposition of an ultimate termination of physical inquiry may come too soon; this has happened in the history of science. The pre-eminent Lord Kelvin supposed that atoms, taken as the ultimate and uncuttable particles that their name implies, were to be explained solely by the direct sustaining action of God. New knowledge compelled us to deal with subatomic "particles," and further investigation continues vigorously today. Such errors should not make us lose sight of the problem that gave rise to them, namely, that no physical explanation can be ultimate.

Then at what point should an investigator acknowledge that the mode of explanation used in natural science has gone as far as it can go? The reasonable answer is that the methods of natural science should be continued as long as they can be. When a jumping-off place is finally reached, rationality and intelligibility demand that the explanation be that of God acting.[28]

"I believe, in order that I may understand." Now we can appreciate the meaning of this seemingly merely circular statement of the medieval churchman Anselm of Canterbury, in which he encapsulated a theme of Augustine. There can be no view of life and the world based on experienced facts that are, taken one by one, indubitable. Rather, we experience the interconnectedness of many facts, most of them less than absolutely certain. Taken together, they enable us to form hypotheses of the independent, mutually shared, real world that exists independently of our minds. Like the strands of Peirce's cable, these countless facts and hypotheses corroborate and reinforce each other, bearing witness not only to newly discovered truth, but also to the coherence of the universe. Practically, we inevitably come to consider many such hypotheses as indubitably certain fact.

The seekers who persist come finally to a viable natural theology of Cosmic Care — the knowledge of the reality of God as the fulfilment of coherence. It is our creator, God, who enables us to justify our creator, God. Further, the seeker learns the direction that ethics must take. The method of true natural theology and ethics is the method of natural science. The result is the validation of the system of the world which is plainly the most probable of all hypotheses — indeed, the only plausible one — that of a caring, ethical theism, wherein the believer is to cooperate with God.

If a lingering implausibility persists in the reader's mind, it can be regarded as an effect of novelty, since *every* view of life and the world presents surface enigmas. Indeed, "The mystery of mysteries is that something exists."[29] Any objector who admits that something exists must, if possible, put forth a better hypothesis to explain it than that of the existence and activity of God. In a correct worldview, such surface enigmas will lose their jagged edges of seeming incoherence as one analyzes them in depth.

By contrast, in the elaboration of an erroneous view, the implausibilities increase and lead to insoluble contradictions. The erroneous view is thus left to stand convicted of error. The hypotheses of God's existence, His act of Creation, and His love and continuing care are, *on superficial analysis*, profoundly mystifying. But then, so is the existence of a universe, and the existence of ourselves, or of anything at all. Yet, the acceptance of these singular mysteries is the key to that logical coherence which constitutes an understanding of the world. The fact that our science does not give us sensory verification of God, as though through a telescope, is not cogent as negative evidence.[30]

The solution to the riddle of life is to be known by the *global coherence* that the solution affords. Peirce defines a bad aim as one that cannot be consistently pursued when it is "unfalteringly adopted." A bad aim means an inauthentic cause or goal.[31] Lenin shouted at his advisers, "If the end does not justify the means, then in the name of sanity and justice *what does?*" He received no answer.[32]

Such consistency in allowing an ultimate end to dictate the permissible means is a severe test of the correctness of the end pursued. The trouble with subordinating means to ends is that the choice of an end that is not both fully comprehensive and correct will lead into a morass of problematic means that tend to swamp the end itself. In the matter of Lenin's challenge, the choice of the wrong end, together with the drive to elaborate the initial error, allowed resort to brutal and unproductive means on a seemingly endless scale, with the ultimate nullification of the promises of the planners. Proponents of other ideologies and values as ultimate, including entrenched laisser-faire capitalism, have also repeatedly justified the continuance of racking violence, misery, and waste in order to preserve the status quo, be it "democracy," "national security" or, regrettably, all manner of religions. Yet, as the legal ethicist Michael S. Josephson observes, "The notion that nice guys finish last is not only poisonous but wrong. In fact, the contrary is true: Unethical conduct is always self-destructive and generates more unethical conduct until you hit the pits."[33]

"Blessed are the peacemakers." Yet, even while lauding such benign spirit, one must hesitate to embrace pacifism *with full con-*

*sistency,* for then it becomes, "Peace at any price." Consider what such a commitment entails, when absolute. All other values become subordinate. Loyalty to, and protection of, family and friends becomes subordinate. There is no principle or person that a devotee of peace at any price would not have to betray in order to be true to the one ultimate aim itself. In truth, as G. K. Chesterton says, pacifism (so understood) "is not a cause at all, but only a weakening of all causes. It does not define its goal; it only defines a stopping-place, beyond which nobody must go in the search for any goal."[34]

*A bad end or aim is one that cannot be consistently pursued* — that is, not without unacceptable damage to other interests which make life, or any aim, worthwhile. On the other hand, the filtering influence of a correct and comprehensive end upon the means to be employed in its pursuit excludes unacceptable means. In ethics, a good end or aim is one that can be consistently pursued when all the ramifications of the pursuit are taken into account.[35] By a process of elimination, we identify the one overall aim that does not entail internal contradiction or incoherence. And we attain not merely a tentative, fragile, purely personal belief but we attain secure *knowledge*. This knowledge allows life to be seen as real and as in the care of God, rather than as a series of incoherent scenes like shifting dream images presented in sleep. In place of the aim of contributing to God's happiness, is there another universal aim that is coherent, all things considered?

The concept of coherence deserves more development than even Blanshard, Rescher, and Harris have exerted upon it. Philosophical and psychological work remains to be done to elucidate the concept of coherence as it relates to percepts, concepts, and categories, in scientific knowledge, in belief or faith, in intuition, and in psychology generally.[36] Nevertheless, enough has been said in the foregoing discussion to corroborate and extend the arguments for the existence of God based on the common origins of good judgment, science and philosophical theology, all of them arising in the same way that we have seen science arise. F. R. Tennant has summarized this:

> The probability which is the guide of science turns out to be ultimately the same, in logical and psychological nature, as that which is the guide of life and of reasonable prudence. The world of which we have scientific knowledge may be found to admit of reasonable explanation only in terms of theism.

For inductive science has its interpretative explanation-principles and its faith-elements with which the faith of natural theology is, in essence, continuous. The only broad differences between science and theology are in respect of their data and the degrees in which verification is possible within their spheres.

Tennant further observes that God as known through natural theology is but a continuation of science as it was constituted before its main line of procedure tended towards the abstractly mathematical. At bottom, both theology and natural science are continuous with our own general commonsense knowledge. Tennant's thesis is implicitly upheld by Jaki and Harris. Tennant concludes:

Natural theology, apart from the sciences, is baseless; natural science, stopping short of a theistic culmination, has the appearance of an arbitrarily arrested growth. Theology is not an isolated nor an isolable science; it is an outgrowth of our knowledge of the world and man. In short, science and theism spring from a common root. God, man, and the world constitute a chord, and none of its three notes has the ring of truth without the accompaniment of the other two. To say the same in terms of another metaphor: the cosmos is no logico-geometrical scheme, but an adventure of divine love.[37]

For the sake of intelligibility and logical coherence, we must view the laws of nature as the expression of the rational reason and purpose of One God in the world, the Cosmic Mind who is absolutely rational and absolutely good. God's rational reason and purpose operates in the world in order to guarantee a dominance of order over disorder, a dominance of beauty over ugliness sufficiently to make possible the existence of living beings who can enjoy identity, integrity, and sanity. This is the only way to make any kind of sense of the world. The only alternative is to take refuge in mystery-mongering and despair.

The well-documented, pivotal role of the coherence criterion or test of truth in the building of modern natural science is also the criterion whereby we know ethical and religious truth. Spiritual knowledge is not different in kind from any other knowledge, but a longer road leads to it, one lacking in direct sensory cues — a fact which drastically slows the process of discovery and learning. The learning process is thereby stretched perhaps all the way into old age when, with luck, one finally gets the idea. Illumination is not necessarily sudden.[38]

Apparently, countless people have been fortunate enough to trod this road to the end — some soon, some late. Yet, with their merely intuitive self-guidance, they did not learn the name of the road, let alone its major short cuts. Consequently, they have not been

John Gallagher                                    September 1979

*"Walton always says, it doesn't matter what you believe, just so you believe in something."*

able to tell others what their successful route was, or not in such a way that others, mired in the sophisms of our century, could follow it and arrive at the same knowledge.

The dynamics of ethics seem never to have been clearly understood, either by humanists or theists. We suggest that the wisdom that can come with long experience of life is herewith presented in a form that is available to thoughtful youth. As a result, we have secured an important truth, one that the ancient Greeks with their pantheon of free-wheeling gods did not quite succeed in attaining and retaining but which successful Christian and other missionaries have always known, namely, that *virtue can be taught.*[39] Yet to teach effectively the love of neighbor, one must teach more than the love of neighbor.

"The fear of the Lord" — that is, the revering of the Lord — "is the beginning of wisdom."[40] The imperative that is implied demands total devotion. Jesus of Nazareth cited the Judaic Scriptures: "Hear, O Israel: The Lord our God, the Lord is one, and thou shalt love the Lord thy God with all thy heart, and with all thy soul, and with all thy mind, and with all thy strength, and thy neighbor as thyself."[41] Of these two Great Commandments, the second, regarding one's neighbor, is formally an explication of the first, for God is "the love which embraces all one's loves."

Ethics is simple in its aims and in its basic directives, but it is not simple in its derivation. To see the complexity of human life in its ethical aspect is to gain sympathy for the moral foibles of our two-legged race. Is it any wonder that well-developed moral attitudes have not been widely found in human history? Christianity demands more of its adherents than do other faiths and it has achieved much, yet much remains undone. The historian Crane Brinton reminds us that there have never yet been Christian centuries.[42] Every society, land, and denomination has been plagued with problems of weak faith and of the content of faith. In the context of a renewed vision, that negative fact should be seen as an opportunity.

The causes of moral behavior, like the causes of crime, are not simple, yet they are understandable and traceable. Intelligence may yet prove to be of clear significance to common morality. However, we should expect no perfection of life on earth. We need not fear the onset of Nirvana among our descendants: the freedom of human will cannot fail to keep things forever spiced up.[43]

Theistic religion, it is said, is the morale in morality. In adopting a worldview, a person may ignore the still, small voice of coherence, but only on pain of ignorance and suffering. Our power to perceive global coherence in a system of Cosmic Care is the epitome of the human way of knowing. We may partake of the spirit of Peirce who writes, "I should not rate highly either the wisdom or the courage of a fledgling bird if, when the proper time had come, the little agnostic should hesitate long to take his leap from the nest on account of doubts about the theory of aerodynamics."[44]

> When the religion of a people is destroyed, doubt
> gets hold of the higher powers of the intellect and
> half paralyzes all the others. Everyone becomes
> accustomed to having only confused and changing
> notions on the subjects most interesting to their
> fellow creatures and themselves. Opinions are ill-
> defended and easily abandoned; and, in despair of
> ever solving unaided the hard problems respecting
> human destiny, one ignobly submits to think no
> more about them. Such a condition cannot but
> enervate the soul, relax the springs of the will, and
> prepare a people for servitude.
>
> *Alexis de Tocqueville*

# 10

## *And This, Too, Shall Pass Away?*

The enemy is any man whose only concern about
the world is that it stay in one piece during his
own lifetime. Nothing to him is less important than
the shape of things to come or the needs of the
next generation.

*Admiral Hyman G. Rickover*

A CHILD'S TEARS suddenly turn to smiles. Your
day is made upon receiving a word of appreciation, but bad news
or a snub may spoil the day. Happiness often is evanescent, fragile,
sometimes even irrational. It may seem unimportant because it so
often fails to last. Moreover, what makes for happiness varies from
one person to another. Hence, happiness sometimes may seem
unreal as compared to the solid-seeming attributes of matter. To
begin to doubt the reality of happiness can itself poison our happy
moments, somewhat as with Sir James Barrie's fairy Tinker Belle
whose very existence depends, the audience is told, upon their faith
that fairies exist.[1]

To date, science has mostly avoided the study of happiness. The
accustomed methods and pursuits of science imply that values and
value-experience are merely incidental to reality. Bertrand Russell
claims, perhaps jocularly, that "Happiness comes from pandering
to one's self-esteem."[2] Even the existence of ourselves as persistent,
choosing, feeling entities has been denied in some academic circles

in our era. Such is "the lusty squalour of the twentieth century," as Winston Churchill characterized our time.

So elusive is the reality of happiness that Karl Marx's philosophy of dialectical materialism is still taken seriously by some converts in its aspect wherein feelings are denied any reality. Part of the aim of the present work is to enable a person to speak of happiness, delight, and feelings without any doubt as to their inescapable importance or their reality. Values as immaterial do matter, as some Marxists now admit, and not only as mere reflections of matter.

Pending further argument let us presume, in keeping with common sense, that (1) each of us as a sentient being exists, (2) that each of us has the right — indeed an abiding obligation — to pursue happiness, delight, or joy, (3) that people's actions and attitudes affect their own happiness, and (4) that their thoughts about what they should do are influential in guiding their pursuit of happiness. These presumptions imply further that each of us is free and that fatalism is false.

Happiness and joy are not substantial or abiding aspects of our experience, but rather our moods flicker and pass, as do our earthly lives. "The great globe itself," astronomers tell us, will be swallowed into the swollen sun in perhaps six thousand million years — an event that may leave "not a rack behind." Reflecting on all this — as well as on more immediate problems — one may wonder at times whether there can be a happiness in life that is worth its pursuit, let alone the orderly pursuit of any goal at all. If all our pleasures and efforts are ultimately to end in nothingness, then are they, when seen from a long-range perspective, equivalently nothing right now?

Decades ago, General Mills used a sales slogan for flour and cereal: "Eventually, why not now?" implying that if customers were destined ultimately to learn of the superiority of General Mills flour, they might as well go ahead and learn of it now. Interpreted negatively, this slogan may say, If something is finally destined to oblivion, we should recognize it, when viewed from the broad perspective, as worthless already.

Abraham Lincoln tells of an Eastern monarch who asked his counselors to devise a saying "to be ever in view, and which should be true and appropriate in all times and situations." The counselors finally came up with the words: "And this, too, shall pass away." Lincoln found this saying a needed corrective in "the hour of pride," and "consoling in the depths of affliction. And yet, let us hope," he added, "it is not quite true." For Lincoln it was enough to cultivate the world outside us and "the intellectual and moral world within us" in order that the course of history should continue "onward and upward."[3]

Nevertheless, the fate of everything that we encounter in space and time is that of "swelling, fleeting phantasms," as the fifth-century Christian philosopher Augustine calls them. "Space offers us something to love, but time steals away what we love."[4] In a sense, time is the greatest of destroyers. Augustine explores the concept of time itself — especially important in Christianity, which posits that time and history have both direction and meaning. Despite the Einsteinian revolution in physics, the concept of uniform and universal time put forth by Galileo is still the rock-bottom foundation of practical physics, which supports a ladder upon which all subsequent physical thought depends. What is more, some of the most learned physicists, astronomers, and electrical engineers of today are publishing challenging disclosures of flaws in both the general and special theories of relativity.[5]

The English-American historian Christopher Dawson observes that, in the Christian and scientific idea of time as linear and one-directional, the modern Westerner differs profoundly from people of other ages and cultures. "World history means infinitely more to the Christian than it meant to the ancient Greek or Oriental thinkers," for whom "Time, and consequently History, were without ultimate value or significance." To Westerners, time and history are of the essence of their conception of reality.[6]

The Christian idea of the importance of history may be contrasted with that of the World War II American GI reported as saying: "I don't want to make history, I just wanna make love." The American psychologist David C. McClelland has shown in his book *The Achieving Society* that people who are oriented toward achievement have a longer forward time-perspective than others. They demonstrate this, for instance, by their preference for a larger future reward in lieu of a smaller immediate one.[7]

Time has been called "a perpetual perishing,"[8] a "torrent of forgetting." Must this universal perishing and forgetting be the fate of happiness and joy also? The ancient Epicureans and the Victorian ethical thinkers thought so, as do atheists, agnostics, and humanists, for they are committed to promoting happiness even while believing that every trace of happiness will finally pass away. The resulting sense of futility and despair appears to be a leading reason why such movements are losing ground. We begin to perceive the general truth stated by the American philosopher William Ernest Hocking, that "Duration is a dimension of value."[9]

What are happiness, delight, and joy, that they come and go so readily? In the Judeo-Christian tradition, they have clearly been considered psychological, pleasurable goods, not greatly dependent on material or "worldly" goods such as wealth or power. Indeed, material goods have been despised by some groups since early Christendom. The scriptures of both Judaism and Christianity abound with mentions of joy and how to get it, with special emphasis placed on obeying the will of God. Augustine, for whom true happiness is "a perfect joy," universally pursued by all people, related a psychology of joy to theism, thereby making a basic contribution to Western civilization.[10]

How may we define happiness? For the ancient Greek philosopher Democritus it is clearly psychological: "Happiness and unhappiness belong to the soul" — a view supported by Thomas Aquinas.[11] In Aristotle's writings, the Greek word *eudaimonia* is usually translated as "happiness," but *eudaimonia* means general well-being or welfare, of which psychological happiness or pleasure is only one aspect. It would appear that pleasure, happiness, delight, and joy as qualities of feeling do not differ essentially, and we shall take them as always referring to psychological good.

Pleasure and happiness, considered as simple experience, differ only in their patterns of occurrence through time. The pattern in time of sensory pleasures taken by themselves lacks continuity. In this respect such pleasures resemble the quick jumps of a grasshopper which spends most of its time resting on something fairly solid. But there are other kinds of pleasure. There are pleasures of harmony and of contrast, as well as those of sharing, of admiration for someone or from someone, of memory, of self-congratulation, and of self-consistency.

Happiness is a *configuration* and *patterned harmony* of pleasurable or delightful moments. Sense-oriented pleasures may not result in happiness or even in much abiding pleasure. A person with few pleasures, conventionally speaking, may be happy; for instance, one may find deep happiness in attending to the sick. Schweitzer observes truly: "Lasting pleasure, taken seriously, can be nothing but the pleasure of the mind."[12] The English philosopher John Locke tells part of the reason why this is true:

> If I prefer a short pleasure to a lasting one, it is plain I cross my own happiness. I find the well-cooked meal I ate today does

now no more delight me; nay, I am diseased after a full meal. The perfumes I smelt yesterday now no more affect me with any pleasure. But the good turn I did yesterday, a year, seven years hence, continues still to please me as often as I reflect upon it.[13]

Then what is joy? As with Locke and his pleasant reflections of the past, the word is best used to signify the compounding of many pleasures, even small ones, through mutually sustaining *reverberations* in the psyche. On the other hand, thoughts of things we wish we had not done or regret that we did not do, dampen otherwise pleasant reflections. Observation suggests that, for some, the problem of negative memories is so serious that they seek noise and frenetic activity to block out unwanted thoughts. In contrast, joy is a coherent pattern of simultaneous pleasures that lend substance to each other. Thomas Aquinas points out that some of these pleasures will be pleasures of reason, not merely of sense.[14]

Consider the effect of a good joke well told, when one's mind flits from one element of the humor to another, each element magnifying the others. Again, a mother contemplates her child. The child is good looking, well dressed, well mannered, thoughtful, liked by peers and by older people, good at studies and arts, with every promise of a bright future. The thought of each attribute of her child gives the mother pleasure. In the mother's contemplation, each attribute lends weight to the others; to think of one quality puts her in mind of the others. That is, the pleasant thoughts reverberate, undampened by negative attributes. Thus the whole becomes greater than the parts.

A lover talks with the beloved, whose talk, unique qualities, and very charm bring to mind the loved one's character, good sense, skills, sensitivity, their mutuality of interests, their plans for the future, their love for each other. The loved one's visible attributes are fascinating. The slightest touch is pleasant. To contemplate one quality brings to mind the others; physical attributes bring to mind mental and moral ones, and these in turn bring to mind the physical virtues. True love between the sexes is the epitome of the reverberatory buildup of joy.

To share pleasures is a joy. In part, love is joy taken in the joy of others. To contemplate someone else's pleasure becomes a pleasure for the beholder. To value it as the beloved person's own experience is a higher level of joy. To know that one is responsible for that pleasure is a joy of a yet higher level. In its inherent harmony of personal contrasts, love seeks an ever-enlarging connectedness.

The interplay between desire and fulfillment is an example of the self-reinforcing buildup of pleasures into joy. Augustine's definition of joy is simple but suggestive: "What do you call enjoyment but having at hand the object of love?"[15] Amplifying this, Wilmon H. Sheldon writes:

> To be happy is to welcome the experience while we have it. We joyfully contemplate the friend's gift; we feel, "It's just what I want." We like looking at it. We *want* to look at it while we're looking at it. Desire is present just as truly when we are looking at it as when we are longing for something we haven't got. How could happiness be desire fulfilled if the desire weren't there, being fulfilled?[16]

Where Sheldon says "happy," we might well say "joyous." The meaning ascribed herein to the word "joy" is narrower than common usage, in that it does not include pleasures characteristic of self-centered people. The pleasurable constellation of reverberations described as joyous is normally social or interpersonal rather than merely private.[17]

Even human love must finally fail if there are no reinforcing reverberations of meaning that impinge upon a lover. If joy itself is dampened by the continual thought of its own final annihilation, then only fleeting pleasures remain, unconnected in time, not magnifying each other and not fulfilling any humane patterns of felt value, not even of love.

When pleasures become thereby disconnected, the intense ones stand out, like branches stripped of leaves. They are then sought directly: raw experience becomes the goal. Work becomes drudgery. Nature becomes boring, humor falls flat. Harmonious music fades. Children are seen as nuisances — which they then become. Smiles and laughter fade. Sympathy and affection are perceived as "sticky." Sexuality becomes unreal, dull, or feline. Sexual discretion is no longer worth the sacrifice. Freedom isn't worth a fight. Life becomes merely the pursuit of tarnishing pleasures.

The Golden Rule loses its appeal as selfishness becomes pervasive. The universe is seen as disorderly or purposeless, where nothing troublesome is worth doing. Irrationality and anti-philosophies such as the permissive "philosophies" of existentialism, emotivism, and deconstructionism spread. With the motivation for rationality itself obliterated, there is no longer any point even to philosophize; the victims are to that extent back with the infants and the animals. The nerve of rational effort is cut. For increasing numbers of people, pain and misery are seen as rooted in the nature of things. This perception can lead even to Satan-worship with its compounding of misery.

All this is a view of the decline of a civilization as seen from the inside.

What can be done?

The Chinese peoples long ago circumvented the problem of the continual annihilation of meaning resulting from death and the other ravages of time. During roughly the second millenium B.C. the Chinese were theists, with no idols or evil spirits. Their chief deity's name was Shang-ti, which means literally Supreme Ruler or Lord on High, who was represented as a personal ruler having a surprising resemblance to the God of Hebrew and Christian scriptures. One doctrine was that the wickedness of humanity, especially of rulers, would incur the wrath of Shang-ti.

The Chinese God was no respecter of persons but visited favor and blessing upon the person who was clean in heart, correct, kind and generous, whereas severe penalties were inflicted upon those who, pursuing their own pleasure, inflicted injury upon others.[18]

There seems to be no way to tell at present which concept of supreme deity was first acknowledged in civilization, since the general burning of books and burial of scholars by imperial edict in 213 B.C. was followed by the loss of the imperial library in 206 B.C. in the resulting disorder. These events may have forever blocked access to the facts on the Chinese side. The Chinese apparently espoused monotheism at roughly the same time the Israelites did, but China lost this faith, while the Israelites and Jews have had their faith continually renewed. The vigorous offshoots of Judaism, namely Christianity and Islam, cover much of the earth.[19]

Contemporary Chinese, despite material poverty, nevertheless appear to observers as happy, generally intelligent, diligent, and polite in their private manners. They display ingrained ethical imperatives concerning family responsibilities, tolerance of minorities, forgiveness, self-control, and the Golden Rule. With their primeval theism now only a shadow, what explains the prevalence of these virtues? It would seem that the ethics of Confucius has much to do with it, notably the emphasis on familial values.[20] Another theory is that the character of the Chinese owes much to their persistent belief in an afterlife.

For the Chinese, ancestor-worship has been more than a quaint custom. This belief has been maintained vigorously for millenia, through the worship in each family of their deceased ancestors. For the living, ancestors are still persons who remain concurrently aware of the doings of their descendants' behavior. Hence, the values experienced by the deceased while they were living are preserved and even augmented by ongoing events, notably as they experience the pleasure of being honored in family ceremony. The living can hope for the same preservation and augmentation of their own valuable experiences. Thus the Chinese people have not had occasion to ask Groucho Marx's question: "What did posterity ever do for me?" For posterity will ultimately do something for each deceased person, and do it in the intimacy of a family setting.[21]

In Western civilization, the belief in survival beyond the grave appeared in ancient Egypt and later in Persia (now Iran). Thereafter, it entered Western theism generally. The Latter-day Saints or Mormons are noteworthy in this connection, for much of the time spent by members in their temples is devoted to ceremonies to enlist deceased ancestors into their church.

But is there any validity to this belief of life after death? What of the complete dissolution of the body after death, together with all the immensely complicated phenomena of human biochemistry and neurology? Must every psychical entity be associated with a material entity? Is the preservation of experience and personality in some sense conceivable nevertheless? Natural science tells us much, but how much? What does it fail to tell? Can reason rush in where science fears to tread?

The Fool has said, "There is no experience beyond the grave — no conservation of our personal valuable experience beyond our earthly lives." Now why is it foolish to say such a thing? Because, in essence, foolishness is saying or doing what there can be no essential value whatever in saying or doing. If life is in essence valuable, then it is essential to act to find some way to see it as conservable; i.e., it is essential to stand, both in theory and in practice, for the conservation of that value. Only the experience of some intrinsic value can make a person feel that it is intrinsically better to be alive than not to exist at all. To fully recognize an intrinsic value is to recognize the need to conserve it without respect to the passage of time. What makes a person essentially valuable now is not that he or she can be used as a means to someone else's end; rather, it is precisely that something in him or her is essentially good and so ought to be permanently conserved.

Some will criticize the above thoughts as being mere wish-fulfillment which feels good but which does not contact reality. There is an argument that inexorably drives into absurdity any *expression* of disbelief in the conservation of our valuable experience. "No one can survive the grave" can be shown to be a statement appropriate to a fool, simply because any sincere uttering of the words would undercut the necessary substratum of all fully rational motivation for saying anything at all. The motivation even to think the negation, let alone pronounce it, is undercut by the words themselves, if these are understood in their full implication.

Of course, cynics do pronounce such words and think that they are using them appropriately. The supposition that such words are rational arises simply from the habitual use of one's ability to communicate with words. As an extreme but pure case, let us consider our Fool who has fallen into the trap of disbelief on this matter but who, as a youth, had been untainted with the pale cast of sophistic thought, who had known the joy of exercising the powers of imagination and of language to the point where this youth could speak of joy. For years, animal optimism, hyperactivity, and the vivid novelties of experience mostly displaced disturbing reflections on annihilation and general absurdity.

Finally, years add up and a middle-aged Fool finds nothing new under the sun. Our Fool now definitely disbelieves that there is such a thing as a conserving of the values of our experiences beyond our earthly lives. He or she thinks that those theistic ancestors who built the world and its language were deluded in supposing otherwise. Our Fool now regards himself or herself as a victim of the ancestral delusions which earlier led to the belief that his or her life has some intrinsic, abiding value. In line with the preceding argument, our Fool cannot defend current choices any better than did H. L. Mencken who said, in response to a challenge: "I go on working for the same reason that a hen goes on laying eggs."[22] Had our Fool been fully reflective (as most real people are not), perhaps he would have claimed that the current anguish would have been avoided if someone had continually reminded him from the cradle onward that "This, too, shall pass away."

The words when generally applied amount to an imperfectly formed death rattle. If that reminding had been done thoroughly enough to keep the alleged impending annihilation *continuously* in mind, our Fool would not be burdened now with the habitual joy-affirming powers that make one lurch onward despite such deadening reflections. Had such doleful reflections saturated the heart, our Fool would not have been enticed to develop the living will and skills of an adult and would have slipped into Nirvana — that is, into an extinction of desire and individual consciousness. Our Fool would have remained incapable of knowingly pronouncing the words, "There is no sort of hereafter" — not for anyone nor in any sense.

And had our Fool been fully consistent (as real people are not), he or she would now stop depending on the labor and creations of those whose affirmation of the continuing reality of joy hold one's world together and soften the otherwise crushing impact such a philosophy must produce.

Thus, our Fool uses the human powers of imagination and language to say: "All is vanity, all things are empty, there is no kind of experience that survives death. All enjoyment, all experienced value, is intrinsically so futile and fleeting that, when I see the end result of it, it isn't worth pursuing." In full honesty our Fool might elaborate: "Nothing exists that can rationally motivate my own use of language or my own understanding of what I am now saying since, in the end, it will all amount to nothing." Our Fool, if *consistent* in following out the initial affirmation, will be beyond pleasure and pain, beyond indignation, "beyond good and evil."

But our Fool is most evidently a fool for not shutting up. To avoid reproach such a one must stop arguing and persuading while slipping into Nirvana. Unfortunately for their logical acumen, such people, like the compassionate Gautama Buddha on the same road, may look back. Moreover, they imply that others ought to follow them. Like the Buddha, they are in the impossible logical position of saying: "I desire to teach you my secret of having no desires. Do you desire to learn?" Since ancient times, critics of Mahayana Buddhism in fact have pointed to this inherent contradiction and were answered only with a laugh or shrug, or a bare repetition.[23]

Here, then, is the absurd and *intellectually* intolerable dilemma of our would-be fully rational, unbelieving fools. On the one hand, they can be silent on this matter like the vegetables and refuse to philosophize over the problem. On the other, they can attract others into their unbelief, but if they attempt to proselytize by argument, they thereby commit a subtle bit of circularity that amounts logically to a total undercutting of themselves, thereby committing what we may call a *hoof-in-mouth contradiction,* by which their motivated *performance* of expressing unbelief entails the opposite of what the words *say.* Thus, they shut themselves out of rational discussion. If they can use concepts like happiness, or experience after death, they commit a hoof-in-mouth contradiction in denying them, since their negating words undermine the motivational basis for the act of uttering them. There is simply no point in saying that life simply has no point. It is meaningless to say that life is intrinsically meaningless. It is futile to say that life is futile. It amounts to nothing now to say that life amounts to nothing in the end.

**FRANK and ERNEST®**          by Bob Thaves          June 18, 1982

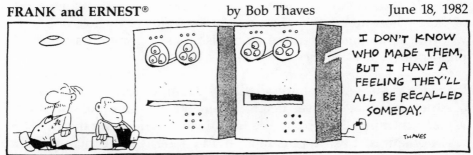

It is of no use to listen to contradiction as genuine communication. Though we may see our Fools passively approaching non-being or death, we are not to become their students if they say: "Because there is no value that abides, there can be no joy, no delight, no happiness." In reality, we will never hear rational people utter these words, for no one can utter them and take them seriously if they fully understand the implications of what they are saying.

Far down deep inside, our Fools know that there is some value that is worth holding onto and that they should continue to strive to hold onto. Plainly, if this were not the case, then there is no possible way to explain why they continue to hold onto this life and utter any statements at all. It is clear that our Fools are saying, in effect: "I am telling you that there is nothing valuable enough that I should tell you about it, or that either you or I should continue to try to see some value in it."

Such irrational, self-contradictory statements must be relegated to the memory of a philosophical culture that, in its zeal to deny too soon, was only "half smart." What may keep the irrational aspect of such talk from being obvious is the trust we accord to our own unexamined habits of speech and thought, which suddenly become inappropriate for expressing the inexpressible.[24] Nobody can rationally express the thought that nobody can express a rational thought.

With the *expressed* denial of belief in the survival of life ruled out, there is no way to oppose a statement of belief in some sort of genuine value conservation that is based on our earthly lives but that goes beyond our life on earth. For Peirce, belief marks the end of an inquiry where the mind is put at ease on whatever matter is at hand. When investigators are working to expand knowledge, their positive beliefs constitute intellectually respectable resting-places, where inquiry may cease for the time being.[25] The reality of value conservation must be regarded as a belief justified by evidence. For both logical and practical reasons, it may also be regarded as knowledge. Plainly, if there is one single intrinsically good reason to stay alive for another moment (to hold onto something of intrinsic value, or to take ahold of other intrinsic values), then for precisely the selfsame reason, a person ought to stay alive forever. If there is no intrinsically good reason to stay alive forever, then there is no intrinsically good reason to stay alive for another minute.

The timeless conservation of value is a fulcrum of rational action — that is, of fully rational motivation to do anything at all at any time. The presumption of some mode of "life after life" is an article of sanity. It is a logically necessary stipulation with which to preface any deliberate act. Even the motivation to consider whether such survival is a reasonable prospect depends on that presumption. It need not be mere desire or wishful thinking or a "leap of faith." Rather, it is justified as one of the minimally essential conditions of argument and of full rationality.

A person has not merely the "right to believe" but something more: there is in this case the intellectual, moral, and emotional obligation not to doubt. We each have the responsibility to affirm whatever is essential to rationality. Nietzsche disputes this kind of argument but gives no reasons.[26] The knowledge or justified belief that human beings must have in order to be fully human, they can have; indeed, it is already theirs for the taking.

Here, then, is the answer to such skeptics as W. K. Clifford who put down such beliefs on the ground that they are founded on "insufficient evidence" and are therefore intellectually sinful.[27] But is evidence insufficient when to deny its sufficiency implies logical and personal havoc? In the present matter, the "sin" is to be found on the side of *dis*belief. The denial of the reality of value-conservation has a result similar to that of denying the laws of logic.

No one can give a logical reason to argue that there are no laws of logic. Likewise, no one can show any value in arguing that no values can be preserved. If there are no laws of rationality, then what possible motivation can there be for any person to pursue rationality? And, if there are no intrinsic values that can be permanently conserved, then what possible motivation can a person have to discover them, hold onto them and to act to preserve them?

This entire indirect proof may be called the *motivational argument* for the conservation of experienced value. It may seem strange, but not all knowledge need arise from experience. Those who have become half smart through philosophy courses may object that the argument of this chapter purports to derive a matter of experience-able fact, namely, life after death, from reason alone. They may contend that David Hume has shown that all knowledge belongs to either one or the other of the two prongs of what has come to be referred to as "Hume's fork," and that any knowledge that applies to matters of experience must come only from experience, never from reason. Hume argued that there are two unconnected, and unbridgeable, realms of truth: (1) truths of reason, and (2) truths of fact. That is, he maintained that there is no intelligible relationship between experientially empty abstractions of logic, mathematics, language, or definition on the one hand, and experienceable matters of fact on the other.

A detailed response is beyond the scope of this book, although the Annex at the end of the book deals with a related matter and guides the interested reader to the literature. Here, some brief observations must suffice to show the unrealism of Hume's fork. As we have seen, scientific knowledge is never a matter of deriving truths purely from experience. This fact alone severely dulls the prongs of Hume's fork. Moreover, even concepts of supposedly pure reason are often derived from an awareness of fact.

There can be no questioning one simple fact: Hume's "fork" theory is an embarrassing scandal to the logical mind. The theory contains a hoof-in-mouth contradiction, namely, that it is intelligible to argue that there is an inherent *un*intelligibility in the relationship between reason and fact in the ultimate structure of reality. Hume tried to use *reason* to show that, *as a matter of fact*, there can be no intelligible connection shown between reason and matters of fact. In other words, he himself tried to connect reason and fact in order to try to demonstrate intelligibly that there can be no intelligible connection between reason and fact. In what more treasonable way can reason and facts be used? Hume's "fork" theory of truth is still likely to be taught as though it were true, but in reality it is one of his most noteworthy perversions.

Truths are classed as "synthetic" when we learn about them through experience. Following an inspiration of Immanuel Kant, some recent philosophers have shown that the alleged gap between the prongs of Hume's fork is bridgeable by the existence of "synthetic" truths of a special kind which we can also learn about by deriving them through logic. Logical theorizing of the kind we have posited in the matter of life after death occurs *before* relevant sense-experience on the part of living creatures. Obviously, nobody can presently have sense-experience of life at a future time, since the future is simply not here for anyone to have a present experience of. Such logically derived truths are knowable "prior to" or independently of the relevant sense-experience — hence the designation of such truths as *a priori* truths. Despite all manner of philosophical attacks, a number of truths that follow from logic "prior to" experience of them but which are at the same time "synthetic," or matters of fact, have survived the attacks. Philosophers call these synthetic *a priori* truths.[28] For example, we conclude in this chapter that there continues to be experience of value after death. The conclusion alleges future experience on the part of living creatures, though it was derived herein from reason, not from experience reportable by the generality of humankind. It is true as a synthetic *a priori* statement.

A critic might claim that the argument of this chapter to prove the reality of experience beyond death depends merely upon language and that disbelief is possible without resort to language. A critic might ask: Why cannot a person simply wake up of a cold, dark morning and silently disbelieve? The answer is that one can do so without self-contradiction, provided that one *quietly* goes all the way into Nirvana without further arguing the matter.

It is the in-between positions that are subtly incoherent. What is left is a rigidly forced choice between affirmation of a worldview adequate to rational motivation or, alternatively, annihilation. No plea of agnosticism, whereby one professes neither to believe nor disbelieve, can release one from this choice. Agnosticism implies doubt, and doubt *when expressed* incurs the same problem that has been discussed. One may compare this choice to the forked path indicated in the benediction uttered by Moses: "This day I have set before you life and death, blessing and curse. And you shall choose life."[29]

Is the present argument any better than that of Romeo, exclaiming in despair, "Hang up philosophy! Unless philosophy can make a Juliet"? In other words, is the argument any more than a heavy case of wishful thinking? If the argument still seems implausible, what about the alternatives? They are all self-destructive. The authors do not claim to know the exact mode in which personal values and their experiencers are to be conserved through time. The world in general is a strange affair in the first place. If it were not for our prior experience of it, the existence of anything at all would have to be regarded as incredible, let alone the universe in its plenitude. When we are faced with the kind of choice here offered, why not take the alternative that does not destroy its own argument?[30]

Judging from personal experience and observation, the nonbeliever suffers a loss of spiritual vitality — indeed, a loss of what may be called integrative strength — over this problem. The Danish philosopher Søren Kierkegaard claims that we are all in a state of despair, whether we know it or not, until we take a "leap of faith" and believe in survival beyond the grave.[31]

Whether by leap of faith or otherwise, those who have dwelt on both sides of this issue affirm that it is an experience at once illuminating and challenging for an agnostic to comprehend the spiritual economy of someone who takes seriously "life after life" — i.e., the continuation of any experience beyond the grave. Such a belief is more important to happiness and proper functioning than scoffers can imagine, quite apart from one's hope or fear of whatever there may be in the hereafter.

Some skeptics mock believers' hopes for a posthumous life. They insist that it is nothing but a naive belief in "pie in the sky." They describe faith in the permanent survival of the soul as nothing but the acceptance of a bribe for good behavior, and as compensation for the hardships they have been willing to endure while here on earth. Believers often have been slow to refute this, but the point is not really "pie in the sky" for believers to enjoy without any responsibility. Rather, a permanent conservation of values makes it possible to view knowledge, and indeed life in general, as *coherent now*, thus setting forth life as a rational and intrinsically valuable enterprise *now*. A reflective person's belief that the value of life in general will be conserved produces the psychic coherence necessary to sustain the motivation to live at a fully human level *now*.[32]

The conviction that there is survival beyond the grave affords additional coherence to the worldview that God's universe exists for the sake of our happiness and His. Both God and the conservation of experienced value are reciprocally essential to a coherent worldview. There is an old Buddhist saying that "Eternity is in love with the productions of time."[33]

Recent theistic Western philosophers who have doubted the reality of individual, personal life after death seek to fill the void by invoking the traditional idea of God's complete knowledge of the past and present. They emphasize the traditional idea that God knows all the past and present, remembers everything and forever contains within Himself all the experience of all the creatures, whether joyous experience or otherwise. Whitehead and Hartshorne believe that this divine remembering constitutes a continuing accretion to God's knowledge and calls the concept "the divine treasure-house of memory."[34] The entirety of the person's life is to be conserved perfectly in God's everlasting memory and nothing is to be lost. This concept would appear consistent with what has been developed herein. But does this position also support the idea of the indefinite survival of our individual souls? Does it lend personally relevant meaning to the divine promise that we read in Isaiah: "For the mountains shall depart and the hills be removed, but my kindness shall not depart from thee"?[35]

At first sight, this concept of the divine treasure-house of memory seems to be a reasonable way to think of life as immortal. Some would say that no more than this is necessary to preserve rationality and would be ready to conclude that when people die, their lives are over; they live no more. However, critical reflections on this view of immortality point to serious difficulties in it.

To preserve memories is not the same as to preserve the persons or the souls who may continue to accumulate memories. If God's memories are all that is to be left, the march of time inevitably will entail much tragic loss. What can value-conservation mean unless the persons involved are to be preserved in at least their psychical aspects? Can persons preserve their sense of rationality if they settle in their own minds for merely the divine treasure-house of memory while disbelieving that they and those whom they love will live on as persons?

**FRANK and ERNEST®**          by Bob Thaves          July 28, 1981

Unmistakably, altruistic love is our most valuable experience in life. Can a person love a mere memory as such? We love persons, not memories. On the fuller view, a person must either possess the possibility of further joyful experiences or else cannot be said to be fully a person. To deny the reality of the personal afterlife is to deny the conservation of the most valuable part of value. Love exists between persons. Can any absolute commitment of love be made to another person without the assumption of permanence?

The logical answer must be no. Whenever people deny the personal continuance of life after death, they thereby tend to shield themselves against any real and lasting close personal commitment and thus deny themselves the experience of absolute value and responsibility in the present. Those who feel with all of their being that their loved ones have sacred value cannot accept a philosophy that does not hold to the full preservation of those loved ones. The destruction of any intrinsic value would be an intrinsic evil, which no totally committed lover can ever accept.[36]

Nietzsche writes, a bit hyperbolically, that all joy wills the eternity of all things.[37] We must believe that God's vast storehouse of creation is adequate to those needs of ours without which we cannot be fully human. The apostle Paul adumbrated the argument of this chapter in the often misunderstood passage: "If the dead are never raised to life, 'let us eat and drink, for tomorrow we die.' "[38]

We have already engaged the question whether we live in the best of all possible worlds, a world in which God exists and is doing the best that can be done, despite some appearances to the contrary. In this chapter we have considered constructively the final objection to that theory — that we all have to die in this world. We now turn to supporting arguments for the worldview of Cosmic Care, starting with the importance of appreciation.

God will endow our fleeting days with abiding worth.
*Jewish ritual*

# 11

## *Appreciation and Self-Esteem*

Every man is said to have his peculiar ambition.
Whether it be true or not, I can say, for one, that I
have no other so great as that of being truly
esteemed of my fellow-men by rendering myself
worthy of their esteem.

*Abraham Lincoln*

**W**E ALL KNOW THAT APPRECIATION and its
opposite are all-important to the quality of life.[1] Jonathan Edwards
writes of the natural disposition of people "to be pleased in a perception of their being the objects of the honour and love of others, and
displeased with others' hatred and contempt." He continues:

> For pleasures and uneasiness of this kind are doubtless as much
> owing to an immediate determination of the mind by a fixed
> law of our nature, as any of the pleasures or pains of external
> sense. And these pleasures are properly of the private and per-
> sonal kind, being not by any participation [in] the happiness
> or sorrow of others through benevolence. It is evidently mere
> [private] self-love that appears in this disposition. It is easy
> to see that a man's love of himself will make him love love of
> himself, and hate hatred of himself. And as God has con-
> stituted our nature, self-love is exercised in no one disposition
> more than in this. Men probably are capable of much more
> pleasure and pain through this determination of the mind, than

by any other personal inclination or aversion whatsoever. Though perhaps we do not so very often see instances of extreme suffering by this means as by some others, yet we often see evidences of men's dreading the contempt of others more than death, and by such instances may conceive something of what men would suffer if universally hated and despised.[2]

In his valuable book *Reflections on Human Nature*, Arthur O. Lovejoy uses the term "approbativeness" for the love of approbation, that is, love of praise, popularity, esteem, fame — indeed, the love of being loved. In Lovejoy's words, this appetite is "that peculiarity of man which consists in a susceptibility to pleasure in, or a desire for, the thought of oneself as an object of thoughts or feelings, of certain kinds, on the part of other persons." He elaborates:

Of this, three varieties or degrees, at least, may be distinguished. There is (*a*) as the minimal form of it, the mere wish to be "noticed," to be at least an object of attention and interest on the part of others. There is (*b*) the desire for affective attitudes — sympathy, friendliness, affection, love. Children, it is to be hoped, usually have an affection for their parents, however little they may approve of them. There is (*c*) the desire for some form or degree of what is called a "good opinion" of oneself on the part of other men.[3]

Moreover, "These all have their negative counterparts, running from mere indifference to contempt." But

the negative counterpart of the least pleasurable of the positive series is, rather notoriously, usually the most unpleasurable; to be in a society and not to be the object of anyone's interest or attention, seems to be, to most human creatures, most intolerable of all — a peculiarity which some have thought that dogs appear to share with us.

Lovejoy is struck by the "strangeness as a biological phenomenon" of this distinctively human trait of approbativeness. Thus the human being is indeed

an animal which has an urgent desire for a thought *of* a thought — and of a thought not its own — and whose action is profoundly affected by this type of desire, more profoundly and more pervasively than by any other. That is man; and he is therefore a singular member of the animal kingdom.

In sum, people are essentially "desirers and fearers of adjectives."[4] The psychologist Kurt Goldstein comes to a parallel conclusion through the study of smiling in infants. One's concern for another's existence is "an intrinsic property" of human nature. A person as unique is not to be understood without a consideration of belonging together with the "other." This relationship is not simply a means of "mutual support in the difficult effort of living in the world." It is by this belonging of individuals to each other that one becomes human.[5]

Ethics as a discipline of the will cannot be merely left to nature. For in that case, there would be no call to exert oneself to improve one's natural tendencies. Again, we might reiterate Jonathan Edwards' distinction between "natural sympathy" and the sympathy that is associated with "true virtue," for in his view sympathy merely as a natural, animal feeling — as merely "emotional infection" — gives rise, when properly assimilated, to cultivated, intelligent, directed, fully humanized sympathy. The Scottish philosopher H. B. Acton would even restrict the word to the latter meaning. Far from being a primitive animal feeling, sympathy in his view is "an exercise of the imagination involving self-consciousness and comparison. Hence it should not be contrasted with rationality but should be regarded as a form of it."[6]

The pursuit of happiness works through internal drives — not only through primary ones like hunger but also through those that may be called secondary or *derived*. That is, pleasure and happiness may arise from the satisfying of needs and interests that have been learned, whatever innate basis they may have. Derived drives include the drive of wishing to afford intelligent, cultivated sympathy to others. They also include the cultivation of all the elements of civilized conscience that make for human maturity in work, love, and play.

We acquire a civilized conscience largely through receiving the reward of timely appreciation. Yet, self-esteem may itself be considered a reward, which from the outside is not always observable. Because of self-esteem, certain habits or traits of character may persist even in the face of punishment designed to break them down. The American psychologists O. Hobart Mowrer and A. D. Ullman note that the fear of externally inflicted punishment, the fear of which an outsider can observe, may be offset by self-administered reward, which an outsider cannot directly observe. The approval of one's conscience may be quite as powerful as its disapproval.[7]

A proud person might think: "I have done right — splendid! I am a good man! Lord, I thank thee that I am not as other men are."[8] Henry Sidgwick draws needed attention to the unwarranted assumption that a person's pleasure and pain are determined independently of that person's moral judgments, "whereas it is manifestly possible that our prospect of pleasure resulting from any course of conduct may largely depend on our conception of it as right or otherwise."[9]

In other words, whether a given conduct makes the agents happy depends on their prior idea of what *ought* to make them so. We cannot have the pleasure of self-esteem unless we ourselves approve of what we choose to do. When we are sure of the rightness of our choices, we do have that pleasure. Yet, in many matters such as artistic, economic or social ones, self-esteem needs confirmation by others. There is more to the matter: the appreciation of others is innately pleasurable to us, unless it is inwardly canceled by consciousness of our unworthiness to receive it.

Adam Smith dwells on the importance of assurance that one merits the appreciation one receives. To receive earned appreciation is a double experience of pleasure. Smith asks, "What so great happiness as to be beloved, and to know that we deserve to be beloved? What so great misery as to be hated, and to know that we deserve to be hated?"[10] In the conduct of life, both appreciation and the pleasure of receiving it are important because they confirm and reward one's tentative opinion of one's own value and so draw people toward values that, more often than not, preserve and enhance life. This confirmation cannot exist when there is no self-esteem to be confirmed. Or rather, it cannot occur without self-deception. Smith says that

> The most sincere praise can give little pleasure when it cannot be considered as some sort of proof of praiseworthiness. The man who applauds us either for actions which we did not perform, or for motives which had no sort of influence on our conduct, applauds not us but another person. To be pleased with such groundless applause is a proof of the most superficial levity and weakness. It is what is properly called vanity.[11]

Similarly, the English essayist Joseph Addison, a predecessor of Smith, well notes: "False happiness loves to be in a crowd, and to draw the eyes of the world upon her. She does not receive any satisfaction from the applauses which she gives herself, but from the admiration which she raises in others. She flourishes in courts and palaces, theatres and assemblies, and has no existence but when she is looked upon."[12]

A modern counterpart of Addison's victim of "false happiness" is the "other-directed" person as described by the social scientist David Riesman in his book *The Lonely Crowd*.[13] Other-directed adults look to friends or to contemporary celebrities as models. These take the place of interior standards communicated through a wholesome tradition. To the other-directed person, it is the signals from one's contemporaries, rather than one's inner "guidance system," that remain all-important. Nevertheless, we are all a bit other-directed in that we crave and need associates who share our basic values. Other-directedness becomes clearly pathological when its victims, in default of something better, look to the nation-state for all moral guidance.[14]

In sharp contrast to the pattern just considered are persons who, though worthy of praise, are not eager for it. Addison adds, a bit hyperbolically, "True happiness feels everything it wants within itself, and receives no addition from multitudes of witnesses and spectators." Smith makes a needful distinction when he claims that creative mathematicians and scientists, who are naturally independent in spirit,

> have little temptation to form themselves into factions and cabals either for the support of their own reputation or for the depression of their rivals. They are almost always men of the most amiable simplicity of manners, who live in good harmony with one another, are the friends of one another's reputation, enter into no intrigue in order to secure the public applause, but are pleased when their works are approved of, without being either much vexed or very angry when they are neglected. It is not always the same case with poets or with those who value themselves upon what is called fine writing.[15]

The French philosopher Henri Bergson suggests an explanation:

> Take exceptional joys — the joy of the artist who has realized his thought, the joy of the thinker who has made a discovery or invention. You may hear it said that these men work for glory and get their highest joy from the admiration they win. Profound error! We cling to praise and honours in the exact

degree in which we are not sure of having succeeded. There is a touch of modesty in vanity. It is to reassure ourselves that we seek approbation; and just as we wrap the prematurely born child in cotton wool, so we gather round our work the warm admiration of mankind in case there should be insufficient vitality. But he who is sure, absolutely sure, of having produced a work which will endure and live, cares no more for praise and feels above glory, because he is a creator, because he knows it.[16]

In some areas of life, we are nearly all insecure and in need of appreciation. Decades ago, a woman attended a party where she met a famous French general who had commanded in World War I. The general did not thank her when she spoke in praise of his victories. But his pleasure was unbounded when she mentioned the twinkle in his eye.

Lovejoy stresses the fact that, as a matter of feeling, there is more to internally administered reward and punishment than mere awareness of our acts. He says, "Man is a self-conscious animal. As a consequence, man is a habitually self-judging and self-appraising animal; and he has, as no one, surely, can deny, an intense desire to think well, or at least not to think ill, of himself and his qualities and acts and performances."[17]

Accordingly, Lovejoy asks us to distinguish two irreducible kinds of motivation. One is the desire for the *ends* of action. The second is the desire for affirmation of our *qualities as agents* — qualities of ourselves as responsibly acting persons. These two kinds of motivation correspond to what Lovejoy calls (1) "terminal values" as attributes of the desired *ends* of action, and (2) "adjectival values" as attributes of the *agents* as worthy performers of the acts. Lovejoy asks us to consider how the same action may be prompted by either a terminal value or an adjectival one or by one reinforcing the other. "The consideration that if I eat Welsh rabbit this evening, I shall much regret it tomorrow, may not suffice to deter me from the eating — that is, if I like Welsh rabbit. But the addition of the consideration that those who obtain trivial present pleasure at the cost of future pain are gluttonous fools, or weak-minded, may suffice to turn the scale in favor of abstinence."

Similarly, consider the thoughts of a young person who is considering the pleasure of taking up smoking. Perhaps the prospect of lung cancer at a remote date might not deter, but the added reflection that anyone injudicious enough to take up smoking must have scrambled eggs for brains might do the trick.

Countless people have endured physical hardship, social punishment, and even death to affirm some principle. It may be that martyrs are motivated to endure martyrdom by their desire to affirm themselves as principled, ethical beings. Presumably they shrink from denying their beliefs or from seeming to be renegades or cowards.[18] In martyrdom there would be, in Sheldon's words, "the terrible strain of concentrating on the goodness of the right."[19]

Or, stated differently, the strain could be that of maintaining one's will to see oneself as preserving one's integrity. If a martyr is dedicated as much as John Stuart Mill (or countless theists) to the promotion of happiness, the martyr will endeavor to affirm his or her self-identity as one who is unable to conceive the possibility of personal happiness consistently with conduct opposed to the general good. In this way one would affirm, as Mill says, the indissoluble association between one's own happiness and the good of the whole.[20] The American ethical philosopher Philip Blair Rice asserts that it is what goes on inside a person that is decisive.[21]

Adam Smith puts forth a problematical theory of self-sacrifice where he thinks martyrs are motivated by "that fame which in future times was to be bestowed upon them. Those applauses which they were never to hear rung in their ears, the thoughts of that admiration whose effects they were never to feel played about their hearts, banished from their breasts the strongest of all natural fears, and transported them to perform actions which seem almost beyond the reach of human nature."[22] Perhaps, but we have considered that fame with honor is not the only motive for noble actions. Besides, fame is notoriously capricious, a well-known fact that should give pause to an ambitious person.

To receive expression of deserved esteem from others is especially important to the young, for they are less certain of the validity of their self-esteem than their successful elders. Without such support, young people fail to develop their powers. Yet, for all of us, the receipt of appreciation is so needful in most areas of life that, even when fitful and uncertain, it entices us to take the trouble to render ourselves worthy of esteem.

Indeed one may doubt that, lacking this impetus, life could proceed at a human level. The psychologist Walter Houston Clark interviewed achievers and noted that "Quite a number made special mention of the appreciation of others, [of] acclaim, or frequently the influence of one particular person. Such comments were perhaps more prominent among the more eminent group."[23] In the words of Thomas Fuller: "They that value not praise, will never do any thing worthy of praise."[24]

Normally sympathetic people find pleasure in imaginatively taking the role of another person, perhaps one close by, and finding their own thought of that person's pleasure itself pleasurable. One may cultivate a sympathetic nature and so take the joyful states of others as proximate ends of one's own conduct, thereby contributing to one's own joy also.

Once a fellow philosophy student claimed that it is irrational, even masochistic, to give away a candy bar. Such a statement tells more about the speaker than it tells about the normal course of human sympathy. People who lack a capacity for sympathy can be absorbed in their self-centered fun and indifferent to concerns that would trouble more sensitive people. At the extreme are those who feel no guilt over their irresponsibility and appear not to desire love or appreciation. Not being moved by natural sympathy, such persons account for many of our criminals, the ones we call psychopaths or sociopaths (though not all people lacking in natural sympathy become criminals).

The aggressiveness and hostility of human beings makes good press, while sympathetic and cooperative behavior does not sell so well. Some fast-selling books afford excuses for beastly behavior to people who otherwise might restrain their antisocial impulses.[25] In ethics, the nineteenth-century German philosopher Friedrich Nietzsche has been accused of writing like a psychopath, though he does not seem to have filled out the pattern in his personal life, and the authenticity of some relevant statements in his writings is in doubt.[26] Encountered in a pure form, the psychopath may be hardly educable to ethical behavior, since being appreciated does not make him, or her, more empathetic.

The deficient personality type we have been discussing seems to arise primarily from lack of consistent parental care in babyhood or early childhood. Orphan asylums were discontinued early in this century, and one may wonder why. Significantly, it was because the babies in them died in great numbers, and most of the surviving ones were retarded in their physical development or evidenced psychic damage. Although the little ones generally received good nourishment and physical care from countless bequests, their problems evidently centered around unfathomable grief, the deprivation of parental love, especially motherly love — which is the special kind of tenderness indispensable at a crucial period of life. The evidence for this explanation is overwhelming and has been summed up by the anthropologist M. F. Ashley Montagu.[27]

So long as such people are around, we cannot seriously think of dispensing with socially sanctioned force. Some recently formed subcultures appear to cultivate the psychopathic personality; for evidence, one need only read the lyrics of some popular music. If cultivation of psychopaths is possible, then encouragement in the other direction should also be effective. In view of the considerable and growing numbers of these people and the damage they cause, such problems must be met in more effective ways than are now customary.[28]

The American psychologist David McClelland speaks of a generally measurable individual need for affiliation and of a similarly measurable need for power. He presents historical evidence to the effect that the ratio of the existence of these two needs in a population is a fairly reliable predictor of their engagement in war.[29]

Psychopathology develops out of the absence of affection. To acquire the self-esteem essential to developing the highest possible capacity for true happiness, a person needs the constant and unconditional love of someone important to him or her. A consistently loving parent, relative, or friend can help nurture a young person who will be able and disposed to give much joy to others. It is also a fact, however, that nothing can better assure the capacity to receive and give joy than the certainty of the unconditional love of God, which is absolutely constant. Happiness comes from security and love. God is the only possible absolute guarantee of such security and love.

> When Nietzsche says, "A new commandment I give to you: 'Be hard,'" he is really saying, "A new commandment I give to you: 'Be dead.'" Sensibility is the definition of life.
>
> *G. K. Chesterton*

# 12

## *Pooled Egotism*

Religion blushing veils her sacred fires, And
Morality, unawares, expires.
*Alexander Pope*, The Dunciad

Despotism may be able to do without faith, but
freedom cannot.
*Alexis de Tocqueville*

DOES PATRIOTISM MOTIVATE? Of course it does.
One need not live through a great war to feel its power. The Declaration of Independence and the American Constitution are sources of patriotism. But patriotism extends beyond the forms of government and embraces the people of a nation and the land itself. Patriotism and religion have often lent support to each other. For example, Mormons regard the U.S. Constitution as divinely inspired, one reason being that it guarantees freedom of religious belief. Moreover, the Constitution is widely and properly regarded as enabling the people to pursue the moral goals enjoined by traditional theistic religion. Our present concern goes beyond a simple love of country. As a development beyond patriotism, nationalism may be defined as the exalting of one's nation to the point where all others are despised. There is a degree of nationalism that is so intense that, psychologically, it occupies the same place as religion. The devotees not only look down upon other nations but view their own nation as entitled to be the ruler of all other nations. They are

willing to obtain such dominance by any expedient means, including warfare.

Nationalism, or rather nationalisms, have rushed into the vacuum left by the decline of traditional religions, displacing them further. Historically, in tribes and city-states, elements of what has come to be called nationalism were sometimes powerful as motivators well before this decline, but in most times and places, there existed nothing nearer to nationalism or statism than the worship of kings and emperors, some of whom ruled by presumed divine right. Theistic or polytheistic religion and, in China, "the will of Heaven," have been potent motivators to socially significant ends beyond those achievable by the family or clan or village.

In the seventeenth century, Oliver Cromwell and the English Puritans were convinced that they were God's chosen people and that the nation was properly the protector of religious belief and practice. Together they would carry out God's will on Earth.[1] Traditional theistic religion is still important as an element of patriotism within those countries where it can be practiced without governmental hindrance.

Nationalism in Europe arose in part from the slowly growing alliance of the rising middle class with monarchs. Together they outflanked the power of the nobility on whom the power of kings had rested under feudalism. With the intellectual challenges to theistic religion in the eighteenth century, increasing numbers of people took their nation as the object of their primary loyalty. During the eighteenth century French Revolution, the Legislative Assembly decreed that an altar in every "commune" bear the inscription, "The citizen is born, lives and dies for *la patrie*."[2]

Such a mentality slowly eroded the cosmopolitan spirit fostered by eighteenth-century intellectuals such as Hume, Voltaire, Helvétius, Goethe, Schiller, Kant, Franklin, Jefferson, and Madison. The German writer Adam Weishaupt observes that, because men were grouping in nations, nationalism or national love was taking the place of general love. "With the divisions of the globe and with its countries, goodwill contracted within limits which it could no longer surmount. Then it became a virtue to expand" at the expense of neighboring lands. "To obtain this end [of expansion] it became permissible to distrust, deceive and offend strangers."[3]

Since that time, nationalism has been at the center of the political and military history of the European peoples and their colonial settlements. In the early nineteenth century there was a need for other European countries to defend themselves from the nationalism

of the French, personified by Napoleon Bonaparte. The new bourgeois fortunes, along with the increasing specialization of labor and
the new facility of communication, rendered people progressively
more dependent upon national governments for safeguarding their
complex economic interests.[4]

Historians themselves have contributed to the growth of
nationalism. The historian H. Morse Stephens in 1916 saw "written in blood, in the dying civilization of Europe, the dreadful result
of exaggerated nationalism as set forth in the patriotic histories of
some of the most eloquent historians of the nineteenth century."[5]
As nationalism spread, false ideologies of race and nation were made
to serve political causes.[6]

Nationalism found philosophical expression in the nineteenth century in the German philosopher Georg W. F. Hegel who played into
the purposes of the Prussian state by claiming that the state is "the
realization of Freedom, i.e., of the absolute final aim, and that it
exists for its own sake. All the worth the human being possesses —
all spiritual reality — the person possesses only through the State.
There only is a person fully conscious; there only is a person a partaker of morality — of a just and moral social and political life."

Hegel continues: "For Truth is the Unity of the universal and subjective Will; and the Universal is to be found in the State, in its laws,
in its universal and rational arrangements." He adds: "The State
is the Divine Idea as it exists on Earth. As high as the mind stands
over nature, so high does the state stand over physical life. Man
must therefore venerate the state as the Divine upon Earth and
observe that if it is difficult to comprehend nature, it is infinitely
harder to understand the state."

Later he says: "Moral claims that are irrelevant must not be brought
into collision with world-historical deeds and their accomplishment.
The Litany of private virtues — modesty, humility, philanthropy and
forbearance — must not be raised against them."[7]

Hegel exalts war as health-giving, and we owe largely to him the
cultivation of the "curious habit" of thinking of nations as existing
"apart from the individuals who compose them" and as having existence rather like that of a living, biological being. Benito Mussolini,
the Fascist dictator and ally of Adolf Hitler, closely echoed the
thoughts of Hegel.[8] Indeed, Hegel spoke the words that sank a thousand ships. Karl Marx's dependence on Hegel's ideas is well known.

The clash of nationalisms is the most salient feature of the military
and political history of our century. The more extreme forms of
modern nationalism are described by Toynbee as "the recrudescence

of Man's ancient worship of himself in the panoply of his corporate power."[9]

Recent history teaches that there is no limit to the demands of the rulers and functionaries of sovereign states.[10] They claim to open the way to Heaven on earth, the secular version of God's realm, without the help of theism. As they have gained access to more and more money and multiplied their bureaucracies, sovereign states have increased their control over the lives of all within their boundaries. Average economic well-being suffers, as experience amply shows.[11]

Nationalism in its single-mindedness falls short of either liberty or prosperity. In the present century, governments have "liquidated" over three times as many people as have been killed in wars.[12] The American historian Herbert Schlossberg writes, "Woebegone as it is, with a record of fatuous incompetence, dishonesty, irrationality, and bloody repression almost beyond description, statism nevertheless boasts a horde of fanatical adherents. Ignorant devotees or cunning and cynical hypocrites, they give it power and, equipped with modern technologies, make it a fierce and implacable enemy."[13]

**FRANK and ERNEST®**          by Bob Thaves          March 23, 1978

THESE ARE THE COMMANDMENTS -- THOSE OVER THERE ARE THE GOVERNMENT GUIDELINES THAT GO WITH THEM.

It appears that nationalism has deep roots in the human psyche. Can nationalism be transmuted into innocuous, benign patriotism? The English lawyer-journalist Arthur Clutton-Brock has a diagnosis and points to a cure for nationalism, in his 1921 article directed primarily to Americans, an article with which the authors are in thorough agreement:

> Because it exists everywhere, and is not only tolerated but encouraged, it must satisfy some need, however perversely. Where there is a great demand for dangerous drugs, it is not

enough to talk indignantly of the drug habit. That habit is but a symptom of some deeper evil, something wrong with the lives of the drug-takers, for which the drug is their mistaken remedy; and the right remedy must be found if the habit is to be extirpated. National egotism, I believe, is a kind of mental drug which we take because of some unsatisfied need.

Clutton-Brock asks: Is this unsatisfied need simply the herd instinct at work within us? No, herds do not necessarily fight other herds. In any event, there is no promise of a remedy in this hypothesis, for "it says, merely, that we are fools in the nature of things, which is not helpful nor altogether true." His well-written and vitally important article appears quite forgotten and deserves to be quoted at length:

> The habit of believing good of our own nation and all evil of another is a kind of national egotism, having all the symptoms and absurdities and dangers of personal egotism; yet it does not seem to us to be egotism, because the object of our esteem appears to be, not ourselves, but the nation. Most of us have no conviction of sin about it, such as we have about our own egotism; nor does boasting of our country seem to us vulgar, like boasting of ourselves. Yet we do boast about it because it is our country, and we feel a warm conviction of its virtues which we do not feel about the virtues of any other country. But, when we boast and are warmed by this conviction, we persuade ourselves that our feeling for our country is noble and disinterested, although the peculiar delight we take in admiring it could not be if it were not our country. Thus we get the best of both worlds, the pleasures of egotism without any sense of its vulgarity, the mental intoxication without the mental headaches.

Clutton-Brock goes more into detail:

> Disraeli said that everyone likes flattery, but with royalty you lay it on with a trowel; and nations are like royalty, only more so; they will swallow anything about themselves while wondering at the credulity of other nations. But when our country is flattered, and by one of our countrymen, we do not feel this uneasiness; at least, such flattery is a matter of course in the newspapers and at public meetings in all countries; there is

such a large and constant supply of it, that there must be an equally large and constant demand. Yet no one can doubt that it is absurd and dangerous, if not in his own country, in others. Englishmen, for instance, however bad their manners, do not proclaim, or even believe, that they are individually superior to all other men; indeed, you hold the bad manners of Englishmen come from their belief, not in their individual superiority, but in the superiority of England. If they could be rid of that, they might be almost as well-mannered as yourselves. It is a national vanity, a national blindness, that makes fools of them.

If we suppose that nations which started the great wars of living memory did so because of perverse national characteristics,

we shall learn nothing from their disaster. They were, like ourselves, human beings. There, but for the grace of God, goes England, goes America even; and whence comes this madness from which the Grace of God may not always save us?

As a world, we shall not cure ourselves of national egotism, Clutton-Brock urges, until we discover the causes of the craving for national flattery, as well as the causes of dislike of other countries:

Somewhere, as in the case of all drug-taking, there is suppression of some kind; and the suppression, I suggest, is of individual egotism. We are trained by the manners and conventions of what we call our civilization to suppress our egotism; good manners consist, for the most part, in the suppression of it. However much we should like to talk of ourselves, our own achievements and deserts, we do not wish to hear others talking about theirs. The open egotist is shunned as a bore by all of us.

But this suppression of egotism is not necessarily the destruction of it, any more than the suppression of the sexual instinct is the destruction of that. Ask yourself, for instance, whether you have ever been praised as much as you would like to be? Are you not aware of a profound desert in yourself which no one, even in your own family has ever fully recognized? True, you have your faults, but, unlike the faults of so many other people, they are the defects of your qualities. And then there is in you a sensitiveness, a delicacy of perception, a baffled creative faculty even, in fact, an unrealized genius, which might any day realize itself to the surprise of a stupid world. Of all this you never speak; and in that you are like everyone else; for all mankind shares with you, dumbly, this sense of their own profound desert and unexpressed genius; and if we were suddenly forced to speak out the truth, we should all proclaim our genius without listening to one another. Though we may submit to a life of routine and suppression, the submission is not of the whole self: it is imposed on us by the struggle for life and for business purposes.

It is, Clutton-Brock states, a point of good manners to conceal our egotism from others

by a number of instinctive devices. One of the chief of these is our humor, much of which consists of self-depreciation, expressed or implied; and *we* delight in it in spite of the subtle warning of Doctor Johnson, who said, "Never believe a man when he runs himself down; he only does it to show how much he has to spare."

By such devices, we as a nation persuade ourselves that we are rid of exorbitant nationalistic ego. Clutton-Brock continues:

We are not troubled by the contrast between our personal modesty and our national boasting, because we are not aware of the connection between them. But the connection, I believe, exists; the national boasting proves that we have not got rid of our [inordinate] self-esteem, but only pooled it, so that we may still enjoy and express it, if only in an indirect and not fully satisfying manner.

The pooling is a last resort, like the floating of a capital stock issue when you don't have enough capital to finance some enterprise of your own. Yet "it is the best we can do with an egotism that is only suppressed and disguised, not transmuted."

Clutton-Brock points out that those who have an exorbitant opinion of themselves even learn to repress it in consciousness, lest they blurt it out and be criticized. Even so, one unconsciously seeks to justify it:

It becomes impossible for me to believe that I am a wonder in the face of surrounding incredulity; so I seek for something, seeming not to be myself, that I can believe to be a wonder, without arousing criticism or incredulity; in fact, something which others also believe to be a wonder, because it seems to them not to be ourselves. The largest, the most convincing, and the most generally believed in, is Our Country.

A man may, to some extent, pool his self-esteem in his family; but the moment he goes out into the world, he is subject to external criticism and incredulity. Or he may pool it in his town; but, as I have heard, the Bostonian-born is subject to the criticism and incredulity of the inhabitants of other towns. What, therefore, we need, and what we get, is a something which at the same time distinguishes us from a great part of the human race, and yet is shared by nearly all those with whom we come in contact. That we find in our country; and in our country do we most successfully and unconsciously pool our self-esteem.

This great common vice, this pooled self-esteem, we confuse with true patriotism, which is love of something not ourselves, of our own people and city and our native fields, and which, being love, does not in the least insist that that which is loved is superior to other things, or people, unloved because unknown. We know that where there is real affection, there is not this rivalry or enmity. True love increases the capacity for love; it makes the loving husband see the good in all women. [But] the patriotism that is pooled self-esteem, though it make a man boast of his country, does not make him love his countrymen.

Pooled self-esteem is self-esteem afraid to declare itself, and it exists because the self has not found a scope for the exercise of its own faculties.[14]

In the epigraph to this book, General MacArthur states, "The problem basically is theological." A curious fact about power is that it is apt to be sought when the seeker's personal life goes askew. According to Plato:

All goes wrong when, starved for lack of anything good in their own lives, men turn to public affairs hoping to snatch from thence the happiness they hunger for. They set about fighting for power, and this internecine conflict ruins them and their country. *Access to power must be confined to men who are not in love with it.*[15]

Plato's observation applies with special force in a democracy, where the votes of malcontented people have overturned a society as advanced as Germany was in 1933. As Confucius saw millenia ago, there will not be peace in the nation until there is peace in the home and in the souls of the people. So far as that may ever happen on a wide scale, power that does not serve the common interest may ultimately come to be forfeited by the very people who hold it.[16]

> If bad men can work together to get what they want, so can good men work together, to get what *they* want.
>
> *Count Leo Tolstoy*

# 13

## Music and Romantic Love

Let me write a nation's songs, and I care not who
writes its laws.
                    *Richard Wagner, after Fletcher of Saltoun*

When love's well-timed, 'tis not a fault to love. The
strong, the brave, the virtuous, and the wise, Sink
in the soft captivity together.
                    *Joseph Addison*

# M

USIC MOLDS MINDS AND MOLDS VALUES.
So say sages of antiquity. Western music up to about the twentieth
century may be said to mirror parts of the Universal Web of Love
in its infinite dramatic aspects. Such music has been called "the
radiance of truth." Music is unique among the arts in its persistence
and pervasiveness in consciousness, in its penetration into "the
inward places of the soul," and in its ability to unite people by
eliciting similar emotions among them. As such, it is an adjunct
to leadership of whatever kind. A piece of performed music may
be said to be a metaphorical representation of a person or group.
To hear music, as Robert Browning said, is to have one's solitude
peopled.[1]

The Islamic Moors of Spain, whose schools provided much of
Europe with the literature of antiquity,[2] also brought to Europe the
ideal of romantic love — that is, if such love is to be thought of as
more than an obscure accident and as a generally fulfilling experience. For evidence, we need look no further than the *Arabian Nights*.[3]

On the other hand, the development of the spiritual aspect of romantic love took place later and in medieval Europe.[4] Romantic love seems to have pervaded the Russian ethos but little.[5]

There is one characteristic that theism, music, and romantic love all have in common: each in its insinuating way forms a persistent backdrop for consciousness in general. During our turbulent century, family life and sexual morality have decayed, and some would say music has decayed, too, whether serious music or popular.[6] This may be more than coincidence. Religion, the family, and sexual conduct are interrelated, and the status of one affects the other.

The naturally pleasant sexual thoughts, their pervasiveness, their spontaneous, self-maintaining quality, the persisting psychic reverberations of sexual experiences, their power to enlarge the horizons of concern and to bind persons — all these afford a unique power of cumulative psychic web-weaving and motivation. Sexuality can magnify either love or hate. It can strengthen people by enhancing their self-esteem; indeed, that is partly why sexuality is so strong a force. It can also burden people with guilt over the waste of such a power to produce social coherence and joy. Joy can arise from meaningful psychic reverberations of sensuality, tied by reverberating associations of affection, sympathy, and admiration within a larger network of meanings stretching into the surrounding society and into eternity.

As the words of a certain waltz inform us, love between the sexes is a matter of "Two Hearts in Three-quarter Time." On its psychic side, sexuality has been thought of as constituting a kind of fusion: "Let me dream once the dear delusion that I am *you*, O heart's desire."[7] The desire for fusion is found in Plato's *Phaedrus* and *Symposium*, but there it tends to deny the individuality of the parties. In ancient Greece as in most times and places, women have been the heavy losers of individuality.

The Apostle Paul, in Ephesians 5, has been accused of being a chauvinist (though some scholars regard this epistle as the work of an intellectual descendant of Paul).[8] The British philosopher Shirley Robin Letwin cogently maintains that the marital relationship in Christendom is better understood primarily as a shared celebration of the uniqueness of each party and as an experiencing of valuable contrast of personal characteristics within a basic harmony of them.[9] It seems doubtful that the earth's other creatures know much about these matters.[10]

At its best, sexuality is a shared refuge for each person's inward uniqueness — a mutual expression of appreciation that strengthens inward wholesomeness and creativity, within the framework of a shared worldview and shared values and experiences. The biological significance of such a psychical refuge from the world is that a person receives thereby a seconding motion to one's uniqueness. Even though often mistaken, such a seconding affirms that one is not living merely in a private world in which the fruit of one's hands or mind or heart are in vain.

Sexually inspired motivation within a faithful monogamous union can strengthen the race both biologically and culturally. Hence, the unique pleasures of sexuality can acquire value beyond themselves and beyond reproduction. Members of the American counter-culture, seen much during the 1960s, often talked of creativity and individuality, but they tended to mangle their preconditions. Many of us have been compelled to read the late American anthropologist Margaret Mead, notably to study her 1928 idyll of uncomplicated free sex in Samoa. Now after nearly sixty years of misguidance and confusion abetted by most behavioral scientists and most institutions of "higher" learning, this work has come under attack as being sensationalist and misrepresentative of the facts.[11]

Despite his many critics, the influence of Sigmund Freud remains very great. He claimed to be offering a theory that would enable people to civilize themselves, but he reduced human beings to sex machines and created, in effect, a religion of sexuality. He erred in denying that a human being is a spiritual agent possessing freedom of choice for exercising varying degrees of control over both the conscious and unconscious life. By attacking the very concept of right and wrong, this avowed immoralist became arguably the greatest single destroyer of culture and civilization. Yet, in leveling right and wrong, he was clearly anticipated by Marx.[12]

Unfortunately, too few women are encouraged to study philosophy. There still lingers in departments of philosophy the sexist bias of the ancient Greek intellectuals. Another reason why so few women study philosophy may be their intuition that philosophy as currently taught in secular schools, with its profusion of tedious blind alleys and open manholes, may amount to a plot against their integrity — an intuition that too often proves right. Whatever reasons there may be for so few women studying philosophy, lack of native ability is not one of them.

The fusion view of sexual love may be compared to the Brahman-Hindu view of immortality wherein one is at last to become merged into the static godhead — that is, into Brahman-Atman, where all individuality vanishes. By contrast to both of these views, consider Letwin's view of sexual love as parallel to the traditional Western view of the afterlife, wherein individuality and uniqueness are retained and valued.

Some complain that an ethic of happiness-promotion amounts merely to everybody going around "tickling" one another, notably sexually, in a circularity that respects no further meaning. If the complainers take pleasure or happiness to be only a matter of ephemeral tickles, then they are right; sexuality is then seen as of no more spiritual or even emotional value than elimination and hence nothing to get excited about, unless one can perhaps create fleeting illusions that individuality has significance. In atheistic belief, sexuality tends to lose its spiritual importance, as it does generally among people who allow their individuality to be downgraded. The increasing claims of the nation-state have something to do with this. In such ways, the clash among sexual values at present may be partly accounted for.

When physical pleasures are seen as augmenters of the pleasures of the mind, they contribute to the happiness of God and the creatures. Responsibly experienced physical and mental pleasures become magnified by association with each other, culminating in joy, in reverberations wherein one pleasing thought leads to others. The life-aims of partners may appear on the surface to be unrelated, but by sharing a common theism, the differing aims can be seen as contributing to the common divine end of pleasing God through pleasing His creatures. In this way, a sense of unity between partners, and between one another and God, is attainable.

Decades ago, when Christian missionaries were still welcome in India, a Western woman at a mission school reported on what fun it was to see recently converted young men fall in love with their own wives. It appears that Hinduism, so far as it glorifies sexuality without romantic love, is a path to pleasure but not to joy. By contrast, Christianity has provided a number of paths to joy, one of them being that of more meaningful sexuality.[13] It may be speculated that the value of sexuality as it develops more deeply in both Judaism and Christianity constitutes a large reason for their historical successes as religions, notwithstanding the much discussed sexually negative influences therein. Hartshorne writes, "The spontaneous conviction of all exalted moments of life is the sense that love, which is to say, in its lowest terms, the sensitiveness of living beings for each other, is the key to the nature of things."[14]

We may agree with Count Tolstoy's character Pierre who, in reply to a question of what the good life is, replies, "To be able to believe in God, to cause happiness, to love."[15]

Sexual unity resonates with and reinforces other kinds of unity. Effective sex therapy treats the soul and the heart. Such therapy is a reasoned Christianity, or a reasoned Judaism or a reasoned Islam if the ethical teachings of Jesus be added. A shared love of God can enhance a couple's pleasure and joy in their sexual relationship. It simply brings the couple closer together and prevents tension that would diminish their mutual pleasure. "Perfect love casteth out fear."

Sexuality has often been held to be evil in and of itself, indeed even by Tolstoy, who adumbrates for us his own early escapades.[16] The view of sexuality as evil is also found in the Psalms, by tradition ascribed to King David: "Behold, I was shapen in iniquity, and in sin did my mother conceive me."[17] Paul is equivocal.[18]

Of course, there is plenty of evil and waste to be encountered, inasmuch as most people fall short of experiencing true love in a setting where it can flourish. One inadvertent source of evil is that of supposing that romantic love can be made the sole basis for one's worldview and general motivation. The popular view of Hollywood in the 1930s and '40s reflected and promoted the fiction that romance alone is sufficient. The attempt to substitute the worship of the opposite sex for a receding ancestral faith really amounted to a special kind of humanism.

Some negative statements of the Church fathers Ambrose and Augustine about sexual love are well known, even though they did not consider marriage evil. Augustine, who put away his two successive live-in mates and turned to a life of Christian scholarship, speaks of "the taint of generation." He characteristically equates the Fall of Adam in the Garden of Eden with sexual sin, a fall which, he claimed, was moreover "occasioned by woman."[19] Augustine coined the term "original sin," whereby the sin of Adam was thought to be transmitted by inheritance to everyone. He saw original sin as the reason for the existence of death — part of God's mysterious plan. Original sin as inflicted by God has often been held to be a large part of the explanation of sin in general. As such, it has weakened the sense of moral responsibility by providing an excuse for sin.[20]

Among Roman Catholic scholars in medieval and modern times, the Fall has not itself been taken as essentially a sexual matter, but it was viewed as giving rise to sin in general, including sexual sin. Like Aristotle, Thomas Aquinas gives preference to intellectual pleasure, but Aquinas explicitly avoids the error of denigrating pleasure generally, and indeed he forcefully vindicates sexual pleasure.[21]

John Calvin, Martin Luther and other influential Protestant leaders have asserted the "total depravity" of natural persons. Some commentators have seen in the idea of original sin a splendid instance of the inflation of a personal hangup into an ontological principle. This may be too harsh a judgment; yet Pelagius, who was the contemporary antagonist of Augustine on this matter, well notes that there are enough willful, destructive acts for which each of us is morally accountable, without blaming ourselves for things for which we are not responsible.[22]

The Puritans are frequently said to have been ascetics and prudes in sexual matters. In America at any rate, they were not what they have been painted to be. Although they condemned the exercise of sex outside of marriage, they were thoroughly favorable to it within marriage, so long as sexuality, like other goods, was "subordinated to the greater glory of God."[23] Indeed, the American philosopher Edmund Leites informs us that the Puritans believed in "the possibility and desirability of the integration of the ethical and carnal elements in marriage."[24] Ralph Barton Perry states while discussing the Puritans, "To live well requires the forging of a will which is stronger than any natural appetite."[25]

Side by side with Augustine's view, such positive views as those of the American Puritans are widely held among religious folk. The twentieth-century Mormons or Latter-day Saints generally follow the positive Puritan and Pelagian views. Like Roman Catholicism and some other denominations, they place an explicit and correct emphasis on the value of family life and on anything that strengthens family ties. The exaltation of the family unit is typical in Christianity from its earliest days, as well as of Judaism after polygamy was left behind millenia ago.[26] The family has long been held sacred in China. The historians Will and Ariel Durant have appropriately named "lasting affection" as "the most precious gift of life."[27] Families historically have been the primary means of cultivating lasting affection. The journalist Maggie Gallagher states:

> Sex is paradoxical, it establishes sex differences in order to create the possibility of union. Sex creates gender so that we may overcome it in desire. Sex creates people who need each other, erotically — a perpetual adult act of joining which replaces the perpetually adolescent act of breaking free. Sex is dangerous, which is another way of saying sex is powerful. Sex leads to babies, and having a baby is a sexual act. Sex binds. It reconnects the soul to the body, the man to his lover, the woman to her child, children to their parents, parents to other parents and to the future.[28]

Perhaps the best thing that psychologists could do would be to discover the basis for marital compatibility and incompatibility.[29] But it appears that progress here can follow only upon the dissemination of a reasoned and teachable theology and ethics. Otherwise, goals that are intensely self-centered will continue to cause conflict.

As men, the authors hold that the creation of women is the best thing that ever happened.[30] Women's liberation was and is a real need. Our social and moral problems will grow progressively worse until we develop a culture that enables people to live together as equals, sharing life's intrinsic values. Leadership must be earned, and if a man is to use his gifts to lead a woman in some aspects of life, he must do so through a full recognition of her needs and rights, just as he would lead other men by recognizing their needs and rights.[31] And the converse is true. Men and women differ in their anatomy and neurophysiology. To neglect this fact in a drive to erase sexual identities is folly.[32] Yet men and women do not differ in their basic intrinsic life needs, nor in their basic human rights. Unfortunately, the promoters of women's liberation in America have sometimes allowed extraneous matters to muddy the political and legal picture. It is equally as unfortunate that men in America often still practice old chauvinistic habits plus now a variety of subtle new modes to counter feminine rights.

The question is not: What can men accomplish that women can't? Gross biology aside, the answer is Nothing; people in general can do what has to be done. Rather, the question is: Given our natures, what conventional arrangements turn out to be the most fulfilling for all concerned? It seems that men who are just a bit feminine and women who are just a bit masculine "have more fun than anybody."

Whether on the part of male or female, sexual motivation is dangerous when it comes only from the loins. To be responsibly

Whitney Darrow                                    October 20, 1980

*"Some relationship, huh, kid?"*

exercised, to result in real joy or lasting happiness, it must come also from the heart and a rational mind. Sexual motivation is wrong when it involves insincerity, deception and the manipulation or exploitation of the other person as a means to one's selfish ends.

A true concern for the other's well-being and lasting happiness must be as great a fervor as flaming desire.

An Old Testament commentator has mused, "No man originally meant to become the sinner he has become. He only intended, like Eve, to taste."[33] Richard Wagner's last opera, *Parsifal*, tells a story of redemption from sexual sin. The story is couched in symbolism, but the redemptive later parts are clear. The music is majestic, exalted, and ethereal. This singularly beautiful, spiritually healing work of Germanic art deserves to be widely witnessed — preferably in a language that the audience understands.[34]

Two rules should be stressed. First, conjugal intentions should be publicly declared, preferably in a religious ceremony. The willingness to do so is evidence of soul-searched commitment —indeed, evidence of love. As the cartoonist Al Capp said of free sex, "The price is right." The other time-tried rule is "Be ready for happiness." But such conservative thoughts have been well elaborated by others.[35]

"My peace is gone," lamented Goethe's unfortunate young Gretchen.[36] One may wonder how much radical politics stems from the self-hatred of people who regard themselves as marred by barren sexual choices.[37] By contrast, radiant, joyful, committed love seems to arise from an initial period of thoughtful delay in acting on one's newly found passions.[38] This sublimation of the sexual instinct is an aspect of human life which many, especially young Westerners today, do not discover. An insensitive "macho" sexual philosophy is still transmitted from generation to generation, without much realization of what is being lost or of what conflicts may be prepared by committing one's psyche to banal sexual experiences that entail no moral or spiritual motivations.

Can the world bear the confounding of the chaste and faithful by the promiscuous? It has been doing so for a long time. Is the world perhaps even enriched by some combination of these lifestyles? We cannot claim to know. Albeit, those who do survive the storm and stress of irregular passion may find that there is more to life than sexuality. Jonathan Edwards, late Puritan as he was, well observes:

> How soon do earthly lovers come to an end of their discoveries of each other's beauty! How soon do they see all that is to be seen; [how soon] are they united as near as 'tis possible and have communion as intimate as possible! How soon do they come to the most endearing expressions of love that 'tis possible

to come to, so that no new ways can be invented, given, or received!

And how happy is that love in which there is an eternal progress in all these things, wherein new beauties are continually discovered, and more and more loveliness, and in which we shall forever increase in beauty ourselves. When we shall be made capable of finding out, and giving, and shall receive more and more endearing expressions of love forever, our union will become more close and communion more intimate.[39]

The twentieth century American theologian Henry N. Wieman is not cynical about erotic love:

Sometimes a magic union of favorable conditions enables love between a man and a woman to transfigure the whole appreciable world, revealing what life might be if this transfiguration could be more commonly attained and stably conserved. The magic union of sustaining conditions is swiftly swept away by the fatalities of existence. Yet not in vain. These rare occasions carry a promise — they tell us of what might be and whisper of a wonder that is hidden. Sometime, somewhere, to some degree, it may be revealed. A social order and a personal discipline, a culture and a sustaining group, a tradition and an art, abounding in vitality and tender grace, may all be so developed and combined that the great transfiguration will be attainable. Meanwhile, on rare occasions of love between the sexes, heaven has touched our earth timidly and fleetingly. The sweetness and the magic of that touch may keep us faithful to a high devotion. We know wherefore we labor, having had that visitation. The hope and the dream of a world more fit for love shall henceforth be the goal of our endeavor.

When any man and any woman meet in love, the world trembles with the beginning of a new creation. It may fail. The new emergent may die in the bud. The failure may even cause their world to lapse into evils too drab or too terrible to endure. But the undreamed transfiguration of a world hovers over every union of man and woman where love breaks the constraints of self-protective concern.[40]

# 14

## *Humanistic Love Is Not Enough*

Such is the tragi-comedy of our situation—we continue to clamour for those very qualities we are rendering impossible. In a sort of ghastly simplicity we remove the organ and demand the function. We make men without chests and expect of them virtue and enterprise. We castrate and bid the geldings be fruitful.

*C. S. Lewis*

JUST WHAT IS LOVE? A current characterization is: "Love is giving what you need to get." This might be a good beginning, yet love needs to be distinguished from mere reciprocity, which is giving with the motive of getting. As Wilmon Henry Sheldon states, "To love others is to seek their true welfare as just theirs."[1] The American theologian H. Richard Niebuhr elaborates:

By love we mean at least these attitudes and actions: rejoicing in the presence of the beloved, gratitude, reverence and loyalty toward him. Love is rejoicing over the existence of the beloved one; it is the desire that he be rather than not be; it is longing for his presence when he is absent; it is happiness in the thought of him; it is profound satisfaction over everything that makes him great and glorious. Love is gratitude; it is thankfulness for the existence of the beloved; it is the happy acceptance of everything that he gives without the jealous feeling that the self ought to be able to do as much; it is a gratitude that does not seek equality; it is wonder over the other's gift of himself in companionship. Love is reverence; it keeps its distance even as it draws near; it does not seek to absorb the other in the self or want to be absorbed by it; it rejoices in the otherness of the other; it desires the beloved to be what he is and does not seek to refashion him into a replica of the self or to make him a means to the self's advancement. As reverence love is and seeks knowledge of the other, not by way of curiosity nor for the sake of gaining power but in rejoicing and in wonder. In all such love there is an element of that "holy fear" which is not a form of flight but rather deep respect for the otherness of the beloved and the profound unwillingness to violate his integrity. Love is loyalty; it is the willingness to let the self be destroyed rather than that the other cease to be; it is the commitment of the self by self-binding will to make the other great. It is loyalty, too, to the other's cause — to his loyalty. As there is no patriotism where only the country is loved and not the country's cause — that for the sake of which the nation exists — so there is no love of God where God's cause is not loved, that which God loves and to which he has bound himself in sovereign freedom.[2]

We are often advised by humanists and theists alike to love humanity in general. Assuming the validity of Niebuhr's description of love as highly personal, one may ask, Is such broadly distributed love possible? Karl Marx's collaborator Friedrich Engels denies the possibility, going so far as to claim that "Universal love toward humankind is stupidity." Teilhard de Chardin is more moderate, saying, "To love all and everyone is a contradictory and false gesture which only leads in the end to loving no one."[3]

A benevolence whose quality is proportioned according to closeness of relationships of blood, region, or nation has not worked well in China. Confucius was a child of his time 2,500 years ago when feudal governments abounded. He said that it is correct to love relatives more than others, though he is also quoted as granting priority to universal love.[4] The sage Mo-tzu, his contemporary, foresaw correctly that a preferential love of one's family and state would in practice lead to wars, rebellions, and nepotism and recommended instead something closer to the spirit of Christianity. He was branded an arch-heretic by the increasingly dominant Confucian orthodoxy, which followed the later sage Mencius in emphasizing the graded love of preferring those who are close by. Military rampages, at least those through the Communist revolution culminating in 1949, can be laid in part to this restricted ethical scope.[5]

Jesus, who enjoins us to "Love thy neighbor as thyself," answers the question "Who is my neighbor?" with the parable of the good Samaritan.[6] The parable prefigures the growing awareness today that all of the shrinking earth's people are neighbors to each other. We find ourselves in relationships in which our unrequited acts or lapses may affect any number of people whom we shall likely never see and whom we cannot love in any affective sense. An error can blind or kill a hospital patient, poison a water supply, crash a train or an airliner in a distant land, or merely smash a couple of automobiles. We know the results of some of these lapses all too well, and we do not approve of those who care nothing for the good of strangers. Nor need we suppose that Newton or Pasteur or Washington should have taken less satisfaction than they did in their achievements because they did not personally know, hence not consciously love, each of the multitudes of persons whom they benefited.

Is it the mark of a badly ordered love to care especially for those close to us? The American educator George Herbert Palmer says no in his forgotten little book, *Altruism: Its Nature and Varieties:*

> I read a while ago of a famine in China. Crops had failed and there was wide-spread suffering. Tragic tales were reported. The same day a man I knew broke his leg. An awful affair! I hurried to his bedside and could think of nothing else than how I might help. Then it occurred to me how disproportioned were my sympathies. Thousands of squalid deaths on the other side of the globe made a spectacular newspaper item. A broken leg next door engrossed me and called out all my resources. We have all had the experience and, on first reflection, have called ourselves selfish brutes. But I believe that is an error. Helpful sympathy waits on knowledge and proportions itself by this, rather than by objective need. The sufferings of China are known to us only abstractly and in outline, and only in outline can our sympathies be accorded. But a case which comes under our immediate inspection, disclosing all its significant details, is a different matter and lays upon us a claim of

giving which the other rightly does not. Nearness counts. Knowledge heightens obligation.

Palmer's reflections lead him to conclude that the measure of understanding is the measure of duty:

> All men are not alike. Relation to me does constitute a special claim. Shall I treat my mother as I would any other old lady, as the apple woman at the corner? I say no; and the ground of different treatment I do not find in selfishness but in superior knowledge. I have known my mother ever since I was born. In early years she studied my needs and now she is my special charge. I comprehend what she requires in heart, mind, and person as I can comprehend those of no other woman. It is at least uneconomical to lay aside all this equipment for service and give her only the care a stranger might receive from me. The family tie means something. The tie of country means something. I know the habits of thought, the half-conscious turns of feeling, of my own people. In understanding a person of another nation I go about so far and then run up against a brick wall, beyond which all is blind. The measure of possible understanding is the measure of duty.[7]

G. K. Chesterton sums up the whole matter from a Christian perspective:

> Christ commanded us to have love for all men, but even if we had equal love for all men, to speak of having the same love for all men is merely bewildering nonsense. If we love a man at all, the impression he produces on us must be vitally different to the impression produced by another man whom we love. To speak of having the same kind of regard for both is about as sensible as asking a man whether he prefers chrysanthemums or billiards. Christ did not love humanity; He never said He loved humanity; He loved men. Neither He nor anyone else can love humanity; it is like loving a gigantic centipede.[8]

By way of ironic contrast, Charles Schulz's cartoon character Lucy remarked, "I love humanity, it's *people* I can't stand." One wonders how valid such professed general love may be, if it cannot also be concretely realized toward individuals.

Why are non-theistic philosophies not reliable as motivators for the pursuit of desirable goals? Suppose, for a moment, that all the altruism conceivable in the fondest hopes of, say, Count Tolstoy had come to pass in a world committed to a belief simply in the happiness-promotion program of godless utilitarianism, according to which no human was to survive the grave. Let us further suppose, in this hypothetical world, that love was universal and that it was reciprocal, such that the objects of one's love would be as deserving of care as one's altruistic self. With all this altruism, we would then be spared the conflict and the incoherence of the present clash of selfish wills. Would we then have Heaven on earth?

It may be doubted that we would. As a preliminary observation, we might note that something approaching this state of affairs appears not to have worked well in one historical situation. Many people of Victorian England approached a high moral condition but, arguably, they and their offspring backed off from the good of it.

**FRANK and ERNEST®**          by Bob Thaves          May 9, 1987

OH, I HAVE PLENTY OF KNOW-HOW, I JUST NEVER HAD MUCH KNOW-WHY.

THAVES

Why? Let us try a theory. The influential English philosopher John Stuart Mill presented to his fellow Victorians the seemingly congenial ethics of utilitarianism, the way of general happiness-promotion. As often expressed, the goal of this ethic is the greatest possible happiness of the greatest number. While Mill does not exactly deny that there is a God who is to be taken into account in ethics, he does not affirm it.[9]

Many critics complain that utilitarianism invites concentration on whatever is pleasing to everybody. In this way, it is said, utilitarianism has centered attention on the more animalistic appetites. The Scottish essayist and historian Thomas Carlyle, Mill's contemporary, even calls it a "pig-philosophy." In attempting to meet such objections, Mill proposes in his essay *Utilitarianism* that pleasures be divided into higher and lower kinds. Of the lower pleasures, there are simple pastimes — smoking, drinking, and the bodily pleasures and satisfaction of passions generally. These are set against the higher pleasures, for example, helping others, performing useful work of all kinds, and attending to good music and literature. In short, the higher pleasures include the pleasures of increasing the happiness of others, or of putting oneself in readiness to do so, as music and literature ideally should assist in doing. Mill theorizes that one who has experienced both the higher and the lower pleasures will prefer the higher pleasures, including the pleasures of altruism, as the way to maximize one's own pleasures or happiness. Mill, though aware that the pursuit of the higher pleasures can be frustrating, thinks that those with experience of both kinds of pleasure will prefer to be like "Socrates dissatisfied" rather than like "a pig satisfied." The Victorian novelist George Eliot remarks through one of her characters:

> We can only have the highest happiness, such as goes along with being a great man, by having wide thoughts, and much feeling for the rest of the world as well as ourselves; and this sort of happiness often brings so much pain with it, that we can only tell it from pain by its being what we would choose before everything else, because our souls see it is good.[10]

One cannot deny this. But how can one evaluate the happiness of others as important enough to be placed first in our personal priorities and, more, be motivated by it? The American philosopher Josiah Royce disputes Mill's claim that experienced people will prefer the higher pleasures:

> How do we learn that? Because men always choose [the higher pleasure]? In fact they do not. So Mill has to shift the ground a little. They do not all of them actually seek it, but they would seek it if they knew it. Most of them are ignorant of what they would prize most, namely, of these "higher pleasures." But here again Mill meets a disheartening fact. Most men, if they ever love "higher" pleasures at all, are found loving them more for a while in the ideal enthusiasm of youth. Men who have known the "higher" happiness do then deliberately turn away from it. This is a regular fact of life, well known, and often lamented. How does this agree with Mill's doctrine? Alas! it

does not agree, and only by worthless devices can he conceal from himself the fact. The people who enjoy the higher know the lower and reject it. The people who enjoy the lower do not know of the higher, or, if they ever knew it, they have forgotten it, or if they have not quite forgotten the higher, they have "lost capacity for it." As if all this could not just as plausibly be said from the side of the "lower" pleasures. Just as if it were not constantly said from that side in every good drinking-song, with a result precisely opposed to Mill's.[11]

Royce thus knocks down Mill's plausible split-level utilitarianism. Are we then left only with that simple, single-level utilitarianism of Bentham in which the childish game of "push-pin" is, at one point, said to be "as good as poetry, provided the pleasure is as great"? Or does the problem rather suggest the imperfection of an otherwise high culture of a particular time and place, namely, that of the highly educated classes of Victorian England with their secular utilitarian ethical philosophy serving as a substitute for a moribund Christian faith? The latter interpretation is arguably true.

The practical difficulty of living by a philosophy is not of itself convincing proof that the philosophy is deficient. We still must ask why the secular humanistic utilitarian philosophy was not an adequate program then and is not now. To repeat the prior question: If everyone were as altruistic as the utilitarian ethic demands, then would the world be a place of our heart's content? It may be doubted, and in this vein George Herbert Palmer reports:

> A couple of little children, a girl of four and a boy of five years old, had just been tucked into their beds. Their mother in the next room heard them talking. Listening to learn if they needed anything, she found them discussing one of the vast problems for which the infant mind seems to have a natural affinity. They were inquiring why we were ever put into the world. The little girl suggested we might have been sent here to help others. "Why no, indeed, Mabel," was her big brother's reply. "Of course not: for then what would the others be here for?"[12]

Jonathan Edwards faced this difficulty almost two hundred years earlier:

> If the highest end of every part of a clock is only mutually to assist the other parts in their motions, that clock is good for

nothing at all. The clock in general is altogether useless [even though] every part is useful to turn round the other parts. So, however useful all the parts of the world are to each other, if that be their highest end, the world in general is altogether useless.[13]

An ethic whose ultimate basis is the love of creatures for other creatures suffers of necessity from a curious circularity which leads to an infinite regress of decision and hence no rational decision. Decision becomes a never-ending tour of the same finite circle like that of two men at a doorway, saying, "After you, Alfonse." "No, after you, Gaston." "No, after you, Alfonse," and so on. The final practical result of such an incomplete decision procedure is arbitrary, unreasoned decision.

Brand Blanshard notes that a community of altruistic people, all of whom were committed to giving of themselves for others, would admittedly be a much more amiable society than that found in the "state of nature" in which life would be "nasty, brutish, and short." But the members of the altruistic society would be at a loss to resolve their "chivalrous rivalries" so long as they had only humanistic love as their arbiter.[14]

Given the present state of the world, any need for "an application of brakes to love" may be rare. The fixing of the point at which the brakes should be applied may be difficult. But to the extent that there may be much moral progress, the need to do so becomes no longer rare. Indeed, one finds it notably in friendly rivalries of service among dedicated Christians or other religionists within large extended families. Of course, the only immediate danger is that of an experience of futility.

There are more serious difficulties to face, all of them being quiet, pervasive problems rarely brought to the surface of consciousness and so all the more dangerous. Mostly subconsciously, these problems subtly sap the vitality of incompletely founded ethics. The greatest happiness of the greatest number — the aim of utilitarianism — is surely a noble objective. But can people maintain such motivation in that direction? Can they pursue this goal in an orderly way?

The reader has perhaps seen the automobile bumper sticker that reads, "Honk if you love Jesus." Suppose that there were a bumper sticker which read: "Honk if you promote the greatest happiness of the greatest number." How many such promoters would honk? Would you? If not, why not?

In the first place, you have to pause and think what such an abstract statement means. By the time you have done that, the occasion for honking is fast receding. More pointedly, the concept of "greatest happiness" of some large number of people lacks vividness and concreteness. It is abstract and you put it before your consciousness only through a series of deliberate mental operations.

The general happiness of creatures can be conceived only as a mathematical sum or aggregate. For one to make use of this concept, one must consider all the separate, individual happinesses of creatures as constituting an undifferentiated pool in which all individuality is reduced to calculation and submerged into an abstraction — the abstraction of total quantity of happiness or happinesses. Such a summated pool is of itself a merely logical entity. It does not enable a person to form, as Kant puts it, "any determinate and assured conception" of the goal of ethical activity. Teilhard de Chardin adds, "It is impossible to give oneself to anonymous number."[15]

When a secular humanist adheres to such an ideal, such devotion appears to be what the English economist John Maynard Keynes calls a "lugubrious duty," or what Schweitzer calls "a purely intellectual act."[16] Schweitzer adds, "Abstraction is the death of ethics." Charles Hartshorne elaborates the matter as follows:

> If my aim is the happiness of creatures, then it's the happiness of many creatures. But now the aim loses its unity. Now you've got this fellow happy because I did something, that fellow happy because I did something. But what is the value of the sum of these happinesses? This fellow is happy here for a while and that fellow is happy there for a while. How does that add up to one good that I'm aiming at? How can you add up the happiness of all and get something? Everybody's happiness isn't anybody's. The concept of everybody's happiness is just an *ad hoc* invention.[17]

Hartshorne points out further that it is psychologically impossible to worship or love an abstraction with all of one's being — to respond integrally to it. The simple reason for this is that we are all naturally interested in more than abstraction. To act coherently, a person requires "a love which embraces all one's loves," as Hartshorne has said — a concrete whole to which one can devote oneself. The abstraction "humankind," on the contrary, constitutes "a collection without concrete inclusive unity." Therefore, it does not afford a suitably motivating content for a universal ethical goal or criterion. On the other hand, some less abstract goal or task —that is, some unitary, personalized overall task — can embrace one's several interests and powers. If the task moreover reaches beyond the temporally finite human race and involves at least God's "divine treasure-house of memory," then one may avoid the discouraging thought of all earthly meaning ultimately passing away.

Devoting oneself to the greatest happiness of the greatest number may engage some because of one's religious heritage, whereby one fulfills thereby the will of God as stated in the Bible. This may be the case even if the agent is not a believer but one who is still unconsciously under the influence of the remnants of a theistic heritage.

The problem of abstraction is more graphically seen as a problem of social incoherence. Say that you are watching passersby on the street. Say imaginatively that you and they all hold solely to the simple, altruistic ethic of general happiness-promotion. You point to this one and that one; in what sense can you say that you and they are pursuing the same goal or task? What sense of unity can you experience with these strangers? Some of them may be loyal to factions that propose to destroy your interests and to do it in the name of the general happiness. As much could be said of relatives of some of us.

Such considerations indeed render the general happiness too abstract as a nexus of motivated effort. Such a tenuously shared ideal requires an effort even for you to conceive of it, if indeed you can form a conception of it at all, for there inheres in it only a bit more conceivability than the critters described by Lewis Carroll in his delightful philosophic spoof, *The Hunting of the Snark:*

> The warranted genuine snark has a taste
> Which is meagre and hollow but crisp,
> Like a coat that is rather too tight in the waist,
> With a flavour of will-o'-the-wisp.

The upshot is that neither you nor your group can feel that, together, you are doing the same kind of thing. Certainly, there is nothing of unifying emotional significance here to compare with one's loyalty to one's home town, one's ancestors or nation, let alone to the God of theistic religions with their prophets, symbols, and verbal tenets. One may object that similar oppositions may occur among members even of the same church. However, in a church, some basis of shared precepts and ritual obtains.

Possibly the abstractness of mutual ideals among secularists accounts for the dourness and grimness that were noted among leaders of the secular utilitarian movement in nineteenth-century Britain. James Mill, father of John Stuart Mill, was said to be "nothing more than a man of abstract convictions" who did "not separate his existence from his ideas."[18] John Stuart Mill describes in his autobiography his mental crisis, a lapse of motivation for intellectual reasons. Such *ad hominem* fragments are not conclusive evidence against a philosophy but, like the history of Britain from Victorian times, they do constitute a kind of witness. Without experiment and observation at some point, whether in natural science or in the discipline that can be called ethical science, one becomes the victim of uncontrolled theory-spinning. True ethical science and natural theology should cohere and mutually support each other in a scientifically defensible way.

It may be objected that the argument from abstraction against secular utilitarianism gains its strength, not from theoretical considerations, but merely from some practical limitations of human psychology. A utilitarian might hold that some descendant of ours, belonging to an as yet nonexistent, more highly evolved and more highly educated human species, should one day have the mental power to love even foggy abstractions wholeheartedly — indeed, to love them as much as we now may love those few souls whom each of us may know well. Even though the Mills, father and son, may have not been entirely up to that task, the task is nonetheless conceivable, utilitarians might claim. If that is possible, then the argument from abstraction would tell only against utilitarianism as seen merely in our epoch, and so the argument against secular utilitarianism would lack universal validity.

This objection can be refuted. Our psychological limitations are part of our humanity, part of our contingent creaturehood. The removal of our finitude would entail that we become essentially what we are not. We are men and women and not gods. Yet, as a race we do possess sufficient mental powers to solve our deepest problems. The faith that we can do so is a presupposition of this book, as it was of the founders of natural science. Indeed, our poor ability to love a bare abstraction as such may be regarded as an instance of that inner light which directs our attention to that Reality we should love above all our loves, thereby to perfect them all. Secular utilitarianism is the cut flower of Judeo-Christian theism.

Recent history in the democratic West affords evidence of the moral bankruptcy of a political variation of utilitarian-humanist philosophy. Political activists assert various novel individual rights and have pushed through new laws to enforce them. Promoters of the newly defined rights claim to be acting upon utilitarian moral or even Christian grounds, for in the sayings of Jesus, each person is sacred in the eyes of God.[19] Yet, a strange coalition with narrow self-interest has developed. American sociologist William A. Donohue points out that, as a result of the work of such activists in the 1970s,

> Authority, tradition and custom were pinpointed as the enemies of freedom. To be free meant to be free from traditional representatives of authority: parents, teachers, clergymen, policemen, judges, employers. Rights mania began, once liberty was seen as rights alone, and freedom from responsibility became respectable.

According to the "rights industry," all of us are victims of our fellow humans and hence should look to our legal resources to defend ourselves in the growing competitive war. Donohue continues:

> The language of rights mania has increasingly become the language of the narcissist, as any contemporary profile of male-female relationships will disclose. Relationships cannot be sustained without a sense of responsibility, restraint, sacrifice, commitment, duty and obligation. That's what is needed in order for compromise to be attained, and no relationship will last long without a willingness to compromise. But these values are hard to come by in a society which thinks that individual rights are both a necessary and sufficient cause of freedom.[20]

For example, some women, seeking total independence, are liberating themselves "straight into total abandonment."[21] The reason is simple:

> Women's liberation has also meant men's liberation, and this has led to an emancipation from all the constraints that make

for lasting relationships. It's every man, and woman, for himself: commitment is a dirty word to those who embrace the ethics of a conditional relationship. The convenient nature of [mere] cohabitation explains its popularity, but also accounts for its failure to satisfy. The mark of a good relationship has never been convenience.

Of course, the above is true only if one thinks of women's liberation as meaning total independence. There are, in fact, many women who seek no more than responsible recognition of their real rights, and who are not at all interested in total abandonment or independence. Such independence could entail no meaningful or ethical relationship between men and women and would soon result in the dying out of both men and women.

The preference of the eighteenth-century French philosopher Jean-Jacques Rousseau for the elimination of all personal dependencies was, Donohue tells us, based on the supposition

> that only in a state of society-wide dependence could all of us be conjoined together in real community. As Rousseau said, "Each, in giving himself to all, gives himself to no one." And that is exactly what the rights activists want: to be free from the burden of providing a particular service to a particular person.

The latest generation to reach maturity has, by and large, come to think of community affairs as the proper business only of government, not of the citizenry. John F. Kennedy's injunction is turned around: "Ask not what you can do for your country, ask what your country can do for you." Donohue muses:

> There is no community without a moral hierarchy. A clear-cut articulation of value priorities is absolutely essential to any community. There must be boundary lines, parameters of acceptable behavior, and the will to stigmatize deviants. But this isn't popular in today's culture of moral neutrality. Rights mania is bent on equality, and that means moral equality, as well as political, economic, and social. Rights activists would rather witness the dissolution of community before they would penalize the deviants who would destroy it. Their blind faith

in the cause of the individual has left them without an appreciation for the social and cultural context of freedom. They imagine chains where there are none, and seek to sever those social harnesses which restrain the individual and allow him to conform to the common good. They passionately believe that the creation of more and more rights is in the best interests of individuals. But someone forgot to tell them that even they must exercise their rights in something called society.[22]

Examples abound. There are now some laws forbidding tests for drug abuse among employees or applicants for employment. They were passed and signed in the face of instances of multiple death and destruction caused by misusers of drugs or marijuana — for instance, the tragic 1987 rail wreck in Maryland. Various laws and ordinances are also in place to protect the rights of victims of the contagious disease AIDS. Of course, persons with AIDS, like anyone else, should have their rights protected as long as they are obligated to avoid spreading their disease to new victims. However, at least one municipal ordinance in California has forbidden even minimal segregation of those infected in hospitals, doctor's or dentist's offices, or restaurant kitchens, thus making AIDS perhaps the first legally protected infectious disease in history.

In a strange juxtaposition, anti-smoking campaigns are increasingly fashionable, while in some places carriers of AIDS are given privileges beyond all reason. The highest elected officials of an Eastern state demeaned President Reagan's recommendation to require AIDS tests for marriage license applicants, prisoners, and patrons of venereal disease clinics. The testing of all marriage applicants is arguably inadvisable on technical grounds, but the testing of high-risk groups appears defensible.[23]

One may question the psychological and moral soundness of those who would oppose *any and all* boundaries drawn around AIDS victims. Perhaps the cynicism of such dangerous permissiveness is suggested by the remark: "I'm no good, but neither is my neighbor." For such people, the Golden Rule loses its force.[24] The nineteenth-century Scots poet James Thomson in his eloquent poem of despair refrains: "But I strode on austere, no hope could have no fear." No fear, that is, of guilt or shame.[25] Or perhaps the motive is simply that of saying, in effect, "If you'll leave me alone to sin as I please, I'll leave you alone to sin as you please."

Rights are properly limited by the rights of others. The "rights" philosophy in these curious forms is an absurd vestige of secular utilitarianism which omits the insight that, in order to do generally as one pleases, one cannot do exactly as one pleases.[26] Aristotle reports the ancient jibe of Demodocus: "The Milesians are no stupid crew, except that they do what the stupid do."[27]

Keynes and his friends were students at Cambridge University around the turn of the century, where they encountered atheistic utilitarianism in the form in which it had just been extended and blurred by their professor, the English philosopher G. E. Moore. As noted earlier, these students sighed over the "lugubrious duty"

**FRANK and ERNEST®**          by Bob Thaves          May 27, 1978

UNEMPLOYMENT OFFICE

A to L

THE PROBLEM IS THAT HALF THE TIME I DON'T FEEL GOOD ENOUGH TO WORK, AND THE OTHER HALF I FEEL TOO GOOD TO WORK.

entailed by secular utilitarianism, for no matter how sensible utilitarianism standing alone may sound, life teaches that, in the long run, it does not work. We have considered why it cannot work.

There is more to humanism than a utilitarianism of the thoughtless and degenerate form just considered. The proponents of the explicitly political faiths of socialism, Communism, and statism, along with their hybrids have, like the adherents of traditional religions, sought some object around which to *cohere* their lives — some task with timeless, humane meaning. They have seen, as we have, the ultimate absurdity of the old secular utilitarianism as a sufficient faith to live by. Unfortunately, in their version of coherence, everyone should think alike in the projected non-theistic, ideal society.

Advocates of political humanisms would have us picture the unbroken and regimented cooperation within a great choir and orchestra, in which the conductor knows all that is needed, and each chorister and player knows what to do and does it on cue. The members of the orchestra are like a kind of staff, who need prior training to fulfill the design of the conductor, but the choristers hardly need to create, for the original work has already been done by the composer. Competent choristers do not need cues from their fellows, for their eyes are never far from the conductor. The ideal humanist-socialist nation-state or world-state would be like that choir and orchestra, pervaded by coherence and joy; each would seek the good of all.

Older readers may remember seeing around 1937 in newsreels the joy on the faces of Russian men and women as they marched in review on May Day in Red Square. The joy did not last. State socialism as political humanism harbors an inherent dynamic pattern of violence. Repeatedly, the violence has surfaced under doctrinaire leadership in lands lacking a strong tradition of liberty. Buoyed by widespread hopes, the leaders of a humanist-socialist government persuade a broad base of people that temporary dictatorial power is needed.

Having gained this trust, the leaders find that their drive for social cohesion still meets widespread resistance, if only because of the inevitable economic malaise attendant on the socialist anti-market policies. When the leaders find that persuasion and manipulation do not suffice, they persuade themselves that no human sacrifice, no limitation of freedom, can be judged too great to stand in the way of the realization of their ideal socialist-humanist society. The more vicious leaders seem to gain the ultimate power. In the name of the ideal, millions of kulaks in the Ukraine were sacrificed in the 1930s, at least a million literate Cambodians in the 1970s, and so on in a dreary history of death that adds up to over a hundred million in this century — far more than the numbers killed in war meanwhile.[28]

Cooperation within a society is a fine thing; we need much more of it, though explicit cooperation is not for every occasion, as we have seen. Creativity, while not necessarily competitive, requires personal initiative. This is the case whether the objective of the innovator is altruistic or merely that of making money. Creativity seems to be intrinsic to the human race when not suppressed. The need for it is immense and never ending. The suppression of creativity by any politically imposed order entails, for one thing, a shadow-existence for creative persons who know how to enjoy their own creativity.

To continue the musical metaphor, not every person should remain in a chorus, for composers are needed, and there is no telling where they come from or what free acts will cultivate their abilities. Eric Hoffer wrote that even the humble people he rubbed elbows with were "lumpy with talent." No one can either define or mandate creativity ahead of the fact; neither can one create all that needs to be created, or know or communicate all that needs to be known. Simply put, none of us is God, notwithstanding a contrary religious belief emanating from India and just now pervading the West. In an ideal society, the cues or information that anyone needs in order to function well should not come through one person, one computer, one bureau, or one system; they must come from all around, pluralistically, from wherever they may.

We may sympathize with the drive for coherence that has energized socialist-humanist leaders. Yet, freely acting theists can achieve the alleged benefits of humanist collectivism without its stifling problems. The collectivist kind of coherence must be likened to those chemical compounds of the element silicon which make up inert rocks. In them, the constituent particles are rigidly locked to each other. In contrast, the rarer element carbon, with an equal number of electron bonds, is the nexus of an almost infinite variety of compounds that form the physical basis of life. The electron bonds afforded by carbon are not only inherently stronger than those of silicon but also more flexible. The stable existence of countless otherwise impossible compounds is thereby enabled.[29] Similarly, in a polity of human freedom under theism, flexibility combines with strength, enabling achievements otherwise impossible.

Among other humanists, Marx perpetuates the dominant myth of the twentieth century, which has it that ethics above a barbarian level does not depend on theism. Marxism and secular humanism in their cosmic isolationism would have the human race worship itself. Even Schweitzer's nobly intended and brilliantly stated ethic of Reverence for Life hardly advances beyond humanism and the lessons of ecology. The inherent contradictions within humanism or any other this-worldly ethic subtly sap the vitality of its followers and lead to cynicism. As Augustine warns, "By craving to be more, mankind becomes less; and by aspiring to be self-sufficient, they fell away from Him who truly suffices them."[30]

By contrast, Karl Marx can only write, "The abolition of religion as the *illusory* happiness of the people is required for their *real* happiness. Religion is only the illusory sun, which revolves round man as long as he does not revolve round himself."[31] Lenin can only heap scorn: "Every religious idea, every idea of God, even flirting with the idea of God, is unutterable vileness of the most dangerous kind, 'contagion' of the most abominable kind. Millions of sins, filthy deeds, acts of violence and physical contagions are far less dangerous than the subtle, spiritual idea of God."[32]

In denying God, humanists of all kinds may insist that they are only applying the healthy skepticism inherent in science and may even claim to be scientific. But this skeptical claim we have found reason to deny, if only because there is more to the roots of scientific method than even scientists usually are prepared to discuss.

One might wonder whether, with all the foregoing objections to humanism and secular utilitarianism, we have thrown out the subject-matter of ethics. Not so. The all-embracing earthly good that is called "the general happiness of society" is certainly good and certainly ought in some sense to be furthered, no matter how fuzzy or unmanageable this concept may be in philosophical discussion. The foregoing has been simply an investigation of why the *sole* promotion of general creaturely happiness has failed to rid the world of human evil and indifference. Humanism and its sub-faiths of socialism, Communism, and statism present splendid but unrealistically simplified vistas. Effective ethical motivation is subtle. We may consider sympathetically the appellation of Keynes, who calls both utilitarianism and Marxism "economic bogus faiths."[33] All these must go the way of shimmering mirages. One must look beyond humanism for viable religion and ethics.[34]

> If it were not so terrible it would be ridiculous,
> with what pride and self-contentment we, like
> children, take a watch to pieces, pull out the
> spring, make a toy from it, and then wonder why
> the watch has stopped going.
>
> *Count Leo Tolstoy*

> It is disconcerting that present-day young who did
> not know Stalin and Hitler are displaying the old
> naiveté. After all that has happened they still do
> not know that you cannot build utopia without
> terror, and that before long terror is all that's left.
>
> *Eric Hoffer*

# 15

## Rules and Rights

The central problem of the legal enterprise is the relation of love to power.

*John T. Noonan, Jr.*

THE SINGLE BASIC RULE of earthly conduct has been derived herein. It is the chief end of humankind, namely, to glorify God — that is, to increase His joy, through increasing the joy of His creatures. To follow the rule consistently and faithfully is itself a person's basic satisfaction, even one's joy. Some reward of following it is immediate, whatever the disadvantageous situations into which one may land as a result.[1]

The English legal reformer Jeremy Bentham, though not a theist, insists that it is right and good to bring about the greatest happiness of the greatest number — that is, to do in every case the act which will bring about the greatest amount of happiness. Bentham and his fellow reformers left God out of account — a fatal error, as we have noted. Nevertheless, some of the literature of utilitarianism remains enlightening.[2]

The question, much discussed by philosophers, is whether in some cases it may be better to follow some widely accepted specific rule of conduct rather than to do something else that seems, under the unique circumstances of the moment, to be right and good and productive of happiness but which necessitates ignoring the rule that normally applies.

A case in point: we are enjoined from childhood not to tell lies. But say that a girl runs into your house and begs to be hidden. A deranged man with a knife runs in and asks where she is. Do you tell the truth and say, "In the broom closet"? Or do you say, "She went out the back door, toward the police station"? Only a fanatic (and among philosophers there are a few) would admonish one to tell the truth in this case.

In such a matter, we do not apply the rule of truth-telling and so to that extent would side with Bentham. His view of subordinating rules to results is known by the technical name of *"act-utilitarianism."* It is to be set against an opposing view, *"rule-utilitarianism,"* in which the rules or precepts themselves are held to have ethical value, simply because, being generally known and respected, they afford a structure of reasonable expectations of each other's behavior. If everybody was assumed to be lying much of the time, the result must be a weakening of the mutual confidence necessary to all social cooperation.[3]

A judge has to decide at each sentencing whether to temper justice with mercy. Afford too much mercy, and sins will multiply. But to impose justice rigidly without mercy: could the world bear it? Who would be guiltless?[4]

What about rules against murder or killing — for example, tyrannicide? The Sixth Commandment is properly rendered, "Thou shalt not *murder.*" Whether a tyrannicide is to be called murder or else justifiable killing is more than a linguistic matter. The eighteenth-century German dramatist J. C. Friedrich von Schiller, in his historical play *Wilhelm Tell*, eloquently expresses a right of tyrannicide in an extreme case.[5]

Feodor Dostoyevsky imagines a situation where millions of people can remain happy only on the one condition that a certain unfortunate child kept well out of sight should lead a life of lonely torture.[6] As a society, we do encounter analogous dilemmas. For example, the governments of the free world do not usually force despotic governments to give up one unjustly detained prisoner or hostage, or even a hundred on occasion, for fear the world might be plunged into war. Whatever justification of such timidity is to be put forth, the spirit of the Parable of the Lost Sheep is thereby violated — the sort of ideal that is supposed to distinguish free governments from despotic ones.[7]

From these examples, must we assume that moral rules, though necessary for education and general guidance, cannot be inviolate? In 1966 the Episcopal cleric Joseph Fletcher published his best-selling book *Situation Ethics: The New Morality,* in which he claims that "Love is the only measure."[8] By this he means that the applicability of every moral principle is to be determined according to each momentary situation and not by rules. Fletcher uses this argument to batter down rules of sexual morality. In this, his influence has been pervasive. Analogously, a school of legal thought has arisen known as "legal realism." It doubts the validity of all legal rules or precedents. Can such extremes be correct? Was Bentham right, after all? Should rules be ignored when it appears that greater general happiness ("utility") would result in particular cases if some rule were ignored?

Before prematurely deciding in the affirmative, let us examine one more candidate for an inviolate rule, namely, that every person ought to be treated as an end in himself or herself, rather than *merely* as a means to someone else's ends. This maxim is usually associated with the name of Immanuel Kant.[9] Undeniably, there is much wisdom imbedded here, for this would preclude our hurting others for our own pleasure or aggrandizement. On the other hand, when we act as judges or lawyers or policemen, we sometimes subject people, say psychopaths, to imprisonment or something more drastic. To do so is hardly to treat them as ends in themselves.

According to committed secular humanists, there can be no value higher than the self-assessed sanctity of human life; this is their chosen fundamental presumption. In consistency, humanists should not do away with human life, neither in war nor in capital punishment. Many of them subscribe to both prohibitions. Yet, in the world we still live in, the alternative to military defense is at times slavery or extermination, in which all ideal principles, including those of humanism, are lost.

The American Civil Liberties Union, Marxist in origin, can be described as humanist in that it has regularly put down theistic religion in public affairs, as opposed to the alleged Constitutional rights of others. It has defended the rights of murderers regardless of public safety. It has defended the right to purvey pornography to minors, and to purvey child pornography. All this and much more. A reason for such odd defense actions may be that the victims of such criminal activities ordinarily are not in need of the kind of condescending ministrations that many humanists like to perform. That is, the victims ordinarily are not underprivileged or mentally or morally disadvantaged. Hence, in the priorities of such humanists, the victims cannot compete with the criminals.

Humanists do not explain how a society can operate in so unjust a manner without life eventually becoming hardly livable.[10] The upshot is that the rule of never using a person as a mere means is sometimes at least awkward to apply and, in view of other values, should not be taken as a universal rule.

Has Bentham finally won, then? Is his rule of acting as though there were no (other) rules sound? This hardly sounds right. Let us investigate why. To put Bentham down in this matter, we must identify some overall guide or rule of behavior of a higher level than Bentham's, for the sake of which the applicable specific rule is sometimes to be broken. One who has read thus far already knows what this supreme rule is and how it was reached. As for derivative

**FRANK and ERNEST®**       by Bob Thaves       February 3, 1982

rules, such as the Ten Commandments, it does not require a doctorate in philosophy or psychology to see that life in society is happier when the specifically ethical commandments are widely respected. And the reader can by now understand the ethical importance of the theological or ceremonial commandments. Of course, the Ten Commandments do not limit the extent of needed moral rules.

We still have not determined whether Bentham was correct in holding that it is *always* right and good to perform that act which will, under the circumstances, bring about the greatest happiness, regardless of any rule. Philosophers like to argue whether it is vital to an orderly society to observe the rule of keeping one's promises. A classic case is that of the desert-island promise made to a dying man by his surviving friend to convey the dying man's wealth to his wastrel son. Say that our survivor is an act-utilitarian — a man, let us here suppose. As such, he keeps before his mind only the general good without regard to rules; hence he may ignore the promise and keep quiet about the matter.

If the survivor is, on the contrary, a strict rule-utilitarian — let us say for the purpose of discussion, a woman — she won't. Why not? Because, she may reason, a breach of promise might become widely known and so erode for many the trust that people habitually place in promises — that is, in the rule that one should keep all promises. If people couldn't trust in promises, cooperation would disappear — e.g., appointments would be made to be broken; neither business relationships nor friendships nor marriages could be maintained. Our rule-utilitarian lady muses that promise-keeping usually has good results but that, if in some one case before her it doesn't, the promise should probably still be kept; the preservation of the practice of promise-keeping is worth some sacrifice of immediate advantage.

Is this social practice of keeping promises then partly inconsistent with the general happiness? Not at all, says our lady rule-utilitarian; the institution of promise-keeping is a part of the structure of social expectations that enables us to promote each other's happiness, as well as one's own.[11] Keeping one's promises is important, she might say, though not all-important. As a hostess, she would not expect her friend to keep a luncheon appointment if the friend's house were being flooded; should the invited guest appear, the hostess would be chagrined to learn the result of such disproportioned priorities.

The act-utilitarian may dispute even this tempered stance, saying that rules are not at all needed to promote the general good —not even a rule about promise-keeping. He claims that, acting without rules, he would keep the promises that promote the general happiness, all things considered, but not the other promises. Let us say that he made the desert-island promise in order not to offend the dying man and had no intention of keeping it, nor would he let the matter ever be known to others. Can he therefore be excused from the rule to keep one's promises?

The answer is no, not generally. The reason is simple, as the Oxford philosopher John Leslie Mackie has made clear in a brilliantly reasoned article, "The Disutility of Act-Utilitarianism." The main point of promising in our present society is that it enables people with more or less divergent aims to make mutual plans and so to cooperate to some extent. Mackie gives an economic example:

> Alf, say, would like best to get his work done and not pay any wages for it; Bill would like best to be paid wages and do no work; but Alf would rather pay the wages and get the work done than not get the work done and pay no wages, and Bill would rather work and be paid than neither work nor be paid. They can reach a compromise between their divergent interests if Alf promises to pay Bill if he first does the work, and Bill trusts this promise, and does the work, and Alf then keeps his promise and pays Bill. But if there had been no divergence between their aims or perceptions, if they had each been concerned only for their common welfare, no promising or promise-keeping would have been needed. One is reminded of what Humbert Wolfe said about the British journalist: "You cannot hope to bribe or twist, thank God! the British journalist. But, seeing what the man will do unbribed, there's no occasion to."

> In much the same way, you cannot hope to bind, by a promise, an act-utilitarian to perform an act that will have, or even one that apart from the promise would have had, less than the maximum possible utility. But seeing that what he in any case will do is what you, as a fellow act-utilitarian, want him to do, you have no occasion so to bind him.

We may agree with Mackie's example so far as it is relevant to mundane matters where compromise is usual. But to characterize promises in general as compromises, as Mackie does, seems strained when it comes to considering a promise of marriage or of commitment to a religious order. Such promises touch the essence of one's integrity and as such can hardly be considered as occasions for compromise. Rather, they are confirmations against irresolution and against temptations to compromise.

With that qualification, we can analyze Mackie's position more closely and sympathetically. He points out that in a thoroughly act-utilitarian society in which there are no conflicts of interest or purpose, the need for our ordinary conventional rules is eliminated at the same time that the conventional and utilitarian reasons for observing them are cast aside. "Such a society could enjoy the benefits of cooperation as it arises from an automatic harmonization of effort without requiring the devices that we now need if we are to erect some measure of mutually beneficial cooperation on a foundation of divergent purposes."

The Australian philosopher D. H. Hodgson has examined the situation of a lone act-utilitarian in an ordinary, non-act-utilitarian society. Will the efforts of this fellow to maximize general happiness be inevitably self-frustrating, so that he will produce less happiness than would various kinds of non-utilitarian agents? In reply, Mackie reasons that

> It is quite true that if he shows his hand and makes it plain to everyone that he will act, on every occasion, so as to maximize utility, then he will be unable to enter into bargains with his fellow citizens, and they may well not believe what he says, since they will reasonably suspect him of deceiving individuals in order to promote the common good, for which these individuals have no concern. He may therefore be frustrated in most of his efforts to promote utility, and achieve less in this direction than would some agent who was not even aiming at utility. This must be conceded, but this is hardly paradoxical. It is not surprising if the efforts of too candid a saint are frustrated in a wicked world.

But what if our hypothetical act-utilitarian is prepared to conceal his own motives? In that case, Mackie finds that

> then — *mistakes of judgment apart* — there can be no reason why he should fail to achieve whatever maximum utility the circumstances allow. Since we are assuming that utilitarianism is not being misapplied, that there are no mistakes of judgment, nothing can prevent our act-utilitarian from asking himself, and answering *correctly*, the question, "What course of action, step by step, will produce at least as good results as any possible alternative course of action?" and, having answered it, acting accordingly. This course of action may well include quite a lot of promising, making of bargains — and keeping them often enough not to lower one's credit rating — and various other procedures of ordinary life, apologizing,

praising, blaming, and so on. All these activities would be insincere: the act-utilitarian must expect his fellows to interpret him as being guided by motives other than those which really guide him, that is, as feeling *bound* by promises, as feeling that he *ought* to respond to conventional moral pressures, ought not to tell beneficient lies, and so on. Therefore, the act-utilitarian can consistently succeed in choosing the act which would have the best consequences possible.

This would be the case under the hypothetical situation of the act-utilitarian in a conventional society.

Of course, this hypothesis puts a strain on our imaginations. In practice, of course, we have learned to be on our guard against people who aim so single-mindedly at what they take to be the welfare of the community, or of the human race, that they regard veracity, the keeping of bargains, and what are commonly called the rights of individuals as of no importance. But this is because we either do not share their concept of welfare, or aim obstinately at more limited goals, or think that these well-meaning fanatics are very likely to make mistakes. If we take seriously the hypothesis that none of these qualifications is in order, then we can no longer argue that an act-utilitarian will necessarily fail to maximize utility in his dealings with a non-act-utilitarian society.

It is, after all, absurd to say [as critics of Bentham have said], that it is not consonant with utility to consult utility — *except in so far as mistakes of judgment are likely to be made.* This danger, together with the difficulty of reaching agreement about what constitutes welfare or utility, is the source of the real objections to [act-] utilitarianism as an immediate practical guide to conduct.[12]

What seems in any case repugnant about act-utilitarians is the idea that one could permit oneself even to entertain the notion that sacred promises could be continually exposed to denial by proud, fallible human judgment. In practice, of course, promises are not only so endangered but are broken, every minute of the day. Nevertheless, the point is that rules can be dispensed with only on the impossible condition that there can be no mistakes in judgment. Thus moral rules do have a place, because no one, however well intentioned, can be infallible or know everything. Hence we need a few ready anchors for our behavior. For anyone to suppose otherwise is to play the role of God.

Besides such broad rules as that of promise-keeping, we need rules or ordinances regarding technical matters such as one about turning on automobile lights in a tunnel. A reason for this particular rule is that novice drivers may not appreciate the problem of other drivers whose eyes have not fully adjusted from the daylight. Again, for the conduct of any sizeable meeting, rules are necessary — that is, procedures for sorting out priorities of business and of speaking. Else the result is chaos. The same goes for any democratic government.

Fletcher claims that "Love is the only measure" of conduct — love, not rules. It should be clear by now that Fletcher has lost the argument and that "situation ethics" is a mirage covering a chasm. Having affirmed with Mackie the need of having some moral rules to constrain us, we are now in a better position to return to the problem of the dying man on the desert island. How could the survivor be sure that the wastrel son would remain a wastrel? There are turnarounds now and then that are simply unknowable in advance. How could the act-utilitarian survivor be sure that he himself would keep the secret? Confession is good for the soul, the survivor may one day decide. Such factors lend weight to the rule about keeping promises.

All of which brings us back to the inherent human fallibility and lack of omniscience that distinguish each of us from God. Hence, we need rules and laws, but not too many of either, please, lest honest folk be confounded by that artificial complexity which is loved by some uncreative folk and by eager wielders of power who spin legal spider webs. Rules and laws should be servants, not rulers.[13] In any case, no society does without rules. Indeed, there is a large area of sameness in basic moral rules among the societies of the world.[14]

A new question arises. Suppose that a person sees the value of rules without making them absolute. How is this person to decide whether to follow a rule, or to ignore it and do what would seem best in the momentary situation? In the case of the friend whose house was being flooded, the answer is clear enough: the rule about promise-keeping should be ignored. Other examples are less clear. For instance, the standard medical rule is to preserve life by any available means — an application of the rule of "Reverence for Life." A debate rages about who should decide, and how to decide, when it is time to withdraw preciously expensive life-support systems from terminally ill patients.[15]

The question is: What rule can there be for the application or non-application of the more specific rules? The lack of a clear procedure for deciding has caused more than one philosopher to despair of happiness-oriented ethics and of goal-oriented ethics in general.[16] Yet, such despair is out of place. For would not life be dull if all of our planning were fully rationally determinate? — if we did not have to sweat out some decisions by our own fog-bound lights and take our chances?

Whether or not to abide by a rule is only one kind of decision that is not rationally predeterminate. Decisions that have to do with feelings, sensations, and emotions are obvious further examples, and most personal decisions are so entangled. Computers in their *sang froid* are not about to supplant us. Jesus resisted the idea of inflicting injury according to the letter of the law, yet He respected the law in other contexts. Wrong decisions and inadvertent injuries that result from ethical conflict must forever remain part of life. We can accept this much of what Schweitzer means where he says that "The good conscience is an invention of the devil."[17]

We have mainly considered teleological, i.e., goal-oriented ethics, of which the ethics of happiness-promotion is the most interesting kind. Another kind of ethic is often proposed, in the hope of finding simple rules without depending upon so many practical angles as have been alluded to. Kant states: "I ought never to act but in such a way that I can will that my maxim become a universal law."[18] Some philosophers wish to confine ethics to such seemingly unconditioned, pure rules as those of Kant in his "deontological" ethics, as the class is technically known. Herein, it will be termed "formalistic" or "rationalistic" ethics.[19]

What people in fact *mean* by the idea of ethics is that of a goal-oriented pursuit. This is the conclusion of the American ethical philosopher Frank Chapman Sharp, who queried thousands of his students without finding any contrary instances. Purely rationalistic or formalistic ethics, denying any relevance of feeling or emotion, winds up in empty dogmatic abstractions.[20] Even a moralist like Kant must have loved his pure, independent, non-vulgar rules and loved them with emotions of pride and pleasure.[21]

Consider Kant's rule: I should always act in such a way that I can will the principle of my act to be a universal law. This rule is seemingly unconditioned by practical considerations and is valuable but only when set against a less abstract context. Despite all the discussed strictures on formalistic ethics, it is possible to combine fruitfully the promotion of divine and human happiness on the one hand, with the Golden Rule and the principle of justice as fairness on the other. And when commonsense psychology is added, we can pretty well derive the Ten Commandments.[22] We can also arrive at the following simply stated, practical ethical principles, which inherently do not require to be applied with great precision in complex situations. This brief statement of human rights and duties gives us some direction:

1. No one has the right to inflict needless harm or suffering on either oneself or others.

2. Everyone should examine oneself, should judge oneself cautiously and critically, and judge others by the same criteria with which one judges oneself under identical circumstances.

3. Every individual has the right to freedom of independent and creative thinking and acting, the right to be different, as long as this same right in all others is recognized and honored, and as long as, in one's differences or disputes, one does not cause needless harm or suffering for either oneself or others.

4. Every individual has the right to recognition of his or her needs and to act freely to fulfill those needs, as long as this same right in all others is recognized and honored.

5. Everyone should see oneself as an end in oneself as opposed to being a means to some other person's selfish ends; and likewise, should see all others as ends in themselves rather than as means to one's own selfish ends.

6. Everyone has the right to defend oneself from injustice or tyranny, and the duty to do so insofar as one is capable.

7. Everyone has the duty to fulfill oneself insofar as one is capable, and to fully utilize one's capacity to help others fulfill their lives.

8. The individual should seek that alternative to act on which will bring about the greatest amount of need fulfillment or joy, and the least amount of need frustration or joylessness, into life as a

whole — into the life of humans, the other creatures, and God — on a long-range basis.

Existentialists are fond of saying that, in the anguish and desperation of the great crises of life, rules are useless and that a creative and unique response is required. Indeed, it is possible to find examples of difficult situations that are not much amenable to rules. Yet, countless decisions exemplify obedience to simple rules and are nonetheless valiant or difficult for being so.

Victor Hugo's *Les Misérables* presents the valor of Jean Valjean in surrendering to the police, in order to forestall the detention of an innocent victim. Arguably, a greater good could have been obtained for many others by Valjean's quietly staying in his responsible and productive position. A famous case from early in this century is that of the English explorer Titus Oates, who decided to walk out to his death in the Antarctic snow so that he would not be a burden to his endangered companions. Indeed, countless such selfless acts in military situations, exploration, police work, or rescue work could be instanced, to mention only the more colorful situations.

Leading existentialist Jean-Paul Sartre put forth ambiguous rules of his own — a convenient arrangement for the libertine that he was.[23] Other existentialists have done the same, likewise lacking precision or consistency. While existentialism is of course not to be identified with criminality, there can be no denying that the basic tenets of existentialism afford to those criminals who are so disposed the opportunity to justify themselves in their own eyes.

Even though a criminal may not have studied philosophy, the messages of popular philosophers seep everywhere. Notably in Sartre's view, the uniqueness of the person entails that he must regard the world as hostile and as inciting nausea when it intrudes.[24] The followers of Sartre appear to pride themselves on not being their "brother's keeper" — or sister's either. Indeed, historian Paul Johnson relates in shocking detail that the genocide in Cambodia in the 1970s was "entirely the work of a group of intellectuals, who were for the most part pupils and admirers of Jean-Paul Sartre."[25]

In the mid-nineteenth century, Dostoyevsky foresaw that the acceptance of humanism as the highest value would gradually lead to such aberrations and even to senseless suicide, murder and revolution — carried out perhaps merely for the sake of demonstrating one's absolute freedom.[26] "By their fruits ye shall know them."[27]

Of course, such adversarial views of reality are without reasonable basis. Secular existentialism in its ramifications is the *reductio ad absurdum* of the belief that human beings contain within themselves the sole source and criterion of all values.

**ANIMAL CRACKERS®**            by Roger Bollen            January 1, 1971

The American mathematician Harold Willis Milnes draws attention to the Egyptian religious manual *The Book of the Dead*, which evidently dates from before 4000 B.C. and is mostly tedious liturgical ritual. It contains a jewel, the so-called Negative Confession, which was for that time a remarkably advanced moral code. At the last judgment or "Psychostasia," the deceased was required to recite the forty-two statements of the Negative Confession before the assembly of all the great gods, among which are the following:

> I have not stolen. I have not slain man or woman. I have not made light the bushel. I have not uttered lies. I have not attacked any man. I have not pried into the affairs of others to make mischief. I have not slandered any man. I have not been wroth without reason. I have not debauched another's wife. I have not terrorized any man. I have not turned a deaf ear to truth. I have not stirred up strife. I have made none to weep. I have not committed acts of sexual impurity. I have not abused anyone. I have not judged in haste. I have not multiplied my words in speaking. I have not cursed the king. I have not stopped the flow of waters. I have not spoken with arrogance. I have not blasphemed a god. I have not acted insolently. I have not made myself unduly great. I have not increased my wealth with what is not mine.

Milnes suggests that the god Osiris must have remained rather lonely in the Tuat or Heaven for lack of qualified candidates. Nevertheless, he observes that the form of each confession affords "a sense of accomplishment that is available to anyone, regardless of his talents, wealth, social status or paternity. The individual is left free to act as he chooses, but it is he, by his own volition, who has made the better decision."

Milnes wonders whether such a Confession might be more effective than a "code like the Ten Commandments for inculcating the virtues of humility, self-control, respect for persons and property, and sympathy for weaker beings." He wonders how many people have strayed simply to find out what happens if forbidden fruits are tasted.[28] We cannot but note, however, that the "Negative Confession" is only a statement of the evil things one has not done. We could attribute the same negative morality to a stone. No rock has done any immoral thing. On the other hand, to require the constant performance of positive, specific acts to achieve good ends could be very restrictive and even tyrannical. For instance, it is good that most people devote themselves primarily to a family, but should everybody do so?

**FRANK and ERNEST®**          by Bob Thaves          October 12, 1985

WELL, THE "LOVE THY NEIGHBOR" PART SOUNDS EASY ENOUGH.

Excessive positive rule-making need not be a problem for the theist. In the ethically ultimate case, the theist takes as the basic rule of conduct "benevolence to intelligent being in general," which amounts to actively and positively contributing ultimately to the joy of God. This becomes a habit — indeed a person's firm *identity* that cannot be violated without serious internal conflict and incoherence. It is possible to pursue this basic rule, not out of narrow, private self-love or selfishness, but rather out of a brightly enlightened pursuit of happiness, motivated in one sense by "simple self-love," to use this term as defined in the discussion of Jonathan Edwards. To the believer, the love of God is its own reward. "You cannot take a more direct course to make life pleasant," says Edwards.[29]

"Love [God], and do as you will."[30] The foregoing arguments buttress this advice of Augustine — provided, of course, that one love God as an end in Himself, not merely as a means to one's own selfish ends. The psychic structure of the ethical human being is subtle and manifold, but it can be understood, communicated and taught. Indeed, the fact that it can be learned is one evidence of God's love as it enters into the design of the universe.[31]

> It's pretty hard to tell what does bring happiness.
> Poverty an' wealth have both failed.
> > *Kin Hubbard as Abe Martin*

> The most delicate, the most sensible of all
> pleasures, consists in promoting the pleasures of
> others.
> > *Jean de la Bruyère*

# 16

## Freedom of the Will

In all things people begin with the simple, the
complex comes later, and with superior enlightenment one often comes back to the simple at last.
This is the course of the human mind.

*Voltaire*

Man is many things — he is protean, elusive,
capable of great good and appalling evil. He is
what he is — a reservoir of indeterminism. He
represents the genuine triumph of volition, life's
near evasion of the forces that have molded it.

*Loren Eiseley*

VOLUNTARY CHOICE is a singular aspect of con-
scious life. It is another example of the "inexhaustible queerness"
of the universe.[1] The American philosopher Clarence Irving Lewis
writes, "The concept of a deliberate act is peculiarly fundamental
to ethics because it is only to acts which can be done deliberately
that any directive of doing can apply."[2] A corollary is that robots
have no morals. Mechanistic philosophers hold that there is no
freedom of the will, no such thing as voluntary action, that all is
predetermined and that we are mere cogs in the great universal
machine, driven by fate or by a presumed tyrannical will of God.
This belief is called determinism.

Suppose, however, that people really were to consciously believe,
every minute of the day, that their acts were not at all the result
of their own deliberate decisions but were entirely the outcomes
of forces over which they had no control. To be in mind of such
a thing every minute is unrealistic, but no matter. One result would
be that the greater sources of happiness would no longer be

available. Strictly speaking, there could be no pleasure of accomplishment or of proficiency, no self-congratulation, no pleasure in appreciation received from others, and no joy of freely interacting with others. Similarly, great sources of unhappiness would be missing, especially guilt and self-deprecation. If determinism were true, there could be no morality or, for that matter, immorality. The quality of life appropriate to a human being, or for that matter to a dog, would cease.

However, such a prospect need not be a source of worry. All alleged disproofs of the voluntariness or the freedom of voluntary actions are readily shown to be empty or invalid. This result follows from the fact that any verbal expression of disproof must be understood as being itself a voluntary act. The objector, by any spoken attempt at disproof, implicitly and foolishly assumes exactly what is being denied. That is, *voluntary* self-reference is implicit in the objector's disproof, and that spoils the disproof.[3]

No matter how many constraints may be placed upon our options of action, the possibility of free human choice and action must always be regarded as real in some degree and as directed toward the attainment of some planned consequence. Insofar as one is a normal human being, one freely chooses within whatever the imposed constraints may be. Quantum mechanics has successfully denied the universality of the Newtonian mechanics that formerly appeared to allow no possibility of freely willed action. Newton himself did not see how his own system of mechanics in any way denied the reality of human freedom of choice. In the following century, however, Pierre-Simon Laplace argued that if the mechanical world is governed by ironclad Newtonian laws, then it would follow necessarily that these laws govern all of our physical motions, and the notion that we are free to influence our own bodies must be a myth. In modern quantum theory, it is generally considered that the principle of the conservation of energy is transitorily but ubiquitously violated at the quantum level. This means that, since the movement of particles in space is not governed by ironclad laws, the particles are amenable to the influence that we as spiritual agents can exert upon them with the strange but unmistakable capacity we possess to control our bodies and the bodies around us.[4]

We need not here be concerned with the lack of freedom in involuntary actions or of thoughtless or merely habitual or instinctual actions. Only such action as is voluntary is considered, that is, action which is motivated within one's consciousness and which is the result of one's willful choice — that is, the act of one's own mind in pursuing a goal, in what to most people seems certainly to be freedom.

Curiously, a most prominent strain of Christian theology, classical theism, has unfortunately lent support to a form of determinism. Around the time of Jesus, Philo Judaeus held that God does not exist in time as we know it, but in eternity. That is, the past, present, *and future* are all laid out to God now and eternally within His private eternal present. More pointedly, Philo held that God not only knows the general direction of the future but infallibly knows every detail of it, i.e., that all time is *present* within God's mind. In this way, all of the future is already effectively an existing set of facts. By implication, the natural human belief in free will is held to be an illusion since all of our actions are predetermined, rather like the vibrational movement of a needle that follows the wavy groove of an old-fashioned phonograph record. We may feel that we are acting outside of that all-confining groove, but we never do, on this account.[5]

Several Biblical verses would support such a view — for example: "When I was being made in secret, thy eyes beheld my unformed substance; in thy book were written, every one of them, the days that were formed for me, when as yet there were none of them."[6] This extravaganza of praise is from a psalm attributed to King David. In implying detailed foreknowledge, the verse effectively contradicts what is implicit in the rest of the Bible, namely, human freedom of choice. Taking this verse seriously, we would have to disregard everything in Scripture that ascribes the responsibility of doing right or wrong to each one of us — a situation that would entail losing the ethical value of the Bible and of theism in general.

Philo has proved influential up through the present. In the fifth century, Augustine tried to have it both ways, affirming both determinism and freedom. As a result, countless people today think that both sides of this dilemma are true, whereas the plain truth is that all attempts to escape it are illogical. How can *any* being *know* infallibly in advance what you are going to do while in fact you may not do it at all because you are free to choose not to do it? The effects of the unfortunate passages in Augustine's *Confessions* is described by the otherwise sympathetic historian Adolph Harnack as being "narcotic," even in Augustine's own time.[7]

Other theologians who subscribe to classical theism have less subtly deprived mankind of free will and responsibility by claiming that
God is absolutely omnipotent, possessing all power while the
creatures have none.[8] This idea of God's omnipotence is properly
seen as awkward when we consider the evil that indeed exists in
His world. That is, if God knows of an impending evil, has the
power to prevent it, and yet does not act to prevent it, then is not
He a party to the evil? The American philosopher William Pepperell
Montague puts the matter, "The puzzled, mounting wretchedness
of a single dog lost on the streets of a city would be enough to damn
with shame any God who ever lived in heaven if, with omnipotence
to draw on, he had ordained it so."[9] Such a thought has led many
to conclude that God is inhumane and tyrannical.

This leaves us confronting a trilemma between the ideas of God's
total power, total knowledge, and total goodness. Something has
to give way if logic is to be honored. The Reformation scholar

**FRANK and ERNEST®**          by Bob Thaves          January 22, 1982

Erasmus eliminated one untenable choice in saying, "Let God be
good." For if God is presumed to be less than good, then we might
as well give up efforts to be rational or ethical, or to write or read
books on how to be rational or ethical.[10] We must assume, then,
that any correction is to lie with the other two premises of the trilemma. Some modern philosophers have supplied excellent arguments to show why the assumptions of classical theism are logically incoherent as well as ethically pernicious.[11]

How could the ethics of Jesus have become half subdued by
classical theism in its incoherence? Through the centuries, there has
been too much deference accorded to the dogmas of some Greek
metaphysicians, whereby theologians obsequious before God have,
as Whitehead puts it, been "paying to Him metaphysical com-

pliments."[12] By implying that God is a divine tyrant or is insensitive to the creatures, such "compliments" turn out to be insults. Hartshorne discusses a recent theologian's concession to such "negative theology":

> At first blush, it seems a reasonable doctrine. Does not a modest estimate of our human capacity to understand God imply that our concepts cannot properly apply to him? So it is held to be quite safe to say, without qualification, that he is *not* finite, *not* relative [to the creatures] or open to influence.

But Hartshorne finds such modesty only apparent. Such theologians

> dare to forbid God to sustain relations, to accept the definiteness that comes through limits, to respond to the creatures and thus be influenced by them. He may, we concede, do these things "symbolically," whatever that may mean, but we tell him in no uncertain terms that he must not literally do them! Is this modesty — or is it monstrous presumption? Have we this veto power upon divinity? Not to sustain relationships, not to respond sensitively to the existence of others is to be wooden, stupid, or an utterly empty abstraction.[13]

If God in absolute immutability is totally unaffected by what we do and say, then in what possible meaningful way can He be said to have any interpersonal relationship with us? Quite plainly, a god who is in no way affected by us can in no meaningful way be personally related to us.

The fifth-century religious scholar Pelagius, by all accounts personally a blameless man, was primarily a moralist who challenged Augustine and asserted the freedom of human will unambiguously. Pelagius regarded himself as an orthodox Christian, but after prolonged arguments and church trials, Pelagius was excommunicated.[14] Augustine was the person primarily responsible for the successful persecution of Pelagius. While generally recognized as a saint, Augustine was in fact capable of being vicious towards people who did not share his ecclesiastical and theological dogmas. Pelagius, an innocent and sincere Christian, suffered enormously at his hands. Nevertheless, any system of theology that has survived as classical theism has survived must have some attractions or even benefits.

There are good reasons for not completely denigrating classical theism. But let us first consider two of its attractions that seem not altogether constructive. With some, a denial of the reality of freedom of choice may exemplify the endless ingenuity and self-deception of the human race in trying to wiggle out of moral responsibility. Classical theism opens the door to such a view. In similar fashion, the atheistic English philosopher Gilbert Ryle told a professor of ethics: "When I was young, I saw a lot of people being hurt because they thought they were free."

Some Christian theology professors and ministers have acknowledged that there are "paradoxes" (a euphemism for con-tradictions) in classical theism. They would presume to get around the embarrassment of being exposed in their contradictions by sim-ply claiming that reality is ultimately paradoxical in its nature, or that revealed truths about God should not be held accountable to the laws of "human logic." The fact is, the real laws of logic are not human any more than the laws of mathematics or physics are human; they are inscribed in the nature of things and discovered by humans, not invented by them.

The effort to escape from accountability to the laws of logic —that is, from the duty to be rational in one's thinking about God by claim-ing that the laws of logic are merely "human" — is a form of both intellectual and spiritual dishonesty. Some classical theists defend the contradictions in their thinking about God in no more sophisticated a way than merely shrugging their shoulders and saying, "Well, that's just the way it is." They have acted as though theology is too sacrosanct to be meddled or tinkered with by realistic logicians. In effect, they would have us believe that we cannot be real Christians unless we can be illogical.

Some people are uncomfortable in laying their problems before a God who is concerned, even saddened, with the problems of all of us here below. They prefer to believe that there exists a cosmic Person by whose will all happenings occur and yet who is unmoved by any of those happenings. To understand the motive for such belief, consider an analogy involving the role of royalty in history. A commoner would look at the soaring castle of the inaccessible ruler and say to himself: "The king rules by a right that is rooted in the nature of things. Surely, the royal residents of yonder castle are happy; surely, they have conquered the problems of life and should not have to endure the discomfort of knowing about mine. One day, either the monarch or an anointed successor will so order the kingdom that my own problems will melt away. Their power will raise us all from our miserable condition." In like manner, those who prefer a life free from need for initiative — indeed, free from freedom — may prefer the God of classical theism.

Thomas Aquinas was the thirteenth-century theologian who had the ambitious aim of integrating spiritual knowledge with natural knowledge. This book also attempts that goal. Thomists hold to classical theism. They claim that if God were in any way dependent on a creature, then He would be a caricature and could not have been the Creator. So stated, this argument seems to be a *non sequitur*, but Whitehead gets at the valid point when he states, "The task of Theology is to show how the World is founded on something beyond mere transient fact."[15] Classical theism does avoid the thrust of questions like the following: If God were created out of some other entity, or if God were mortal, would God be truly worshipful? If God's ethically relevant powers depended on something prior to His own being, would allegiance and worship be inspired? The answers must be no.

Can the theory of God as sensitive, growing, and sharing power with the creatures, match or exceed classical theism in cogence? In considering the ways whereby God can be known, neoclassical theists such as Charles Hartshorne give a coherent reformulation of six pre-existing *a priori* arguments: the ontological, cosmological, and the design arguments, as well as the epistemic, the moral, and the esthetic arguments. All the conceivable options regarding these arguments are restated by Hartshorne, analyzed, and used in mutual support. He renders explicitly what is entailed in a denial of theism — that is, the tragic intellectual, axiological, and emotional price that must be paid for denial. All Hartshorne's arguments are, he states, "phases of one 'global' argument, that the properly formulated theistically religious view of life and reality is the most intelligible, self-consistent, and satisfactory one that can be conceived."[16]

The neoclassical theism of Hartshorne identifies God with universal creative power, wisdom, and goodness, the unsurpassable orderer of the universe. God can do anything He wants to do, and what He wants to do is always good.[17] God is not static but can be self-surpassing over His prior achievements, growing in knowledge and experience. God is the supreme recipient of all influence from creatures, knowing and remembering the value of every individual and the value of the self-creativity of each. As for God's needs, Hartshore asserts:

> God "needs" only one thing from the creatures: the intrinsic beauty of their lives, that is, their true happiness, which is also his happiness through his perfect appreciation of theirs. This appreciation is love, not something extra as a motive to love.[18]

Regardless of whether one agrees with Hartshorne on every point, he enables serious inquirers to think about God and the universe for themselves. Such public freedom of independent thinking is also offered by natural science. No intellectual or cultural discipline can bear up, and be progressive, if it does not encourage open, creative, and logical thinking. Hartshorne's works stimulate such thinking and should be required reading in seminaries.[19]

In polytheism, there is no necessary Person. For example, belief in a literal eternal Devil, eternally coexistent with God and independent of God, is one form of polytheism. In monotheism, God is God simply by being the one Person whose existence is essential and necessary — the Person with a capital **P** who cannot fail to be and cannot fail to love. In polytheism, every god has an origin in time and is preceded by some other gods who had origins in time, and so on. Every god is therefore contingent — that is, not necessarily existent. Since in polytheism there is no necessary being, the polytheist has an insoluble problem in trying to make a case for intrinsic values in anyone's life.

> Faith on the human level is trust that the nature of things insures the appropriateness of ideals of generosity, honesty, and esthetic refinement, or goodness, truth, and beauty, to such an extent that despite all frustrations and vexations, despite disloyalty or crassness in our fellows, despite death itself, it is really and truly better to live, and to live in accord with these ideals, than to give up the struggle in death or in cynicism.
>
> *Charles Hartshorne*

# 17

## *The Stuff of Motivation*

Nothing is more than an instrument save living
feeling and emotion. Consciousness and feeling are
not devices for achieving ends, they are the only
ends. The end of all existence is enjoyment, inten-
sified by contrast, harmonized by similarity, and
enriched by the realization of meanings.

*Charles Hartshorne*

AN ENGLISH PHYSIOLOGIST, H. J. Campbell,
arranged a pair of mildly electrified "goal posts" in an aquarium.
A slight current between the posts could be switched on by the
breaking of a light beam that crossed the area. "Much was my joy,"
Campbell writes, "when the fish stopped their usual aimless
wanderings. They swam backward and forward through the light
beam and so provided themselves over and again with that little
tickle of electricity that must be like fondling and kissing to you
and me." Campbell's fish ceased swimming through the light beam
when no electricity was supplied or when local anesthetic was added
to the water.

"Most impressive to me," continues Campbell, "is my little
crocodile's wearying search for joy. Left alone, he sits motionless
for hours, but when the goal-post is put into his tank he lumbers
through it some fifty times in fifteen minutes; hard work for a
crocodile, but presumably worth it."

Campbell puts forth a theory:

> It is postulated that an absolutely essential requirement of the animal nervous system is that the pleasure areas of the brain be kept activated. To do this, animals engage in one piece of behavior after another, as each [kind of behavior] ceases, on repetition, to bombard the pleasure areas with nerve impulses. The ramifications of the theory are enormous, explaining the rise of religion, the cause of extinction and survival, most social institutions, the importance of sex — and the division of all people into human and sub-human. Only when the pleasure areas are activated by thinking behavior are we distinct from the lower animals.[1]

This means that if people can't get their "kicks" in ways appropriate to the human level, they will get them any way they can. Hence, exclusively negative ways to educate children, to control crime, drug abuse, or misdirected sensuality must fail. Seven centuries ago, Thomas Aquinas also figured this out: "No one can live without delight, and that is why a man deprived of spiritual joy goes over to carnal pleasures."[2]

Three backdrops of consciousness were mentioned earlier — sexuality, music, and theism. Campbell's thesis might be extended by speculating that no person can well bear to be without at least one of these three pleasing backdrops of conscious for any great length of time. The thread common to these backdrops is that each can afford *a continual felt unity of persons*. Theism is the reliable one which moreover lends meaning to the other two.

Campbell's thesis is a corollary of the thesis that pleasure or happiness is the stuff of conscious choice or motivation in general. That has been rather assumed herein, if only to facilitate discussion. For instance, coherence not only is the essence of rational thinking behavior, but coherence in ideas is *pleasing* to reflect on. Inner, psychological coherence is experienced as steadfastly pleasant. The idea of the superior status of pleasure in motivation goes back, according to Aristotle, to the ancient Greek mathematician and astronomer Eudoxus, who argued, "No one ever asks the question for what purpose a man is feeling pleasure, because we assume that pleasure is in itself desirable."[3] Augustine, Thomas Aquinas, Joseph Butler, and others take it for granted that the pursuit of happiness or joy as a psychological good is the inward universal stuff of rational motivation.[4] Some people dispute this and claim that happiness is only one among other motivations. Moreover, many claim that happiness-motivation may not always be moral.

Misunderstanding about the role of pleasure and happiness in motivation has been going on at least since Plato wrote the *Philebus* dialogue. There, Protarchus is asked whether he would consent to be an oyster possessed of the greatest possible pleasures while at the same time bereft of reason, memory, knowledge, intelligence, true judgment, and consciousness.[5] Protarchus says no, he prefers a life of pleasure mixed with reason. Plato here ignores the alternative consideration that the activity of reason may itself be a kind of pleasure. Ever since, philosophers have often thought it their duty to attack pleasure or happiness when regarded as a state worthy to be generally sought. Perhaps it was seen as too undignified to undergird motivation. Or perhaps, in the eyes of powerful rulers, it was seen as politically dangerous.

Value judgments, including judgments about happiness, have long been widely belittled among materialistic scholars. This view must be challenged. We first consider the allegations that happiness, pleasure, and joy are not important in the scheme of things and for that reason cannot explain motivation, if indeed motivation itself is to be taken as something other than mechanical causation. Strangely, some academic bellwethers have alleged that it is not even meaningful or scientifically interesting to speak of happiness and pleasure.

Do such terms refer to anything fully real or important? Peirce in 1868 seems to have been the first to seriously doubt whether our power of introspection, that is, our attending to our own private processes of thought and feeling, is a means to knowledge of "man's glassy essence" — the internal world of our psyches. There have been other attacks against the feelings of pleasure and pain as objective scientific concepts.[6] Some philosophers who philosophize mainly about language, notably Gilbert Ryle and R. S. Peters, have denied that pleasure or pain may properly be said to have any causal or explanatory influence of their own, or even that pleasure is a sensation or emotion at all.

The physical side of reality is pervasively impressive in our time. In recent centuries, so much of reality has been explained in physical categories, and so much has been added to our comfort, safety, and convenience thereby that, with the decay of religious faith, materialist philosophies have flourished. Strict Marxists deny the importance of anything that is not physical. For them, the only thing that is real is the material world; so-called consciousness is *only* a complex expression of chemistry. They may be asked why largely unknown recondite brain chemistry should in itself be as important as it certainly is, as compared to all other physical happenings. For instance, why is it important to them that a dentist use a local anesthetic when filling one of their teeth? The questions answer themselves.

The concept of happiness or pleasure gains stature in relation to the physical world from the work of the American neuropsychologist James Olds, who implanted low-voltage electrodes in the brains of rats. The current could be turned on and off through a treadle-switch by the rat itself. Suitably wired rats pressed the treadle up to five thousand times an hour; meanwhile, the rat was not attracted by food or the opposite sex. Insertion of a similar electrode into certain other areas of a rat-brain was followed by perhaps only one press of the treadle and then no more, ever.

Such behavior has been replicated with cats, dogs, sheep, dolphins, and monkeys. It has been done with people, too, who report many kinds, shades, and intensities of feelings.[7] The procedure substantiates a link between physics and pleasant feeling. Of course, some links between body chemistry and the quality of feeling have long been known, through the subjective effects of alcohol and drugs. All these facts and others contribute to the scientific admissibility of the concept of happiness.[8]

Happiness as a concept would gain further in scientific stature if it could be reliably measured in physical terms. But it has been truly said that human beings make poor subjects in psychological experiments or tests. Genetic data and past experiences are mostly unknown, always different in countless ways, and generally relevant to one's present disposition and outlook on life. It would take a powerful influence to shine through such clutter. Such powerful influence is likely to be found in religious systems.

The neglect of happiness-measurement in behavioral science has not been total. Enough has been done to make the point that happiness can be measured at least well enough to *rank* various degrees of happiness as more than a subjective matter.[9] A program of happiness-measurement could explore correlations between different techniques of measuring happiness. As in measurements of

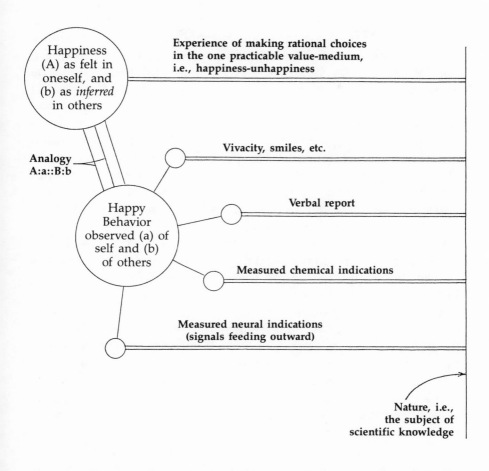

*Validity of happiness as a scientific concept, following Margenau's analysis of multiple connections.*

I.Q. or intelligence quotient so called, the correlation of findings between different modes of measurement may be expected to strengthen the credibility of the overall results, through their coherence.

The arguments henceforth through most of Chapter 18 are relatively technical and dry, since they tackle the more vexed questions in philosophical ethics. Those who so prefer may skip to Chapter 19.

The accompanying chart shows the logical relations in our knowledge of the concept of happiness. Its form is suggested by the American physicist Henry Margenau to illustrate essential criteria for scientific concepts in general. The circles are constructs or concepts and are examples of that component of science which is neither pure observation nor pure logic. In psychology this includes the class of "intervening variables," of which felt happiness is one. The presence of only one path to a construct signifies that it lacks logical fertility, meaning that there is nothing to which the construct may relate or to which it may cohere. In fact, such constructs are intuitively rejected by capable scientists as explaining nothing. For example, when we are told that Homer didn't write the *Iliad* or the *Odyssey*, that it was another fellow of the same name, we are not thereby enlightened. Homer is known to us only through the narrative poems under that name; we have no second path to enable us to say any more about his identity.

When we see in others vivacity, smiles, and positive words spoken in a certain way, we do not need the special tools of science in order to infer felt happiness within these persons. This is because we know how we feel when we spontaneously behave or express ourselves in similar ways. When we see others who are behaving similarly, we attribute similar feelings to them. By analogy between the behavior and experience of oneself and others, one can know that others are experiencing happiness. Multiple such experiences result in multiple connections in the chart, adding to the validity and logical fertility of the concept of happiness itself.[10] Similarly, Hartshorne notes the similarity in the cries of dogs, cats, birds, human beings when they are obviously in distress.[11]

Why should anyone subordinate the psychical side of life to its material side? The nineteenth-century German physiologist and philosopher Hermann Lotze considered the importance of mental phenomena such as perception, in comparison to material entities. He asked, "Must all the glory revealed by the senses be changed into an illusion of our mind that, incompetent to discern the true nature of things, consoles itself by creating a show without objective validity of any kind?"

Lotze's answer was no. He spoke of the significance of a world of sensation coming into being under the influence of physical entities such as brains, nerves, and light waves. To him, this event is

one of the greatest, if not the greatest of all events. As we prize a blossom for its brilliance of colour and its fragrance, without requiring of it to exhibit a representation of the form of its roots, so we must prize this inner world of sensation for its own beauty and significance, without measuring its value by the fidelity with which it reproduces its less important foundation.

For why, in fact, should we not reverse this whole relation, to which a crude mode of conception has accustomed us? Instead of setting up the external as the goal to which all the efforts of our sensation are to be directed, why should we not rather look upon the splendour of light and sound as the end which all those dispositions of the external world, whose obscurity we deplore, are designed to realize? Let us therefore cease to lament as if the reality of things escaped our apprehension.[12]

A main question of ethics is whether we should pursue happiness, pleasure, joy, satisfaction, etc. That is, should we exclusively pursue this feeling, making it our sole motive? We cannot answer that question until we consider in what sense we do in fact already and inevitably pursue our own maximum happiness or highest pleasure, etc., at every rational moment. The theory that we do pursue our own pleasure or happiness as the *sole* essence of our motivation internally speaking is called *psychological hedonism*. It was stated too simply by the British legal reformer Jeremy Bentham in the early nineteenth century. The theory has recommended itself to many, including the present authors, as affording the only reasonable way to talk about motivation or even to talk about the making of ethical choices.

Many others deny the theory of psychological hedonism. They consider it unprovable, unfalsifiable, sterile of predictive power, and ethically repugnant. There is some substance to these objections. However, the force of the objections is avoidable. The position to be defended here is a qualified psychological hedonism. In a unified view of rational motivation or decision the theory is, in some restricted sense, inescapable. For without such a theory of rational motivation, it turns out that ethics can at best amount to no more than idle talk, unrelated to action. "Hedonism" is here to be taken as only as a technical term for the pursuit of pleasure, happiness, etc.; it is not to be taken in its common meaning of a merely narrow pursuit of private pleasure such as the seeking of thrills and the avoidance of pangs. Our concern in all this is only with voluntary actions, or actions for which one is to accept responsibility for consequences.

First, we shall consider whether it is possible for a person to pursue and maximize two or more ultimate values or ethically relevant criteria at the same time. One value to be pursued might be peace of mind; the other might be the accumulation of wealth. *Can a person voluntarily serve two (or more) masters as ultimate goods or aims?* The answer will turn out to be no.[13] Hence, one and only one ultimate value can be of service to ethics. Readers already know which one this is to be.

A person who is weighing alternatives for action might well tend to choose a particular course of action by applying one criterion but would choose another course if the other criterion were applied. In that case how is one to choose between the alternative courses? Can one decide according to more than one criterion? On trying, even as a thought-experiment, curious consequences result.

For example, during World War II, Allied military commanders found it necessary to place a dollar value on the lives of American servicemen, namely two hundred thousand dollars, a sum which would amount to perhaps a million current dollars. Crass as such a procedure may seem, a little thought will show that some unified measure of projected losses must be used for rational decision-making among military options. As with an individual's actions, only one military plan or group of plans can be followed at one time with one set of resources. If the criterion were solely that of minimizing the loss of life, any fight with lethal weapons would be ruled out; surrender would be indicated. If the measure were solely money, that would be plainly barbaric and would redound to the disadvantage of the foot-soldier and the wounded, not to mention the damage to the morale of all the armed forces and the people at home. Because of these awkward facts, the two measures were combined into one criterion according to a consistent scheme, so that possible strategies and tactics could be *ranked* and the superior one chosen. The way to do that was to equate a sum of dollars to the life of each member of our forces, in relation to resources actually available at the time.[14]

The attempt to use a decision procedure based on two different criteria has not worked well in classical utilitarian ethics. Jeremy Bentham with his intellectual forebears — Francis Hutcheson and Cesare Beccaria — contended that the true criterion of action which is to be called fully ethical is "the greatest happiness of the greatest number," a concept that is to be internalized and taken by the agent to be one's own good — one's own happiness or joy. But there is an innate problem with this criterion, in addition to that considered earlier. The criterion is really two criteria: two independent goods are to be maximized, namely, the degree of happiness of some people, and the extent of the spreading of whatever total happiness there is.

As a specific example: How many children should be brought into the world? Should people aim in concert to maximize the population of the earth, or should they aim to make some smaller number of people happier through immersing them in less congestion, less pollution, and more natural resources? Secular philosophy has not found a justifiable answer. If there are to be still larger multitudes of people, the quality of life would suffer, but then there would be more people to enjoy whatever good things are to be had. On this course, the aim would be to maximize an alleged total amount of happiness even at the expense of average happiness. Under such a scheme, it would count as an improvement to plan for only fifty-one per cent of the present average happiness per person, provided that the population which experienced that diminished happiness were doubled. But would anyone in his or her right mind recommend such a state of affairs, whatever may be meant by a degree of happiness so specified?

Perhaps the reason for reacting negatively to the above question is that our heritage has already put us in mind of a divine Impartial Spectator who would find such an unhappy idea inconsistent with divine care for us.[15] For us to suppose that God would indulge in such dismal number-juggling would hurt our perception of Him and diminish our attraction to Him. An intuitive weighing of the matter will place heavy emphasis on the quality of life. While we cannot know exactly what God may think of the matter, theism does afford a way to focus somewhat an answer which God should find pleasing. That is, God's presumed pleasure would enable us to conceptualize a single criterion to be used for such decisions and so render the problem more nearly ponderable.

The problem of trying to maximize two independent variables at once is made graphic by a simple thought-experiment. Suppose that you like hamburgers that comprise a maximal amount of pickles and a maximal amount of onions. That is, the best hamburger for you is the one with the greatest amount of each. Then say that you have to choose an optimum hamburger from a randomly prepared assemblage of hamburgers, each of which contains randomly varying amounts of onions and of pickles. You can choose the one with the most onions, perhaps even finding one with the maximal amount, or you can likewise choose the one with the most pickles. But you are not likely to find in the randomly prepared assemblage a hamburger that has the maximal quantity of onions while at the same time the maximal quantity of pickles. So long as your goal remains *both* and not simply a maximal sum of the two, there can be no decision procedure that will qualify as reasonable.

In 1944 the Hungarian-born scholar John von Neumann first conceived of the marvelous, versatile computers into which the user can insert independently stored electronic programs. One such device is being used to complete this book. Von Neumann and Oskar Morgenstern with their logical minds state: *"A guiding principle cannot be formulated by the requirement of maximizing two (or more) functions at once."*[16]

Following this principle, we may conclude that an action, to be fully consistent and rational, must be directed to maximizing only one criterion of value, not two or more — that is, unless both criteria are taken as additive parts of some one unifying higher criterion. To act fully rationally is to serve one master — that is, one goal or task. In order to be consistent and rational, a person must select one and only one criterion for the ranking of possibilities among all of one's evaluative or comparative decisions. Either a person decides according to one principle or preference, which eliminates the other, or else the person acts basically at random. In the latter course, one is bound to fail to maximize anything; one thus behaves so far non-rationally.

Moreover, the indecision entailed in attempting to serve two or more masters is persistently uncomfortable to the agent. "Purity of heart is to will one thing," Kierkegaard tells us. The one criterion, whatever it is to be, must encompass all the partial value-systems and partial criteria used by the person, such as money, health, job, honesty, courage, the good of one's family, etc. By now in this study we know what that criterion is to be, whereby our inward sense of the valuable is hopefully to correspond with what is objectively valuable in the universe.

We may conclude, then, that there can be only one essence of rational motivation. What is that essence to be?

As anticipated earlier, the most interesting candidate is pleasure, happiness, etc. But it is time to say just what is meant by such terms. The American philosopher Clarence Irving Lewis holds that there is one (and only one) kind of value (and disvalue) that needs no conceptualizing, for it is psychically *immediate* and unmistakable to everyone. It may be called "immediately or directly findable value," or pleasure or joy or their opposites such as unpleasure, displeasure, pain, or algedonic feeling (painful, as in neuralgia). Or they may be called just satisfaction or dissatisfaction. C. I. Lewis writes that, by any name, "everyone knows what it is, and if anyone should not, we could hardly tell him."[17]

We may follow Lewis further:

> If "pleasure" or any other name is to serve as synonym for the immediately and intrinsically valuable, then it must be adequate to the wide variety of what is found directly good in life. It must cover the active and self-forgetting satisfactions as well as the passive and self-conscious ones; the sense of integrity in firmly fronting the "unpleasant" as well as "pleasure"; the gratification in having one's way, and also the benediction which may come to the defeated in having finished the faith. It must cover innocent satisfactions as well as those of cultivation; that [satisfaction] which is found in consistency and also that of perversity and caprice. [It must cover] the enjoyment of sheer good fortune, and that which adds itself to dogged achievement. All this in addition to the whole range of the sensuously pleasing and the emotionally gratifying. And the immediately disvaluable has its equal and corresponding variety. Such immediate goods and bads are ill compressed into any single term or pair of terms.[18]

The "immediately valuable" is directly and continually felt. It is *in*trinsic; in comparison to it, all other values are *ex*trinsic — valuable only because they contribute to "immediate value," which is the intrinsic value.[19] Whatever these feelings may be, they seem "to extend to and to affect the very center of experience, the self."[20]

All this, then, and only this, is to be included in the term "immediate or directly findable value." Indeed, if we conclude that there is nothing else that in an inward sense is rational to pursue, then we would in fact pursue happiness, pleasure, satisfaction, so far as we might be said to be rational. This is a statement of psychological hedonism that is qualified by the requirement of rationality. Let us call it *rational psychological hedonism*. Given the idea that value as immediately felt is the only sort of thing that is valuable, inwardly speaking, then the only rational thing to do is to pursue such inward value, and to do it with all of one's heart, soul, and mind, though we shall find that this intense-sounding way of putting the matter is misleading in its seeming exclusivity and repulsiveness.

An objector may first ask whether the pursuit of "immediate value" really defines a unified pursuit. Does such a "happiness-imperative" or "joy-imperative" require us to do anything different than the multitude of different things that we would be doing without the imperative? The only addition made by acknowledging the truth of the theory seems to be that we are to be single-minded in the pursuit of true joy and lasting pleasure and that we should not hesitate over thoughts that we should not.

It is alleged that the theory of rational psychological hedonism predicts nothing, or nothing that common sense wouldn't have predicted. The objector may insist that any theory which, with one simple idea, purports to explain every action, even altruistic pleasures and the pleasure of renunciation of pleasures, explains nothing. The objector may hold further that the theory is unfalsifiable, since everything that anybody ever does is to be subsumed under the theory, as the theory itself states. For instance, there is the pleasure of fulfilling one's intention to act, which pleasure is alleged to always occur, whatever that act may be. Thereby, the act has at least a minimal rationality of motive. As Peirce puts it, "All action in accordance with a determination is accompanied by a feeling that is pleasurable."[21] Even this usually slight pleasure is to be included in a list like that of Lewis. An objector might ridicule the theory on this basis, though a defender can say that the pleasure is generally experienced as real, even important sometimes, if one introspects suitably about it.

There is a bite in each of the objections. What good, then, is such a theory as rational psychological hedonism? Can it be true if it neither improves predictions of behavior nor admits of its own disproof? Yes, it is true anyway because, as we shall find, no other theory enables rational choice to permeate life. Rational psychological hedonism honors the common sense which we in fact all honor in practice and without which we can hardly function. In ethics, it supports the idea that we each cannot well be expected to afford to others anything but that sort of feeling which we ourselves find valuable. However, before coming to such a conclusion, we should examine more counter-arguments. Along the way, the seeming crassness of this *psychological* theory will become softened as we learn the difference between it and an *ethical* theory.

It is often alleged that love, in order to be genuine, must be selfless and that its essence is altruistic self-sacrifice, as though no consideration of the state of mind of a person who is attending to the needs of someone else can be allowed to compromise the value of the love. However, the psychology of love is not so simple. The American thinker Nathaniel Branden writes that love may be considered as one of the most profound forms of self-regard:

> If the reader wants proof of this, I suggest that he ask himself what his reaction would be if the man or woman he loved were to tell him: "Don't imagine that I want to marry you out of any selfish expectation of pleasure. Don't imagine that I see anything to admire in you, or that I find your company interesting, or that I enjoy our relationship in any manner whatever. In fact, I find you boring and thoroughly unappealing. But I wouldn't be so *selfish* as to seek anything personally valuable from our marriage. Don't imagine that your thoughts or feelings are of any *actual* interest to me, or that I do any of the things I do for you because I *care* about your happiness — don't think there's anything in it for *me* whether you're happy or not. I'm not an egoist, after all. I'm marrying you out of pity, out of charity, as a *duty*, because I know that you *need* me. I'm marrying you out of compassion for your flaws, not admiration for your virtues — I'm doing it as an act of *self-sacrifice*.

Branden asks, "Would the reader feel romantically inspired as the recipient of such a statement? No, he would not? Then so much for the theory that love is selfless."[22]

Branden's example is cogent in proving that totally selfless love does not promote the happiness of either the lover or the loved. We begin to see that motivation is double-ended; it arises from feelings within oneself but is directed outward. We may conclude that there is, in actuality, no such thing as totally selfless love and that to suppose otherwise is to invite unhappiness all around. Therefore love, however important, however indispensable to happiness, however unavoidable in a workable ethic, is not a psychologically independent concept in the sense that pleasure, happiness, and satisfaction themselves are, even the satisfaction of God. For true and ethical love is the inwardly felt concern for the happiness of the beloved and of God. A person may love to hate, love to domineer, love to indulge in petty vicious gossip, love to hurt, love to kill, etc. Therefore, immediately valuable feeling such as happiness or satisfaction should not be crowded out of consideration by the idea of love when we are talking about the basis of motivation. However, we shall find that, in ethics, the logic of talking about love is quite different.

The following chapter continues the sequence of arguments relating to rational psychological hedonism.

> In every science, those who make it their business
> to dive into the depths of it, find a very different
> scene of things from those who take only so much
> as is requisite for common use. As such as have
> bestowed much thought on the foundations of right
> and wrong discover many contradictions and absur-
> dities in the popular notions, so on the other hand
> their refinements appear unintelligible and absurd
> to the generality of men.
>
> *Abraham Tucker*

> The only simplicity to be trusted is the simplicity
> that is on the far side of complexity.
>
> *Alfred North Whitehead*

# 18

## *The Benign Quality of Pleasure*

Contemporary English writers on ethics are quite
as convinced as Nietzsche that God is dead. But
being committed to the British practice of
understatement, they would never dream of uttering dramatic Zarathrustra-like pronouncements on
the subject. They would only treat defenders of
God or of a moral order with supercilious contempt, much as they would treat a man who ate
peas with his knife.

*Henry Veatch*

A DEVOTEE OF SOME POPULAR CAUSE might
say that he or she is not pursuing it for any pleasure it might afford
but rather is pursuing it as a substitute for pleasure itself. In the
case of an ascetic reformer — say, a Peace Corps volunteer or a sincere
revolutionist — there could be a bit of plausibility about such a statement. Remember the young, zealous revolutionist in *Doctor Zhivago*
who could say, "The private life in Russia is no more."[1]

Such people might even hold that no one can have any significant affective existence. They might so despise their own perhaps
pale and twisted personal life that they enter their whole selves into
some collective cause or crusade, such as the promotion of
nationalistic interests at the expense militarily of other nations. Or
it may be: "Save the snail-darter"; "Support CEPTA, the Committee to End Pay Toilets in America"; or "We must have peace at any
price." In *The True Believer* Eric Hoffer discusses several possibilities.[2]
It seems that one can learn to value almost any good or alleged good
that one can conceptualize, and then one can use it as a criterion

for *ranking* the attractiveness — the prospective satisfaction — of various possible prospective actions.[3] It further seems that nearly all persons must regard themselves as moral in some area, however narrow or remote.

But a criterion for decision that affords priority to some such specific item must be unfaithful to the facts of existence. Any such criterion which leaves out the inner life inevitably fails to enlist "the warm response of our total natures" — that is, of "our global sense of directedness." These are the words of the American ethical philosopher Philip Blair Rice. We have in pleasure, joy, and happiness "concepts which are more comprehensive than the various species of conation" or striving toward some goal. "Joy and suffering may be the accompaniments of striving, its results, and, when we are reflective, its guiding lights."

A universally applicable ranking criterion would be, as Rice suggests, "fitted to make the multiple distinctions forced upon us," and "it would have to enlist and fulfill our general sense of directedness, as that manifests itself progressively in our buffeting by the world." Can anything else than pleasure or satisfaction or joy do nearly as much? Can any other criterion for evaluating and ranking possible actions render living according to reason worth the trouble? Rice proposes some thought-experiments that each person might perform, and he presents a negative answer.[4] So may we. By a process of elimination through the process of *reductio ad absurdum* then, the "immediately valuable," joy, pleasure, etc., win over the other contenders.

G. E. Moore, twentieth-century British philosopher, denied that ethical motivation pivots only on the concept of happiness but claimed instead that quite a few different concepts of the good are ethically ultimate and that happiness is only one of them. In his attack he poses his "open question" argument against the truncated ethic of classical, secular utilitarianism by stating correctly: "It will always be pertinent to ask, whether the feeling itself is good." Therefore "good cannot itself be identical with any feeling."[5] For one thing, Moore suggests that some pleasures are bad and that therefore pleasure cannot be taken as the criterion of what is good.

It will generally be allowed, at least in the Western world, that happiness or pleasure, etc., is at a minimum one good among others. But Moore urges, in presenting his alternate theory of "ideal utilitarianism," that there are other goods which are coequal with happiness and which would even be good in some other world in which there were no beings present to perceive them as good. Moore and all of us acknowledge the importance of personal characteristics such as integrity, industriousness, honesty, loyalty, courage, magnanimity, politeness, etc. But Moore claims that each such item has a value in and of itself — a value independent of any conscious happiness that may be so induced in any earthly person. Thus in Moore's scheme, these various goods are each absolute and not amenable to comparison or addition; their importance is not that of contributing to a single goal such as widespread happiness. Moore emphasizes the values of "personal affection and aesthetic enjoyments."[6]

This early general position of Moore must be denied. Each item commonly considered to be good can indeed be shown to contribute to, say, widespread human happiness. For instance, honesty or truthfulness is an abiding precondition of the fruitful use of language to communicate or preserve knowledge. As such, it is important to everyone's pursuit of happiness. We have seen how integrity — i.e., personal coherence — is for one thing an abiding, essential, pervasive part of happiness. People's habits and principles, together with their dispositions of character that tend toward specific kinds of virtuous actions, all add stability to their production of happiness. Health and security, though not essentially moral matters, are obvious underpinnings of happiness. Finally, beauty contributes to creaturely pleasure and happiness; if it did not, it would not be beauty in any world. Arguably, it would not be beauty for God, either, unless it was beautiful to His creatures. In any case, Moore in 1942 retracted the core of his argument about "other worlds."[7]

A question is left over from Moore's challenges, namely the question, Is all felt happiness or pleasure good, or is some of it bad? Would all of it be good in the sight of an impartial, God-like spectator who could know all its probable consequences for everyone? What about the ephemeral happiness of rash young lovers who are bound to break up with bitterness and scars? What about the pleasures of the infamous Marquis de Sade or his recent imitators, or of the pleasure of Josef Stalin when he said, "To choose one's victim, to prepare one's plans minutely, to stake an implacable vengeance, and then go to bed — there is nothing sweeter in the world."[8]

Some ethical theorists have supposed that all pleasure is of itself good, that the bad thing about the starkly selfish kinds of pleasure is not the pleasure as such but the frustration of the possible joys of the victims, including their continuing fears of repeated bad incidents.[9] In the case of gluttony or drug abuse, the victim would be primarily oneself. Such answers have not satisfied everyone, nor should we ourselves be satisfied with them. Some say that Stalin's very satisfaction in destroying his victims compounded the evil of his deeds if only because, had there been no such joy in Stalin, there likely would have been no killing. More to the point, many have thought it absurd to suppose that pleasure taken in evil could

**FRANK and ERNEST®**          by Bob Thaves          April 29, 1982

"PEOPLE"? -- IT'S NOT CONTAGIOUS, IS IT?

cease to be evil, even when instrumental to greater good. There seems to be no good answer to this objection.[10]

In the case of the sadist, would God as the Cosmic Knower merely weigh the sadist's pleasure against the overwhelming pain of the victims? If we were to suppose that God reckons the matter in this calculating way, then He would determine that the pleasure of the sadist, though wrapped in a wrong, would counterbalance to some slight extent the grief of his victims. But this does not sound like a judgment of a God who is a Person who cares.

Why should we think God's personality to be more limited than our own? Why should we think of God as a mere cosmic adding machine? Is it not more plausible to suppose that God would be outraged morally as we would be and that He would condemn the pleasure of the sadist and refuse to partake of it? If God is a person and a good person, as we have found reason to believe, then the only portion of our joy that He enjoys and cherishes is unselfish or *benevolent* joy — that is, joy consistent with the joy of others. God would have no need of any other kind. Thus, we may presume that He did not share either Sade's pleasure or Stalin's but sorrowed over both.

Moore was not visibly a theist. If he had been, he could have seen that the paradox of evil pleasure can be seen as resolved in God's pleasure taken as the absolute good. Despite a general and fundamental need for joy, joy does not exist as an independent accounting commodity apart from the circumstances of its realization. It does not exist in a vacuum. It cannot be separated from desires, choices, or motives. The enjoyment of evil is evil, apart from the other consequences of the evil act. Human pleasure in evil cannot be a pleasure for God in the role of Impartial Spectator. Thus the "joy" attendant on occasions of evil is intrinsically evil.

We, like God, need benevolent, unselfish joy, not selfish, joy-killing pleasure. A felt good or a joy may itself be valued by its compatibility or coherence with other joys in the world as a whole. To repeat Edwards' words: "A virtuous benevolence will seek the good of every individual being unless it be conceived as not consistent with the highest good of being in general."[11]

Another attack on the essential unity of inward hedonic motivation points to the frequency of behavior which perversely spoils one's own satisfaction or joy. That being so, how can it be said that happiness is a universal motive? Specifically, an imprudent neuro-psychiatrist might say to you, "I'll put some micro-electric probes into a certain place in your head, and when you press the button, all of your dreams will come true. Or they might as well come true, because you will feel so good." Of course, one need not have resort to the especially problematic electrical means; highly varied chemical ways to such temporary bliss, or seeming bliss, are now all around us. Does not this possibility pose a serious challenge to the validity of promoting one's own happiness as a proper goal?

No sensible adult needs to be told that the general use or misuse of mind-altering drugs, including alcohol, has serious disadvantages. Even tranquilizers are receiving similar medical criticism as this is written. One may lose the incentive to relate well to others or to be productive. The natural processes of motivation are thereby short-circuited. With good reason, God so made us as to be less than happy some of the time. That is, it is well that our state of happiness depends upon what each of us might or might not be doing.[12]

What thing so good which not some harm may bring?
Even to be happy is a dangerous thing.[13]

The euphoria produced by drugs and probes, while useful in treating pathologies, will in other cases diminish one's consciousness of one's own real life needs and those of others. The euphoria can only diminish one's ability to act effectively to fulfill those needs. Such artificial euphoria must diminish moral insight and strength; consequently, it is incompatible with one's own best interest and that of society and of God. Seeking the pleasure of drugs can make only for internal *in*coherence, not coherence.

Before one becomes addicted to mind-altering drugs or devices, the thought of becoming the equivalent of a "happy" oyster or dangerous monster should be enough to prevent the fateful steps. That this does not prevent multitudes of people in our affluent society from falling out of control is an indication of how unsatisfactory life can be without a coherent total commitment. The result can only be a downward spiral of general ruin. On the other hand, living by a theistic religious philosophy that is validated by the coherence theory of truth should finally prove more attractive than the decision to start or continue taking mind-altering drugs.[14] But either pursuit is, under psychological hedonism, a pursuit of pleasure or happiness.

The theory of happiness-motivation does not stand or fall on the claim that everyone *rationally* pursues value in one's voluntary actions at all times. Irrationality is possible, even practically certain at some points, if only in the form of sins of omission. We dawdle; we are slugabeds. We rationalize that we need the relaxation, perhaps saying to ourselves that ideas come more readily to us thereby (sometimes they do!) We eat too many snacks. Such pastimes are pleasant in their way, but we overdo them, and in moments of truth we know it. Again, we procrastinate in confronting the unpleasant and hope that it will just go away. But in insightful or "hindsightful" moments, we know differently.

Could it be that wasteful dawdling often is a sign of sloth, or that procrastination is a sign of cowardice — that one's own explanations are really rationalizations designed to conceal from oneself such unpleasant self-images? Unfortunately, this is all too possible. Such perversity often hinders the kind of self-understanding which is essential to personal growth. It amounts to the substitution of a lower value in place of a higher one — perhaps of easy comfort in place of active, real achievement.

Worse cases of rationalization occur, as we learn from the reports about drug addicts and abusers. Again, suppose that a college teacher of philosophy who is a theist has been falsely accused of using his classroom for proselytizing, instead of skillfully defending and criticizing each well-known standard philosophy, of which theism is only one. Further, say that a colleague knows of this conspiracy and that an exposure of it could save the teacher from defamation or ostracism. But the powerful academic managers to whom all the teachers are responsible are either atheists or cowards, who are not interested in seeing justice done to the teacher. The colleague knows this and so remains discreetly silent, leaving the philosophy teacher to sink or swim, rather than expose himself to a danger of having his own cushy position threatened or his personal comfort disturbed. This is a case of rationalization that actually occurred.

We all have a natural impulse to avoid imminent suffering. Thus a person can choose to act on an unworthy ground — i.e., on a substitution. In the above case, instead of striking an influential blow for truth, academic freedom and self-respect, a number of professors chose the comfortable way. They chose a lower in place of a higher value, for the sake of escaping possibly painful immediate consequences. Unfortunately, to do right, a person may have to suffer now or later. If one clearly knows and professes loyalty to the morally better but does not choose it, we can call that person a hypocrite.

**FRANK and ERNEST®**     by Bob Thaves     February 25, 1983

More often, self-deception operates by the subtle process of self-repression, wherein one makes oneself unconscious of the choices made.

Self-deception starts out with a conscious act, namely, that of freely deciding to repress something from one's own awareness. Repressors lie to themselves and concomitantly repress from their consciousness their awareness of the fact that they are lying to themselves or playing a game of erasing from their minds an awareness that their choice of action is wrong. They deliberately construct a blind against their own moral vision. Thus they make their choices perversely, cheating themselves of greater joy in the long run, rigging the contents of their minds to convince themselves that they are acting for the better alternative.

In deliberately squelching their insightfulness as to their own long-term good, they cheat themselves of joy in the short run, too, for there is a concomitant self-division that follows from this perversity — that is, a splitting of oneself into two — a divided, incoherent self. In ordinary terms, this is a bad, or repressed, conscience. The guilt is still *within* such persons but is doing its damage out of sight. Their repressed consciences are working against them, insidiously sapping spiritual vitality and subtly poisoning whatever happiness they might tend to experience. Eric Hoffer well says, "We lie loudest when we lie to ourselves."[15]

The phenomenon of self-deception may be treated as a kind of "snare" of the sort Tolstoy analyzes. By snares or traps he means a subtler kind of self-deception wherein people tell themselves that their sins were, or continue to be, demanded by the spiritual life itself. For instance, there are snares of preparation, whereby one plans to sin just for a time. The decision is to temporize, to get past the "need" for the sinning and thereafter to lead a productive life. Tolstoy puts these words into the mouth of such a person:

> "I know the meaning of my life is not in service of self, but in service of God or man," says the man who has fallen into this snare. "I must first acquire knowledge, finish my term of service, re-establish my health, marry, secure a livelihood for the future. While attaining these ends, I cannot fully obey the demands of conscience; but having accomplished this, I will then begin to live exactly as my conscience demands."

Tolstoy notes that the victim so snared serves his or her own person, committing sins, such as sensual sin, the sin of idleness, of amassing property, of self-centered ambition, and even of depravity and intoxication. The victim does not regard such items as important, because the indulgence is to be only temporary, to last only during the time that all one's powers are directed to preparing for future active service of others. But having begun to serve one's person — protecting, strengthening, "perfecting" it — the object for which one is doing so becomes forgotten. One gives up the best years, sometimes one's whole life, in preparing to perform a service that never occurs.

> In the meanwhile, the sins so committed for a good object become more and more habitual; and, in place of the supposed useful activity for others, one passes one's whole life in sins which ruin it, and by serving as a temptation to others, injure them also. This constitutes the snare of preparation.

Perhaps more insidious is the family snare, wherein the needs of one's spouse and children — say, the costs of children's education — entice one to commit sins of avarice. It is sometimes observed that a person might make, in the course of a lifetime, just one underhanded financial "killing" at the expense of others, in order to be in position to do well by one's family, and others, for the rest of one's days. Again, others remain in jobs where they are compelled to spend their time at tasks that they know to be valueless or perverse; yet they stay because they have lucrative or prestigious positions.

There are other snares.[16] Tolstoy's examples show that people may not always choose the alternative that, at some point, they know to be truly their highest-ranked, most preferred value, failing to do so simply by willfully choosing to repress self-awareness of the thing that is to be ignored and hence forgotten. Or one may choose to block some piece of information from coming to awareness, such as the knowledge that, at some point, one knew better.

There is some pleasure, albeit an immoral one, in escape from responsibility. Immorality is always a choice between cheap pleasure and noble pleasure. In a conflict of values, the moral way is to choose a noble suffering now for the sake of more happiness in life on a long-range basis, setting aside the cheap, perverse pleasure. The motive in sinful choosing is to avoid paying the price of responsible care. One perversely holds this self-directed relief from responsibility to be more satisfying than the pleasure of integrity. That is, we may *choose* not to do the best we can in an ethical sense; we may repress from our minds our consciousness of the unwisdom of our choice, in order to escape from the pang of responsibility to stand up and do what should be done for the sake of all concerned on the long-range view.

We may indeed choose perversely, but this fact is to be subsumed under the present point, which is that, if hedonic motivation is real and universal, then we can choose to distort our decision-making process so that even choices made against one's own rational interests come out on top of the ranking of possible actions and are in this weak sense rational; else they would not be deliberately executed as they often are.[17]

An educated conscience will choose the noble alternative as being more personally satisfying, or less dissatisfying. There is a substantial *present* pleasure for the agent or actor in making a decision by this criterion; that is the substance of the motive. One has at the moment of decision a present interest in the future; the matter is not confined to the future.[18] Though such prudence may be exercised in the light of personal and divine happiness beyond the present, one nonetheless renders oneself better off in the present, not only later. Else one is not speaking of motivation as a psychological matter. Hartshorne declares, "To really love others is to find reward now in promoting their good."[19] As before, we may suppose that God shares in this kind of *present* pleasure and magnifies it in the divine life, knowing that it is associated with more pleasures in the future.

An ethically educated conscience is developed more readily in a human being who is brought up affectionately, which is a matter that has been discussed already. The point for now is that the argument from the existence of perverse behavior does not cut against the reality of rational psychological hedonism.

Is it psychologically possible to choose a course of action which one foresees as finally being evil *for oneself?* Is there such a thing as one's deliberately choosing a sum of experience that is predictably unpleasant *on the whole?* Some will answer yes, that masochists deliberately pursue suffering for its own sake. But the American ethical philosopher Philip Blair Rice rejoins, "What is called masochism can be plausibly accounted for by the tendency to replace a greater suffering by a lesser, as when we incur physical pain in order to distract ourselves from the greater suffering of anxiety, or when we punish ourselves to relieve feelings of guilt."[20] In a milder sense, a woman might welcome the pains of labor, since they mean that she won't have to carry the child around anymore. Thus, masochism may be an expression of some degree of rationality, an instance which may be subsumed under rational psychological hedonism.

It has been alleged that motivation, rather than being a unitary matter, is of two kinds, depending on the situation. The German-American psychologist Karl Duncker challenges the theory of happiness-motivation by seeking to show a fundamental chasm between two kinds of pleasure: the sensory pleasure of a glass of beverage on one hand, and the joy in the victory of one's cause on the other. In challenging the unity of motivational theory, Duncker notes that joy is the "pleasant consciousness that something we value has come about." Joy is always "about" something, he continues. "We rejoice 'over,' are glad 'at' something. In sensory pleasure the object, e.g., the wine, is a means sought on behalf of the experience caused by it. We aim at the experience. But in the joy [of having helped the good cause to win, Duncker says], the object, the victory of the good cause is not a "means." In hoping and fighting for it [Duncker continues], we do not aim at the experience of it. Much as we enjoy the victory, much as the feeling in knowing it is a pleasant one, we do not seek the victory in order to enjoy the feeling."[21]

"One cannot kill a difference," Duncker adds. We may agree that there is a difference, but is the difference one of essentially different motivation? Jonathan Edwards would consider the pleasure taken in the wine as an exercise in "private self-love," a matter of "pleasures and pains that are originally our own, and not what we have by a participation with others."[22] On the more joyous side of Duncker's dichotomy, one may include one's work — one's job or task — in the service of some cause or guiding aim. Sheldon notes that "We are happiest when in working we forget our happiness."

This is an aspect of the old paradox of happiness-pursuit: "Fly pleasures and they'll follow you." That is, "We have as it were to keep a secret from ourselves, and to hit the mark by pretending to look in the opposite direction."[23] Sheldon provides us with an answer to Duncker:

> Happiness is the motive for forgetting happiness, even for suffering the painful quality that attends toil and exertion. The athlete, striving his hardest to win the race, isn't thinking of the pleasures of victory; he is thinking of the race, the speed he needs, the closeness of his rival. But what is the motive power, forgotten during the struggle, that gave rise to the struggle? It is the joy of victory. Because the motive is usually beneath the surface-consciousness of the moment, the critic overlooks it.[24]

Henry Sidgwick offers a perceptive supplement:

> Our greatest happiness is generally attained by means of a sort
> of alternating rhythm of the two kinds of impulse in conscious-
> ness. A man's conscious desire is, I think, more often than not
> chiefly extra-regarding; but where there is strong desire in any
> direction, there is commonly keen susceptibility to the corres-
> ponding pleasures; and the most devoted enthusiast is sus-
> tained in his work by the recurrent consciousness of such
> pleasures.[25]

Sidgwick here has explained the observation of the British
economist Walter Bagehot: "Business is really more agreeable than
pleasure; it interests the whole mind, the aggregate nature of man
more continuously, and more deeply. But it does not look as if it
did." Although happy reflections flash in and out of consciousness,
we need not concentrate on happiness continuously in order for
it to be a motive.

In gazing at an apple, we don't concentrate on the quality of red
to see the apple, not any more than, while making a speech, we
need to recall the rules of grammar. Our time is spent *alternately*
in each of two modes: *inwardly* attentive and *outwardly* attentive.
While outwardly attentive, we are hardly aware of what is going
on in our heads, attending instead to what is outside each of us
without attending just then to how we feel. Even pain can be "gated
out" by suitably directed external attention (adults seem better at
this than children). Hence, explicit happiness-pursuit is possible
along with the quest of a cause or pursuit of business; thus Duncker's distinction is not a fundamental one. There is not "room" for
both kinds of thought — inward and outward — at exactly the same
time. These attentions should not occur at the same instants, for
trouble lies in that direction. Decades ago, a cartoon by Bud Fisher
shows Mutt and Jeff in a baseball game, near the outfield fence.
Each is running from different directions toward each other to catch
a fly ball. Each is looking only at the descending ball up high, and
each is saying to himself, "This catch will make baseball history."[26]

The English philosopher R. S. Peters objects to hedonic psychology
and ethics: "It is difficult to see what properties the alleged hedonic
states have in common [given all of their unique, hardly describable
qualities] if they are thought of as species under a genus." The

answer is simply the capacity of one's hedonic states to be *ranked* in the making of one's choices.[27] Embedded somehow in each of our minds, we may suppose that there is an ever-readjusted hierarchical array of countless remembered or anticipated possibilities of action — a ranked "bank," so to speak, or *rank-bank* of memories and anticipations. So far as we are rational, we sort out, evaluate and select, from moment to moment, the action that has the highest rank according to the *ranking criterion* of delight or satisfaction at the moment of decision, all things considered. To this end, we each rank possible choices to fit within our "rank-bank," even though the ranking is constantly influenced by novel experience, thought, and shifting inclinations, as Bosanquet has pointed out. To affirm the reality of this procedure is equivalent to saying that rational psychological hedonism is true and that the ranking criterion is hedonic.

Say you are reading a restaurant menu. You think of buying an ice-cream sundae for dessert. You choose to buy it or not, based upon your rank-bank of memories — that is, on your nearly lifelong file of remembered personal impressions of flavors and after-effects. You remember how good a hot-fudge sundae tastes when you are not eating one. A contrast or *evaluational discrepancy* is presented — to use Whitehead's term. Your remembered pleasantness is matched against whatever feeling you have aside from that remembered pleasantness. One point on the evaluational scale is where you want to be, and the other point is where you are.

The discrepancy motivates you to make a choice — i.e., to order the sundae or not to order.[28] A stimulus by itself is not a motive; the newborn baby who touches a hot stove may not instantly move its hand away, because it has not yet learned the value of doing so.[29] But a stimulus as contrasted to a remembered state — the memory of a past sundae — does constitute a motive. Thus at the critical moment, you come to *rank* the imminent eating of a sundae over not eating it. With experience, you may rank a hot-fudge sundae over a pineapple sundae, and both of them over a coffee-flavored sundae. Your overall scheme of rank ordering of possible courses of action is the unique pattern of your identity.

One element that influences the ranking process may be the prospect of becoming overweight (or more overweight). Again, you would not ordinarily prefer a sundae at the beginning of a meal, since your taste for the other foods might be dulled thereby; at such a time, you habitually elect — that is, confer top rank upon — the use of another hierarchy or ranking of foods. In that new situational ranking, the sundae does not come out high.

At first thought, your personal rank-bank should be just one hierarchy or ordered system of hierarchies at any given moment. However, a little reflection reveals that our multitude of scintillating evaluated possibilities or recallable memory elements cannot, at any moment, be precisely and unilinearly ranked into a linear spectrum of ready possibilities for choice, though we continuously and inevitably try. For such reasons, decision typically cannot be fully reasoned. In getting on with life, we all do the best we can at this. Or do we? As we have seen, deliberately perverse choice is possible.

By now we can affirm that deliberate pursuits all have in common the inward motive of "simple self-love," whether it be the drinking of Duncker's glass of wine, the anticipated joy of the victory of one's cause, the true love of others, or the consciousness of the "true virtue" of "benevolence to being in general." All these are inwardly motivated, involving in an inward sense one's pursuit of one's own satisfaction, even though at the same time there are always outward motivations that may regard something or someone else. All motivation is double-ended.

**SESAME STREET**®            by Cliff Roberts            May 26, 1972

Why do people do anything voluntarily or willfully? We may at last say simply that it is because, at the time of decision, they find the idea of it pleasant — that is, relatively pleasant. Most people who are innocent of philosophy would admit that this is at least part of the answer, that the thought of satisfactions or dissatisfactions does provide direction, at least in part, toward what they exert their will to do. If you asked them why they listened to music or played a tennis game or did anything that they did not regard as a means to something else, they would say that they did it because they enjoyed doing it. If you were to ask them why enjoyment or enjoyable activities motivated them, what would they say? There is only one appropriate answer, for the common person as for the scholar, namely, that no further explanation is needful or even possible. Common sense wins, strengthened however from its ordeal at the hands of philosophers.

Introspection strongly suggests that no one of us acts unless he or she feels that it is rationally more valuable to act than not to act. Nobody ever acts in a given way at a given time without having a motivation to act in that way at that time. Joy is the very essence of the experience of positive motivating value. Real value (joy) is our sense of well-being — our sense that something is rewarding enough to act for. Joylessness, or pain, is never an intrinsic value; it is never worth pursuing as an end in itself. Well-being, in the sense herein clarified, is always worth pursuing as an end in itself. We have found that there is neither need nor reason to suppose that motivation is basically other than unitary in essence. In this way, among others, the theory of rational psychological hedonism is confirmed.

So far as we are rationally pursuing value, are we then completely determined in our actions by the pursuit of the pleasant as we see it at the moment? Are we to conclude further that we have no intrinsic freedom but are determined in our respective courses as hapless slaves of whatever pleasure happens to seem the strongest at the moment?

To put the matter this way is to make a false distinction. In reality, the complex and ramified pattern of things that a person finds pleasant *is* one's identity as a chooser, a decider, an experiencer, a rememberer. Take away your preferences, and your identity would be that of someone else. "Take away my faults," says R. William Hazelett, "and I wouldn't be *me*." Moreover, to find something to be pleasant or the reverse is often an act of our free will, or of habits previously formed by the exercise of our free will. Recall now an earlier chapter, in which the importance of derived drive was discussed, wherein one's joy in a given pursuit was influenced by one's idea of what *ought* to make him or her joyous. For instance, a couple may appreciate their marriage partly because of their *decision* so to commit themselves. Or, one enjoys writing a book partly because one has decided to write it, thinking it helpful and important to do so. That is, though the strongest motive determines action, one's pre-existing priorities can determine the strongest motive.

More broadly, one has hereby a foundation for ethics in that he knows what to give to others in the way of feeling, because he likes that kind of feeling himself and, after this discussion, knows that he has the right to like it. Failing this knowledge, why should you give something to others about which you are dubious yourself? Such hesitation can cut against truly moral behavior. In such light, we need see no harm in supposing that rational psychological hedonism, asserting as it does the sovereignty of the delightful or joyous, is true but that it is also innocuous when fully understood.[30]

The theory of rational psychological hedonism is unfalsifiable since, as a matter of experience, its truth rests on the data it affirms, namely, the alleged fact that every instance of motivation involves pleasure in some sense and not necessarily anything else. In this respect, the theory hardly goes beyond common sense. As discussed in an earlier chapter, unfalsifiability in a scientific theory is usually fatal to the theory. However, in this instance, we may say that the truth of the theory rests most securely on the fact that it makes ethics as an intellectual endeavor possible. Otherwise we drift irrationally. This is an instance of truth known by coherence.

A popular saying, probably inspired by the early nineteenth-century German philosopher Arthur Schopenhauer, has it that one can do as one wills but that one cannot *will* as one wills. The message is that one's freedom of action, one's volition, is no more than apparently real, resulting perhaps, as Schopenhauer would have it, from the allegedly unchangeable nature of each person. As a general proposition, the saying is but a half-truth. Yes, we do build our character partly in response to the precepts and examples our parents put before us and the quality of our associates and teachers. Yes, one's parents and friends may have been less than ideal — likewise the schools one has attended. But we are all born with the potential to develop a conscience, and generally we do develop a more or less humane conscience that we can and should attend to, despite the strictures we have discussed.

Be that as it may, your authors argue that if you have read and understood this book then you have lost any right to complain much of your upbringing — that is, of the state of your volition resulting only from your upbringing. If you sin henceforth, then it will be because you have exercised your choice and must assume responsibility for the sinful choice that you have made. Schopenhauer, alas, lived and died much too soon to benefit from reading enlightened and realistic writing on the subjects of right and wrong and human freedom to choose.

**PEANUTS®**　　　　　by Charles Schulz　　　　　October 5, 1988

# 19

## *Joy, Spark of the Infinite*

Let joy be founded on reason, and then sorrow
will be a stranger to you.
*Dindimus, third century B.C.*

Man has no reason for devoting himself to
philosophy, other than to become happy.
*Augustine*

No man truly has joy unless he lives in love.
*Thomas Aquinas*

F OR MILLENIA there has been an antithesis between
the Greek and Judeo-Christian ideas of goodness, that is, between
reason and joy. As a result, a tension runs through the history of
Western thought between an ethics of reason on the one hand and
an ethics of feeling on the other. The history of Western ethics has
been in large part an attempt to define the part played in good
conduct by the Greek concept of ethics and by the Judeo-Christian
concept, and then to bring them into harmony without resort merely
to authority.[1] The present chapters exemplify the effort to unite the
two conceptions.

The contribution of ancient Greece to the study of reason, including logic and epistemology, would be hard to overestimate.
Though reason is mighty, it is not everything. Something about
experience makes it worth the trouble to apply reason to it, and
that something cannot be reason. Motivation is a matter of felt
value — of feeling. Hartshorne has said, "Logical argument implies
commitment to truth but, unavoidably, implies something within
that commitment, namely the motivation to consider the truth

important." We may conclude that reason is not to be regarded as existing for its own sake but is properly applied to furthering the pursuit of joy.[2]

In the previous chapter, we concluded that we in fact always do pursue happiness, satisfaction or joy so far as we can claim to be rational. This is a psychological matter and not itself an ethical one. However, it becomes a precondition of ethics since it enables one to regard others as having the same need for joy as oneself.

What makes one feel good is affected in large part by one's conscience, that is, by one's conviction that one is doing the right thing or that which *ought* to make one feel good. As discussed in an earlier chapter, the inward aim of opting toward one's own joy is not usually a selfish aim, and is not necessarily even a self-centered one. Finney notes:

> Many say, "Who will take care of my happiness if I do not? If I am to care only for my neighbor's interest, and neglect my own, none of us will be happy." That would be true, if your care for your neighbor's happiness were a detraction from your own. But if your happiness consists in doing good and promoting the happiness of others, the more you do for others, the more you promote your own happiness.[3]

Once one properly esteems one's own joy, then one's natural affection, i.e., sympathy, affords the motive to afford joy to others. One's own happiness is thereby promoted. A psychopath or sociopath may presume that he or she has no obligations toward others. That is the problem, not the aim at happiness which, being inescapable, cannot be regarded as a problem to be solved. Of course, society has set up a legal and penal structure to slant the pursuit of happiness of psychopaths by rendering some choices too expensive for them. What has been demonstrated herein is that one who aims to be rational will pursue his or her own happiness or satisfaction, whether this is done directly and unsuccessfully by continuously *concentrating* on *it*, or by the indirect but fruitful path of concentrating on productive matters involving other living beings.

As previously noted, John Stuart Mill, in his split-level secular utilitarian ethical philosophy, problematically proposes that pleasures be sorted into higher and lower ones. Mill's problem of motivating the pursuit of the higher pleasures is solved in theism. Mill may have suspected as much: his last written words imply a thwarted wish to become a theist.[4] Had he surmounted the intellectual roadblocks to religious belief, he could have solved the problems of his style of ethics. Like the other earnest, influential Victorian intellectuals, he failed to see how he could joyfully choose what was best. Finally lacking a basis for the needful distinction of higher and lower pleasures, the Victorians were left merely with Bentham's earlier utilitarian philosophy — a simple, unqualified atheistic utilitarianism.

Now that we see how the pursuit of the higher pleasures is best motivated, we may consider what these pleasures are. We concluded earlier that some pleasures would not please God as an all-knowing Person. Conversely, some "higher" pleasures would please God more than ordinary pleasures. One distinguishing characteristic of these higher pleasures is a concern for the future — even the remote future — as opposed to the merely immediate and sensuous. The more publicly oriented services pay off additionally in pleasures that continue for all. The difference is ultimately a matter of quantity, but of so much quantity in the cascading, cumulating effects that the higher pleasures may be said to be of "a higher dimensionality" than the merely sensuous pleasures.[5]

Hence, prudence pays off, for it affords continuing pleasures for oneself. "One ought to have as much regard for future good or evil as for present, allowing for differences in certainty."[6] Should you spend money for a pleasure trip now, a pleasure trip later, or use the money for the sound education of a child? To put the trip off decreases its certainty, but to spend the money for good schooling will multiply the potential of the child to enjoy life and to serve productively. Thus, the pleasure of providing the good schooling would be the higher pleasure, one in which you can surmise that God as Impartial Spectator and Seer would take more pleasure. When we comprehend this, we ourselves take more pleasure in this decision.

We may now consider some arguments of Jeremy Bentham, who is best remembered for elaborating the secular utilitarian ethical philosophy of universal happiness-promotion into a system of legal reform that has been deeply influential for good around the world.[7] In his ethical theorizing, Bentham suggests that the happiness of a society might be measured, and its prospective happiness calculated, by a "*hedonic calculus*" which is intended to become the basis for rational ethical decision-making. A person or a society would *rank* the possible courses of action and choose the actions of highest rank.[8] Bentham is concerned to promote actions that would increase the general happiness. In a dispute over a course of action, one would say, "Ladies and gentlemen, let us calculate."

The hedonic calculus is a bold suggestion, one that works smoothly in the case of evaluating flavors or odors. However, it presents problems when used in ethical decision-making. Even so, we must find in it a residue of validity if happiness is to be the ethical criterion, whether that happiness be vaguely and unsatisfactorily conceived as a sum of worldly happinesses or as the happiness of God, the Universal Sympathizer.

Critics have held that an agent would have to know the entire future of the world, the future of its people and their problems, in order to make rational ethical decisions. Critics add correctly that even if this detailed knowledge were obtainable, impossible amounts of time would be required to perform the calculations. Probably more time would thereby elapse than would elapse in the natural working out of events.

We do make fairly precise evaluations in economic matters, perhaps every day.[9] In the non-market part of life, one can make only general and probable projections of the results of one's actions. Still, critics may insist truly that it is hard to know even that much. The inventors of television hoped that it would be a more constructive influence than it has proven to be in our turbulent times. The fire fighter who saves a baby cannot know whether it will grow up to be a Joan of Arc or a Lucrezia Borgia, a Francis of Assisi or a Charles Manson. If it turns out to be a Charles Manson, who will blame the fire fighter?

But mathematical precision, while desirable, is not required. The tendencies of the motives of such actions to produce good are beyond dispute and, with increasing knowledge to guide the motives, they bring about still more good. The impatience of John Stuart Mill in answering objections along this line is understandable:

> This is exactly as if any one were to say that it is impossible to guide our conduct by Christianity, because there is not time, on every occasion on which anything has to be done, to read through the Old and New Testaments. The answer to the objection is, that there has been ample time, namely, the whole past duration of the human species. During all that time,

mankind have been learning by experience the tendencies of actions, on which experience all the prudence, as well as all the morality of life, are dependent.[10]

The human race has developed some rules worth relying on, for instance, the commandment, "Thou shalt not murder."[11] We evaluate actions according to their conformity to rules that have pointed generally the ways to personal and general happiness. Consequently, these rules themselves can be evaluated by their general hedonic results. We can and do fare without arithmetical precision in most of our affairs. Bentham observes that one does not need a thermometer to tell a hot day from a cold one.

But what of decisions to which rules seem not to apply? No rule can tell each of us whether it is truly best to learn carpentry or metalworking, secretarial work or accounting, or whether to buy a dog or a cat. Moreover, one's desires shift as one matures and as one learns from experience what works and what doesn't. Our ancestors wrested North America from the wilderness and the indigenous peoples, thus winning time for our generation to pursue material, scholarly, or effete interests. Knowledge and technology continue to advance. Some of the world progresses intellectually and perhaps morally. All these changes affect everyone's priorities. Thus, even if one calculus of personal or general happiness were to work at one time and place, it would need adjustments to do its work at another.

Even this residue of validity within a hedonic calculus must be qualified. In a profound critique, the early twentieth-century British philosopher Bernard Bosanquet objects that

> A pleasure which seems strong at first simply fades away in the light thrown upon it by a certain combination of objects of action. The prima facie magnitudes of pleasures and pains change their amount or their sign with the combinations in which they are considered, because of the way in which those combinations alter the direction of our interests and our wants. Interest, satisfaction, expected pleasure, are not constant magnitudes attaching to particular acts or objects, but are determined by the whole fabric of purposes and satisfactions which life presents before us from moment to moment. Now, it is the essence of deliberation to change this presentation by readjust-

ing the emphasis of its outlines, completing some and obscuring others. In this process some things which fell prima facie in a main line of interest are shown not really to be so. Other things, not attended to at first, take the place of the former and promise a satisfaction which they cease to offer.

Bosanquet offers a clarifying example:

A man is reading an ordinary novel with enjoyment. A newspaper comes in with exciting intelligence, perhaps with the continuation of a controversy in which he is profoundly interested. He does not subtract the enjoyment of going on with his novel from the great enjoyment of reading and discussing his newspaper, and turn to the second in virtue of the surplus of pleasure to be gained by doing so. The momentary adjustment of his interests is modified. The novel, for the time, has ceased to please. Our interest, as we say, is called away. This is not an effect of relations of magnitude. It is an effect of the peculiar bearings of the various objects of life upon one another, according to the shape which our plan of satisfaction is able to adopt at the moment. Relations of magnitude are the effect, but not the cause. It is as if one thing were not merely outweighed by another, but lost weight in a certain comparison, or as a colour which is pleasant in one combination becomes painful in another. The new fact is not, or at least need not be, pain of discord less pleasure of colour, leaving overplus of pain of discord. The colour is now differently seen, and now seen as painful throughout. And deliberation just means readjusting the combinations in which things are seen. The object itself is altered. There is not a persistent hedonic effect which is overbalanced.

Bosanquet deals with comments from the utilitarians:

It might be objected that these consequences cannot be lawless or irrational, and that if we knew the actual nature of the interests concerned we could, theoretically, deduce or derive their bearing on each other's hedonic effects from their nature, and this would be the required hedonic calculation. But my point is, that the laws of the combination, though certainly not irrational, are yet not arithmetical. They are the laws of the logic of desire, by which its objects include, modify, reinforce or supplant each other; and they deal in every case with the growth of an individual concrete whole, perpetually modifying itself. Deliberation which consists in a phase of the life of such a whole differs in principle from the type of [activity which is] calculation.[12]

Anyone who has watched a house cat slowly preparing to do something forbidden will have surmised that the cat weighs alternatives in a simpler way than we are apt to do. The cat's act of deciding may be largely that of addition and subtraction of motives and fading inhibitions. But in human motivation, we must affirm the truth of Bosanquet's observations.

After Bosanquet's critique of the idea of a hedonic calculus as a procedure for ethical decision-making for the good of all, is anything useful left? Despite every objection, the lack of viable alternatives requires us to take it completely seriously, though not with pencil and paper usually. In truth, we each select or choose actions according to how we feel about them, given our character, inclinations, information, and values. If we have each firmly taken as our absolute value the rule that we will glorify God — that is, increase His joy through increasing the joy of the creatures — then the following of this rule is our joy. In that case, we should trust our own private hedonic motivation, *untroubled by the thought that we shouldn't*, for our feelings then encompass all that is ethically relevant to us.

The valuing of states of consciousness, people, objects, or external affairs is comparative; it has degrees. Hence, notions of *better* rather than *good* are involved. Most often, to say that something is good is to say that it is better than the alternatives.[13] Turnips are better than nothing, but a better alternative might be strawberries and cream. Similarly, in order to rank alternative courses of action, the point is not to be able to call a prospective action good but rather to be able to call it better than its alternatives.

A study by Philip Brickman and associates shows that the experience of winning a large state lottery is apt to dull simple pleasures thereafter, in a kind of negative compensation. What was formerly good enough becomes no longer so, when one has at hand new and more impressive standards of comparison.[14]

Opponents of happiness-oriented ethics such as G. E. Moore have claimed that such an ethic commits the *"naturalistic fallacy."* This is a stumbling block alleged to invalidate the ethics of happiness-promotion. The naturalistic fallacy consists in identifying goodness with some natural characteristic, notably, humanly felt pleasure or happiness. If one defines the good as something so naturally sought after as human happiness, but still also uses the word in its ordinary

**THE FAR SIDE** by Gary Larson

*"Just think: Here we are, the afternoon sun beating down on us, a dead bloated rhino underfoot, and good friends flying in from all over. I tell you, Frank, these are the best of times."*

evaluative or prescriptive sense, then one is properly accused of committing a fallacy, that of confounding as identical two things that are not the same at all.[15] Indeed, if one erroneously follows David Hume, Charles Darwin, and Herbert Spencer in taking the innate, biologically normal feeling of sympathy for others as a *sufficient* foundation for ethics, then ethics means merely "doin' what comes natcherly," as goes the song from the operetta *Annie Get Your Gun.*

The objectors are conditionally correct, but their objection can be escaped here. Of course, it is comforting to learn from Darwin and others that sympathy and the capacity for altruism are given naturally in our biology — a hopeful fact. In the animal kingdom generally, cooperation is at least as normal as its contraries.[16] But we have unsocial feelings and impulses, too — even anti-social ones. Which are we to obey? If one's innate sympathy is not qualified by the effort to reason, the resulting behaviors, though partly altruistic, will not be reliably so. As the Canadian philosopher F. F. Centore observes, "In nature, everything is natural."[17] The various feelings and the behavior elicited by them are all equally "natural," whether constructive or not. If nature unqualified by reason is to be taken as our guide, then everything must be regarded as acceptable. In that case, is the human being to be considered merely natural and so in no need of reason in making ethical decisions? In such an incomplete view, the only thing that ethics could do is to clarify for us what our innate feelings of sympathy are and how important they may be.

That is the situation into which Darwin dropped ethics. But we must not suppose that one's study of biology or of the subdiscipline of "sociobiology" will inspire ethical behavior, for we are then studying merely what was already there and how it may have got there. In most species of mammals, parents naturally enjoy caring for and sympathizing with their offspring, and this natural pleasure is a motive for the care. But in humankind, much of the parental enjoyment comes from reason and hope — that is, from something more than thoughtless natural sympathy. This added human dimension makes the care more likely to occur, and at a high level.

The naturalistic fallacy is a real fallacy, but it is not committed in the present scheme, which avoids identifying individual, situational human pleasure with the corresponding contribution to God's pleasure. The jump between these two modes of value may be called the *naturalistic transformation*. This is neither a fallacy nor a blind "leap of faith." The relation between the two modes of value was described earlier where it was found that not every instance of human pleasure can be counted good. Those who draw attention to the naturalistic fallacy are properly objecting to the ways of thoughtless nature being taken as a touchstone for ethics, an error which would amount to supposing that we cannot ascend above nature, nor for that matter descend below it.

Ethics is more subtle than that. Albert Schweitzer says, "Ethics consists in this: that natural happenings in man are seen, on the basis of reflection, to carry within them an inner paradox. The more this paradox is removed into the sphere of that which goes back to instinct, the weaker do ethics become." One of Schweitzer's fine metaphors has it that altruism always appears in human nature as "the backward twin" of egoism, "who can be reared only with the most careful nursing."[18] Note Schweitzer's use of the word "natural" above, which he has extended to include reason. And why not? Both meanings are normally used.

The conclusions of ethics can be stated as imperative sentences, such as "Thou shalt not steal," or "Do unto others as you would be done by." The argument of David Hume to the alleged effect that values or statements of obligation cannot be derived from facts or factual statements remains highly influential in academic life at the present day. It remains at the root of ethical relativism, a position that, despite the fact that it cannot even be consistently stated, has largely taken over the educational establishments of the Western world at all levels. Hume is answered on his own ground in the Annex to this book in a discussion which, of necessity, is more abstract and technical than those so far. This demonstration will show that ethical commands and values are derivable from facts. The key technical device employed is here named *Bohnert's bridge,* after its principal discoverer, the American philosopher Herbert Bohnert.

Given that God is a caring Creator, we may suppose that He created us that we might pursue joy, for ourselves and for each other. J. C. F. von Schiller's "Ode to Joy" was made world famous in Beethoven's Ninth Symphony. In the first line, this eighteenth-century German poet and playwright speaks to "Freude, schöner Götterfunken, Tochter aus Elisium (Joy, beautiful spark of the gods, daughter of Elysium)." Despite Schiller's indecisive resort to classical paganism in this poem, the line is appreciative of the divine nature of joy.

The Bible and the Koran are replete with promises of joy for believers. The word "joy" and its derivatives such as "rejoice" and "enjoy" — also "delight" — appear about five hundred times in the Bible as attainable to believers and doers of the injunctions therein.[19] This emphasis is congenial to the overall ethical argument herein, the result of which may be called *theological utilitarianism,* in which the all-encompassing ethical criterion is the happiness of God, which we have concluded is served mainly through promoting the happiness of His creatures. Still, the end is not the happiness of God as wrapped up in Himself. Hartshorne writes, "Our God is the God of the creatures. We don't have to love God without the creatures."[20]

What about ordinary pleasure? Of course, the unqualified pursuit of pleasure is a grave danger. Yet Philip Yancey, quoted earlier, points out that creaturely pleasure, even in its misuse, bears witness to its proper function. If "Hypocrisy is the homage vice pays to virtue," then drug abuse is homage to true beauty, promiscuity is homage to sexual fulfillment, greed is homage to stewardship, and crime as a general shortcut is homage to genuine and lasting pleasure. Yet, pleasure becomes full and durable only when intentionally shared with God, eschewing the destructive routes to it. To repeat Yancey's questions: "Why is sex fun? Why is eating fun?" Why do we experience the pleasantness of colors and sounds?[21] Because these are God's gifts. God bestows them in fullness if we remember Him as our Creator. If there is another solution to the philosophical problem of pleasure, Yancy for one would like to hear of it.

Considerations of coherence have led us to the reasonable theological suppositions that God is an unselfish Creative Genius whose joy is primarily in giving, in benevolence. God experiences joy in receiving, simply because He is a person. God knows that we ought to love our Creator, and He has a need to be loved. If He had no need to be loved, then it would make no difference whether we loved Him or not.

In creating the world, God created a variety of goods. There is not just one kind of goodness. There is an infinite variety of beauties, and yet all are beautiful. Each one is a different kind of beauty. Unless one wants to end up with a cosmic soup of a monism which destroys all meaningful distinctions and eliminates the very multiplicity and variety that sustains life, one will presume that God has a variety of needs and seeks a variety of goods. Not only do God's creatures have a variety of needs, but so, too, does God. God does not need just simple joy; He needs a variety of qualitatively different kinds of joy. God's aim is to bring the greatest amount, the greatest quantity, the greatest sum of joy into the world, into His life and the life of His creatures. Yet, each instance of pleasure in us does not necessarily mean a corresponding pleasure in God.

As there is an infinite variety of beauties, so there is an infinite variety of truths, and there can be an infinite variety of joys. There is an infinite variety of experiences — even of divine experiences, we may speculate. God being a person surely craves variety. This means that He is not absolute simplicity but has a complex nature. The less one is able to understand this, the more dangerous one's theology will be. The more one's theology predicates simplicity in God, the more simplistic will be one's conduct of one's responsibilities toward Him. But such a consideration is not to be taken as a pragmatic argument for complexity in God's nature; we have already considered reasons to suppose that God cannot be less than a person.

If evolution is a correct theory, then simple self-love must have appeared on earth earlier than benevolence. Consider a person who has received and internalized sound ethical education. Which item qualifies as the ultimate factor in that person's motivation: the "simple self-love" implicit in rational psychological hedonism, or else concern for the happiness of God and all of being? Put this way, the question appears no more answerable than that of which originated first, the egg or the chicken. "Simple self-love" is the internal aspect of motivation. The motives are to be directed toward ethically oriented external motivating objectives. To take the one to the exclusion of the other is futile, for neither could exist without the other. At the human level, both self-love and benevolence toward all of being constitute an intelligible coherence.

In terms of practical moral judgment, responsibility is the key concept. Responsibility presupposes free choice between responsible and irresponsible alternatives for acting. In sinning, people exercise their freedom of choice irresponsibly and deceive themselves into thinking that they really are pursuing the maximum of joy. But in doing this, they make themselves their own victims. The ancient Greek philosopher Democritus presumably had this in mind when he said, "He who does wrong is more wretched than he who is wronged."[22]

Sin is not only perverse: it is, in sum, irrational. It is *irrational* to refuse to suffer now, to refuse to accept short-range pain in order to avoid paying the price for greater long-range happiness or benefits. But sin as a habit can be corrected in a way that it is not correctible when it is regarded, in the modern fashion, merely as "sickness." For instance, alcoholism, now usually classified as a disease, is a disease of a special kind, one from which the patient may not be anxious to recover.[23] Anger leading to injustice or crime amounts to emotion sinfully allowed to go out of control. Sin is correctible through the *choice* of virtuous action. Virtue is fully rational. Facing arrest at Gethsemane, Jesus paused, saying, "Let this cup pass from me." Yet, who will deny that He chose aright, even from His own point of view?

Egotism is self-esteem out of control. It is based on the self-deception that one is worthy in ways in which one is not. To be egotistical is to be in love with oneself to the disadvantage of others. Egotism is generally not obvious to those afflicted with it; hence it is even harder to control than the sexual instinct, which it exceeds in persistence. Egotism may cause one to thwart the talent of another when one is afraid of competition. In this way a person is sundered from truth, beauty, and constructive power. Augustine incisively states how to escape from this and other perversities:

> In all the wickedness men commit, they always desire happiness. A man steals. You ask: "Why?" For hunger, for need. So he is wicked for fear of being unhappy, and all the more unhappy for being wicked. For the sake of driving away unhappiness and obtaining happiness, all men do whatever they do, good or bad. They invariably, you see, want to be happy; but not all attain to what all desire. All wish to be happy; none will be so but those who wish to be good. And then, lo and behold, someone or other, although doing wrong, wants to be happy. How? With money, with silver and gold, with estates and farms, with houses and servants, with worldly magnificence, with fleeting and perishable honors. He wishes to find happiness in possessing something. Well then, find out what you want to possess to be happy. Look for what is better than yourself, so that by that means you may become better off than you are. Gold, even though you desire it, you may perhaps never possess; God you will possess as soon as you desire Him.[24]

# 20

## *Cultivation of Morality*

To what extent are we now living on moral savings
accumulated over many centuries but no longer
being replenished?

*Glenn Tinder*

The terrible danger of our time consists in the fact
that ours is a cut-flower civilization. Beautiful as
cut flowers may be, and as much as we use our
ingenuity to keep them looking fresh for a while,
they eventually die, and they die because they are
severed from their sustaining roots.

*D. Elton Trueblood*

HOW DOES A PERSON LEARN the fundamentals of ethics, these days? Such learning takes place hardly at all at public or secular schools. The American journalist George Will says, "Contemporary education often teaches that there is only one permissible ideal — a world cleansed of dangerous confidence in our ability to know the good."[1]

The philosophy of Cosmic Care culminates in the concept of the Universal Web of Love. Full comprehension of this concept requires an inner moral development that may be analyzed into successively elaborated steps. To have spelled most of these out is the contribution of the late American social scientist Lawrence Kohlberg.

Kohlberg's leitmotif is the concept of fairness. It develops from stage to stage. At level one, the base level, fairness is seen as bare, mechanical reciprocity, which does not go much further than the negative rule: "An eye for an eye, a tooth for a tooth." At level two, bare reciprocity is qualified by awareness that other people have needs that are like one's own and that each may justly pursue those needs. At level three comes the Golden Rule or empathy. Kohlberg quotes a ten-year-old on the Golden Rule: "Well, it's like your brain has to leave your head and go into the other guy's head and then come back into your head but you still see it like it was in the other guy's head and then you decide that way."[2]

To progress this far in ethics is important. The idea is not foreign even to many toddlers, a fact that makes one wary of taking Kohlberg's steps to be a strictly temporal succession. The Golden Rule is, by itself, not enough to settle the conflicting claims of two or more persons upon the agent. For instance, should one act on what one's parents want, or on what one's spouse wants? At level four, this problem can be faced, and some consistency achieved, by resorting simply to authority, either that of the state or of an authoritarian religion or, in pre-industrial societies, the elders and customs of the village — that is, to convention, law and order, without reasoning over the applicability of the convention or its validity. In level five, however, one does consider such questions. There, a person adheres to principles concerning, for example, rights and their reciprocity. From this there follows the obligation of honoring one's contracts.

In level six, Kohlberg's highest level, reflective and rational moral reasoning — "ideal role-taking" — is to be achieved. For Kohlberg, the full flower of ethical behavior in level six appears to be that of intellectually justified civil disobedience. Kohlberg, an atheistic humanist, encounters problems especially here. It is not clear that his level six is so distinguishable from level five as to justify designating it a separate level or developmental stage. Indeed, Kohlberg admits that the evidence is unclear.[3]

The obstacles to focusing Kohlberg's level six are not obstacles for those who have arrived intellectually at the concept of God as the Ideal Impartial Spectator. Properly speaking, level six is not realized without the concept of God's happiness, a happiness that, as we have seen, is to be regarded as partaking of our own.

Unfortunately, Kohlberg closes for himself this way out of his difficulties. After his misinformed statement that deceit occurs heretofore at only a low level in the Soviet Union,[4] and after ineptly lumping Islamic faith together with Christian faith, he concludes that "Religion is not a necessary or highly important condition for the development of moral judgment and conduct."[5] To support this judgment, Kohlberg refers to the 1928 study of Hugh Hartshorne and M. A. May which reveals, on the average, no significant correlation between the fact of one's receiving Protestant Sunday-school instruction and some testable points of the students' morality. But in our century, the Sunday schools have evidently diverged widely in this matter, and the study shows that divergence.[6] More positively, the evidence is overwhelming that Sunday schools in the nineteenth century were an important constructive force, indeed, a massive indirect political force — a matter well documented for England and seen plainly by Tocqueville in America.[7]

Kohlberg's cross-cultural comparisons of averages are striking in their diversity; they seem to contradict his own view that religious heritage is not important in eliciting moral behavior. He admits that one's knowing the good does not necessarily motivate one to do the good.[8] Otherwise, Kohlberg does not talk much of behavior. He champions the development of formal moral reasoning — that is, the cognitive or abstract side of morals as opposed to the affective or emotional side. He even says, "Affect is neither moral nor immoral."[9] If by this he means that the pursuit of individual pleasure in every circumstance is not necessarily either moral or immoral, we may agree. But if Kohlberg means that the pleasure or happiness of our fellows generally, or of God, is not a moral matter, we must most strenuously disagree.[10] This distinction parallels the one as to the market system and profit made in Chapter 2 herein. Kohlberg holds that children should not be instructed in virtues, that they will figure it all out for themselves when they are ready — a view so foolish as not to require response here.

Religious conversion generally brings about a favorable disposition toward moral ideas, but civilized morality is not created all at once upon conversion. In our culture, we are heirs of up to two thousand years of ancestral experience under Christianity, in addition to the early Judaic heritage of Christianity. All this has its cumulative effect upon each of us, whether or not one has had much contact with churches or synagogues.[11] Conversely, people who reject their ancestral faith do not shake off its influence suddenly. Christopher Dawson tells us that "A civilization cannot strip itself of its past in the same way that a philosopher discards a theory. The religion that has governed the life of a people for a thousand years enters into its very being, and moulds all its thought and feeling."[12] Dawson justly complains:

In fact every great civilization that exists in the world today has a great religious tradition associated with it, and it is impossible to understand the culture unless we understand the religion that lies behind it. This is accepted by the orientalist and usually also by the student of more primitive cultures. No one pretends to understand Arab or Persian culture without knowing something about Islam and the beliefs and institutions that are common to the whole Moslem world. Only in the case of Europe has this elementary consideration been neglected. We have had countless studies of Western culture and histories of European society which leave out Christianity or treat it as of secondary importance.

In the past all the great civilizations of the East and the West have recognized this world of spiritual experience as the supreme end of human culture in general and of education in particular. It is only during the last two centuries that Western man has attempted to deny its existence and to create a completely secular and rationalized form of culture. For a time the experiment succeeded, but only so long as it was carried on by men who had been trained in the tradition of the old humanist culture and who accepted its moral values and intellectual ideals with almost religious conviction. We are still living internally on the capital of the past and externally on the existence of a vague atmosphere of religious tolerance which has already lost its justification in contemporary secular ideology.[13]

The American author Herbert Schlossberg writes:

The good pagan is running on his memory and is receiving no sustenance from any external source. When he and his fellows begin wondering *why* they have those convictions and cannot come up with a satisfactory answer, the society begins coming apart at the seams. That is what is happening now.[14]

Dawson's theory of history contradicts that of Marxism, whose basic assumption is that economic and material forces ultimately explain not only what is but what can be. There is something to be said for Marxist determinism so far as people emphasize material goods as their main interest. So far as people emphasize matters that are more fruitful of happiness, such as theistic religion and ethics, the Marxist analysis is unhelpful. Even political forces seem more powerful than economic ones, as Sir Karl Popper suggests and as has been demonstrated anew by the events of 1989 in China.[15]

In observing the fortunes of Western religion of recent centuries, Whitehead observes, "Each revival touches a lower peak than its predecessor, and each period of slackness a lower depth."[16] The main reason surely is that the revival process has been making no substantial concession to the increasingly insistent claims of natural scientific facts. The highly successful revivalist Charles G. Finney did make substantial appeals to reason and facts —which, unfortunately, is not always true today. Hence the valid complaint has been heard that the churches in selling themselves hold aces but play deuces. Fundamentalists and ecclesiastical athletes do not, in general, care about an intellectual approach to religious belief, even when there is afforded thereby hope of verifying some of their basic beliefs.

Too often fundamentalists condemn their young, probing intellectuals to truncated, drab lives, rather than tolerating any serious questioning of the orthodoxies. Naturally, fundamentalists are reluctant to acknowledge that there could be any independent basis for sorting and picking through their religious beliefs. Indeed, their leaders exhort the followers to hold all tenets of their faith at the same unchallengeable level. Even though religious intolerance is largely the fear of being upset in one's own belief, we should respect the fragility of belief in some, lest we learn too late that an intellectual path can be too arduous or abstract for them.

At the opposite end of the religious spectrum, one finds religious liberals who are mainly interested in politics. Neither extreme need dominate, though moderates will be carelessly judged by extremists as being too light for heavy work and too heavy for light work.[17]

In having learned how ethics and theology are constructed and how they may be considered as publicly verifiable knowledge, one can hope the time will come when they will be taught in a manner similar to that in which other knowledge is taught.[18] It would appear that it is time for ethics and natural theology to be somewhat partitioned from philosophy so as to form a unified science, just as other sciences have been split off from philosophy. The publicly supported teaching of such a science should not be counted as "an establishment of religion" and so ought to escape this stricture in the First Amendment of the U.S. Constitution. The last words about this science have hardly been stated here, yet no claim is made that all of theistic religious belief must come under the heading of science. No ceilings have been set herein. But the time is approaching even for specialists to put much of the history of philosophy into the background. We should take seriously certain constructive modern philosophical writings that are mostly ignored.

Well-known philosophers of modern times have had disappointingly little to add to ethics beyond the adventurous investigations of the ancient Greeks. If the study of philosophy puts one in mind of a vast junkyard, it remains true that a valuable implement may occasionally be found in a junkyard. Experts can find these and are always helpful in pointing out what is junk and what is not.[19]

Some modern philosophers have explicitly denied the possibility of ethical knowledge, for example, Ludwig Wittgenstein, Rudolf Carnap, Charles L. Stevenson, Albert Camus, Lord Russell, Sir Alfred Jules Ayer, and Jean-Paul Sartre.[20] Such thinkers have created a wasteland and then called it ethics. Were they all sincere? One may have doubts; there are too many ways to "cop out" of responsibility by pseudo-intellectual means. Many students seek through philosophy a way to avoid personal responsibility, though not always consciously — which may help to explain the creation of some modern philosophical movements. Jaki reminds us that "While

**DOONESBURY**          by Garry Trudeau          June 23 and 24, 1987

immorality was rampant even in times characterized as Christian, it was at least not systematically talked away."[21]

We have considered why the popular views denying the possibility of ethical knowledge are self-contradictory gibberish when expressed. It is no wonder that Paul the Apostle cautioned the Colossians: "Beware lest anyone spoil you through philosophy and vain deceit."[22] In reviewing Paul's warning, we may note that some things haven't changed. The English essayist William Hazlitt says, "The worst kind of disputing is that which tends merely to overturn, without establishing any thing. For I can have no right to pull down my neighbour's house till I have furnished him with materials for building a more convenient one."[23] Lovejoy muses:

> Reason, as the history of philosophy and that of religion abundantly show, has a perverse inclination to turn against the business and traditions of the house of which it is sprung and from which, in truth, it derives all of its support. The hardwon capital of life is thus turned against the ends of life. In intellectualist philosopher, in ascetic moralist, in other-worldly mystic, the will to live, active even here, is strangely set in activity against itself.[24]

The basic sin of modern philosophy is its refusal to think big. The British philosopher and humanist Bertrand Russell advises his fellow philosophers to attempt to solve only small problems and not to tackle the allegedly overambitious task of building a viable and coherent system — advice obviously not followed here. One may now see broadly how the general good, conceptualized as God's good, can become the interest of each and all. With this knowledge, ethical behavior should be intrinsically enjoyable and hence more likely to occur. Even those who erroneously remain skeptics should entertain the idea that the moral psychology of Western civilization has been delineated herein.[25]

We can now see how profoundly misleading and shallow is the evaluation of theistic religion delivered by Russell in his book *Why I Am Not a Christian.* He holds forth: "Religion is based, I think, primarily and mainly on fear. It is partly the terror of the unknown, and partly the wish to feel that you have a kind of elder brother who will stand by you in all your troubles and disputes. Fear is the basis of the whole thing — fear of the mysterious, fear of defeat, fear of death." This book of Russell's contains many examples of cleverly phrased bad reasonings and half-truths. Yet it is hard to think of a more influential modern book among college students.[26] The damage done by such writers exceeds that done by whole armies in the field. Yet, similarly misleading writers continue to be supported in prestigious academic positions and receive countless honors.

Russell and other skeptics deny themselves the key that would enable them to build an acceptable philosophical system. Previous approaches to theistic religion have all suffered from the fact that, the more one learns about traditional religions and about the world, the more one finds unanswered, troubling questions. The same is true of atheistic philosophy. The opposite happens with the moral psychology and philosophical theology of Cosmic Care. The more a person knows about it, the less pressing are the remaining questions and the stronger one may become. Cosmic Care is the worldview upon which informed opinion appears destined to converge into an ultimate unanimity.

There is a special irony in the example of Russell. His diatribes against Christianity are blunted by his following candid report, late in life:

> I had never before been in Greece and I found what I saw exceedingly interesting. In one respect, however, I was surprised. After being impressed by the great solid achievements which everybody admires, I found myself in a little church belonging to the days when Greece was part of the Byzantine Empire. To my astonishment, I felt more at home in this little church than I did in the Parthenon or in any of the other Greek buildings of pagan times. I realized then that the Christian outlook had a firmer hold upon me than I had imagined. The hold was not upon my beliefs, but upon my feeling. It seemed to me that where the Greeks differed from the modern world it was chiefly through the absence of a sense of sin, and realized with some astonishment that I, myself, am powerfully affected by this sense in my feelings though not in my beliefs.[27]

Jaki relays to us Russell's plea for "Christian love or compassion," delivered at Columbia University in 1950.[28] Such revelations are dizzying, in view of the incalculable spiritual, moral, and political damage done by Russell's writings. "The greatest of all thefts," Jaki has said, is "the one which deprives man of God."[29] But perhaps the reputation of philosophy may yet be redeemed, even in Christian, Jewish, and Moslem circles.

In the cultivation of morality, the world can learn from China. The esthetic and ethical residue of China's ancient theistic religion thoroughly penetrated many aspects of life and is evident even today at all social levels.[30] The original light of ancient Chinese theism shone brightly on the Chinese, but the light has long since been only that of an overcast sky. Nevertheless, it has been adequate to the support of their pervasive cultural ideals. In the West, the sun of theism has shone, between thunderstorms, upon turbulent, separate and incompatible groups. From the Chinese experience we can infer that even a diffuse, vague religious ideal can contribute mightily to the quality and technical achievement of a people when that ideal is generally and persistently held. How much more, then, might a reasoned theism achieve since, being supported by reason, it too could be generally and persistently held.[31]

So far, we have defined pleasure, happiness or joy only negatively or sketchily. No positive verbal definition can be fully adequate, but we can posit that pleasure or joy is that which makes integrated motivation conceivable and coherent. Stated in a more novel way, joy is that which fulfills psychical *need*. All deliberate action is thus rooted directly or indirectly in need. Life is pursuit. Need is a liking for something good — a correction of genuine lack.

"Need was the first experience," writes the American sociologist William Graham Sumner, "and it was followed at once by a blundering effort to satisfy it."[32] One starts with need; otherwise, there is no need to start. If a person didn't need anything, then there would be no logical foundation for an act. Before people will pursue joy, they first have to feel a need that calls for satisfaction. They then may act to satisfy that need which pains them or makes them feel dissatisfied.

Life's most basic need is for need itself. Without need, life would seem needless, and hence senseless. One has to have potential joy, actual joy, and real need, before there is any responsible motive to act at all. Motivation is the felt tension between need and potential joy. Potential joy is known through past joy. There is a categorical need for need; it is intrinsic in human nature.

Also, there is a need for desire. Desires are justifiable to the extent that they fulfill need. But some desires are unjustifiable: they frustrate both need and the attainment of joy. One may desire something that is bad for one, but one does not *need* it: a person does not need to be joyless and does not need selfish joy.

As there are various joys, so are there also various needs that these joys fulfill. To act intelligently to fulfill a need, one has to know what the need is about. There are vital life needs that all human beings share, although not always consciously. Eighteen are listed here. These may well be regarded as crucial to any practical study of human nature. They are to be distinguished from mere desires, which may be falsely regarded as genuine needs. These are:

1. The need to be loved and to love.
2. The need for positive self-esteem.
3. The need for self-discipline, for a sense of accountability for one's decisions and acts.
4. The need for a sense of personal accomplishment — a sense that one has done something, or produced some effects in the world that are of lasting importance.
5. The need for a basic sense of security, a feeling of well-being.
6. The need for emotional and intellectual integrity — an inner order, a unity of being.
7. The need for freedom of self-expression, self-realization, and growth.
8. The need for intrinsically valuable knowledge (those things that are always worth knowing).
9. The need for constructive creativity (to bring fresh effects into one's life and the world).
10. The need for the ability to communicate constructively, both with oneself and others.
11. The need for a communion with nature, namely, finding intrinsic value in the world around one.
12. The need for a sense of priorities — that is, for a knowledge of intrinsic values, whereby one can distinguish between what is important and what is trivial.
13. The need for faith that existence makes sense — that one's life in the world has a permanent rationale.
14. The need for faith in the conservation of values.
15. The need for beauty.
16. The need for hope.
17. The need for a compassionate and constructive sense of humor.
18. The need for unselfish happiness or joy — joy that regards the joy of others.

The last need includes all the others, as we have seen. The difficulty of accurately assessing one's real life needs, and the needs of others, sometimes is very trying, and under complex circumstances may be impossible. But the problematical nature of implementing this ideal in practice (correctly assessing and fulfilling these needs) does not undermine the validity of the ideal in principle, nor alter the fact that the endeavor of pursuing it is crucial. It only obligates us to continue to seek for a successful means of implementing it. Countless volumes already have been written on practical methods of fulfilling these needs.

In summary, our basic ethical obligation is to bring the greatest amount of need-fulfillment — that is, joy — into life as a whole on a long-range basis — and the least amount of need-frustration — i.e., joylessness or suffering — into the lives of humankind, the other creatures, and God, whose needs and joys include those of all the creatures. The purpose of ethics is to guide and motivate action by distinguishing between justifiable and unjustifiable desires, between real life needs and imagined needs. The right thing to do is what most *needs* to be done. Modern culture has produced much unhappiness because its kaleidoscopic glitter and tinsel distracts persons from some of their real life needs, especially their integrity and their need to know and to serve God.

The imperative of any sound philosophy of morality is that we seek to find ways to act that will bring about as much joy into life as possible — into our own life, into our fellow human beings' lives, into the lives of the other creatures, and into God's life. We are well advised to make the joy imperative our personal "law," unmuddied by any and all pressures and false admonitions to the contrary. We ought in this sense to "learn to become [better] hedonists,"[33] using this term in its non-pejorative root sense. We ought to allow superior satisfaction to be "the cement that makes learning stick."[34]

> In the world to come, each of us will be called to account for all the good things God put on earth and which we refused to enjoy.
>
> *Benjamin Franklin*

> Power makes no noise. It is there, and works. True ethics begins where the use of language ceases.
>
> *Albert Schweitzer*

# 21

## *Homiletic Epilogue*

And let those learn, who here shall meet,
True wisdom is with reverence crowned,
And science walks with humble feet
To seek the God that faith hath found.

*Caleb T. Winchester*

THE CULTIVATION OF MORALITY through theology inevitably tends toward preaching. Homiletics when presented to a philosophical audience is apt to result in the loss of that audience. Among many philosophers, argumentation is a form of sport held to be more important than finding useful conclusions and making corresponding commitments. For where conclusions are reached, little is left to argue about. The present chapter reaches beyond argument.[1]

Ultimate reality centers around *Care* — not perfection as supposed in Greek philosophy, but Care as proposed in Judeo-Christian cosmology. God *is* love — a love that is absolutely righteous, long-suffering, patient, creative, and sacrificial. This is what constitutes His perfection. In a world order where there is no risk that things can go wrong, nobody would have to exercise any responsible care to see that things go right. In a world in which there was no risk of failure, nobody could feel the need to act carefully to succeed in doing what ought to be done but which will not be done unless one acts carefully to see that it is done. Ultimate reality is Care (God), and care is inconceivable for either God or His creatures where there is no need, risk, freedom, challenge and responsibility.

In a world in which no evil could possibly happen, we could have no meaningful concept of God and we could not exist as human beings experiencing our free will. God exercises power in an absolutely rational way and in an absolutely loving moral way. But there are self-imposed limitations on this divine power, and these are primordial in the divine nature. The possibility of some *unnecessary* evil is itself a necessity, one that may be regarded as good because, without it, care here below could not emerge. And care is what ultimate reality is about, not absolute bliss.

Well-chosen Judeo-Christian scripture offers a drastic shortcut to ethically relevant knowledge. The authors of the present work have allowed their ancestral Christianity to be refined by the life of the mind. They owe a most special rever ?nce to Jesus of Nazareth, born and raised a Jew, whose influence shaped the better parts of Western civilization. Indeed, we find that most of what we have finally learned about God by an intellectual route, we had first learned as children from being told of Jesus, the friend and protector of little children. God, we must conclude, is like Jesus. Informed peoples of whatever theistic persuasion may reflect on Paul's insight that, in Jesus, "all things *hold together.*"[2]

Without such an exemplary figure, theism is apt to be a vague, abstract business. Christians commonly hold that Jesus is more than exemplary, that He is divine, the literal Son of God, and that God exists as the primordial Holy Family in three persons. If seen only as an abstract, disembodied non-personal being, God may be unable to command the general allegiance of us more limited minds to whom it may seem that "life is human relations, the rest is tinsel."

Can a further-extended coherence theory of truth be applied to make a case for the divinity of Jesus? William Ernest Hocking finds reason to think so. He compares the Christian faith with other faiths:

> The stricter monotheists (Jews and Moslems) consider that they have still to wage the fight against idolatry in the other religions. The Trinity is interpreted by them as a limited polytheism: the Koranic refrain to the effect that Allah neither begets nor is begotten is directed against it. Nevertheless, these religions also have their own mediators and their mystics; their own origins

are referred to some kind of conversation between God and man; they also cannot do without the human aspect of God.

And while the doctrine of the Trinity remains a mystery over which subtleties may be endlessly poured out as intellectual libations, in its total tangible effect it is an admonition that pure monotheism is not enough, whereas tri-theism is too much and too many; the true idea of God lies between them; it must at least contain a procession out of the infinite reserve into the life of the universe and of men, and without abandoning its absolute self-hood. This doctrine is probably much more valuable as a mystery to be jealously guarded from solution than in any possible philosophical translation. For as a mystery, it stands simply for the indispensable parameters of any tenable idea of God.[3]

Nearly a century ago, before the modern solvents of faith had penetrated widely, the British theologian and minister Andrew Martin Fairbairn wrote his monumental volumes entitled *The Philosophy of the Christian Religion* and *The Place of Christ in Modern Theology*.[4] It is indeed unfortunate that Fairbairn, a thinker with such an extraordinarily penetrating mind, is now virtually totally unknown to the world of Christian intellectuals and scholarship. This is one of the saddest ironies of intellectual history, that those who have had the most to contribute to it have become forgotten before their influence could take hold deeply and spread widely.

Neither Fairbairn nor Hocking refer to the "coherence theory of truth" and have not developed the concept in the same manner or to the same degree of elaboration as has been done herein. Nonetheless, Hocking and Fairbairn are in effect applying it in order to make sense out of the concept of the Trinity, but they are not unique in this. In considering the history of Christology, one may see a striving for coherence in many places, as in the works of Thomas Aquinas. A caution must be repeated, namely, that a proper application of the coherence theory of truth must embrace with consistency everything that is, while at the same time Ockham's razor must be kept well honed, lest concepts be multiplied needlessly.

Although he did not use a term like "coherence theory of truth," Finney applied it in his practical writings about the relationship between God and humankind. For instance, he elaborates Paul's insight that one can coherently perform both one's earthly duties and one's service to God. He comments at length on the standard excuses for spiritual escapism. Finney hears a mother ask:

> "How can I be religious? I have to take care of all my children." Indeed! and can't you get time to serve God? What does God require of you? That you should forsake and neglect your children? No, indeed; He asks you to take care of your children — good care of them — and *do it all for God.* He says to you: These are *my* children; and He puts them in your hands, saying: Take care of them for Me, and I will give thee wages.

> The farmer pleads: "I can't be religious; I can't serve God — I must sow my wheat." Well, sow your wheat; but *do it for the Lord.* If God did require us to serve Him in such a way as would compel us to neglect the practical duties of life, it would be truly a hard case. But now the whole truth is, that He requires us to do precisely these duties, and do them all honestly and faithfully *for Him,* and in the best possible manner. Let the farmer take care of his farm, and see that he does it well, and above all, do it *for God.* It is God's farm, and the heart of every farmer is God's heart, therefore let the farm be tilled for God.[5]

The right spirit of prayer, performed in some way, is more important to ethical behavior than nonbelievers can know. The main point of prayer is our need to be reminded continually that all happiness, all value, is ultimately one, and of everlasting significance in God's Universal Web of Love. Thereby, the believer remembers his or her right relation with all that exists, by acknowledging the reality and the love of the Entity whereby joy becomes real. If we enter into this right relation, our own wishes gain an impetus toward fulfillment. To give thanks for what we have is a proper part of prayer, but the primary thanks is that of the ancient doxology: "We give thanks to Thee for Thy great glory."[6]

Johann Sebastian Bach made this passage the climax of his glorious masterwork, the Mass in B Minor, the foremost of the hundreds of musical compositions by which he expressly hoped to make people better Christians. He would modestly sign his manuscripts, "S. D. G." standing in Latin for "Soli Deo gloria" (To God alone be glory).[7] This may seem to be attributing egotism to God, but a previous conclusion based on considerations of coherence may be sharpened by Finney who says, "God seeks his own happiness, or glory, as the supreme good. But not because it is his own, but because it is the supreme good." Hartshorne amplifies this:

> God cannot benefit another without benefiting himself. In his case self-interest and altruism are indeed coincident, but not because he is clever enough to do us good so as to satisfy his own egoistic desires. He has no egoistic desires, if words are properly used. He wants only to enjoy creaturely good, seeking for the creatures the happiness they seek for themselves.[8]

You cannot make anyone feel a need for God by making abstract arguments for His existence. To make somebody feel a need for God, when it can be done at all, you must bring into that person's life some values that are so priceless, some beauties that are so exquisite, some meanings that are so profound that it makes that person feel a need to find some way to conserve them permanently. And that need becomes a need for God. In short, the individual has to find some *great joy*. The only thing that can bring that joy into a person's life is love. Abstract theological arguments or abstract metaphysical arguments cannot bring into a person's life the experience of love. One has to experience that first.

You cannot make anybody feel a need for love by arm-twisting. People cannot be compelled; you cannot force love; you have to give them some concrete life values that are so great that it makes them feel a need to conserve them permanently. Then, when they see the value of that love, when they experience it concretely, it makes them ache. People get security from God, but unless they have some security to start with, there can never be an open relationship with Him. The only way we know to help atheists is to love them.

Once people feel this need, the second requisite is to understand the possibility of its realization. They first have to see the need for God, and then secondly, see the unmistakable factual and logical possibility that He can and indeed must exist. Once they see that the existence of God is at least a logical possibility — indeed, a necessity for the sake of intelligibility and love — then thereafter it is no longer a question logically whether they can or cannot believe; it becomes a purely personal question of whether they will or will not believe, i.e., whether they *want* to or not. So, once people feel a need for God and then see that the arguments against His existence are tissue-paper, they then have to decide, and that is the third requisite. At that point, if one *decides* to believe in God, the resulting belief will not be the result of environmental conditioning but the result of one's own experience of truly felt religion, which then becomes a truly meaningful part of oneself. Belief is most meaningful when one decides to believe. It is not really a part of oneself in the deepest sense unless one has decided to believe.[9]

We hope that the spirit of Jesus will come to touch the lives of people in the professions of philosophy and psychology and ultimately to touch all. There is a vast, untapped reservoir for faith in those brilliant, promising persons who have slipped into humanism, socialism, statism, or Communism as quasi-religions. Hopefully, young people can be spared the sorrow of irretrievable errors and the despair of forsaking the ideal of the examined life. Inspired youth can lead with new ideals better than those elders who are fearful and who are engrossed in the problems of security, whose minds often are proven by the facts to be overflowing with useless knowledge that has resulted in generations of failures in the fields of applied religion, marriage, morality, loving one another, politics, economics, and peace.

Woodrow Wilson writes, "Societies are renewed from the bottom." The tragic failure of the successful to follow up their worldly success in abiding spiritual ways, or even in abiding material ways, becomes the opportunity of the underprivileged and the downtrodden. Yet, these lowly people may not be underprivileged in the matter of religious belief, since they may not have had enough money to become students of aggressively atheist professors. Women should make themselves more prominent in philosophy, psychology, and theology than they have heretofore.

What you do can make a difference. That is an exciting thought. When taken seriously, the whole course of one's life can be greatly affected. Schweitzer writes:

> You are fortunate, they say; therefore you are called upon to give much. Whatever more than others you have received in health, natural gifts, working capacity, success, a beautiful childhood, harmonious family circumstances, you must not accept as being a matter of course. You must pay a price for them. You must show more than average devotion of life to life. To the fortunate, the voice of the true ethics is dangerous, if they venture to listen to it. It assails them to see whether it can get them off their smooth track and turn them into adventurers of self-devotion.[10]

Young people should ignore all adults who do not follow the Commandment to love one another. The youth of the world should train their minds for the task of spreading the principles upon which a world of peace and happiness may be built. They should associate with altruistic people; this factor is of great importance and is often neglected in psychology and counseling, though Paul the Apostle did not neglect it.[11]

So far, the human race has coped with adversity better than with prosperity. It is conceivable that the West in its present irreligion, corruption, frivolity, ignorance, and general self-indulgence has too much backward momentum to save itself. Many peoples of Europe and a growing number of people in America have become shut off from hearing or pondering any intellectual understanding of cosmic reality or even day-to-day news critical to their future.[12]

Fear and despair help to explain one's willful avoidance of bad news. Those who depend on a humanist faith can hardly bear to hear that their faith isn't working. Some politicians and powerful men deliberately lead the public to despair of political progress, in order to manipulate them into passivity. The muckraking reporter Lincoln Steffens learned in Philadelphia eighty-five years ago that unscrupulous politicians can commit so many abuses so quickly that the public may become bewildered and lose hope. Boss Iz Durham confided to Steffens that "public despair is possible" and is "good politics." The lesson has been learned by others.[13]

Schweitzer expresses a "hearty admiration" for the work of American and French missionaries in central Africa:

> It has produced among the natives human and Christian characters which would convince the most decided opponents of missions as to what the teaching of Jesus can do for primitive man. In proportion as he becomes familiar with the higher moral ideals of the religion of Jesus, he finds utterance for something in himself that has hitherto been dumb, and something that has been tightly bound up finds release. Thus redemption through Jesus is experienced by him as a two-fold liberation; his view of the world is purged of the previously dominant element of fear, and it becomes ethical instead of unethical.[14] The Gospel of Jesus in its very essence aims at being the supreme ethical enthusiasm.[15]

Frank Laubach, the American missionary who devised many phonetic written languages for the world's peoples, devised also the effective pedagogical method of "Each one teach one." A generation ago, he wrote a book called *Wake Up or Blow Up: America: Lift the World or Lose It*.[16] In this concern, he is surely right. Laubach leads his readers to imagine that they are teaching an illiterate. You are apt to be "the first educated man who ever looked at him except to swindle him," and he "will be so mystified by your unusual kindness that he is likely to stop and ask: 'How do you expect to get paid for this?' " Then, Laubach says, you have your chance to say:

"I do not want any pay. I have learned this from Jesus. He spent all His time helping people free of charge. From the moment He awoke in the morning until He closed His eyes at night, He was looking around asking whom He could teach, or heal, or encourage, or defend, or save. I think that is a beautiful way to live. If we were all like Jesus, this world would be a paradise. So I thought I would try helping people just because I love them. And I have discovered the secret of happiness! When I am teaching you it makes my heart sing. When I have finished teaching you, I want you to go and teach your neighbors. Don't take any money for it, and your heart will sing!"[17]

The fruits of Laubach's efforts have fallen largely to political opportunists as indeed he feared they might. Religious missionary efforts have lost most of their effectiveness, because, it appears, they did not address the sort of questions that have been treated herein and so too often have failed to build a Fellowship of Mind and Heart.

We have seen that China enjoyed a monotheistic culture in the mists of remote past time, between four and three millenia ago. One wonders whether the Chinese will rediscover their forgotten heritage — a heritage which they may have first discovered and which was the source of the spiritual and intellectual power of Western civilization. Will the inquisitive minds among the Chinese peoples thereby find within themselves a motivation to do basic science and nation-building that would extend and exceed the achievements of the West? If Asians were to rediscover their theism, could they save the West from itself?

If theism were added to their work ethic and the humane Confucian values such as self-control, mutual service and forgiveness, it would be a magnificent combination. Whatever the deficiencies of Confucius, he was among the greatest of civilization builders. Christianity in China survived the brutal efforts of the "great Cultural

Revolution" to exterminate it. The segments of Christians who went underground and have now come into the open are said to have grown to something like 50 million. In 1949 there were only about 4 million. This history appears to parallel that of the Roman empire when Christianity, on being driven literally underground, survived, flourished, and ultimately became dominant.

Hopefully, the world may yet learn how to cope with prosperity without losing its way. In the ensuing scientific and material success of those who find the way, there may be pleasant occasion to reflect on the injunction: "Seek ye first the kingdom of God and His righteousness, and all these things shall be added unto you."[18]

The providence of a loving, caring God is, all things considered, the only plausible worldview, all the others being less credible. Upon this worldview one may base a lasting personal happiness and the power to rebuild civilizations. No "leap of faith" is required. Rationally, the chief end of humankind is to glorify God. This means that we are to increase God's joy by celebrating His being, by delighting and pleasing Him and the creatures, through His endless Web of Love forever. One may even dare to hope that humankind is on the verge of moral progress that will surpass any in recorded history.

The ultimate practical response to the problem of the existence of evil is, after all, to use our God-given abilities to quash evil — both natural evil and human evil. Some Christians, by invoking original sin, deny the possibility of moral progress. This book denies that denial without denying the possibility of sin. One may now hope that intelligence will become noticeably correlated with benevolent conduct — a situation that has been only weakly observed heretofore.[19]

With the present newly backed knowledge, readers should find it decidedly more fun to be ethical than not. In this way, their children, sensing their parents' joy, may follow after them. The contrasting choice is stated repeatedly in the Hebraic prophetic scriptures. Amos announces:

> The time is coming, says the Lord God,
>     when I will send a famine on the land,
> not hunger for bread or thirst for water,
> but for hearing the word of the Lord.
> Men shall stagger from north to south,

> They shall range from east to west,
> seeking the word of the Lord,
>   but they shall not find it.
> On that day fair maidens and young men
>   shall faint from thirst.

Isaiah looks further forward:

> Young men may grow weary and faint,
> Even in their prime they may stumble and fall;
> but those who look to the Lord will win new strength,
> they will grow wings like eagles;
> they will run and not be weary,
> they will march on and never grow faint.[20]

Lincoln said, "Most folks are about as happy as they make up their minds to be." That was truer among the generality of nineteenth-century Americans, who were religious, than for nonreligious folk. From that period comes the proverb, "Those who bring sunshine to the lives of others cannot keep it from themselves." A Dutch friend, Charlotte Beckers, tells us that, in Europe, people do not laugh much anymore. In some urban areas of America, smiles are hard to come by. Some among us are like the gingerbread children in Humperdinck's charming opera *Hansel und Gretel* who, while still half under the dead witch's spell, sing softly: "O touch me, that I may awake."[21]

To generalize the fine American patriotic hymn of Katherine Lee Bates, we are admonished not to stop building our societies

> Till all success be nobleness,
> And every gain divine!

So high an ideal may be beyond the possibility of this world. Only if we do not despair shall we even passably approach it. Meanwhile, we in the West should heed the observation attributed to George Bernard Shaw: "The world's best reformers are those who start on themselves." Miss Bates continues more specifically:

> Confirm thy soul in self-control,
> Thy liberty in law![22]

Jonathan Edwards, anticipating the heavenly city on earth, describes the day when "all the world shall then be as one church, one orderly, regular, beautiful society."[23] It will be

> a time when the whole earth shall be united as one holy city, one heavenly family, men of all nations shall as it were dwell together, and sweetly correspond one with another, as brethren and children of the same father — a time wherein this whole great society shall appear in glorious beauty, and excellent order, as a city compacted together, the perfection of beauty, an eternal excellency shining with a reflection of the glory of Jehovah risen upon it, which shall be attractive and ravishing to all kings and nations.[24]

Is Edwards' vision a realistic hope in our time? We may be already too far sunken in the quicksands of sin to actualize such an ideal life on earth, unless some truly miraculous changes occur. Sometimes, it appears that nearly everything good is being frittered away. Statistics on human behavior indicate that we probably are living in apocalyptic times. The present generation of Americans

**FRANK and ERNEST®**              by Bob Thaves              November 4, 1982

Copyright © 1982 by Newspaper Enterprise Association Inc. Reprinted by permission

has experienced the highest rate of alcoholism in our history, and also the highest rate of divorce, babies born out of wedlock, crime, juvenile delinquency, drug addiction, mental illness and suicide. Some of these problems tend to expand almost exponentially. For example, the children of alcoholic parents are forty to sixty per cent more likely to become alcoholics than are the children of non-alcoholic parents.

Considering the fact that over ten per cent of junior-high school students in America are alcoholics, we must be aware of having to face greater problems ahead. It is equally true that the children of drug-addicted parents are more likely to become drug addicts. Children born out of wedlock are more likely to bear children out of wedlock. Children with mentally ill parents are more likely to become mentally ill, etc. The past decade has been the worst one in American history for children. One out of every eleven is born a drug addict, with the possibility of lifelong brain damage. Scores of thousands are born with fetal alcoholic syndrome that damages them permanently. Millions are "latchkey" children (with both parents working), who spend little time with their mother or father, and precious little quality time. Multiple thousands are born with AIDS virus. Every year hundreds of thousands of children are physically or sexually abused. Presently, according to a statement from a House committee, nearly five hundred thousand American children have been abandoned by both of their parents, and this number could surge to over eight hundred thousand in four or five years. In recent years, there has been a massive abandonment of children by their fathers, so that we now have an incredible number of children living in single-parent homes.[25]

The world has never been more saturated with lethal weapons; yet, they continue to be manufactured and distributed in all directions in an utter frenzy. In 1985, 35 billion dollars were spent in the arms trade. Fifty-four thousand nuclear weapons were ready for use in the world in 1980. Six nations now belong to the "Nuclear Club." Eight more are about to enter. Thirty-four ethnic flash wars are occurring on an average day. Twelve protracted wars are being waged on an average day. Since World War II, 12 million people have been killed in wars. The world's essential rain forests are being progressively destroyed by greedy exploiters who are seemingly devoid of responsible ecological consciousness. Every day, the wholesomeness of our environment declines. There is more pollution in the air and in the earth's food and water supplies. Soils of countries having indoor plumbing are being depleted of essential nutrients. Vital energy sources are declining. In these respects, America may well be the most culpable nation on earth.

In both capitalist and socialist countries, we have witnessed new heights of corruption and unethical practices in financial and industrial affairs. For example, as mentioned earlier, literally hundreds of billions of dollars deposited in savings and loan institutions in America have been misused in ways that will heavily burden the populace for decades. The ethics of the elected politicians have plummeted to a new low. There are now more greedy vested interest groups influencing governmental decisions than ever before. America has become a progressively more litigious society, conducting endless numbers of law suits. America has more lawyers than the rest of the world put together. Many suits are downright silly, serving the predominant purpose of fattening the bank accounts of lawyers, not to mention the fact that there are too many lawyers in government who have vested interest in the vague, complex, even conflicting laws they design and pass. These Byzantine laws create a market for ever more lawyers. In the confusion, the rule of law is fast degenerating into the rule of lawyers.[26]

Of course, lawyers are not the only professional group needing to be checked. The cost of medical care in America has grown outrageously out of hand. After every allowance for the costs of expensive technical equipment, and for the costs of legal liability insurance and of the extra tests and therapies that mainly protect themselves from the lawyers, the medical doctors and dentists are still accumulating wealth at the expense of people who cannot afford it. Many people are going uncared for because they cannot pay the high cost of medical attention and pharmaceuticals. One of the responsibilities of a humane society is to take reasonable action to guarantee that good health is affordable for all people who responsibly pursue it.

Mountains of problems already are converging upon us because of the ravages of overpopulation. For example, the population growth in the tiny nation of Bangladesh is completely out of hand. It is projected to reach 235 million by the year 2030. To see this problem clearly, visualize this large a number of people in an area even smaller than that of Illinois. Never before has humankind been subjected to such all-pervasive threats to its well-being. There are dark clouds ahead. In the free West, we survey the disorder among other peoples and congratulate ourselves that we are comfortable and safe because we are better than they. In the long run, we are not better and we will not be safer.

We dare to hope that Malcolm Muggeridge, an extraordinarily perceptive and wise man, is wrong in his declaration that " 'Western civilization' is irretrievably over."[27] There is hope in noting what our friend Linda McKenna points out, that small children are collectively the same in one generation as in another. Happily, some things of this world remain in place. In any case, we must hold to an essential moral optimism. To give up hoping for the greater life, and to desist in striving to bring it about, is but to diminish our own decency and dignity; it is to alienate ourselves even farther from our fellow human beings and God. At a minimum, we should hope that the good we do here and now will not be lost but will prove, in the catastrophic sweep of history, to be the seeds of fruitful new beginnings.

Most adults now alive have experienced great changes in technology or in their worldview. Whitehead observes that great changes all but wreck societies. Yet, Whitehead continues, societies may survive if changes do not take place too rapidly. The Russo-American sociologist-historian Pitirim A. Sorokin finds moreover that "The periods of comparative stability, order, and material well-being, and hence of complacency, have scarcely ever given birth to a truly great religion or a truly lofty moral ideal."[28]

The versatile Austrian-American economist Peter Drucker showed clearly in 1939, on psychological and historical grounds, that great social institutions cannot be reformed until they are crumbling: "It is impossible to be a revolutionary from within an existing order." In global political terms, Drucker's well-argued observation and hope is that

> The totalitarian revolution is clearly not the beginning of a new order but the result of the total collapse of the old. Armaments, the suppression of freedom and liberties, the persecution of the Jews, and the war against religion are all signs of weakness, not of strength. They have their roots in blackest, unfathomable despair. As soon as [the masses] are offered an alternative — but no sooner — the whole totalitarian magic will vanish like a nightmare.[29]

A parent of one of the authors passed along Thomas Carlyle's advice:

*Make no small plans.*

Those who, in newly won knowledge, follow this adage will find their reward, no matter what hardships they may endure.

# Annex:
## *The Answer to David Hume*

T HE SCOTTISH PHILOSOPHER David Hume must be answered in a claim of his that is now over two centuries old and all but totally influential in the academic halls of our century. Hume's claim is that facts and values are unbridgeably separate areas of knowledge if indeed knowledge of the existence of values is even possible. Specifically, Hume claims that, when a person starts only from facts — that is, when one starts only from knowledge of what experience shows to exist — it is then impossible to derive any statement of what *ought* to be or of what people ought to do. In brief, his claim is that there is no way to derive an *ought*-judgment from an *is*-judgment. If Hume were right — and few philosophers at present openly disagree — then ethics as a serious study would be impossible, as there would be no foundation of facts in which to anchor it. Whereupon ethics, if more than a mere historical or sentimental study, would be only a detached analysis of meanings that would not afford guidance. Such withered views of ethics have been repeated by Hume's twentieth-century follower, the influential Bertrand Russell, as well as by R. M. Hare, P. Nowell-Smith, and many other philosophers.[1] Here we have a subtle but seemingly lethal stumbling block, the removal of which is absolutely necessary.

Several objections to the universality of happiness-motivation have been answered herein. Those answers are evidence that the correct general theory of motivation has been identified. A relatively formal proof of its completeness is here presented as the answer to Hume's challenge. It will be of interest primarily to those who teach philosophy or who love to persuade through argument.

We have considered the need to have one and only one overall task or goal in order to behave in a fully rational manner. We have considered the need for a single ranking-medium for choices in the world as it is, and why that ranking-medium must be happiness in the sense of joy, satisfaction, or pleasure. By now we have understood rationality in motivation well enough to consider how adherence to rationality necessitates the pursuit of happiness or joy as the only rational overall mode of behavior, *when everything relevant is taken into account*. The impossibility of rationally making certain self-refuting statements or hoof-in-mouth contradictions will be the key to the answer to Hume.

Suppose a sophist guru were to instruct his or her students: "As a matter of principle, do not deliberately choose. That is, do not ponder over choosing according to your highest-ranked possible course of action in terms of joy or for any reason. Perhaps life is but a dream; at any rate, it doesn't matter what you do. So just act at random, on impulse, without reflecting on or evaluating what you are doing."

Let us for the present put something similar into a sentence in the indicative mood — i.e., into a simple statement of fact — rather than as a command in the imperative mood, in order to facilitate logical handling, since our systems of logic do not function directly in the imperative mood. Suppose then our sophist obligingly says instead: "As a matter of principle, I do not waste energy in making reasoned choices. To me, it doesn't matter what I shall do; therefore I do not act out of a reason, I just behave at random, without reflection or evaluation or weighing of alternatives. In short, I have no thought for the future."

In reply, one could say to the guru, "But that is what you just did when you chose to say what you said. You chose to state the principle by which you were choosing. Or if you didn't so choose, then what were you doing? Were you choosing to do what you did not choose to do? Were you willing to do what you were not willing to do? If so, why should we listen to you? What you are saying, in effect, is: 'I do not choose to do what I choose to do.' It would seem, sir, that your utterance was not a true statement — that is, not a meaningful human communication — but merely a syntactically correct but nonsensical sentence without any meaning that could come from a human being who could use the word 'I' and know what was being said. If you will permit me to say it, you were merely fanning the breeze. If I appear to assume a worshipful attitude before you, it is merely that I am warming my hands on the hot air."

To borrow the words of C. I. Lewis, the net effect of such a statement by the guru is "to dissolve away all seriousness of action and intent, leaving only an undirected floating down the stream of time; and as a consequence to dissolve all significance of thought and discourse to universal blah."[2] If the statement, "Have no thought for the future" were to be found "engraved by lightning on a rock," then, since the lightning and the rock have no values and make no choices, there would be no inconsistency. But for the guru to perform the act of stating it, and also to claim to take himself or herself seriously in so doing, is to commit a performatory contradiction or a hoof-in-mouth contradiction (a name with more of a kick).[3]

Hoof-in-mouth contradictions can be turned to good effect by using them in arriving at a kind of *necessary* fact — that is, a fact that cannot conceivably be untrue. A hoof-in-mouth contradiction is a *reductio ad absurdum* of whatever message it purports to communicate. And a *reductio ad absurdum*, when it results in a flat contradiction, has a curious property: it rebounds, so to speak, to support a positive truth, namely, the direct opposite of the message the hoof-in-mouth contradiction was intended to convey.

For example, we can ironically employ this *reductio ad absurdum* line of reasoning to demonstrate an absolute truth — that is, a truth that is true under any and all circumstances. René Descartes uses this method to prove the simplest truth. Descartes writes, "I think, therefore I exist (Cogito ergo sum)." To see why this is a proof, consider somebody's sincerely spoken (or thought) words, "I do not exist." In this form, one may readily see that the act of speaking the words contradicts what is said. The Finnish philosopher Jaako Hintikka comments, "The indubitability of my own existence results from my thinking of it, almost as the sound of music results from playing it or (to use Descartes' own metaphor) light in the sense of illumination results from the presence of a source of light."[4]

The statement "I do not exist" might be spoken either sincerely or ironically. In either case, a contradiction arises from the *implied* words, "I exist," which must be considered as part of the implicit meaning of *every* statement expressed by a person. The words "I exist" are rarely stated by a person talking, since their meaning is implicit in the speech-act itself, not to mention the fact of one's presence. Existing people perform the act of making statements. Statements do not make themselves and do not come into being out of nothing. A non-existent person can make no statements, and a non-existent person cannot doubt his own existence, which follows simply because there is no one to perform the act of doubting. Albeit, the contradiction in the statement, "I doubt that I exist," may go unnoticed by a speaker with an illogical set of mind. When a person does say, "I doubt that I exist" (which Turner has heard several ethical-relativist professors say over the years), the logical listener will readily conclude that the speaker *does* exist but is uttering pure nonsense. It is reported that a slightly distraught young man, a student in Morris Raphael Cohen's philosophy class, came to Cohen and asked seriously, "Professor Cohen, do I exist?" Cohen thought for a minute and then asked the student: "Who wants to know?"

We see that a statement like "I do not exist" is false under every conceivable circumstance of being uttered by a person. Yet this negation of truth can itself be negated, to good effect. Then it becomes, "I exist." The result is a truth that, when expressed by a person, is a *necessary* truth, that is, one that is true under every such circumstance, one that is as necessarily true as the original doubting statement was necessarily false. The *expressed* false statement "I do not exist" is readily converted to the necessarily true statement, "I exist."[5]

A variant example: methodological behaviorism is the theory that consciousness is of no intellectual interest or, specifically, that it has no explanatory value. In the extreme form of behaviorism known as metaphysical behaviorism, the entities of consciousness, feeling, and thought are held not to be real at all. This theory has been espoused in its most blatant form by the psychologists John B. Watson and B. F. Skinner. In this they follow the seventeenth-century English philosopher Thomas Hobbes. A crushing blow against this theory is struck by Arthur Lovejoy in his article, "The Paradox of the Thinking Behaviorist." Lovejoy shows that the true behaviorist is in the absurd position of asserting that that behaviorist does not exist as a thinking, observing, knowing entity — a case of one's hoof in one's mouth as it were.[6]

Unconscious hoof-in-mouth contradictions often are found, even in professional philosophical discussions. What, for instance, is one to make of the judgment, quoted by Blanshard: "No moralist has a right to impose his biases on others"?[7] Or again, the judgment, heard in the faculty lounge: "The world would be better off if we could get rid of all this talk about values." The oldest recorded hoof-in-mouth contradiction, or something close to it, is alleged of Epimenides *the Cretan* in his declaration, "All Cretans are liars."[8] One might object that Epimenides could not have meant to include himself in his problematical statement. But if that was so, he wasn't saying what he meant. Of course, people usually are not conscious of having these blatant contradictions in their speaking or writing.

Some speech acts are almost purely instinctive reactions to a stimulus, such as when a person suddenly stuck with a needle hollers "Ouch!" Mice can do as much. We should not classify this expression as a statement of thought entailing conceptualization, which is a mental act not possible without a thinker deciding to think or speak. Moreover, the electrochemical activities transpiring in one's brain do not speak. A person's environmental history does not speak. The brain is not an entity that speaks. Only a person — a free spiritual agent — can make personal statements, and no one can make them as such without being willing to make them. Actions may possess differing degrees of voluntariness even when they are identical acts performed by the same person at different times. At one time, perhaps one's attention is divided, or perhaps one is half asleep or in some torrent of passion. We are concerned here solely with acts that can be called unqualifiedly voluntary.

Other hoof-in-mouth contradictions may enliven this dullish discussion:

> "And above all, I yield to no one in my ineffable modesty." This one was perpetrated by C. S. Peirce, with tongue in cheek, no doubt, in a letter found by his editor, Charles Hartshorne.
>
> "People from our country never boast." The speaker was from a great island reputed to be pre-eminently *civilised*.

"I've said it before and I'll say it again: Never act on principle."

"I warn every boy I date, I have *no* principles" (Hazelett was warned, during the date).

"My lecture topic today is the Absolutely Unknowable."

Sign seen in the "head" or toilet of a U.S. naval ship: "Reading in the head is not permitted."

Don't tell me my I.Q. score; I want to stay modest, the way I am.

"Exterminate wisdom, destroy science, and the empire will return to order of its own accord," said Chuang Tzu the "wise" Taoist.[9]

"A hundred years from now, it won't make any difference." For instance, it is always important to know that in the long run, nothing is important to know.[10]

Hear again our sophist guru, saying, "I do not weigh my possible courses of action." When this self-contradictory absurdity is negated and generalized, it turns out that any functioning person's choosing of what constitutes, at the time, his or her highest-ranked alternative for action necessarily occurs, in some sense, every time the person opens the mouth and speaks, or pounds the typewriter, making sentences or implied sentences.[11]

Let us be definite. When anyone willfully expresses any statement or renders a judgment, then by that very act, that person does choose one alternative as being the person's highest-ranked course of action at that time. This follows even from the deliberate act of saying something, no matter what is being said or recommended about choice or anything else. That is, choice — at least the decision to speak — is implicit in any voluntary speech act expressing a statement. Anyone who speaks of choice or of anything else is to that extent choosing according to the speaker's highest-ranked prospective action at the time. If the speaker denies this, the speaker is as much as stating the proposition: "It is most important to me now to choose to do what is not most important to me now."

On the contrary, humans "must choose, and for a reason." Anybody who says, "I do not maximize any value" is speaking nonsense similar to that of the celebrated Indian Buddhist monk Bodhidharma (c. A.D. 500) when he asserted, "All things are empty, and there is nothing desirable or to be sought after."[12] Bodhidharma is said to have spent ten years staring at a stone wall. Similarly, all philosophical pessimism about the pursuit of value is proved inconsistent with itself, when it is expressed.[13] The English writer G. K. Chesterton observes, more generally:

No sceptics work sceptically; no fatalists work fatalistically. No materialist who thinks his mind was made up for him, by mud and blood and heredity, has any hesitation in making up his mind.[14]

Clearly, the fact that a functioning person *chooses* to speak when express-ing any real idea cannot be verbally denied without inconsistency. The alternative for anyone who would deny this is silence — perhaps just a long, quiet stare. To be silent is of course neither becoming to philosophers nor congenial to them. A dissenter, philosophical or not, can here choose to be silent and silently believe what he or she will, but this person cannot *verbally* deny the fact of implicit choice by the self without a loss of credi-bility.[15] We may assert simply: Whoever speaks meaningfully — i.e., for a reason — is to that extent and by that very act choosing rationally —that is, according to the highest-ranked option for action at the moment.

Note that the sentence just expressed is in the indicative or declarative mood, not the imperative mood. This is significant because we learn from Herbert Bohnert the vitally important but little-known fact *that imperative propositions may be regarded as condensed or elliptic indicative or declarative pro-positions*.[16] For instance, to say "Please close the door" may be unpacked as truly meaning: "You may close the door and, if you do so, you will thereby please me." Fairly obviously, that is the meaning, but who is going to be so forward and so boring as to say all of this, or even to think of such a string of words to oneself? One says in imperative mood, rather, "Please close the door." A highway sign that says, "Turn lights on in tunnel," may unpack this way: "You will turn on your automobile lights in the tunnel, or else your omission will render you a safety hazard, and you may thereby earn a ticket." Of course, this is not normal discourse; one reads the sign and assumes that there are good, or at least compelling, reasons for obeying it. Again, take the Eighth Commandment, "Thou shalt not steal." In the indicative mood, it could be rendered: "If you steal, you shall grieve both thy victim and the Lord thy God, and moreover, you may be caught and be discomfited."[17]

The above translations from the imperative to the indicative mood are applications of what we may call *Bohnert's bridge*. Like the making of ordinary translations, some judgment and special knowledge is normally involved — a fact discussed by Bohnert. The tests of success are the prac-tical ones used to test any translation. Now we can use Bohnert's bridge for our purpose. We shall derive a value — i.e., a valid command — from facts and shall thereby overturn Hume's long-standing denial of this possibility. We earlier arrived at a *necessarily true* indicative proposition expressing the universality of choice in everything that properly function-ing human beings say, namely:

> Whoever speaks meaningfully — i.e., for a reason — is to that extent and by that very act choosing rationally — that is, maximizing a value in one ranking medium by choosing the highest-ranked option for action at the moment.

This can be translated and condensed into the imperative mood:

*Choose rationally — that is, act on your highest-ranked course of action at each moment.*

This imperative says practically the same thing as the preceding declarative sentence, since there is no consistently expressible alternative, once it is stated. As with previous examples, this statement stands unchallengeable, since it cannot be consistently denied. Let us call it the "ranked-choice imperative" or the "motivational imperative." It may be called a universal or categorical imperative. It is a tidy way to squelch the opposition, who therefore may be expected to greet this result with silence.

The motivational imperative is not a narrowly specific command. That is, it is not limited to specific persons. If it were, no contradiction would result from stating its negation, for you could conceivably say to someone, "Act stupid," in some situation of manipulating a third party, without thereby contradicting yourself. As a merely situational command, there is no logical necessity in it. Its necessity comes about only when expressed as a general imperative, like a moral imperative, which includes the speaker and the moment of its pronouncement within its scope. A moral imperative, or a general imperative of action like the present one, does not single out persons and does not omit any recipient or any moment of time, at least not without giving reasons for such partiality. Thus the motivational

**MOTLEY'S CREW**  by T. G. Forman  April 12, 1989

imperative has a unique force that distinguishes it from all other imperatives, with the exception of one all-important corollary or imperative that may be derived from it. Ordinary imperatives do present more or less live options, no matter how unattractive. We analyzed one above — the Eighth Commandment. At least one Biblical imperative is already set up with an alternative made explicit: "Judge not, that ye be not judged."[18] Penal legislation offers options to the would-be criminal, namely, penalties on one hand, or adherence to socially prescribed behavior on the other, though there is also the unexpressed alternative of evading justice.

The consideration of empty imperatives will illumine Bohnert's translation of imperatives into the indicative mood. For example, a mother admonishes her child, "Stop howling." The child continues to howl, but the mother does nothing. The child gets the idea that all that the mother meant was to say, "I wish you would stop howling." But the expression of a wish is not an imperative, so the child keeps on howling. None of the aforementioned practical examples of imperatives close the door upon rational discussion in the clean way we have been considering.

As another empty imperative, consider the Virgil Partch firing-squad cartoon herewith. Under the untoward circumstances, is a genuine imperative being imposed upon poor Filstrup? If so, what is the enforcement to be?

Our work is not done. The motivational imperative tells us to choose in such a way as to maximize a value but does not say what the value is; the value still requires to be specified. Earlier it was shown that there is one and only one species of value that is adequate to encompass all the aspects of motivation. Accordingly, we may substitute satisfaction or pleasantness or joy — i.e., hedonic value technically speaking — for the bare, logical value in the motivational imperative derived in this annex. Thus we arrive at the following more specific imperative:

> Always act on your highest-ranked course of action — with felt satisfaction or pleasure in the broadest sense as your criterion.

Lest this seem self-centered, the conditions we have discussed should be added, and the result may be called the *joy imperative:*

> *Always act on your highest-ranked course of action, with felt satisfaction or pleasure in the broadest sense as your criterion. That is, so act, all things considered, without self-deception, in view of your interests and what you know of your nature, the character of your community, of the universe and its Creator, and in contemplation of the future.*

If the conditions so stated in the imperative be denied, then the rationality of motivation, together with the probabilities of joyous results, become undercut, as we have seen. The joy imperative, with or without the conditions, is not an ethical imperative; rather, it is the psychological imperative through which ethics must work. It points to the way we necessarily act, to the extent that we behave as rational, language-using beings. The joy imperative is a necessary foundation for ethics: it makes the motivation of both ethical and unethical behavior conceivable and possible.

Virgil Partch

"...And for repeatedly calling the company commander by his first name...
**Filstrup, straighten up that helmet!"**

Ethical imperatives can be derived with its help, including the common ones we all know. As has been discussed elsewhere, its inherent virtue lies in its removal of crippling doubts.

The pursuit of joy is essentially a psychological concept rather than an ethical one. But the pursuit of *unselfish* joy is an ethical concept. For unselfish joy is joy which respects the joy of others. Kindness is a way to experience it. The subject of ethics is the relations among living beings or persons. A solipsist as such can have no ethics. A reader who has been generally persuaded by this book will take the joy of others as the foundation of his or her own joy. Most particularly, one will so act as to glorify God, adding to His joy through adding to the joy of the creatures. In this way, one will fulfill the joy imperative for oneself.

We tell our children that kindness is good — i.e., valuable — and that they should be kind. A Tamerlane or a Stalin or a Mao Tse-tung would hold that unkindness toward those people they didn't like was good. According to David Hume and his twentieth-century followers, such sentences are all empty of fact since they allegedly are not derivable from facts; the choice would be a matter merely of subjective preference or emotion. Is there really an unbridgeable gap between "is"-sentences expressing *facts* on the one hand, and "ought"-sentences expressing particular *values* to be pursued on the other? Has Hume been answered?

The reader possessed of a normally sympathetic nature should be able to say, perhaps with more conviction than previously: "Being kind makes me joyous." This would be a statement of fact. Apply now the joy imperative, which says as a fact that one should pursue joy — with due regard to the many relevant facts. The resulting *obligatory* corollary is: "I ought to be kind." This exemplifies the bypass that is opened when a value is derived from a fact in one unique but all-important kind of situation. The translation from the indicative mood to the imperative mood through the joy-imperative evidently constitutes an exception to the objection of Hume. Other valid, even obligatory values and ideals of ordinary civilized living, can indeed be derived from facts.

So much for the catastrophic sophistry of David Hume in matters of ethical theory. It is time to lay to rest Hume's pernicious intellectual myth. Perhaps Hume half hoped that someone would solve his little puzzle before two hundred years had elapsed. We should give credit to David Bohnert for bringing to full light the missing technical link, namely, the translation between indicative and imperative moods, which may be called *Bohnert's bridge*, whereby the alleged chasm between facts and values becomes bridged.[19]

# Postscript
## by Charles Hartshorne

IN THE FOREWORD I indicated that I have some reservations about this book. The authors have invited me to present them here.

One of my reasons for hesitating to call myself a Christian is that the "incarnation" of deity in a man conflicts with my clear conviction that motherhood is a much more nearly adequate symbol for deity than fatherhood. This I find simply obvious. Turner and Hazelett are against male chauvinism, but they do not mention this difficulty for our inherited religion.

I also question whether they have discriminated clearly enough between two possible interpretations of the philosophy of Brand Blanshard. On the one hand, there is his Spinozistic one-sided exaltation of necessity, hence of unfreedom, in his holding to the validity of (necessary) truth by coherence among extremely general universals used in explicating divine existence or ordinary existence as such. This position of Blanshard's I believe I have refuted. On the other hand, there is a logically very different thing, an epistemic device, that is, (contingent) truth by coherence, as for instance coherence between concepts and percepts as well as simply among concepts. They do mention the distinction.

We are all fallible. But academics need to be aware of the possibility that fallibility sometimes takes the form of self-flattering collective intellectual fashions. Secular humanism seems to some of us one of these fashions. The complaints of fundamentalists on this point are not without foundation. Procedures of public educational institutions do sometimes distort history by grossly understating or misstating the role of theistic religions in inspiring not only ordinary people but great scientists, philosophers, and political leaders.

On the other hand, I side strongly against the traditional ideas of rewards or punishments in careers for human persons after death. Death, for me, is not the destruction of our actuality, our sequences of experiences between childhood and old age, but neither is it the initiation of a new sequence of angelic or diabolic experiences. Rather, as Whitehead with superb genius in the final chapter of *Process and Reality* formulates it, concrete actualities are experiences, and all experiences are everlastingly cherished by the One who Cares for all. Our immortality is the transmission of all that we have been into an indestructible whole in the divine life.

Each of us is finite spatially and temporally, but the Inclusive whole, or the One who cherishes all, is unborn and undying. The story of a human life has a first and a last chapter, but no syllable of that life can ever cease to be in and for God. The ancient Jews asked for no more than this, nor do I. But for less than this I see no need to settle. On this point I side with the Book of Job. Peirce hinted at a similar view. I have read many arguments for posthumous careers. Against every one, I see strong counter-arguments. In every one, I see an unwitting violation of the commandment, Love God with *all* your being. God's everlastingly new experiences suffice to give our lives their full meaning. Deathlessness, like birthlessness, is a divine attribute. Let us not claim them for ourselves. This puts me in disagreement with at least one of the two authors—and with millions of others around the world. But also in agreement with many.

As we all know, philosophers, other than ourselves of course, tend to overstate the force of their arguments. As Peirce once put it, "Give a philosopher an inch and he will take a million light years." Have Hazelett and Turner overstated the force of their long, many-pronged case for theism? On the whole, however, my judgment is that they have understated the pragmatic and metaphysical case for theism. I think that, in a different way, I also have understated it. These writers are strong where I have been weak, in the way they bring out how devastating, indeed frightening, have been the failures of nontheists to provide for our species what the religions (more or less clearly theistic) tried in the past to furnish, a world-view effectively favorable to cooperative, kind, and responsible behavior.

In claiming that my two former students understate the theistic case, I have several considerations in mind. One is their declaration that they lack the natural inclination—and I agree with them that we cannot entirely set such inclinations aside in philosophy—to pursue the evidences that some of us find convincing for a psychicalistic monism. In taking this stance, however, they leave the door open for a dualistic or materialistic view. Dualism, I submit, is a "cop-out," whether in science or philosophy. The togetherness of the mental and the material is either mental or material, or who can say what it is? And materialism I see as a covert dualism. What is wrong in both these other options than psychicalism is the concept of matter as irreducible to mind in some form.

Physicists have been making it more and more clear that for them the constituents of matter have no humanly specifiable positive properties other than the geometrical-causal relations expressible numerically or algebraically. These are not only very abstract but they are purely structural, not qualitative properties. A recent writer on "cognitive psychology" has admitted that psychology has so far given us no explanation of *quality*. We experience the physical in terms of "secondary qualities," but physics uses these merely as signs for the mathematical relations (vibration rates, for example) that condition our experiences of red, warm, pleasant, painful, and the like. A merely physicalistic psychology leaves the riddle of the structure-quality duality where it finds it. The so-called "primary qualities" are merely structures for physics. Left out are terms like beauty, value, hope, fear, love, hate, feeling, sensing, perceiving, remembering, happiness, misery, indeed all those ideas without the application of which our behavior has no intelligible meaning or importance whatsoever.

It is simply not true that we can begin by knowing what atoms or photons are and then try to figure out what concepts like feeling, experiencing, loving, hoping, fearing, desiring add to the material world already known for what it is. Recall the fact that in all ancient Greece *nobody* had a reasonable theory of the so-called inorganic world. Plato, Aristotle, Epicurus each tried his hand at this, but none came close to what we now know. Each was partly right as against the other two, but woefully wrong as judged by current physics and astronomy. Yet what these just-mentioned three authors said about human experience as such is still respectable. They were much closer to a sound psychology or even biology and anthropology than to a sound physics or astronomy. We human animals start our thinking, not with known constituents of matter, but with known psychical functionings — sensing, remembering, feeling, hoping, fearing, loving, hating, desiring, enjoying. To say that we know or experience matter but do not know at all what the words knowing or experiencing mean is absurd. That we could ever set aside these psychical ideas and adopt instead some merely physical correlates seems to me absurd to the point of ludicrousness.

The argument for theism, as not only Berkeley, Kant, Hegel, Marx, but also Peirce, Whitehead, and many others have held, is much weakened *if* the idea of mere, totally insentient as well as unconscious matter can be shown even coherently conceivable. I do not find many scientists of note, if any, undertaking to tell us just how they know that the merely structural concepts of physics could describe any concrete actuality whatever in its concreteness. Who tells us, with careful criteria, just where, or anything like just where, mind emerged into a world of mindless matter? Descartes said it was with the human species. Some say with nervous systems, some with bacteria. Who has told us how one gets inside an atom (or a minuscule vibratory "string") to know that it has *no* form, however remote from our higher-animal-human form, of *feeling* with at least a minimal sense of past and desire for a future? Karl Popper admits he cannot disprove psychicalism, though he has given an argument or two.*

With psychicalism the weakness of nontheistic philosophers begins to take definite shape, provided that we avoid a deficiency found in most idealists or psychical monists until Peirce — that of accepting, or not unambiguously rejecting, strict classical determinism. Leibniz's great achievement of (for the first time) stating sharply in terms of modern science a psychicalistic pluralism was marred by his extreme form of the doctrine of sufficient reason, thus excluding freedom in the structural-causal sense that Epicurus affirmed — here improving, and only here, upon Democritus.

Now that Peirce, Bergson, Varisco and some others, have made a case, even without quantum theory, against strict determinism, but a case for psychicalism, the theistic issue can take a more coherent form. We can now say that there need be no absolute dualism of supremely free creator and simply unfree creatures (the latter all strictly controlled by divine decree or divinely instituted natural laws), or supremely free creator and in lesser ways free human (or angelic) creatures, with the remaining creatures simply unfree. "No," we can now say, "in God is the supreme form of creativity or causal freedom ('supreme' here meaning, unsurpassable by any other being or individual), interacting with a world of non-supreme creatures, surpassable by others, but all in some degree free." Obviously the atheistic argument from evil changes radically if *every* creature has some decision-making power so that its decisions do not merely reiterate portions of any divine decision but introduce something novel even for divine awareness, thus enriching the divine life. Hume's *Dialogues*, like many idealistic systems, can now be seen to have begged the question against a coherent theism by asserting determinism. Hume's

---

* Hazelett wrote a well-documented master's thesis on psychicalism for me in 1969. Turner has expressed quite clearly that he is not in accord with psychicalism. He does not find it to be of practical value in our analysis of problems with the physical world. For example, he says that when he is sitting on a chair, he is sitting on a real physical chair occupying real space; he is not sitting on a mental entity.

Philo, to explain the by him assumed absolute order of the world, assigns all-determining power to God, who therefore is responsible for all evils and cannot in our human sense be good. What multitudes of atheists must have been made so primarily by this assumption that theism affirms a single all-determining power, free mover of all, itself wholly unmoved!

Creatures, none wholly determined in advance (or eternally), even by God, cannot be expected never to fall into more or less unwelcome conflict with one another. Divine power "over all" may still be assumed, but power in this philosophy cannot be monopolized, cannot be coherently conceived as leaving no open options for others. Omnipotence in the problem-of-evil sense was always an absurdity, and religion can do very well without it!

Note too that, as Hume saw, there must be some cosmic order if being a creature is to make sense. Darwinism is a doctrine of mutual adaptation, but one cannot adapt to mere chaos, so that the explanation of order cannot be in terms of adaptation alone. Darwin assumed, did not in the least explain, the basic natural laws. In a philosophy of universal freedom, cosmic order is either a sheer mystery, or else some cosmic, universally influencing though never wholly determining, form of supreme freedom must be its explanation. In this form of design argument no basis for the classical argument from evil is given, and a new level of coherence in the idea of God is achieved. For instance, one no longer has to impute love, purpose, or knowledge to a strictly unmoved mover of all. Rather, with Rabbi Heschel, one terms God "the *most* moved mover." Nor need "knower of all" mean the timeless, immutable knower of all for whom nothing novel can come to be and whose awareness cannot be enriched, since it once for all simply has actually the realization of all possibilities. As John Dewey saw, how there could still be for us in our decisions possibilities rather than actualities or necessities was one of the dismal antimonies in classical theism. Metaphysics today is really new. The old labels no longer serve.

For another aspect of the new metaphysical coherence, consider how psychicalism strengthens the old analogy implied by Plato's idea of God as soul of the cosmos as divine body. A body is, in the human case, no merely single thing, but a vast society of societies of perhaps two hundred thousand kinds of cells. The mind-body relation is then emphatically a one-many, not a one-one relation. The body is that collection of creatures other than one's conscious self with which that self most intimately and constantly interacts. In the theological analogy this mirrors the divine Self. And if the essence of the latter is supreme love, what is it in the human case if not a non-supreme love, truly instinctive and mostly a matter of feeling, not of thought. "Hurt my cells and you hurt me" is the principle here. Merleau-Ponty's generalized, somewhat mystical generalization of "flesh" as universally involved in knowledge and reality fits nicely here, and is closer to theological truth than he imagines.

# Notes and Library Key

**E**LLIPSES in quotations have been omitted in the interest of smooth reading. Assurance is given that meanings have not been altered by selective quotation.

Full bibliographical details of each book or article are usually given only once. At other places, a short entry is given together with bracketed figures indicating the chapter and note in which the rest of a citation may be found. For instance, as to Chapter 9, note 26: "Edwards, *True Virtue* [6:3], p. 15," refers to Chapter 6, note 3, herein, namely, to Jonathan Edwards, *The Nature of True Virtue*.

Works that are deemed to be of unique constructive importance for present purposes are indicated, at one mention only, by the use of **bold-faced type.**

**Book procurement.** Local libraries in the United States can obtain almost any book, or copy of an article, through the efficient interlibrary loan service. Many of the books referred to herein have gone out of print. However, it is legal in the United States to make for "private study, scholarship, or research" a copy of any book in a library collection that is open to the public and is not commercially offered at a "fair price." To determine this, check *Books in Print*, an annual publication of R. R. Bowker Co. (New York), which is found in nearly every library.

To make your own book copies, photocopy two-page spreads on legal-size paper usually, with the image centered on the paper. This leaves room at the edges for binding. Archival acid-free paper may be considered. Do not omit the copyright notice, which is generally behind the title page. Fold each two-page sheet *outward* right along the gutter line, even if the other edges are made crooked thereby. Then stack the folded sheets in book order and take them to a bookbinder with the instruction not to trim the long outside edge, where the folds are. This scheme is known as Japanese fold. Under the law, such a book must become the property only of the user. See the *United States Code*, Title 17, Section 108(e).

**Front epigraph:** General Douglas MacArthur to joint meeting of Congress, April 19, 1951; in *New York Times*, April 20, 1951, p. 4, column 8; *Congressional Record* 97, pp. 4123-4125, at p. 4125.

# 1. The Motivation of Righteous Conduct

**Epigraph:** Eric Hoffer, *Between the Devil and the Dragon* (New York: Harper & Row, 1982), p. 133.

**1:1:** See Albert Schweitzer, *Out of My Life and Thought* (New York: Henry Holt & Co., 1937), Epilogue.

**1:2:** The substance of the latter sentence is from *Collected Papers of Charles Sanders Peirce*, 8 volumes, edited by Charles Hartshorne, Paul Weiss, and Arthur W. Burks (Cambridge: Harvard University Press, 1931-1958), 5.130 (i.e., Volume 5, Section 130).

**1:3:** Plato, *Apology*, translated by Benjamin Jowett, 38a.

**1:4:** Thomas Sheehan, quoted in *Fidelity*, June 1987, p. 21.

**1:5:** See the excellent critique of moral relativism by Frank E. Hartung in *Philosophy of Science* 21 (1954): 118-126. See Brand Blanshard's critique of the book *Ethical Relativity* by Edward Westermarck (New York: Harcourt, Brace & Co., 1932). Blanshard's critique is in his *Reason and Goodness* (London: George Allen & Unwin, 1966), pp. 102-139. Charles Krauthammer attacks the current habit of equating different moral points of view, in *Time*, July 9, 1984, pp. 87-89.

Most recently and thoroughly, see Hadley Arkes, *First Things* (Princeton: Princeton University Press, 1986), Chapter 7 *et passim*. Dennis B. Quinn discusses "Higher Education: The Pluralistic Monopoly" in *University Bookman* no. 1, 1988, pp. 3-7. Perhaps the most influential popularizer of cultural and ethical relativity was Ruth Benedict in her *Patterns of Culture* (Boston: Houghton Mifflin Co., 1934), and in the *Journal of General Psychology* 10 (1934): 59-82.

**1:6:** Leo Tolstoy, *On Life* (1888). The translation of Isabel F. Hapgood has been followed in the main. Omitted is the extreme asceticism of Tolstoy in his later years.

**1:7:** Jean Piaget, *The Moral Judgment of the Child* (London: Kegan Paul, Trench & Trübner & Co., 1932).

**1:8:** A. Clutton-Brock [12:14], p. 723.

**1:9:** For some results of self-centeredness and an unhappy pursuit of pleasures, see Norman M. Lobsenz, *Is Anybody Happy?* (New York: Doubleday & Co., 1962). Paul C. Vitz exposes psychology's "cult of self-worship" in his *Psychology as Religion* (Grand Rapids, Michigan: William B. Eerdmans Publishing Co., 1977). See William Kirk Kilpatrick, *The Emperor's New Clothes* (Westchester, Illinois: Crossway Books, 1985). See Martin and Deidre Bobgan, *Psycho-Heresy* (Santa Barbara: EastGate Publishers, 1987); about 400 references.

Walter Lippmann points out contradictions in modern thought:

> All the varieties of the modern doctrine that man is a collection of separate impulses, each of which can attain its private satisfaction, are in fundamental contradiction not only with the traditional body of human wisdom but with the modern conception of the human character. Thus in one breath it is said in advanced circles that love is a series of casual episodes, and in the next it transpires that the speaker is in process of having himself elaborately psychoanalyzed in order to disengage his soul from the effects of apparently trivial episodes in his childhood. On the one hand it is asserted that sex pervades everything and on the other that sexual behavior is inconsequential. It is taught that experience is cumulative, that we are what our past has made us and shall be what we are making of ourselves now, and then with bland indifference to the significance of this we are told that all experiences are free, equal, and independent. (*A Preface to Morals* [New York:

Macmillan Co., 1929], pp. 285-313, at pp. 306-307: reprinted in *Contemporary Moral Issues*, edited by Henry K. Girvetz [1968+]).

See Garth Wood, *The Myth of Neurosis* (New York: Harper & Row, 1986). An incisive philosophical critique of the behavioral and social sciences is mounted by Holmes Rolston III [4:14]. Modern literature on the whole has been of little help; for a worthy critique see *The God Question and Modern Man* by Hans Urs von Balthasar (New York: Seabury Press, 1967), pp. 119-129. See Duncan Williams, *Trousered Apes* (New Rochelle, New York: Arlington House, 1971). See also parts of Francis A. Schaeffer, *Escape from Reason* (Chicago: Inter-Varsity Press, 1968). *Panic among the Philistines* by Bryan F. Griffin critiques some recent writers (Chicago: Regnery Gateway, 1983).

**1:10:** Perry Miller, *Jonathan Edwards* (Amherst: University of Massachusetts Press, 1981), p. 162; compare p. 140. See the source: Jonathan Edwards, *A Narrative of the Surprising Work of God, in the Conversion of Many Hundred Souls, In and About Northampton*, in any edition of Edwards' works.

**1:11:** In *The Philosophy of Civilization*, Albert Schweitzer presents a profound critique of historical philosophical ethics, with startling insights. Unlike the generality of writers in the field, he understands the motivations and the cultural context behind the dominant movements of thought. Schweitzer's pessimism is at moments profound. Nevertheless, the great amount which he sees correctly, he expresses clearly. The reference here is to p. 107 in *The Philosophy of Civilization* or to p. 25 in *Kultur und Ethik* (Munich: C. H. Beck, 1953); page numbers to this edition will appear in parentheses hereafter — e.g. (25). *Kulturphilosophie* includes "Kultur und Ethik" as the second of its two sections, first published by Beck in 1923. *The Philosophy of Civilization* was translated by C. T. Campion (Tallahassee: University Presses of Florida, 1981), first published in London by Adam and Charles Black, 1923.

Robert C. Neville has perceptively written of "The Social Importance of Philosophy" in *Abraxas* 1 (1970): 31-45.

**1:12:** Thomas Molnar, "Islam on the Move," *Intercollegiate Review* 21 (1985): 17-22, at p. 21. See Molnar on the centrality of religion in the 1989-1990 events of eastern Europe in *Fidelity* (South Bend), May 1990, pp. 28-34. *Fidelity* is a courageously edited Catholic journal.

**1:13:** Schweitzer, *Philosophy of Civilization* [1:11], p. 54.

**1:14:** Compare Arthur Lovejoy, *Philosophical Review* 26 (1917): 123-163.

**Epigraph:** Cornel West in *Christianity and Crisis* 45 (1985); 222-223, quoted in *Religion and Society Report*.

# 2. Socialism as a Motivating Force

**First epigraph:** Hu Yaobang, "Handling Inner-Party Contradictions," *Beijing Review*, July 14, 1986, pp. 12-13, 32.

**Second epigraph:** Arthur O. Lovejoy, "Religious Transition and Ethical Awakening in America," *Hibbert Journal* 6 (1908): 500-514, at p. 513.

**2:1:** Friedrich A. Hayek, *Studies in Philosophy, Politics and Economics* (Chicago: University of Chicago Press, 1967), p. 230. See John D. Barrow and Frank J. Tipler, *The Anthropic Cosmological Principle* (New York: Oxford University Press, 1986), e.g., pp. 99-100, 139-142, 173, 188-189. On the surge of humanitarianism stemming from the eighteenth century see Hermann Kantorowicz, *The Spirit of British Policy* (London: George Allen & Unwin, 1932), Chapter 3.

**2:2:** William James, "Reflex Action and Theism," in *The Will to Believe* (New York: Longmans, Green & Co., 1897; the book is reissued by various publishers as *Essays on Faith and Morals*). See Eric Hoffer, "The

Playful Mood," in *Between the Devil and the Dragon* [1:epigraph], pp. 15-16, 39-42: also "The Practical Sense," pp. 84-91. See Charles Sanders Peirce, *Collected Papers* [1:2], 1.75-1.77: "The Study of the Useless." See Charles Hartshorne, *Reality as Social Process* (Glencoe, Illinois: Free Press, 1953), p. 107; Jane Jacobs, *Cities and the Wealth of Nations* (New York: Random House, 1984), Chapter 14, "Drift."

**2:3:** John Stuart Mill, *On Liberty* (first published 1859).

**2:4:** Eric Hoffer, *Between the Devil and the Dragon* [1:1], p. 388. This book is the final compilation of Hoffer's main writings. Hoffer's blind spot is theism. Nevertheless, until one has read Hoffer, one cannot claim erudition in what may be called the social psychology of civilization.

**2:5:** Aleksandr I. Solzhenitsyn, address at Harvard University commencement, June 1978, as printed in *Solzhenitsyn at Harvard* (Washington: Ethics and Public Policy Center, 1980), pp. 3-20, at p. 17.

**2:6:** Errol E. Harris questions the mutual consistency of the two words "dialectic" and "materialism"; see *The Foundations of Metaphysics in Science* (London: George Allen & Unwin, 1965), pp. 488-489.

**2:7:** William Kingdon Clifford, *Lectures and Essays*, second edition (London, 1886), "The Ethics of Religion."

**2:8:** See e.g. *Abuse of Psychiatry for Political Repression in the Soviet Union* (New York: Arno Press, 1973). This title is reprinted from United States Senate, 92nd Congress, second session, Committee on the Judiciary, Subcommittee to Investigate the Administration of the Internal Security Act and Other Internal Security Laws, September 26, 1972, G. M. Shimanov, pp. 191-224; V. I. Chernishov, pp. 225-228. See *Descent into Darkness* by James Zatko (Notre Dame, Indiana: University of Notre Dame Press, 1965).

Nicolas Berdyaev warned us long ago of inevitable ideological clash, in *The Origins of Russian Communism* (London: Geoffrey Bles, 1937), Chapter 7. V. I. Lenin asserts: "Religion is a sort of spiritual booze, in which the slaves of capital drown their human image, their demand for a life more or less worthy of man. The

yoke of religion that weighs upon mankind is merely a product and reflection of the economic yoke within society." He envisioned a system "cleansed of medieval mildew" ("Socialism and Religion," December 3, 1905, in *Collected Works*, 46 volumes [Moscow: Foreign Languages Publishing House, or Progress Publishers, 1960+], Volume 10, pp. 83-87). The People's Republic of China persecuted religious believers, but evidently both countries are now desisting, unless the congregations meet in secret. The massacre of Tiananmen Square seems to be responsible for further increase in their numbers (*National & International Religion Report*, January 1, 1990, p. 1).

**2:9:** "Resolution of the Central Committee of the Communist Party of China on the Guiding Principles for Building a Socialist Society with an Advanced Culture and Ideology," September 28, 1986, Section 4, in *Beijing Review*, centerpiece, October 6, 1986. See Brand Blanshard, **"Reflections on Economic Determinism"** in *Journal of Philosophy* 63 (1966): 169-178.

**2:10:** V. I. Lenin, "The Tasks of the Youth Leaders," October 2, 1920 (*Collected Works* [2:8], Volume 31, pp. 283-299). See Paul Johnson, *Modern Times* (New York: Harper & Row, 1983), e.g., p. 70. See further Robert Payne, *The Life and Death of Lenin* (New York: Simon & Schuster, 1964), pp. 408-409, 418-420.

**2:11:** Richard T. DeGeorge, *Soviet Ethics and Morality* (Ann Arbor: University of Michigan Press, 1969), Chapter 5.

**2:12:** Eugene V. Debs, American socialist.

**2:13:** On the failures of planning and intervention in western Europe, see e.g. Brian Crozier and Arthur Seldon, *Socialism* (New York: Universe Press, 1986); John Jewkes, *The New Ordeal by Planning* (London: Macmillan & Co., 1968). "National industrial policy" is a quasi-socialism. On the practical details of the inevitable inefficiency of planned economies see Jan Winiecki, *The Distorted World of Soviet Economics* (Pittsburgh: University of Pittsburgh Press, 1988). There are many other articles and books. Some apposite Bible passages are

Micah 4:1, 4: Isaiah 65:22, 2 Thessalonians 3:7-8 and nearby. One effect of the Leninist maxim that the end justifies the means is the long-standing leftist disinformation that the profits of manufacturers are far higher than they are. Dahlberg knocked this one down in *How to Save Free Enterprise* [2:39], pp. 196-209. The ire of hard-working men and women would have been better directed against mega-banking, potentially the last bastion of tyranny, cloaked as it is in a legal smokescreen of complexity and secrecy.

**2:14:** Hayek, *The Road to Serfdom* (Chicago: University of Chicago Press, 1944). See Ludwig von Mises, *The Anti-Capitalistic Mentality* (South Holland, Illinois: Libertarian Press, 1972). For instruction in how to convert from socialism to capitalism see John F. Stehle on the Amana community of Iowa in 1932, how they gave titles to the homesteads and distributed stock shares in all the productive property of the commune (*Wall Street Journal*, November 29, 1989, p. A14). See also Enno von Loewenstein on Ludwig Erhard's spectacularly successful reform in post-war Germany. Erhard distributed the American-made new Deutschemark currency — 40 marks to each person, plus 60 marks per employee to each business. Then he unilaterally abolished most rationing and controls in one surprise stroke (ibid., November 21, 1989, p. A18). Further, see Edgar L. Feigie, ibid., March 9, 1990, p. A12. Of Erhard see further in his *Prosperity through Competition* (New York: Frederick A. Praeger, 1958). It cannot always be so simple; see Piotr Brozyna and Mark Lilla on Poland in *American Spectator*, April 1990, pp. 23-25.

**2:15:** Nicolas Berdyaev, *The Russian Revolution* (New York: Sheed & Ward, 1931), p. 50. His brief psychological analysis of Communism is profound, especially in view of its early date. He had been exiled. See also Eric Hoffer, *The Temper of Our Time* (New York: Harper & Row, 1967).

**2:16:** David Satter, *Wall Street Journal*, May 23, 1984, p. 34.

**2:17:** Arnold J. Toynbee, *A Study of History*, Volume 8 (London: Oxford University Press, 1954), pp. 468-469.

Christopher Dawson, "Bolshevism and the Bourgeoisie," in *The Dynamics of World History* (New York: Sheed & Ward, 1956), pp. 225-230, at pp. 226, 228; this article is reprinted from the *English Review* 55 (1932): 239-250.

In general see H. B. Acton, *What Marx Really Said* (New York: Schocken Books, 1967); Acton, *The Illusion of the Epoch* (London: Cohen & West, 1955), Part 2, Section 2; H. B. Mayo "Marxist Theory of Morals" in *Encyclopedia of Morals*, edited by Vergilius Ferm (New York: Philosophical Library, 1956). Max Eastman writes historically in *Marxism, Is It Science?* (London: George Allen & Unwin, 1941). See Eugene Kamenka, *The Ethical Foundations of Marxism* (London: Routledge & Kegan Paul, 1962).

**2:18:** Toynbee, *Study of History*, Volume 9 [2:17], pp. 618-637, at pp. 622, 584.

**2:19:** Toynbee, ibid., Volume 8, p. 445; *Civilization on Trial* (New York: Oxford University Press, 1948), pp. 236-237.

**2:20:** The British historian Paul Johnson writes of the surprisingly similar lifestyles of prominent architects of the twentieth century in *Intellectuals* (New York: Harper & Row, 1989). The pattern of most of the intellectuals he discusses is one of almost incredible egocentricity, lechery, and disdain for inconvenient truths, together with a flair for self-promotion. Johnson states that

> Marx wrote about finance and industry all his life but he only knew two people connected with financial and industrial processes. Marx declined Engels's invitation to accompany him on a visit to a cotton mill, and so far as we know, Marx never set foot in a mill, factory, mine or other industrial workplace in the whole of his life. What is even more striking is Marx's hostility to fellow revolutionaries who had such experience — that is, working men who had become politically conscious. He attended a meeting of the German Workers' Education Society. He did not like what he saw. These men were mostly skilled workers,

watchmakers, printers, shoemakers; their leader was a forester. They were self-educated, disciplined, solemn, well-mannered, very anti-bohemian, anxious to transform society but moderate about the practical steps to this end. Marx viewed them with contempt: revolutionary cannon-fodder, no more (pp. 60-61).

Marx fathered an illegitimate child by his housemaid, shortly after his marriage to Jenny, who suffered a loss of *Lebensmut* (fortitude) shortly after. The son, Frederick, was alienated and disowned and became an uneducated laborer; see Arnold Künzli, *Karl Marx: Eine Psychographie* (Vienna: Europa Verlag, 1966), pp. 325-341, 835-836. Marx appears early to have flirted with Satanism; see *The Unknown Karl Marx*, edited by Robert Payne (New York: New York University Press, 1971), e.g., pp. 12, 81-83, 86, 116. As to Marx's Christian experience see pp. 33-43.

**2:21:** Phillip Berryman writes as a relatively well-informed socialist in *Liberation Theology* (New York: Pantheon Books, 1987). More negative is Michael Novak in *Will It Liberate?* (New York: Paulist Press, 1986). There is much to learn from Robert McAfee Brown in *Unexpected News: Reading the Bible with Third World Eyes*, despite its blindness to some economic and military realities (Philadelphia: Westminster Press, 1984).

**2:22:** See notably Karl Popper, *The Open Society and Its Enemies* (Princeton: Princeton University Press, 1962), also articles near the end of his *Conjectures and Refutations* [9:21]. See Thomas Sowell, *Marxism: Philosophy and Economics* (New York: William Morrow & Co., 1985). Literate brief criticism of dialectical materialism, so far as it pertains to science, appears in Bernard d'Espagnat, *Conceptual Foundations of Quantum Mechanics*, second edition [7:29], Preface, xvi-xx. See Holmes Rolston III [4:14], pp. 208-209, 248. *Marx* by Peter Singer is short and neutral (New York: Hill & Wang, 1980).

**2:23:** On some recent history of mega-banking see the book *Debt Shock*, by Darrell Delamide (Garden City, New York: Doubleday & Co., 1984). On the structure of the savings and loan swindles culminating in 1989 see James Ring Adams, *The Big Fix* (New York: John Wiley & Sons, 1990). Much more generally, read the Hoover Institution historian Antony Sutton, notably *America's Secret Establishment* (Billings, Montana: Liberty House Press, 1986, or c/o Research Publications, Box 84902, Phoenix, Arizona 85071).

**2:24:** George Getschel, *Wall Street Journal*, June 22, 1983, pp. 1, 26; June 23, pp. 1, 23.

**2:25:** Kenneth Boulding, adapted from "The Principle of Personal Responsibility," *Review of Social Economy* 12 (1954): 1-8, at pp. 6-7; reprinted in Boulding, *Collected Papers*, Volume 4, edited by Larry D. Singell (Boulder: Colorado Associated University Press, 1974), pp. 11-20, at pp. 18-19. See also Boulding, *Beyond Economics* (Ann Arbor: University of Michigan Press, 1968). Boulding is a poet:

Four things that give mankind a shove/ Are threats, exchange, persuasion, love;/ But taken in the wrong proportions/ These give us cultural abortions./ For threats bring manifold abuses/ In games where everybody loses;/ Exchange enriches every nation/ But leads to dangerous alienation;/ Persuaders organize their brothers/ But fool themselves as well as others;/ And love, with longer pull than hate,/ Is slow indeed to propagate.

The above is from his *Collected Papers*, Volume 5 (Boulder: Colorado Associated Universities Press, 1975), p. 147. Paul H. Douglas, economist and U.S. senator, presents many examples to prove *"The Reality of Non-Commercial Incentives in Economic Life,"* in *The Trend of Economics*, edited by R. G. Tugwell (New York: Alfred A. Knopf, 1924), pp. 153-188. Douglas discusses scientists, businessmen and wage-earners. George Gilder, author of the deservedly best-selling book *Wealth and Poverty*, finds the essence of capitalism (at its moral best) to be the risking by entrepreneurs of their money in an imaginative anticipation of people's needs, without reliable assurance of return (New York: Basic Books, 1981).

Contrast "Alienated Labor," in *Writings of the Young Karl Marx on Philosophy and Society* (Garden City, New York: Doubleday & Co., 1967), pp. 287-301, especially pp. 288-289. More cogently in the negative see Paul H. Weaver, *The Suicidal Corporation* (New York: Simon & Schuster, 1988), a study of perverse inclinations toward expediency and psycho-political machinations. Ethically sensitive business people will enjoy the best-selling book *In Search of Excellence*, by Thomas J. Peters and Robert H. Waterman Jr. (New York: Harper & Row, 1982). See also Frank Chapman Sharp and Philip G. Fox, *Business Ethics* (New York: Appleton-Century-Crofts, 1937).

**2:26:** The American sociologist Peter Berger presents a similar insight in Chapter 9 of *The Capitalist Revolution* (New York: Basic Books, 1986).

**2:27:** Jean-François Revel, *How Democracies Perish* (Garden City, New York: Doubleday & Co., 1984), p. 344. Peter F. Drucker urges that capitalism has on occasion been a creed; see *The End of Economic Man* [21:29], e.g., pp. 37-50. Many primitive societies acknowledge incorporeal property including copyrights and monopolies like patent monopolies; see Robert H. Lowie, *Primitive Society* (New York: Boni & Liveright, 1920), pp. 235-239.

**2:28:** Friedrich A. Hayek, *Law, Legislation and Liberty*, 3 volumes (Chicago: University of Chicago Press, 1973-1979), Volume 3, Epilogue, pp. 161-165, etc.; Volume 2, pp. 115-116; try Chapters 10 and 11. For a summary see Hayek [19:16]; Thomas Sowell, *Knowledge and Decisions* (New York: Basic Books, 1980).

**2:29:** Irving Kristol, *Wall Street Journal*, February 20, 1979, p. 16. See H. B. Acton, *The Morals of Markets* (London: Longmans Group, 1971). See Hubert Henderson, *Supply and Demand* (Chicago: University of Chicago Press, 1921); W. H. McComb, *The Businessman Must Save Himself* (New York: Harper & Brothers, 1954). Similarly, see Isabel Paterson, *The*

*God of the Machine* (New York: G. P. Putnam's Sons, 1943). A heap of myths about profit is swept away by Lawrence T. Harbeck, in **"Some Plain Truth about Profit"** (*Wall Street Journal*, January 20, 1972, p. 12). More generally, see Russell Kirk, *Economics: Work and Prosperity* (Pensacola: A Beka Books [Pensacola Christian College], 1989); Donald Paarlberg, *Great Myths of Economics* (New York: New American Library, 1968).

The social scientist Edward C. Banfield treats at length of the inescapable moral component of the problem of poverty and of economic development. One shockingly heretical essay is entitled, "Rioting Mainly for Fun and Profit," in *The Unheavenly City Revisited* (Boston: Little, Brown & Co., 1974). See his book *The Moral Basis of a Backward Society* (Glencoe, Illinois: Free Press, 1958). A startlingly simple and just mode of taxation would be a single tax on energy use; see a letter by Kenneth S. Obenski of San Diego in *Mensa Journal*, March 1984. See also Nicholas Kaldor, *An Expenditure Tax* (London: George Allen & Unwin, 1955).

**2:30:** Dennis H. Robertson, "What Does the Economist Economize?" in his *Economic Commentaries* (London: Staples Press, 1956), pp. 147-154, also in *National Policy for Economic Welfare at Home and Abroad*, edited by Robert Lekachman (New York: Russell & Russell, 1961), pp. 1-6. The internal quotation is from Chapter 9 of *Alice in Wonderland* by Lewis Carroll.

**2:31:** Elizabeth Hoyt, *Science Monthly*, February 1951, pp. 114-119, at p. 118. Medieval historical perspective is afforded by Alejandro A. Chafuen in *Scholastic Economics* (San Francisco: Ignatius Press, 1986), also by Michael Slattery in *Crisis* (Notre Dame, Indiana), April 1988, pp. 24-29.

**2:32:** Schweitzer, *Philosophy of Civilization* [1:11], p. 320 (251-252).

**2:33:** Albert Schweitzer, *Philosophy of Civilization* [1:11], p. 230 (155-156).

**2:34:** Henry C. Simon, as reported by Charles Hartshorne.

**2:35:** Hayek, *Law, Legislation and Liberty* [2:28], Chapters 15, 9.

**2:36:** Under the shocking title *The Art of Selfishness*, David Seabury gives needed practical advice (New York: Simon & Schuster, 1937). A more theoretical treatment comes from Don E. Marietta Jr. in *Ethics* 82 (1972): 232-238, "On Using People," and in the *Humanist*, May-June 1982, pp. 27-29, 46. In ecology, hard choices are presented by Garrett Hardin in *The Limits of Altruism* (Bloomington: Indiana University Press, 1977), especially Chapter 3. See John Wesley's sermon, "The Use of Money" and Thomas Aquinas, *Summa Contra Gentiles*, Book 3, Chapter 25, Section 9.

**2:37:** Joseph Smith, quoted by Truman G. Madsen in a speech at Brigham Young University, c. 1968. Compare Confucius, *Analects* 6:28.

**2:38:** Michael Novak in *National Review,* April 6, 1984, p. 48.

**2:39:** In Germany in the 1920s, the idea of "shrinking" or "melting" money ("Schwungeld") had a popular following of many thousands, who were organized as the Freiwirtschaftsbund, with some academic support. Hitler outlawed the movement in 1933 as being allegedly a political party. See Silvio Gesell, *The Natural Economic Order,* translated from the sixth German edition (Berlin-Frohnau, Neo-Verlag, 1929); skip Part 2. On detailed relevant monetary history see Fritz Schwarz, *Segen und Fluch des Geldes* (Blessing and Curse of Money), revised edition (Bern, 1931-33). John Maynard Keynes had some nice things to say about Gesell while cautioning that the power of a melting-money scheme is limited by the availability of other media of exchange than money. His further criticism appears not to touch the practical proposal (*The General Theory of Employment, Interest, and Money* [New York: Harcourt, Brace & Co., 1936], pp. 353-358). Anglo-American Keynesian economics prevailed after 1945, in Germany as elsewhere.

Gesell had based his proposal upon periodically stamped currency. The late Arthur Dahlberg adapted the Gesell proposal to modern "checkbook" money, proposing a tax on bank accounts at the rate of 0.25 or 0.2 percent per month or, alternatively, an equivalent programmed shrinkage of the dollar amount of bank accounts. See *When Capital Goes on Strike* (New York: Harper & Brothers, 1938); *How to Save Free Enterprise* (Old Greenwich, Connecticut: Devin-Adair Co., 1974). At present, the impossibility of defining money in a forest of novel quasi-monetary instruments (for example, credit cards and certificates of deposit) renders all such proposals unworkable until such time as it becomes politically feasible to restructure financial instruments in such a way as to permit the mild taxing (or shrinking) of highly liquid wealth without undue avoidance. Yet opportunity arises in shattered or less developed economies. Knowledgeable commentary for publication is solicited by the present editors.

Since Roman times and with temporary swings aside, 2 1/2 to 3 percent has apparently been the residual rate of interest after compensation to the money lender was made for risk, bother, and inflation. Arguably, then, an ethical interest rate would be around 3 per cent lower than normal market rates. Such a reduction would be socially desirable to prevent endless exponential accumulations of wealth. The Gesell-Dahlberg sort of tax on, or shrinkage of, money would result in a reduction in all interest rates by about the same amount as the tax. Naturally, the rich, especially rentiers, would hardly support such a cut in their income.

Another kind of employment-stabilizing scheme is Hazelett's "money-pump" plan which uses governmentally-issued, transferable, marketable contractual instruments that pledge the freely-contracting holder to provide a certain amount of employment during a certain period. These would be "sold" by the government by means of an accompanying premium determined by the market for the instruments. The quantity to be pushed onto the market would be sufficient to cover almost the entire work force of a nation and hence would guarantee general employment but would not specify who anyone would work for. The plan is not feasible until such time as the generality of employers can have their fears allayed by receiving instruction into its curious rationale. So far, with rare exceptions, not even economists know of it, let alone employers. An auxiliary transferable permit scheme would allow the banks of a nation to hold only a specified maximum quantity of excess reserves but would not require this of any one bank (see *American Economic Review* 47 [1957]: 136-148, mostly reprinted in *Solutions to Unemployment*, edited by David C. Colander [New York: Harcourt Brace Jovanovich, 1981], pp. 186-200). Both printings contain a comment by Albert G. Hart. A further application of the abstract idea is that of Colander and Abba P. Lerner of *MAP: A Market Anti-Inflation Plan* (New York: Harcourt Brace Jovanovich, 1980). Transferable "permits to pollute," issued in a limited, environmentally acceptable quantity, are now used by the State of California. Hart thought of this application by the early 1960s, but whether the idea was reinvented for California or conveyed by a student of Hart's at Columbia University is not known.

The spirit of all these macro-economic devices is that of a pressure so flexible that the immediate trifling loss of freedom results in effectively greater total freedom. They afford a promise of transparency in government since, if successful, they would render a thousand other governmental interventions superfluous.

**2:40:** See, for instance, among many others, "Will Money Managers Wreck the Economy?" by the editors of *Business Week*, August 13, 1984, pp. 86-93; "The U.S. Needs Patient Investors," by Donald N. Frey in *Fortune*, July 7, 1986, pp. 125-126.

**2:41:** Claire Huchet Bishop, *All Things Common* (New York: Harper & Brothers, 1950); Victor Peters, *All Things Common: The Hutterian Way of Life* (Minneapolis: University of Minnesota Press, 1965); William Bradford, *Of Plimoth Plantation*,

many editions, Book 2, Chapter 14. In general see Howard E. Jensen on "Communistic Settlements" in *Encyclopedia of Religion*, edited by Vergilius Ferm (New York: Philosophical Library, 1945), also Acts 4:32-5:12.

**2:42:** Hazelett must confess to having been a socialist for a few months while 20 years of age.

**2:43:** Of many books, that of David P. Currie, *The Constitution of the United States*, is a brief introduction (Chicago: University of Chicago Press, 1988). Massimo Salvadori summarizes its intellectual prehistory in the latter part of *Liberal Democracy* (Garden City: Doubleday & Co., 1957); at greater length see Thomas L. Pangle, *The Spirit of Modern Republicanism* (Chicago: University of Chicago Press, 1988).

**2:44:** Omar Khayyám, *Rubáiyát*, translated by Edward FitzGerald.

**First epigraph:** Friedrich A. Hayek [2:28], pp. 66-67.

**Second epigraph:** Gilbert Keith Chesterton, *More Quotable Chesterton*, edited by George Marlin, Richard Rabatin, and John Swan (San Francisco: Ignatius Press, 1988), p. 65, March 1, 1919. The book consists of selections from the *Illustrated London News*, with dates as in the American edition (which followed the British edition by two weeks). As to housing and urban planning, much of Frank Lloyd Wright's book *When Democracy Builds* (second edition) is of value (Chicago: University of Chicago Press, 1947).

**Third epigraph:** Thomas Sowell, *Compassion Versus Guilt* (New York: William Morrow & Co., 1987), p. 240.

# 3. The Cradle of Science

**Epigraph:** Stanley L. Jaki, *Duhem* [3:9], p. 433.

**3:1:** Andrew Dickson White, *A History*

of the Warfare of Science with Theology in Christendom, 2 volumes (New York: D. Appleton & Co., 1897).

**3:2:** *Fortune,* "The Scientist and Religion," unsigned, October 1948, 106-112, 166-176, at p. 176.

**3:3:** Jonathan Edwards is an outstanding example of a great thinker who was misled into denial of freedom of the will by a misapplication of Newton's mechanics. Jaki discusses freedom of the will and the limits of physics in general in Chapter 9 *et passim* of *The Relevance of Physics* (Chicago: University of Chicago Press, 1966); *The Absolute Beneath the Relative* (Lanham, Maryland: University Press of America, 1988)—e.g., Chapter 6. See further Jaki, *Road of Science* [3:33], pp. 291, 317, and his note 43 on p. 429.

**3:4:** Jaki, *Relevance of Physics* [3:3], p. 455.

**3:5:** Ibid., Chapter 10; *Zygon* 2 (1967): 187-202. For young people, the Sowers Series of books from Mott Media presents highly readable biographies of Kepler, Newton and others, with religious information not presented in public-school histories. The books are semi-fictionalized to supply dialogue.

**3:6:** See Jaki, "The Case for Galileo's Rehabilitation," *Fidelity* (South Bend), March 1986, pp. 37-41. Subject to Jaki's comments, see Giorgio de Santillana, *The Crime of Galileo* (Chicago: University of Chicago Press, 1955), e.g., the preface. See also Morris Raphael Cohen, *The Meaning of Human History,* second edition (La Salle, Illinois: Open Court Publishing Co., 1961), pp. 254-255. Pope John Paul II announced on May 9, 1983, that Galileo's conviction was "regrettable" and was the result of "grave incomprehension."

**3:7:** Jaki, *Duhem* [3:9], pp. 381-384, quoting William Whewell.

**3:8:** Friedrich Heer, *The Medieval World* (Cleveland: World Publishing Co., 1962), Chapter 12, "Science." See also Heer's *Making of the Middle Ages,* p. 304.

**3:9:** The eminent quantum physicist Louis de Broglie describes Duhem as a theoretical physicist who "bequeathed a beautiful and great work where physicists of today can still find numerous topics worthy of reflection and study" (Stanley L. Jaki, *Uneasy Genius: The Life and Work of Pierre Duhem* [The Hague: Martinus Nijhoff Publishers, 1984], p. 433, p. 309).

**3:10:** Jaki, "On Whose Side Is History?" *National Review,* August 23, 1985, pp. 41-47, at p. 44, reprinted in Jaki, *Chance or Reality and Other Essays* (Lanham, Maryland: University Press of America and Intercollegiate Studies Institute, 1986), pp. 233-244. See also Jaki, *Duhem* [3:9], p. 378; *Science and Creation* [3:14], Chapter 9.

**3:11:** Pierre Duhem, *Le système du monde: Histoire des doctrines cosmologiques de Platon à Copernic,* 10 volumes (Paris: A. Hermann, 1913-1959).

**3:12:** Duhem, *Études sur Leonardo da Vinci,* 3:52, also p. ix, translated by and quoted in Jaki, *Duhem* [3:9], p. 394. See Jaki, *The Absolute Beneath the Relative* [3:3], Chapter 9. The Chinese had the first law of motion by the third century B.C. (Temple [3:31], p. 161, after Joseph Needham [3:32]). However, nothing of further interest seems to have come of it.

**3:13:** Jaki, "On Whose Side Is History?" [3:10], p. 43.

**3:14:** Duhem, *Système du monde* [3:11], 8:340, translated by and quoted in Jaki, *Duhem* [3:9], p. 429. See especially Jaki, *Science and Creation: From Eternal Cycles to an Oscillating Universe* (Edinburgh: Scottish Academic Press, 1974), p. 221.

**3:15:** Duhem, *Les origines de la statique,* 2:iv: 2:286, translated by and quoted in Jaki, *Duhem* [3:9], p. 387, 389; see quotation from Albert Einstein, p. 436.

**3:16:** Jaki, *Duhem* [3:9], p. 386. See as to Buridan on p. 326 therein.

**3:17:** Jaki, *Road of Science* [3:33], p. 239. Duhem's view contradicts that of other writers. But Errol E. Harris is in agreement with Duhem; see Harris' *Hypothesis and Perception* [9:20], pp. 224-231.

**3:18:** E.g., *The New Encyclopaedia Brittanica,* 15th edition (1985), *Macropaedia,* "Europe: The Renaissance: The Italian Renaissance."

**3:19:** Will Durant, *The Renaissance* (New York: Simon & Schuster, 1953), p. 728. Jacob Bronowski, author of the best-selling book *The Ascent of Man* had, in a previous work, *The Western Intellectual Tradition,* referred to Duhem's historical work in a footnote but failed to mention that Duhem meant to prove something more than details of scientific history (New York: Harper & Brothers, 1960), p. 17. Such writers prefer what Jaki calls "the hallowed sleight-of-hand which starts everything with Galileo" (*Duhem* [3:9], p. 426). The historian Herbert Butterfield did briefly reveal an understanding of Duhem's thesis in *The Origins of Modern Science* (London: G. Bell & Sons Ltd., 1957), Chapter 1. David C. Lindberg did likewise in a preface, in *Science in the Middle Ages* (Chicago: University of Chicago Press, 1978).

**3:20:** Jaki, *Duhem* [3:9], pp. 53-55: 160 *et passim*. Jaki teaches at Seton Hall University and is currently a fellow of the Institute for Advanced Study at Princeton.

**3:21:** Jaki, "Science and Censorship," *Intercollegiate Review*, Winter 1985-86, pp. 41-49, reprinted in *The Absolute Beneath the Relative* [3:3], Chapter 11.

**3:22:** On Christianity's relation to Plato see Adam Fox, *Plato and the Christians* (London: SCM Press, 1957). As to Xenophanes see Jonathan Barnes, *The Presocratic Philosophers*, 2 volumes, Volume 1 (London: Routledge & Kegan Paul, 1979), Chapter 5; John Mansley Robinson, *An Introduction to Early Greek Philosophy* (Boston: Houghton Mifflin Co., 1968), pp. 50-55; Dawson, *Religion and World History* [6:25], pp. 97-98).

**3:23:** On the Ionian philosophers and the concept of scientific law see Frederick Copleston, *A History of Philosophy* (several editions), Volume 1, e.g., Chapters 11 and 3; Francis Cornford, *Before and After Socrates* (Cambridge: At the University Press, 1932), Chapter 1.

Jaki is accused of slighting the Greek contribution to science, but see his 1983 essay "The Greeks of Old and the Novelty of Science," in *Chance or Reality* [3:10], pp. 205-224.

**3:24:** Jaki, *Science and Creation* [3:14], p. 130. See Plutarch, *Marcellus*, 14; this is cited in a more general discussion by Lynn White Jr., "Science and Technology in the Middle Ages," in *Scientific Change*, edited by A. C. Crombie (New York: Basic Books, 1963), pp. 272-291, at p. 285.

**3:25:** *Science and Creation* [3:14], p. 214, also Chapter 9; *The Savior of Science* [4:14],

pp. 71-72. Comparisons of Islam with Christianity from a Christian fundamentalist viewpoint are found in John Elder, *The Biblical Approach to the Moslem* (Fort Washington, Pennsylvania: Worldwide Evangelization Crusade, 1978). Christopher Dawson has good words for Sufi mysticism in Islam; see *Religion and World History* [6:25], Part 1, Chapter 10, also in *Dublin Review* 186 (1930): 34-61.

**3:26:** Harris, *Hypothesis and Perception* [9:20], Chapter 12.

**3:27:** Charles Sanders Peirce, *Collected Papers* [1:2], 1.316, 5.47. See also Sections 1.80, 5.591-5.592, 6.12, 6,553, and 7.46-7.48. See further Charles Hartshorne, "Anthropomorphic Tendencies in Positivism," *Philosophy of Science* 8 (1941): 184-203.

**3:28:** Galileo Galilei, *Dialogue Concerning the Two Chief World Systems*, translated by Stillman Drake, second edition (Berkeley: University of California Press, 1967), p. 103. See also Galileo, *The Assayer* (Il Saggiatore), selections of which appear in *Discoveries and Opinions of Galileo*, translated by Stillman Drake (Garden City, New York: Doubleday & Co., 1957), notably pp. 271-272. See further Maurice Clavelin, *The Natural Philosophy of Galileo*, translated by A. J. Pomerans (Cambridge: MIT Press, 1974), pp. 381 to end, especially pp. 393, 414. On *il lume naturale* generally, see Peirce, *Collected Papers* [1:2], 1.80-1.81, 1.316, 5.47, 5.591-5.592, 6-12, 6.553, 7.46-7.48. See Errol E. Harris, *Hypothesis and Perception* [9:20], e.g., Chapter 12: and Chapter 9 herein. See Jaki in *Road of Science* [3:33] — for instance, Chapters 16 and 8. The specialist may consult Abner Shimony, "Scientific Inference," in *The Nature and Function of Scientific Theories*, edited by Robert G. Colodny (Pittsburgh: University of Pittsburgh Press, 1970), pp. 79-172. For a relevant sophisticated psychological view see *Understanding Causality* by Jean Piaget (New York: W. W. Norton & Co., 1974). As to visualization as a component of science see Lewis E. Walkup, *Perceptual and Motor Skills* 21 (1965): 35-41.

**3:29:** Jaki, *Science and Creation* [3:14], p. 183.

**3:30:** Kepler, quoted by Gerald Holton

in "Johannes Kepler: A Case Study on the Interaction of Science, Metaphysics, and Theology," *Philosophical Forum* (U.S.A.) o.s. 14 (1956): 21-33, at pp. 31-32, from Letter to Mästlin, April 19, 1597, evidently translated from *Johannes Kepler in seinen Briefen*, edited by Max Caspar and Walther von Dyck (Munich: R. Oldenberg, 1930).

**3:31:** Jaki, *Science and Creation* [3:14], p. 32. See *The Genius of China* by Robert Temple (New York: Simon & Schuster, 1986). Temple draws on the vast work of Needham (see below).

**3:32:** *Science and Creation* [3:14], pp. 35-43. Joseph Needham, *Science and Civilisation in China* (Cambridge: At the University Press, 1954+), Volume 2, Section 18(*h*): Volume 3, 19(*k*), quoted at p. 581 in Volume 2. See Jaki, ibid., Chapter 2; *Road of Science* [3:33], p. 14. Robert S. Cohen, a Marxist, comments on the conclusion of Needham in "The Problem of 19(k)," (*Journal of Chinese Philosophy* 1 [1973]: 103-117). Cohen's comments do not appear to be damaging to Needham's view. For further insight into the limitations imposed by Chinese traditional religion see Andrew Chih, *Chinese Humanism* [20:30], Chapter 13.

**3:33:** Stanley L. Jaki in *The Road of Science and the Ways to God* (Chicago: University of Chicago Press, 1978). Brief corroborations of Jaki's thesis come from three places. First, see Alfred North Whitehead, *Science and the Modern World*, Chapter 1, paragraphs 33-36 (several editions, first published 1925). Second, see Morris R. Cohen in *The Meaning of Human History*, second edition (La Salle, Illinois: Open Court Publishing Co., 1961), pp. 254-255. Third, see Eric Hoffer's anticipation: "Jehovah and the Machine" (first published by Harper & Row in 1963, in *The Ordeal of Change*), reprinted in *Between the Devil and the Dragon* [1:epigraph], pp. 56-59. Fourth, see Loren Eiseley, *Darwin's Century* [4:14], Chapter 3, Section 2. For occasionally cogent critiques of Jaki on secondary points see Kevin J. Sharpe in *Religious Studies* 18 (1982): 55-75; Frederick Ferré in *Journal of Religion* 60 (1980): 78-80; Frank E. Budenholzer in *Zygon* 15 (1980): 247-249; Frank R. Haig in *Theological*

*Studies* 40 (1979): 206-208. For more favorable reviews, and reviews in general, consult *Arts and Humanities Citation Index*. See also Lynn Thorndike in *Journal of the History of Ideas* 4 (1943): 65-74. Few people appreciate the pains entailed by true and fruitful beginnings, that is, of what it is to take nothing and make something of it. By contrast, reproach for lack of perfect progress is easy.

We do not agree with Jaki at quite every point. Jaki's arguments against the principle of plenitude and against the possibility of life on other worlds seem strained. Jaki makes good arguments against the validity of many philosophies, but his treatment of other philosophers is rather short and rough—for instance, of Whitehead. In addition to Jaki's classical theism (God's omnipotence and omniscience), we have a problem with Jaki's support of the theories of geometry and relativity in the form in which they have become conventions of physics; see [10:5].

A word on some histories of Western philosophy. Will Durant's popular *Story of Philosophy* has gone through several editions and translations, starting in 1927. As intellectual history, Durant is pleasant to read, especially in his detailed and perceptive delineation of personalities. But in presenting the substance of philosophy, he leaves his million-odd lay readers with the impression that philosophy, rather than being a proto-scientific enterprise aiming at knowledge, consists instead of long-winded, personalized literary wisdom that properly has nothing to do with theistic religion. Durant, having spurned theism, spurns epistemology also, to say nothing of logic (see his prefaces). He supposes that the literary residue of the history of philosophy is what makes it worth the trouble to study. It appears that Durant's book killed further interest in philosophy in America, much as sterilized flies spoil their mates' chance for reproduction.

See Hartshorne's list of histories of philosophy in the preface and introduction to his *Insights and Oversights of Great Thinkers* [20:19]. Jaki and Hartshorne when read concurrently with the now available histories will complement them. An excellent introduction to philosophy is *The Fundamental Questions of Philosophy* by the British philosopher Alfred Cyril Ewing, despite our lack of agreement with some of his conclusions (London: Routledge & Kegan Paul, 1951).

**3:34:** Thomas Molnar characterizes phenomenology as asserting that it "was an effort to prove that, although I do not know the real, I know myself in the process of knowing" (*Chronicles* [Rockford], February 1986, pp. 26-27).

**3:35:** See, e.g., Errol E. Harris, *The Foundations of Metaphysics in Science* (London: George Allen & Unwin, 1965), Chapter 22; David Bohm, *Wholeness and the Implicate Order* (London: Routledge & Kegan Paul, 1983). In general see John B. Cobb Jr., *Process Theology* (Philadelphia: Westminster Press, 1976).

**3:36:** Jaki, *Science and Creation* [3:14], pp. 56-64.

**3:37:** Arnold J. Toynbee, *A Study of History* [2:17], Volume 4, pp. 23-39, at p. 30.

**3:38:** *Science and Creation* [3:14], pp. 43, 169-176; Chapter 8. Discussed by Vernon J. Bourke in *Wisdom from St. Augustine* (Houston: University of St. Thomas, 1984), pp. 194-195, 203. See Augustine, *De civitate Dei* (The City of God), Book 12, Section 13. See Roger L. Shinn, "Augustinian and Cyclical Views of History," *Anglican Theological Review* 31 (1949): 133-141. See S. G. F. Brandon in *The Voices of Time*, edited by J. T. Fraser (New York: George Braziller, 1966), pp. 140-157.

**3:39:** Jaki, *Road of Science* [3:33], pp. 269-272: Jaki, *Cosmos and Creator* (Edinburgh: Scottish Academic Press, 1980), pp. 20-22. The importance of the doctrine of creation was anticipated by M. B. Foster in three articles in *Mind*: 41 (1936): 1-27; ibid., 43 (1934): 446-468; ibid., 44 (1935): 439-466. Foster gives several reasons why Greek thought and indeed early Christian thought did not result in science.

**3:40:** See Charles Hartshorne, *International Journal of Ethics* 45 (1934): 90-101, at p. 99. See Chapter 9 herein.

**3:41:** Also Jaki, *Science and Creation* [3:14], p. 203.

**3:42:** Jaki, *Duhem* [3:9], p. 404; see also Jaki, *Science and Creation* [3:14], 243.

**3:43:** As to Engels see Jaki, *Science and Creation* [3:14], p. 313.

**3:44:** As to astrology see Jaki, *Science and Creation* [3:14], the index.

**3:45:** Toynbee, *A Study of History*, Volume 4, pp. 56-63. See also the first part of Augustine's *De civitate Dei* (The City of God). Jaroslav Pelikan analyzes the history impartially in *The Excellent Empire* (San Francisco: Harper & Row, 1987). Toynbee blamed Christianity and Judaism for our ecological problems, since man was commanded in Genesis 1:28 to "fill the earth and subdue it, and have dominion" over everything in it (*Horizon*, Summer 1973, pp. 4-9, abridged in *New York Times*, September 16, 1973, Section 4, p. 15). Much the same people who have followed Toynbee in this matter also blame Christianity for obstructing the growth of science, an inconsistency noted by Norman Lamm in *New York Times*, October 4, 1973, p. 44, and R. V. Young Jr. in *National Review*, December 20, 1974, pp. 1454-1458, 1477-1479. See further J. Patrick Dobel in *Christian Century* 94 (1977): 906-909; Rosemary Ruether, *Christian Century* 95 (1978): 1129-1132; Martin LaBar in *Christianity Today*, July 26, 1974, pp. 8-10. A thorough philosophical treatment of ecological endeavors is that of Bryan G. Norton, *Why Preserve Natural Variety?* (Princeton: Princeton University Press, 1987).

**3:46:** See Pitirim A. Sorokin in *Journal of Modern History* 12 (1940): 374-387, also Paul Johnson, *A History of Christianity* (New York: Atheneum, 1976), e.g., pp. 112, 130, 156.

**3:47:** Henry St. John (Lord Viscount Bolingbroke), as quoted by Jaki, *Road of Science* [3:33], pp. 328, 457.

**3:48:** *Duhem* [3:9], pp. 413-426; Jaki, *Road of Science* [3:33], pp. 12-14: Jaki, "Science and Censorship," *Intercollegiate Review*, Winter 1985-86, pp. 41-49, at pp. 45-46. George Sarton is a special subject of Jaki's negative attention.

**3:49:** Jaki, "On Whose Side Is History?" [3:10], at p. 44; Duhem is quoted in Jaki, *Duhem* [3:9], p. 399.

**3:50:** Wisdom of Solomon 11:20.

3:51: Jaki, *Science and Creation* [3:14], pp. 158, 223.

**Epigraph:** Augustine, *On the Morals of the Catholic Church*, Chapter 7.

# 4. Evolution or Creation?

**Epigraph:** Monsignor Ronald Knox, repeated by John J. McAleer in *Boston Globe*, quoted in *Readers Digest*.

**4:1:** Psalms 19:1 and 139:14 (one number less in most Catholic Bibles). See remarks of Paul in Romans 1:18-22 ff.; Wisdom of Solomon (Book of Wisdom) 13:1-9; Ecclesiasticus (Sirach or Ben Sira) 42, 43.

**4:2:** Plato, *The Laws*, Book 10.

**4:3:** Thomas Aquinas, quoted. For the history of the design argument consult Barrow and Tipler, *Anthropic Cosmological Principle* [2:1], Chapter 2; and David Griffin, *God, Power and Evil* (New York: Seabury Press, 1983). The astrophysicist Stephen Hawking in his book *A Brief History of Time* challenges design arguments (New York: Bantam Books, 1988). A digest of philosophical criticism of Hawking appears in a review in the *Economist*, March 11, 1989, p. 90. Whatever is to be said of Paley's assumption of specific divine intervention in the formation of creatures, such a presumption led William Harvey to discover the circulation of the blood; see Barrow and Tipler [2:1], pp. 52, 55-56, 75.

**4:4:** Robert Shapiro, *Origins* (New York: Bantam Books, 1987). Curiously, Shapiro refutes every form of modern evolutionist theory by a variety of well-informed and compelling arguments, demonstrating that there is no chance that species could have arrived by chance. But then, in the last chapter, he nonetheless clings *ad hominem* to the assumption that it *has* all happened by chance. He decides to believe what he himself has elaborately shown that there is no scientific reason to believe—that is, in evolution by chance. And he does this after chiding the creationists as foolish and sentimental for believing in God as the Creator of life.

Thus, he allows his own atheist religion to take the place of doing real natural science. His atheist hope, that in time we can somehow find a way to scientifically prove the dogma of evolution by chance, is a hope based on no facts or logic. Rather, it is based merely on his personal preference and taste. Of course, Shapiro is entitled to his religion. But he should acknowledge that it *is* religion, not science, while he controverts it with his own scientific arguments.

**4:5:** Charles B. Thaxton, Walter L. Bradley, and Roger L. Olsen, *The Mystery of Life's Origin* (New York: Philosophical Library, 1984). They are aware of Sidney W. Fox, who writes in opposition in Montagu [4:14], pp. 194-239.

**4:6:** Denton [4:14], Chapter 12. See textbooks on genetics or evolution as to comparisons of, say, serum proteins and blood groups.

**4:7:** Norman Macbeth, in *Darwin Retried*. A lawyer and a careful, well-informed challenger—Chapter 4.

**4:8:** Darwin is quoted in Macbeth [4:7], p. 101n; see also p. 74. A negative note is that of Ernest Mayer, quoted in Barrow and Tipler [2:1], pp. 132 ff.

**4:9:** Alan Hayward, *God Is* (Nashville: Thomas Nelson Publishers, 1978). The last two chapters by this devout Christian go further than many philosophically minded readers would be willing to follow. As to the bombardier beetle (pp. 105-107), whatever the form of the evolutionary teleology, the chemical mechanisms of the bombardier did plausibly evolve, according to H. Schildknecht, who presents partial developments in other insects in *Endeavour* 30 (1971): 136-141. Nevertheless, explanation of viable variations as solely random is at least dubious, in this matter as in others.

**4:10:** On Goldschmidt see Macbeth [4:7], Chapter 17. An extension is offered by Karl Popper in "The Hopeful Behavioral Monster," in his *Objective Knowledge*, revised edition (Oxford: Clarendon Press, 1979), pp. 281-284.

**4:11:** Stephen Jay Gould, *The Panda's Thumb* (New York: W. W. Norton & Co., 1980), Part 5. More technically, see Niles Eldredge and Gould, *Models in Paleontology*, edited by Thomas J. M. Schopf (San Francisco: Freeman, Cooper & Co., 1972, pp. 82-115). Asa Gray's "mediate creation," comes physically to rather the same thing as Goldschmidt, Eldredge, and Gould have put forth; see Gray's moderate, literate talk in 1880, reprinted in *Is God a Creationist?* edited by Roland Mushat Frye (New York: Charles Scribner's Sons, 1983), pp. 107-118.

**4:12:** Madge E. Scheibel and Arnold B. Scheibel, "The Physiology of Consciousness," *American Journal of Orthopsychiatry* 30 (1960): 10-14.

**4:13:** Lynn Margulis and Dorion Sagan, *Microcosmus* (New York: Summit Books, 1987), p. 67.

**4:14:** Michael Denton, *Evolution: A Theory in Crisis* (Bethesda, Maryland: Adler & Adler, 1986), pp. 327, 328, 342. Denton's work brings to full light many problems that more biologists ought to become aware of. Holmes Rolston III writes mainly as a philosopher in his *Science and Religion: A. Critical Survey* (Philadelphia: Temple University Press, 1987), e.g., Chapter 3. Neither these authors nor others invoke divine influence in the course of evolution, but they, along with Shapiro, show the insufficiency of all other theories. In *Evolutionary Theory: The Unfinished Synthesis*, Robert G. B. Reid presents many options in evolutionary theory (Ithaca, New York: Cornell University Press, 1985).

Contrariwise, see "Nothing in Biology Makes Sense Except in the Light of Evolution," by the leading geneticist Theodosius Dobzhansky in *American Biology Teacher* 35 (1973): 125-129. At greater length see *Science and Creationism*, edited by Ashley Montagu (Oxford: Oxford University Press, 1984). The reader is forewarned that, in this book, there is much stridency, dogmatism, and close-mindedness, relieved however by Kenneth Boulding's plea for moderation and humility (pp. 142-158).

For moral implications of Darwinism as often interpreted, consult Stanley L. Jaki's works: *Angels, Apes, and Men* (La Salle, Illinois: Sherwood Sugden & Co., 1983), Chapter 2: *The Savior of Science* (Washington: Regnery Gateway, 1988), Chapter 4 *et passim; Road of Science* [3:33], Chapter 18; *Cosmos and Creator* (Edinburgh: Scottish Academic Press, 1980), pp. 112-121; *Chronicles* (Rockford), August 1986, pp. 15-18, reprinted in *The Absolute Beneath the Relative* [3:3], Chapter 12.

Margulis and Sagan in *Microcosmus* [4:13] express the need to humble *homo sapiens*. The case is overstated, though it should not be ignored. The "dominion" over, or the subduing of, other creatures enjoined in Genesis 1:26-28 doesn't mean to kill them off wantonly. Excellent treatments of ethics in relation to other creatures and the environment are those of Holmes Rolston III: *Philosophy Gone Wild* (Buffalo: Prometheus Books, 1986), and *Environmental Ethics* (Philadelphia: Temple University Press, 1988). Job 38-41 is relevant.

For a sympathetic but objective history of Darwinism to mid-century see Loren Eiseley, *Darwin's Century* (Garden City, New York: Doubleday & Co., 1961). See also Søren Løvtrup, *Darwinism: The Refutation of a Myth* (London: Croom Helm, 1987).

**4:15:** Darwin had vague misgivings about postulating unrestricted chance; see discussion by Charles Hartshorne in *The Logic of Perfection* (La Salle, Illinois: Open Court Publishing Co., 1962), Chapter 7, especially p. 207. Alfred Russel Wallace, Darwin's able co-discoverer, doubted that chance was enough; see Eiseley [4:15], Chapter 11, Section 6, etc. For a treatment of theistic evolution see David Ray Griffin in [16:11], Chapter 5.

**4:16:** J. E. Lovelock, *The Ages of Gaia* (New York: W. W. Norton & Co., 1988).

**4:17:** See Rolston, *Science and Religion* [4:14], pp. 67-72, 113; Freeman J. Dyson in *Scientific American*, September 1971, pp. 50-59; Hayward, *God Is* [4:9], Chapter 4, also suggestions in *The New Story of Science* by Robert M. Augros and George N. Stanciu (Lake Bluff, Illinois: Regnery Gateway, 1984). See Barrow and Tipler [2:1], discussing, for instance, the right size for planets on p. 309; requirement of precise nuclear force on p. 322; precarious existence of carbon on p. 326; coincidence between the gravitational and weak interactions on pp. 398-400. See also e.g. their Chapter 8. Barrow beats an unconvincing retreat in *The World Within the World* (Oxford: Clarendon Press, 1988), pp. 363-365. Was peer pressure the cause?

The British philosopher Antony Flew objects that humans do not know, and could never know, what is probable or improbable about universes and their order; if we did know, our present universe might not look improbable and hence in no need of a designing, sustaining Creator. Therefore, Flew concludes, the design argument fails (*God and Philosophy* [London: Hutchinson & Co, 1966], p. 74). But this argument implies, by default of other explanations, either that the universe was built and is sustained by chance, or that it is not to be explainable at all. We have dealt with the matter of chance.

As for non-explanation, we should apply the principle of sufficient reason, which may be stated: Whatever exists has a reason or ground for its existence. If we do not make such a metaphysical assumption about the causal or genetic series of things, we thereby block the path of inquiry in science and indeed block consideration of the universe as a subject of thought and language. In that case, to be consistent, we should at once stop our inquiry and indeed all inquiry. Flew's expedient here is one of arbitrarily setting a lower limit of admissible discussion in the genetic series of things. He would have us discuss the alternately possible universes, about which we can only "wildly gabble," while not admitting discussion of what would have made any universe possible. More on the principle of sufficient reason is to be found in *Christian Belief in a Postmodern World*, by Diogenes Allen, notably in Chapter 4 (Louisville: Westminster/John Knox Press, 1989). The proof of this principle depends formally on coherence, which is a mode of establishing truth to be discussed later.

# 5. Universal Design

**Epigraph:** Wernher von Braun in *Plain Truth* (Pasadena), June 1976, p. 21.

**5:1:** David Hume, *Dialogues Concerning Natural Religion*. For rebuttal see note [9:25] and index herein.

**5:2:** Ethan Allen, *Reason the Only Oracle of Man*, Chapter 1, Section 2.

**5:3:** Jacques Monod, *Chance and Necessity* (New York: Alfred Knopf, 1971).

**5:4:** Alfred North Whitehead, *The Function of Reason* (Princeton: Princeton University Press, 1929), p. 16.

**5:5:** J. B. S. Haldane, quoted by Jaki, *Road of Science* [3:33], p. 277. All of Chapter 17 therein bears on the topic. See further

Jaki, *Angels, Apes, and Men*, e.g., pp. 78-81.

**5:6:** Charles Hartshorne, *Reality as Social Process* [2:2], p. 49. Such a thought about "historicism" is generalized and stated at greater length by Peter Medawar in the essay "Expectation and Prediction," in *Pluto's Republic* [9:25], pp. 298-310.

**5:7:** Jaki, *Cosmos and Creator* [3:39], p. 107. Jaki presents his entire case in brief in **"Science and Christian Theism: A Mutual Witness,"** *Scottish Journal of Theology* 32 (1979): 563-570. Nicholas Rescher laments from a humanist perspective how "some of the best scientific minds of the day unhesitatingly proceed to shroud the issue in mystery and mysticism." He then attempts a non-theistic explanation (*Rationality* [Oxford: Clarendon Press, 1988], Chapter 11).

**5:8:** Frederick Robert Tennant, *Philosophical Theology,* 2 volumes (Cambridge: At the University Press, 1930), Volume 2, pp. 88-89. The second volume is especially recommended, especially Chapters 4 to 8. English philosopher C. D. Broad, though always an incisive critic, said of theologians and candidates for the ministry that "They could not be better employed than in studying Dr. Tennant's work" (*Mind* 38 [1929]: 94-100, at p. 95). Unfortunately, Tennant has no noticeable following, not even in divinity schools. Nearly all Christian establishments simply turn their backs on natural theology. Tennant's Volume 1 is less useful to this discussion. His plunge there into Kantian noumena poses intractable problems.

As to Kant see John H. Lavely, "Comment on John N. Findlay, 'The Central Role of the Thing-in-Itself in Kant,'" *Philosophical Forum* 13 (1981): 66-74. See Brian Hebblethwaite, *The Ocean of Truth* (Cambridge: Cambridge University Press, 1988), Chapter 5. See Jaki, *Road of Science* [3:33], Chapter 8, *Angels, Apes and Men* [4:14], pp. 26-34, *The Savior of Science* [4:14], pp. 121-123 *et passim*. C. D. Broad has entered some objections to Tennant's Volume 2; they appear in *Mind* 39 (1930): 476-484. In turn Peter A. Bertocci answers some of Broad's objections in his book *The Empirical Argument for God in Late British Thought* (Cambridge: Harvard University Press, 1938), notably Chapters 6 and 7. As to Bertocci's challenges to Tennant (pp. 221-226), one may have reservations. A Roman Catholic appreciation of Tennant appears in *Ways of Thinking about God*, by Edward A. Sillem (London: Darton, Longman & Todd, 1961), pp. 181-183.

Aristotle thinks it obvious that there is a rational cosmic order and that any demonstration of it would be attempting to prove "what is obvious by what is not" (*Physics* 193a). To test one's own ability to handle challenges to the argument from design of the universe, one can do no better than to consult the wide-ranging but

ultimately non-cogent arguments of the American philosopher John Hospers in Chapter 7 of his book *An Introduction to Philosophical Analysis*, second edition (Englewood Cliffs, New Jersey: Prentice-Hall, 1967).

**5:9:** Tennant, *Philosophical Theology* [5:8], Volume 2, pp. 79, 105, 85.

**5:10:** Bertocci [5:8], pp. 228-229.

**5:11:** Actually, Paley's argument was not confined to specific examples of organic adaptation to the environment, for he had made note of the laws of nature as a framework in which the adaptations could occur. But this fact is almost universally forgotten. See Turner, *Commitment to Care* [5:23], pp. 377-378.

**5:12:** Even a celebrated humanist like the Polish-British mathematician J. Bronowski backs into a position that sounds suspiciously like theism in referring to "the potential of [life-supporting levels of] stability that lay hidden in the primeval building blocks of cosmic hydrogen" ("New Concepts in the Evolution of Complexity," *Synthese* 21 [1970]: 228-246, at p. 242). It appears that some support to such a view is provided by *Chaos: A New Science*, which is the title of a book by James Gleick (New York: Viking Penguin, 1987). The chaos-scientist Joseph Ford there concludes, "God plays dice with the universe. But they're loaded dice."

The missing explanation may conceivably involve unknown quantum effects. Such effects might be supposed to be guided by a deity, or one may prefer to suppose some more overt form of divine intervention.

**5:13:** Tennant, *Philosophical Theology* [5:8], Volume 2, pp. 87, 188-189, 199-203.

**5:14:** Thomas Henry Huxley, "The Romanes Lecture" (1893), which is Chapter 2 of Huxley's *Evolution and Ethics* (New York: D. Appleton & Co., 1905).

**5:15:** Tennant, *Philosophical Theology* [5:8], Volume 2, pp. 101-103.

**5:16:** Stanley L. Jaki, *Science and Creation* [3:14], pp. 99, 109-110.

**5:17:** See D. Elton Trueblood, *The Humor of Christ* (New York: Harper & Row, 1964). This is one of the finest contributions made to modern theology.

**5:18:** Compare Arthur Lovejoy, "Pragmatism and Theology" [9:29], Section 4. See Holmes Rolston III, his section entitled, "The Way of Nature as the Way of the Cross" (*Science and Religion* [4:14], pp. 144-146).

**5:19:** On freedom of the will, see Chapter 16 herein. Hartshorne asks: "Is there order? The fact that the question can be asked proves that there is."

**5:20:** Karl Popper, *The Logic of Scientific Discovery*, second edition (New York: Harper & Row, 1968), e.g., Sections 6, 11, 15 (first published in German, 1935). In the *Kritik der reinen Vernunft* (Critique of Pure Reason) Kant argues against the apodictic certainty of the "physico-theological argument" — i.e., the design argument (A 620 = B 648 to A 630 = B 658). The present claim is the more modest one of the practical certainty of the existence of a God who is less than omnipotent. Kant goes on to question the idea of God as primordial Creator. Holmes Rolston III explores the considerable extent to which the theory of evolution is unfalsifiable and therefore not fully explanatory [4:14], Chapter 3.

**5:21:** Philip Yancey, "The Problem of Pleasure," *Christianity Today*, June 17, 1988, p. 80.

**5:22:** In the Book of Job, Chapter 40, God suggests ironically that Job assume His power and knowledge, as though Job could do better. This interpretation is sup-

ported by such scholars as Emil G. Kraeling in *The Book of the Ways of God* (New York: C. Scribner's Sons, 1939), James Strahan in *The Book of Job* (Edinburgh: T. & T. Clark, 1913), and Samuel Terrien in *The Interpreter's Bible* (Nashville: Abingdon Press, 1954). Some traditionally accepted passages, namely the prologue and epilogue, hinder a meaningful interpretation of the Book of Job and must be regarded as unperceptive accretions to, or redactions of, the original book-length poem (Job 1:1-2:12, 42:7-17). These verses are *prose* and do not match the style of the great bulk of the book in Hebrew.

**5:23:** In general, see two articles of the versatile mathematician Eugene P. Wigner in his book of essays, *Symmetries and Reflections* (Bloomington: Indiana University Press, 1967): "The Probability of the Existence of a Self-Reproducing Unit" (pp. 200-208), and "The Unreasonable Effectiveness of Mathematics in the Natural Sciences" (pp. 222-237). See Floyd F. Centore, "Mechanism, Teleology, and Seventeenth-Century English Science," in *International Philosophical Quarterly* 12 (1972): 553-571. An extensive treatment of the themes of the design argument with hundreds of references appears in Dean Turner's book *Commitment to Care* (Old Greenwich, Connecticut: Devin-Adair Co., 1978). On its Chapter 10 see [10:5]. On esthetics see Tennant, *Philosophical Theology* [5:8], Volume 2, pp. 89-93.

# 6. The Levels of Ethical Motivation

**Epigraph:** Francis Bacon, *Essays*, "Of Atheism."

**6:1:** "Lincoln's Idea of Selfishness," *Outlook* 56 (1897): 1059; found in Frank Chapman Sharp, *Ethics* (New York: Century Co., 1928), p. 75. This story suggests that Lincoln had read Bernard Mandeville's *Fable of the Bees*. The epigraph to Chapter 11 suggests that he was acquainted with Adam Smith's *Theory of Moral Sentiments*. "The things I want to

know are in books; my best friend is the man who'll git me a book I ain't read"; quoted by Carl Sandburg in *Abraham Lincoln: The Prairie Years*, Volume 1 (New York: Harcourt, Brace & Co., 1926), p. 71. (Some other biographies of Lincoln are more highly recommended.) Sharp's book is unique and highly readable, arriving at some of the same conclusions as the present book.

**6:2:** Joseph Butler, *(Fifteen) Sermons*

*Preached at the Rolls Chapel* (first published 1726), Sermon 11. The English writer and philosopher Bernard Mandeville gained notoriety in 1723 by publishing *The Fable of the Bees*, in which he offers a variation on the thesis of his predecessor Thomas Hobbes that everything which everybody ever chooses to do is done purely out of narrow self-interest. That is, gluttony and charity alike are said by Mandeville to be pursued solely to satisfy one's self-interest or what Edwards calls "private self-love." Lincoln must have known of Mandeville. Bishop Butler delivers an effective answer to Mandeville.

**6:3:** Jonathan Edwards, *The Nature of True Virtue* (Ann Arbor: University of Michigan Press, 1960, first published 1765), Chapter 4, emphasis omitted.

**6:4:** *The Philosophy of Jonathan Edwards from His Private Notebooks*, edited by Harvey G. Townsend (Eugene: University of Oregon, 1955), "Miscellany" no. 530.

**6:5:** Adam Smith, *The Theory of Moral Sentiments* [11:10], "Of the Sense of Duty." See William James, *Principles of Psychology* [11:2], Volume 1, pp. 315-316. Roderick Firth suggests that an ideal observer has various general interests though not particular ones; see *Philosophy and Phenomenological Research* 12 (1952): 317-345, at pp. 335-341.

**6:6:** On the Golden Rule see Marcus G. Singer in *Philosophy* (U.K.) 38 (1963): 293-314, and W. T. Blackstone in *Southern Journal of Philosophy* 3 (1965): 172-177.

**6:7:** Frank Chapman Sharp, *Good Will and Ill Will* (Chicago: University of Chicago Press, 1950), pp. 158, 157. A most practical book. The universalizability requirement stems explicitly from Richard Cumberland (1631-1724), Samuel Clarke (1675-1729), Jonathan Edwards, and later Immanuel Kant; see Ernest Albee, *A History of English Utilitarianism* (New York: Macmillan Co., 1902), Chapter 17. As to Clarke see *British Moralists* [7:17], Volume 2, p. 14.

**6:8:** Edwards, *True Virtue* [6:3], Chapter 5. This is one of Sidgwick's four "self-evident" principles; see article, "Sidgwick, Henry," by J. B. Schneewind, in the section "Self-Evident Moral Principles," in *Encyclopedia of Philosophy* (New York: Macmillan Publishing Co., 1967).

**6:9:** Edwards, *True Virtue* [6:3], Chapter 5, rearranged.

**6:10:** John Rawls, **"Justice as Fairness,"** *Philosophical Review* 67 (1958): 164-194. Widely reprinted.

**6:11:** This principle of Rawls is valid so long as it is not pushed so far as to inhibit the freedom and the incentive of any one person to become, by his own will, more qualified than another. See Charles E. Harris Jr., "Capitalism and Social Justice," *Intercollegiate Review* 20 (1984): 35-49. See also Brian Barry in *Oxford Review*, no. 5, Trinity term, 1967, pp. 29-52, at 33-43.

**6:12:** Edwards, *True Virtue* [6:3]; preceding quotations are from Chapters 2, 4, 7. "Love to God" has been changed to "love of God," emphasis omitted.

**6:13:** See Arthur Lovejoy, *Reflections on Human Nature* [11:2], Lecture 3, as to "pooled self-esteem," especially pp. 117 ff. Nationalism and statism are apposite here but are discussed later.

**6:14:** Max Scheler, *The Nature of Sympathy*, translated by Peter Heath (London: Routledge & Kegan Paul, 1954), Chapter 2.

**6:15:** Edwards, *True Virtue* [6:3], Chapter 5, 6, 7. See Albert Schweitzer's essay, "The Problem of Ethics in the Evolution of Human Thought," in *Albert Schweitzer, an Introduction*, edited by Jacques Feschotte (London: A. & C. Black, 1954), pp. 114-130.

**6:16:** Edwards, *True Virtue* [6:3]; preceding quotations are from Chapters 6, 7; emphasis omitted.

**6:17:** Edwards, *The Great Christian Doctrine of Original Sin Defended*, Part 4, Chapter 2, in any edition of Edwards' *Works*.

**6:18:** Waldo Beach and H. Richard Niebuhr, *Christian Ethics: Sources of the Living Tradition* (New York: Ronald Press Co., 1955), Chapter 13, p. 388.

**6:19:** Edwards, *True Virtue* [6:3], Chapter 7.

**6:20:** Ibid., Chapter 5, emphasis omitted.

**6:21:** Ibid., Chapter 1, rephrased; Chapter 7, emphasis omitted. "Love to" has been changed to "love of."

**6:22:** Beach and Niebuhr [6:18], Chapter 13, pp. 387-389. Norman Fiering's book *Jonathan Edwards's Moral Thought and Its British Context* affords many cross-lights, even though one sighs for Fiering in that he labored so hard without (as it seems) coming to realize within himself what theism was about (Chapel Hill: University of North Carolina Press, 1981). A good summary article on Edwards' ethics is one by Rufus Suter in *Journal of Religion* 14 (1934): 265-272.

**6:23:** Alexis de Tocqueville, *Democracy in America*, translated by George Lawrence, edited by J. P. Mayer (New York: Harper & Row, 1966), Volume 1, Part 2, Chapter 9 (Volume 1, Chapter 17 in the Henry Reeve text), "The Main Causes Tending to Maintain a Democratic Republic in the United States"; Volume 2, Part 1, Chapter 5, "How Religion in the United States Makes Use of Democratic Instincts." First published 1835 and 1840.

**6:24:** T. E. Jessop, *The Christian Morality* (London: Epworth Press, 1960), Lecture 6. Sydney G. Dimond, *The Psychology of the Methodist Revival* (London: Oxford University Press, 1926), e.g., pp. 113-114, 138-139, 203-205, 257-260, 271-273. See Richard M. Weaver, *Ideas Have Consequences* (Chicago: University of Chicago Press, 1948).

**6:25:** Some of the books of Christopher Dawson, all published by Sheed & Ward (New York and London) unless otherwise noted, include: *The Age of the Gods* (London: John Murray, 1928), *The Formation of Christendom* (1967), *The Making of Europe* (1932), *Medieval Essays* (1954), *Religion and the Rise of Western Culture* (1950), *The Dividing of Christendom* (1965), *The Gods of Revolution* (London: Sidgwick & Jackson, 1972), *Understanding Europe* (1952), *Religion and the Modern State* (1935), *The Movement of World Revolution* (1959), expanded as *Christianity in East and West* (La Salle, Illinois: Sherwood Sugden & Co., 1981), *Progress and Religion* (New York: Longmans, Green & Co., 1929), *The Historic Reality of Christian Culture* (New York: Oxford University Press, 1950), *The Modern Dilemma* (1932), *The Judgment of the Nations* (1943), *Religion and Culture* (1948), *The Dynamics of World History* (1956), *The Crisis of Western Education* (1961). Most highly recommended is *Religion and World History: A Selection from the Works of Christopher Dawson* (London: Sheed & Ward, 1975); this volume

was not properly entered into American library indexes. The highlighting of the titles is a bit arbitrary as Dawson's basic messages are widely spread through his works. Some of Dawson's comments will be appreciated more by Roman Catholics than by Protestants.

One may well read the books of the American Protestant religious historian Roland H. Bainton. The multi-volume, highly readable *Story of Civilization* (1935-1967) of Will and Ariel Durant is recommendable except that the Durants did not themselves get inside of theism and did not understand why it has been a force in history. However, the works of Dawson are a corrective.

One of our two favorite shorter pieces by the English historian Arnold Toynbee is his *War and Civilization* (New York: Oxford University Press, 1950), selected by Albert V. Fowler from the twelve volumes of *A Study of History* (1934-1961). Toynbee has a computer-like ability to detect analogies from diverse times and places, in order to form his insightful and sensitive generalizations, stated with literary skill. Perhaps the best result of his Olympian work was to enable him to write the first parts of *An Historian's Approach to Religion* (Oxford: Oxford University Press, 1956). It is, for one thing, a superior introduction to comparative religion. For another, it amounts to a revelation in the dynamics of statecraft, deserving to stand alongside Machiavelli's *The Prince* but far more constructive. In Part 2 and in the Appendix added to the 1979 edition, the reader may well ignore Toynbee's intellectual despair, his avowed agnosticism, and his diffuse ecumenism which, in embracing too much, comes to but little — not to mention what we find to be outright theological errors. Nevertheless, it is ironic that this great, flawed book should, at this moment, be out of print.

Toynbee has received criticism from Pitirim A. Sorokin in *Journal of Modern History* 12 (1940): 374-387; also from Popper [2:22], Chapter 24. A helpful brief introduction to Dawson's thought as contrasted with Toynbee's is that of Thomas

P. Neill, in *Christianity and Culture*, edited by J. Stanley Murphy (Baltimore: Helicon Press, 1960), pp. 21-31. Dawson makes his own comparison in his *Dynamics of World History*, pp. 390-404. Toynbee's deep appreciation of Dawson's work appears in a review: **"Religion and the Rise of Western Culture,"** *Hibbert Journal* 49 (1950): 3-10. Those interested in the growing hostility to Christianity should read José M. Sánchez, *The Spanish Civil War as a Religious Tragedy* (Notre Dame, Indiana: University of Notre Dame Press, 1987).

**6:26:** Dawson, *The Making of Europe*

[6:25].

**6:27:** Thomas Molnar in "The Culture of Corruption," *National Review*, October 24, 1986, p. 46.

**6:28:** George Gallup Jr., *Who Do Americans Say That I Am?* (Philadelphia: Westminster Press, 1986), pp. 71, 127 (Table 32); see [13:13].

**First epigraph:** Charles G. Finney [19:3], Section 9, p. 41; also see p. 44.

**Second epigraph:** Charles Hartshorne, from an unpublished manuscript dated 1965, p. 120.

# 7. Self-Consistency

**Epigraph:** Abraham Lincoln, "Reply to Missouri Committee, 1864," in *A Concise Lincoln Dictionary*, edited by Ralph R. Winn (New York: Philosophical Library, 1959), p. 20.

**7:1:** Charles Darwin, *The Descent of Man*, Chapter 4. Compare the "conscience" of the Thags, a secret society of ritualistic murderers that flourished in India until toward 1850 (J. N. Farquhar in *Encyclopaedia of Religion and Ethics* [Edinburgh: T. & T. Clark Co., 1910-1927]). For Biblical suggestion of conscience see 1 Kings 19:11-12.

**7:2:** Compare L. S. Kubie, *Neurotic Distortions of the Creative Process* (Lawrence: University of Kansas Press, 1958), pp. 54, 58, 84. See William James, *The Meaning of Truth* (New York: Longmans, Green & Co., 1909), p. 99.

**7:3:** Henry Winthrop, *Journal of Social Psychology* 24 (1946): 149-175, at p. 149. See Winthrop, *Journal of General Psychology* 40 (1949): 177-218.

**7:4:** Douglas S. Freeman, *George Washington: A Biography* (New York: Charles Scribner's Sons, 1948-1957), Volume 5, p. xiii.

**7:5:** Malachi 3:6; James 1:17. God in the Bible did change His mind at times (not His general disposition); see 2 Kings 20;

Genesis 6; also 1 Samuel 15; Exodus 32; Deuteronomy 32; Judges 2; Jonah 3 and 4.

**7:6:** Ralph Waldo Emerson, *Essays*, First Series, "Self-Reliance," paragraphs 14, 16. Contrast somewhat Rescher [5:7], Chapter 5. Both of the present authors read Emerson early in life, with profit. But see Richard Brookhiser in *National Review*, October 9, 1987, pp. 50-53. See William James, "Humanism and Truth"; there are many printings since *The Meaning of Truth* [7:2]. See William Shakespeare, *Hamlet*, Act 1, Scene 3, line 78.

**7:7:** Prescott Lecky, *Self-Consistency*, second edition (Hamden, Connecticut: Shoe String Press, 1951), p. 191. See Arthur Lovejoy, *Human Nature* [11:2], Lecture 3, pp. 66-127, at pp. 102-105; Charles Sanders Peirce, *Collected Papers* [1:2], 1.608; Edwards [6:3], pp. 61 ff.; Henry Winthrop, *Journal of Social Psychology* 24 (1946): 149-175, especially p. 151.

**7:8:** Bertrand Russell, *The Conquest of Happiness* (New York: H. Liveright, 1930), Chapter 14.

**7:9:** Feodor Dostoyevsky, *The House of the Dead*, Chapter 2.

**7:10:** John H. Lavely, "Reflections on a Philosophical Heritage," in *The Boston Personalist Tradition*, edited by Paul Deats and Carol Robb (Macon, Georgia: Mercer University Press, 1986), pp. 253-272, at pp. 264-265.

**7:11:** Lecky, *Self-Consistency,* Chapters 7 and 8 in second edition (Chapters 8 and 9 in Doubleday Anchor edition, 1969). See also O. Hobart Mowrer, *The Crisis in Psychiatry and Religion* (Princeton, New Jersey: D. Van Nostrand Co., 1961). See Leon Festinger, e.g., "Cognitive Dissonance," in *Scientific American,* October 1962, pp. 93-102, 27, 177-178. This latter line of thought has on occasion been distorted to defend the view that religious faith is merely the result of wishful thinking. Specialists may consult William J. McGuire in *Attitude Organization and Change* by Milton J. Rosenberg et al. (New Haven: Yale University Press, 1960), Chapter 3 with its appendix. On rigidity see John M. Rehfisch in *Journal of Consulting Psychology* 22 (1958): 372-374.

**7:12:** Lecky, *Self-Consistency,* Chapter 11 (Chapter 12 in Doubleday Anchor edition). On perfectionism see W. F. Lofthouse, "Wesley's Doctrine of Christian Perfection," *London Quarterly and Holborn Review* 159 (1934): 178-188. It can be overdone: see Karen Horney, *Neurosis and Human Growth* (New York: W. W. Norton Co., 1950), Chapter 3. On discrepancy between one's perceived self and ideal self see Thomas Achenbach and Edward Zigler in *Journal of Abnormal and Social Psychology* 67 (1963): 197-205 and the reference to John Altrocchi there.

**7:13:** Lavely [7:10].

**7:14:** See Peirce, *Collected Papers* [1:2], 1.411.

**7:15:** G. A. Tawney, *Journal of Philosophy, Psychology and Scientific Methods* 3 (1906): 113-123, at pp. 116, 115. On the concept of inconsistency in logic see P. F. Strawson, *Introduction to Logical Theory* (London: Methuen & Co., 1952), pp. 1-13.

**7:16:** Richard L. Bushman, "Jonathan Edwards as Great Man: Identity, Conversion, and Leadership in the Great Awakening," *Soundings* 52 (1969): 15-46, at pp. 15-16; reprinted in *Critical Essays on Jonathan Edwards,* edited by William J. Scheick (Boston: G. K. Hall & Co., 1980), pp. 41-64. Bushman paraphrases a psychological theory of Erik H. Erikson. See

in general Fiering [6:22].

**7:17:** John Gay, *Preliminary Dissertation Concerning the Fundamental Principle of Virtue or Morality* (first published 1731), in British Moralists, edited by L. A. Selby-Bigge, 2 volumes (Oxford: Clarendon Press, 1897), Volume 2, pp. 267-275, at pp. 273-274. Gay is the first to express the now forgotten full design of utilitarianism. His insight was soon occluded by the emasculate secular utilitarian philosophy prominent in college ethics courses of the past century or so. Thomas A. Nairn perceptively discusses whether Hartshorne is a utilitarian in *Process Studies* 17 (1988): 170-180.

The comments of Ernest Albee should be read, including those on Gay's successor John Brown (1715-1766), all in Albee's *History of English Utilitarianism* (New York: Macmillan Co., 1902), Chapter 4.

**7:18:** Sterling McMurrin, *The Theological Foundations of the Mormon Religion* (Salt Lake City: University of Utah Press, 1965), pp. 104-105. The Biblical quotation is 1 Corinthians 3:9. As to the general idea of labor and its dignity see Aaron Levenstein, *Why People Work* (New York: Crowell-Collier Press, 1962). See also Donald Scott, *The Psychology of Work* (London: Gerald Duckworth & Co., 1970).

**7:19:** Charles Hartshorne, *The Divine Relativity* (New Haven: Yale University Press, 1948), pp. 124-134, at p. 133. See *Edwards from His Private Notebooks* [6:4], p. 193, "Miscellany" 3, though this statement of Edwards is untypical of him. For his more usual view, in conformity with classical theism, see especially his *Dissertation Concerning the End for Which God Created the World,* notably Section 4, in any edition of his *Works.*

**7:20:** On divine immanence see Charles Hartshorne, "Transcendence and Immanence," and "Pantheism and Panentheism," both in the *Encyclopedia of Religion,* edited by Mircea Eliade (New York: Macmillan Publishing Co., 1987). See F. R. Tennant in *Philosophical Theology* [5:8], Volume 2, Chapter 8.

**7:21:** Romans 8:8; Hebrews 11:6; 1 Thessalonians 2:4, 4:1; Ephesians 4:30.

**7:22:** Hartshorne, *Divine Relativity* [7:19], p. 44; *Man's Vision of God* (Chicago: Willett, Clark & Company, 1941), p. 117; "The God of Religion and the God of Philosophy," in *Talk of God* (London: Macmillan & Co., 1969), p. 161, after Matthew 5:48.

**7:23:** Plato, *Philebus*, 33b.

**7:24:** Aristotle, *Works*, edited by W. D. Ross (Oxford: Clarendon Press, 1908-1952): *Ethica Eudemonia*, 1244b-1245b, cf. 1323b; *Magna Moralia* 1208b. See *Philosophers Speak of God* [7:25], Chapter 2. Aristotle, *Metaphysics*, 1012b. Boethius, *The Consolation of Philosophy*, Book 5.

**7:25:** Philo Judaeus, *Works*, translated by C. D. Yonge (London: George Bell & Sons, 1890), Volume I, pp. 196-197; this appears in Charles Hartshorne and William L. Reese, ***Philosophers Speak of God*** (Chicago: University of Chicago Press, 1953), at pp. 78-80, Sections 40, 51, 57, 52.

**7:26:** Quoted in Arthur Lovejoy, *The Great Chain of Being* (Cambridge: Harvard University Press, 1936), p. 157.

**7:27:** Augustine, *The City of God*, Book 10, Chapter 5. A similar view appears in the Koran, Sura 35, though there are modern counter-examples, as in the book *Ethical Viewpoint of Islam*, by S. A. A. Maududi, third edition (Lahore, Pakistan, 1967). For contrast see Sir Rustom Masani, *Zoroastrianism: The Religion of the Good Life* (New York: Macmillan Co., 1968, first published 1938), p. 91.

**7:28:** Augustine does better elsewhere. In the words of his interpreter Étienne Gilson, love—at any rate earthly love—"is essentially active, a principle of motion and action," which expands spontaneously into "meritorious and productive works" (*The Christian Philosophy of St. Augustine*, translated by L. E. M. Lynch [New York: Random House, 1960], p. 141). Thomas Aquinas, though he affirms God's love, rejects "passion" as an attribute of God (*Summa Theologica*, Part I, Question 20, Article 1). Aquinas does attribute "beatitude" to God but claims it to be of a purely intellectual nature, whatever that may mean (Question 26).

**7:29:** Bernard d'Espagnat, **"The Quantum Theory and Reality,"** *Scientific American*, November 1979, pp. 158-181, 18, 206, plus letters in May 1980 issue, pp. 8-9. A readable digest regarding Bell's theorem by N. David Mermin is in *Physics Today*, April 1985, pp. 38-47. A brief introduction to philosophical problems of quantum mechanics appears in the *Economist*, January 7, 1989, pp. 71-74. Many essays appear in *Philosophical Consequences of Quantum Theory: Reflections on Bell's Theorem*, edited by James T. Cushing and Ernan McMullin (Notre Dame, Indiana: University of Notre Dame Press, 1989). See Peirce [1:2], 6.61 ff. Einstein's descriptive words of the now successful interpretation were "spukhafte Fernwirkungen" (March 1947, quoted by Mermin, ibid., at p. 38).

**7:30:** Henry P. Stapp should be consulted, in *Foundations of Physics* 12 (1982): 363-399. D'Espagnat has elaborated his earlier thoughts into a book, *In Search of Reality* (New York: Springer-Verlag, 1983), for the searching lay person. D'Espagnat seems now to prefer to speculate of abstract theistic influence and not of the earlier "man-centered objectivity" of which Jaki complains. On the metaphysical significance of all this see Charles Hartshorne, **"Bell's Theorem and Stapp's Revised View of Space-Time"** in *Process Studies* 7 (1977): 183-191. The American-English physicist David Bohm is on a variant quest similar in intent to that of d'Espagnat. An introduction to Bohm's work for present purposes is that of Robert John Russell in *Zygon* 20 (1985): 135-158. The book *The Forces of Nature* by P. C. W. Davies is also recommendable (Cambridge: Cambridge University Press, 1986).

**7:31:** As to Newton and space see Alexandre Koyré, *From the Closed World to the Infinite Universe* (Baltimore: Johns Hopkins Press, 1957), pp. 235-243, 301.

**7:32:** Compare George Berkeley, *A Treatise Concerning the Principles of Human Knowledge*, Sections 6, 28-33, 60-66, 145-156.

**7:33:** For a critique of mysticism see F. R. Tennant, *Philosophical Theology* [5:8], Volume 1, Chapter 12, pp. 311-324.

**Epigraph:** Christopher Dawson, *Reli-*

*gion and Culture* (New York: Sheed & Ward, 1948), p. 50; *Religion and the Rise of* *Western Culture* (New York: Sheed & Ward, 1950), last sentence.

# 8. Ethics and the Cosmos

**Epigraph:** Søren Kierkegaard, title of a book.

**8:1:** Henry Sidgwick, *The Methods of Ethics*, seventh edition (London: Macmillan & Co., 1907), p. 501. See Jeremy Bentham, *Introduction to the Principles of Morals and Legislation* (1823), Chapter 6, Sections 21, 26.

**8:2:** Bernard Rimland, **"The Altruism Paradox,"** *Psychological Reports* 51 (1982): 521-522; *Southern Psychologist* 51 (1984): 8-9. The result could have occurred by chance far less than one time in a thousand. For validity of altruism as a factor of personality see Robert W. Friedrichs in *American Sociological Review* 25 (1960): 496-508.

**8:3:** Douglas R. Hofstader, "Metamagical Themas," *Scientific American*, June 1983, pp. 14, 19, 22, 24, 28. In Martin Gardner's department see "Mathematical Games," September 1983, pp. 18-28, at pp. 25-28. See Charles Sanders Peirce, *Collected Papers* [1:2], 2.654.

**8:4:** Matthew 11:30.

**8:5:** Jonathan Edwards, *True Virtue* [6:3], p. 16.

**8:6:** Jonathan Edwards, *Edwards from His Private Notebooks* [6:4], p. 195, "Miscellany" 97.

**8:7:** Charles Finney, *Systematic Theology*, abridged (Minneapolis: Bethany House Publishers, 1976), p. 78 (first published as *Lectures on Systematic Theology*, Oberlin, 1846; London, 1851). See Peirce [1:2], 2.654.

**8:8:** Finney, "True and False Conversion," in *True and False Repentance* (Grand Rapids: Kregel Publications, 1966).

**8:9:** *Edwards from His Private Notebooks* [6:4], p. 147, "Miscellany" 1208. Edwards writes of "love to God," which has been herein changed to read "love of God."

**8:10:** Finney, *Systematic Theology* [8:7], pp. 31, 30. Emphasis added; paraphrased to suggest what Finney presumably intended to say.

**8:11:** Durant Drake, *Problems of Conduct*, second revised edition (Boston: Houghton Mifflin Co., 1935), pp. 310-312. There remains much of value in Drake's *Problems of Religion* (Boston: Houghton Mifflin Co., 1916). See Ralph Waldo Emerson's lecture, *The Preacher*, paragraph 13. Henry Nelson Wieman and Regina Westcott-Wieman have an insightful chapter: "Progressive Integration of Personality," Chapter 17 of *Normative Psychology of Religion* (New York: Thomas Y. Crowell Co., 1935). All write as Protestants.

**8:12:** Charles Hartshorne, *Divine Relativity* [7:19], p. 133. See Ignatius of Loyola, *The Spiritual Exercises*, "The First Week (Principle and Foundation)." See also John Stuart Mill, *Theism* (1874), last paragraph.

**8:13:** Augustine, *De genesi contra Manichaeos*, I, heading 20 or paragraph 31; also *Encyclopedia of Philosophy*, edited by Paul Edwards (New York: Macmillan Publishing Co., 1967), "Augustine."

**8:14:** Alexander Sutherland, *The Origin and Growth of the Moral Instinct*, Volume 1 (London: Longmans, Green & Co., 1898), p. 10.

**8:15:** Hartshorne [7:19], p. 141.

**8:16:** John Maynard Keynes, *General Theory* [2:39], p. 106. The bright remark is that of R. William Hazelett, a hard-working brother.

**8:17:** For William James, the most crucial habit of an effective democracy is "a fierce and merciless resentment towards every man or set of men who break the peace"; quoted by Eric Hoffer in *Between the Devil and the Dragon* [1:epigraph], p. 434.

**8:18:** See Terence E. Fretheim, *The*

*Suffering of God* (Philadelphia: Fortress Press, 1984); the book treats of the language of the Old Testament.

**8:19:** See Nicolas Berdyaev on the position of suffering in world religions, in *The Destiny of Man* (New York: Charles Scribner's Sons, 1937), p. 151; also in *Philosophers Speak of God* [7:25], pp.

285-294, at p. 292. For further pithy comparisons see S. E. Georgeoura in *Toth-Maatian Review* 4 (1986): 2173-2182.

**8:20:** Finney, *Systematic Theology* [8:7], "Attributes of Love."

**Epigraph:** Albert Schweitzer, *Philosophy of Civilization* [1:11], Chapter 9, p. 112 (30).

# 9. Coherence, Truth, and Reality

**Epigraph:** Charles Sanders Peirce, *Collected Papers* [1:2], 5.265, from "Some Consequences of Four Incapacities." Compare Rescher, *Coherence* [9:13], p. 319.

**9:1:** Errol E. Harris, *Hypothesis and Perception* [9:20], pp. 224-231, also Chapter 9.

**9:2:** Peirce, *Collected Papers* [1:2], 5.406-5.408 ff., at 5.407; the selection is from **"How To Make Our Ideas Clear,"** originally from *Popular Science Monthly* 12 (1878): 286-302, reprinted in selections of Peirce's writings. In this passage, Peirce writes as a realist, not as a pragmatist. See also 5.565. For a statement of Peirce's realism see [1:2], 5.384, (in "The Fixation of Belief," originally in *Popular Science Monthly* 12 [1877]: 1-15). A statement of realism in the context of modern physics is given by Bernard d'Espagnat [7:29-30]. See further *Scientific Realism*, edited by Jarrett Leplin (Berkeley: University of California Press, 1984). For a variant view see Rescher [5:7], Chapter 10.

**9:3:** As to Kepler, see Harris, *Hypothesis and Perception* [9:20], the index under "Kepler." Harris may have made some slight errors in reporting the details of Kepler's work; however, the argument is not thereby affected. See also Peirce, *Collected Papers* [1:2], 1.65-1.74; Arthur Koestler, *The Sleepwalkers* (New York: Macmillan Co., 1959), Part 4: "The Watershed"; see various block quotations as in Koestler's Chapter 6; and Gerald Holton in *Philosophical Forum* (Boston) 14 (1956): 21-33.

**9:4:** See Joseph Agassi, *Faraday as a Natural Philosopher* (Chicago: University of Chicago Press, 1977), p. 167 ff.

**9:5:** On Galileo see note [3:28].

**9:6:** As to Dalton's alleged priority in the modern atomic theory, the British chemist and Nobel laureate Frederick Soddy gives the credit to Dalton's contemporary William Higgins. See Soddy's book *The Story of Atomic Energy* (London: Nova Atlantis, 1949), pp. 11-18.

**9:7:** Peirce gives valuable suggestions on dealing with the problem of doubt vs. knowledge, later herein.

**9:8:** Jean Piaget, *The Construction of Reality in the Child*, translated by Margaret Cook (New York: Basic Books, 1954), notably, Chapter 1, Sections 3 to 6. Compare Harris, *Hypothesis and Perception* [9:20], pp. 258, 289. Piaget's entire book is of substantial epistemological interest. The point about realism and coherence is inadvertently corroborated by Karl Popper in his essay "Realism," in *Popper Selections*, edited by David Williams (Princeton: Princeton University Press, 1985), Chapter 17—from his *Objective Knowledge* (Oxford: Clarendon Press, 1972), Chapter 2, Sections 4 and 5 (pp. 37-44).

**9:9:** Brand Blanshard, *The Nature of Thought*, 2 volumes (London: George Allen & Unwin, 1940), Volume 2, p. 227. See notably Chapters 25 and 26. The overall thesis that was dearest to Blanshard must be doubted, namely, that of the seventeenth-century Dutch philosopher Baruch (Benedict) de Spinoza that everything is essentially a monistic whole in which *all* relations are internal to The One all-encompassing entity and that all things and all events are predetermined necessarily therein. Although one may agree with Blanshard that there are indeed necessities in nature and not merely in logic and mathematics, Blanshard's position that the correspondence theory of truth has no basic place must be denied. Indeed, Blanshard has implicitly qualified his position in *The Philosophy of Brand Blanshard* (La Salle, Illinois: Open Court Publishing Co., 1980), pp. 589-600, which is his **"Reply to Nicholas Rescher,"** at pp. 593-594. Charles Hartshorne has commented on the matter cogently in two places: first, in *The Philosophy of Brand Blanshard*, pp. 629-635. Blanshard's reply on pp. 636-645 is valiant but problematic. Bernard Bosanquet briefly anticipated Blanshard and Rescher; see his *Logic, or the Morphology of Knowledge*, second edition (Oxford: At the Clarendon Press, 1911), Book 2, Chapter 9, e.g., pp. 281-292. See Hartshorne, *Creative Synthesis* [16:16], **"The Prejudice in Favour of Symmetry,"** pp. 205-226, also pp. 96-97. See also "The Neglect of Relative Predicates in Modern Philosophy," *American Philosophical Quarterly* 14 (1977): 309-318; "Hume's Metaphysics and Its Present-Day Influence" (*New Scholasticism* 35 [1961]: 152-171). Both of these articles are reprinted in Hartshorne's *Insights and Oversights* [20:19]. Karl Popper ably defends the correspondence theory of truth in his *Objective Knowledge* [9:8], though the argument is not squarely to the present point. Michael Williams deals clearly with numerous questions in "Coherence, Justification, and Truth" (*Review of Metaphysics* 34 [1980]: 243-272), though the restrictiveness of his conclusions seem unwarranted. Edgar Sheffield Brightman finds coherence to be the criterion of truth that the congenial philosophy of *personalism* uses as metaphysical method; see his *Person and Reality* (New York: Ronald Press Co., 1958); *A Philosophy of Religion* (New York: Prentice-Hall, 1940); *An Introduction to*

*Philosophy,* revised edition (New York: Henry Holt & Co., 1975); see indexes under "Coherence."

**9:10:** Harris, *Hypothesis and Perception* [9:20], pp. 354-358.

**9:11:** Nicholas Rescher, *Coherence* [9:13], pp. 48-97, 117-118, 176-177. See also Blanshard, *Nature of Thought* [9:9], Volume 2, pp. 275 ff.

**9:12:** Blanshard, *Nature of Thought* [9:9], Volume 2, p. 215.

**9:13:** Nicholas Rescher's monumental work **The Coherence Theory of Truth** (London: Oxford University Press, 1973) has an intimidating apparatus of symbolic logic; however his basic points are intelligible without the symbols. He is decidedly sympathetic to the coherence criterion of truth, but he rejects coherence when taken as the nature of truth. This rejection is stated early in his book (pp. 27-32). It is summarized in Rescher's contribution to *The Philosophy of Brand Blanshard* [9:9], at pp. 574-588. Blanshard replies to Rescher on pp. 589-600 to the effect that coherence is scientifically descriptive of the presumed cosmic *reality* to which a coherent system of knowledge must correspond. He permits a restricted use of the word "correspondence" in his theory of knowledge, since he acknowledges an independently existing reality to which our knowledge is to correspond, in whatever manner our knowledge may be won.

The validation of logical truths may be included under coherence broadly; see Blanshard, *Nature of Thought* [9:9], Volume 2, pp. 252-259 and 422-423. But as Rescher notes, the coherence theory as criterion of truth is aimed primarily at the extralogical realm; see *Coherence*, pp. 177-180. Anthony Quinton, *The Nature of Things* (London: Routledge & Kegan Paul, 1973), Chapter 8, is noteworthy as to what it means for the elements of a coherent set to support each other. See generally Alan R. White in his survey article, "Coherence Theory of Truth," in *Encyclopedia of Philosophy* (New York: Macmillan Co., 1967), even though the restrictiveness of White's conclusion is open to question. For the historical view see F. (Francis) H.

Bradley, *Essays on Truth and Reality* (Oxford: At the Clarendon Press, 1914), Chapter 7. The British philosopher Richard Swinburne has conducted a thorough study of relevant concepts in his work entitled *The Coherence of Theism* (Oxford: Clarendon Press, 1977). See the Annex herein on the principle of noncontradiction.

**9:14:** Compare Aristotle, *Metaphysics* [7:24], 1005b-1009a. Albert Einstein is relevantly quoted in Stanley L. Jaki, *The Road of Science and the Ways to God* [3:33], quoted in turn from G. A. Coulson, *Science and Christian Belief* (Chapel Hill: University of North Carolina Press, 1955), p. 64. See also Jaki, *Cosmos and Creator* [3:39], p. 97.

**9:15:** Einstein, quoted in *Hypothesis and Perception* [9:20], p. 114.

**9:16:** Harris, *Hypothesis and Perception* [9:20], p. 332.

**9:17:** Otto Neurath, quoted in Rescher, *Coherence* [9:13], pp. 25-26; see also e.g. pp. 207-210, 316-319, 332-333.

**9:18:** Harris, *Hypothesis and Perception* [9:20], pp. 79-80.

**9:19:** Carveth Reed, quoted in Bertocci [5:8], p. 4n.

**9:20:** Errol E. Harris, ***Hypothesis and Perception: The Roots of Scientific Method*** (London: George Allen & Unwin, 1970). Also see Harris in *Idealistic Studies* 5 (1975): 208-230, notably his reply to Clarence Irving Lewis. Harris' metaphysical assumptions of being and substance do not please process philosophers; nevertheless, his position seems to be a justified simplification in his retracing of the path of the founders of classical physical science. Other reservations on the treatment of modern physics and geometry will be discussed later. Brand Blanshard argues specifically against logical atomism in ***Reason and Analysis*** (La Salle, Illinois: Open Court Publishing Co., 1964), Chapter 4. Also the argument of Harold K. Schilling is slightly related to coherence in *Science and Religion* (New York: Charles Scribner's Sons, 1962), in index under "Circularity." Bernard d'Espagnat discusses Baconian positivism in Chapter 20 of *Conceptual Foundations of Quantum Mechanics,* second edition (Reading,

Massachusetts: W. A. Benjamin, 1976).

**9:21:** Perhaps the earliest modern treatment of the hypothetico-deductive method is that of Immanuel Kant; see Kant's *Introduction to Logic* (New York: Philosophical Library, 1963), pp. 75-76 [263-264 in original]. See Karl Popper, *The Logic of Scientific Discovery,* [5:20], Chapter 1 *et passim; Conjectures and Refutations* (New York: Basic Books, 1963), Chapter 8, also other of Popper's writings. For critique of Popper see Harris, *Hypothesis and Perception* [9:20], e.g., pp. 72-79. Popper slips into a physicalism that would exclude the entire present endeavor in Section 28 of *Scientific Discovery* [5:20].

**9:22:** Harris, *Hypothesis and Perception* [9:20], pp. 131, 138, 85-91, 131 *et passim.*

**9:23:** Ibid., pp. 102-109, 217, 365, 224. Harris credits Kant for an epistemology of coherence, despite inconsistency in Kant's work (Harris, *Nature, Mind, and Modern Science* [London: George Allen & Unwin, 1954], pp. 197-198). Illumination on the uses of coherence in science is provided by Pierre Duhem, *The Aim and Structure of Physical Theory* (Princeton: Princeton University Press, 1954), notably Chapter 6. See also Carl Hempel in *Analysis* 2 (1935): 49-59.

**9:24:** Harris, *Hypothesis and Perception* [9:20], p. 299. Compare Popper, *Scientific Discovery* [5:20], Preface, 1959.

**9:25:** Harris, *Hypothesis and Perception* [9:20], Chapter 2 *et passim.* As to David Hume see the item "Cause" in the indexes to the Selby-Bigge nineteenth-century editions of Hume's *Enquiries Concerning the Human Understanding* and *A Treatise of Human Nature* (Oxford: At the Clarendon Press). C. S. Peirce was aware of the two kinds of induction; see the indexes of his *Collected Papers* under "Induction" and "Abduction" [1:2]. Peter Medawar has written a rewarding and literate book of scientific essays, ***Pluto's Republic;*** the first 135 pages are pertinent to this discussion (Oxford: Oxford University Press, 1982). His briefer treatment appears in *The Limits of Science* (New York: Harper & Row, 1984), pp. 13-18. The problem of induction is more generally solved only in theism.

Some intellectual games of Hume, apparently deliberate, are analyzed by John Herman Randall Jr. in *Freedom and Experience*, edited by Sidney Hook and Milton R. Konvitz (Ithaca, New York: Cornell University Press, 1947), pp. 289-312. Hume would start out with innocent-seeming but wrongheaded premises or definitions, or with subtly self-contradictory statements, and then push them to their nonsensical conclusions. Further on Hume see R. G. Swinburne, "The Argument from Design," *Philosophy* (U.K.) 43 (1968): 199-212. Hume is worth some trouble to get past as a matter of self-immunization. A good preparation is found in Richard H. Popkin, *The High Road to Pyrrhonism* (San Diego: Austin Hill Press, 1980).

It is arguable that Hume's skepticism could never have been honored if the coherence theory of truth had been presentable to Kant and to Hume's nineteenth-century followers. Hume dismisses anything of the sort in the *Treatise*, Book 1, Part 3, Section 5 — also in Book 1, Part 4, Section 2 near end. Hartshorne shows how Hume's choice of method predetermined the negative outcome of Hume's *Dialogues Concerning Natural Religion*; see *New Scholasticism* 35 (1961): 152-171. See F. F. Centore in his 1990 manuscript "God Against God: Theism in a Scientific Age," and *Philosophical Studies* (Ireland) 28 (1980?): 212-220. See Jaki, *Road of Science* [3:33], Chapters 7, 16. Jaki says, we think correctly, "In Hume's case philosophy was less important than an irreligious peace of mind" (*The Savior of Science* [4:14], p. 126). See Peirce, *Collected Papers* [1:2], 1.145, expanded by Charles F. Wallraff in *Philosophical Theory and Psychological Fact* (Tucson: University of Arizona Press, 1961). See Brand Blanshard, *Reason and Analysis* [9:20]; and Dean Turner, *Commitment to Care* [5:23].

**9:26:** Edwards, *True Virtue* [6:3], p. 15. Matthew 25:40.

**9:27:** On blocking of inquiry see Peirce, *Collected Papers* [1:2], 1.135.

**9:28:** See Turner, *Commitment to Care* [5:23], pp. 304-306.

**9:29:** F. R. Tennant, *Philosophical Theology* [5:8], Volume 2, p. 104. Arthur

Lovejoy analyzes meanings of the term pragmatism. He rejects most pragmatic approaches to knowledge but sees potential value in a restricted sense of the pragmatic principle in theology ("Pragmatism and Theology," *American Journal of Theology* 12 [1908]: 116-143; reprinted in *The Thirteen Pragmatisms and Other Essays* [Baltimore: Johns Hopkins Press, 1963], pp. 40-78).

**9:30:** Jaki, *Relevance of Physics* [3:3], e.g., pp. 455-457.

**9:31:** Peirce, *Collected Papers* [1:2], 5.133; Hartshorne [16:16], p. 198.

**9:32:** V. I. Lenin, quoted by Joseph Fletcher in *Situation Ethics* (Philadelphia: Westminster Press, 1966), p. 121.

**9:33:** Michael S. Josephson, *Time*, May 25, 1987, p. 29.

**9:34:** G. K. Chesterton [2:epigraph], p. 332, August 3, 1918.

**9:35:** Clarence Irving Lewis, *The Ground and Nature of the Right* (New York: Columbia University Press, 1955). One thinks hopefully of William Penn's remark: "To do Evil, that Good may come of it, is for Bunglers in politicks, as well as Morals" (*Fruits of Solitude* [Richmond, Indiana: Friends United Press, 1978; first published 1693], second series no. 56). For a colossal example of following a mistaken absolute see Lenin [12:12].

**9:36:** A helpful introduction to the categories of the understanding is Borden P. Bowne, *The Theory of Thought and Knowledge* (New York: Harper & Brothers, 1897), Chapter 4.

**9:37:** F. R. Tennant, *Philosophy of the Sciences* (Cambridge: At the University Press, 1932), pp. 184-187 and Lecture 6 generally; also *Philosophical Theology* [5:8], Volume 2, p. 259.

**9:38:** The suddenness of many of the conversions by Wesley is described in Chapter 9 of *The Psychology of the Methodist Revival* by Sydney G. Dimond (London: Oxford University Press, 1926). More generally, see William Sargant, *Battle for the Mind* (New York: Doubleday & Co., 1957). Hazelett's conversion was not sudden. For an account of gradual conversion see the Book of Mormon, Alma 32, also the chapters entitled "Conversion" in William James, *The Varieties of Religious*

*Experience* (New York: Longmans, Green & Co., 1902). Whatever the merits of James' treatment, hope for rational religion is not among them.

Mystical religious experience as discussed by James does not enter into this book, which is restricted to evidences that are available to all. Such experience is discussed, critically but sympathetically, by John Lavely in "Faith and Knowledge: Is the Ineffable Intelligible?" which are on pp. 116-152 of *Contemporary Studies in Philosophical Idealism*, edited by John Howie and Thomas O. Buford (Cape Cod: Claude Stark & Co., 1975). Hazelett had one mystical experience which, while not specifically religious in content, did occur in the intensely religious milieu of Utah.

**9:39:** See Lawrence E. Harrison, *Underdevelopment Is a State of Mind* (Lanham, Maryland: University Press of America and the Center for International Affairs, Harvard University, 1985).

**9:40:** Proverbs 9:10.

**9:41:** Mark 12:29-31. See Deuteronomy 6:4-5; Leviticus 19:18; Luke 10:27; and Matthew 22:37.

**9:42:** Crane Brinton, *A History of Western Morals* (New York: Harcourt, Brace & World, 1959), p. 209.

**9:43:** On the personally internal causes of crime see e.g. Morgan O. Reynolds, *Crime by Choice* (Dallas: Fisher Institute, 1985).

**9:44:** Peirce, *Collected Papers* [1:2], 7.48.

**Epigraph:** Alexis de Tocqueville [6:23], Volume 2, Chapter 5.

# 10. And This, Too, Shall Pass Away?

**Epigraph:** Admiral Hyman Rickover, *U.S. News and World Report*, October 22, 1973, p. 128. Curiously, Rickover doubted that nuclear power in its danger should be permitted to exist; he engineered the nuclear propulsion of ships out of patriotic necessity (*New York Times*, January 30, 1982, p. 8).

**10:1:** Sir James Barrie, *Peter Pan*, Act 4.

**10:2:** Bertrand Russell, as expressed to Yousuf Karsh during a photographic sitting, in *Portraits of Greatness* (London: Thomas Nelson & Sons, 1959), p. 170.

**10:3:** Abraham Lincoln to Wisconsin State Agricultural Society, Milwaukee, September 30, 1859.

**10:4:** Augustine, *De vera religione* (Of True Religion), xxxv or 65. In *Augustine: Earlier Writings*, The Library of Christian Classics, Volume 6, translated by John H. S. Burleigh (Philadelphia: The Westminster Press, 1953). Eminently readable.

**10:5:** Not many know that serious paradoxes remain in the Einstein theories of relativity, requiring arbitrary interpretations of abstruse mathematics in order to make them correspond to reality. The matter is important here. First, the intellectual despair fostered by relativity theory leads some pundits to allege that knowledge of objective reality is impossible. Such a position dishonors proven human ability to determine much of what is true and what is false. Second, the relativity of time, asserted by Einstein, Minkowski and their followers, implies to many that morals, too, are properly relative. For instance, there is no point in being prudent for a future that is not to be future; this argument pops up in philosophy classes. Such matters do not bear on the truth or falsity of relativity theory but do suggest that questions of physics deserve probing before a wider audience. See N. Rudakov, *Fiction Stranger than Truth* (Victoria, Australia [3 Wirth Court, Newcomb, 3219], 1981), Chapters 1 to 3.

The Czech-American electrical engineer Petr Beckmann sums up much when he writes that his own book "is for those who will accept the Einstein theory as a brilliant, powerful and productive equivalence, but not as a physical reality" (*Einstein Plus Two* [Boulder, Colorado: Golem Press, 1987], p. 6). Beckmann addresses those who "strive for insight rather than mere description." He addresses those occasional young engineers or physicists who go to college "thirsting for real knowledge rather than just for a degree" (p. 193).

Beckmann's physically intelligible theory is based in part on the local-ether concepts of George G. Stokes (1845) as modified by Max Planck (1898) and as being somehow associated with gravitational fields. Mercury's advance of perihelion is explained without relativistic assumptions, harking back to Paul Gerber, a German schoolteacher, in 1898. Beckmann's own crucial experiment with P. Mandics (1965) completes the embarrassment of the ballistic theory of light propagation by which relativists have explained the aberration of the direction of starlight in response to the earth's revolving round the sun. Beckmann's theory finds no need of the Einsteinian blurring of past, present and future with odd contractions and curved space-time "in the intangible Temple of Tensors" (p. 175). Even the slowing of atomic phenomena as a result of atomic motion is accounted for in classical terms. When discussing electromagnetics or gravitation, Beckmann uses some higher mathematics; however, his words are usually clear in themselves. Peirce muses, "The only possible justification of any theory is that it should make things clear and reasonable" ([1:2], 6.24). The physics publication establishment has, to this date, stonewalled Beckmann.

As an embarrassment to the theories of geometry that have become conventions of relativity physics, see Hazelett and Turner, **"Space and the So-called Parallel Axiom,"** in *Speculations in Science and Technology* (SST) 7 (1984): 207-216. For a condensation of Jeremiah Joseph Callahan's book *Euclid or Einstein* (New York: Devin-Adair Co., 1931) see Part 5 of *The Einstein Myth and the Ives Papers*, edited by the present authors (Old Greenwich, Connecticut: Devin-Adair Co., 1979). Ives'

devastating critique of relativity theory remains valid, but some of his positive concepts, which Lorentz had shared, are now in doubt. Ives does not deal with the failure of light to aberrate its direction in traveling between two earthly points in response to the earth's motions. The Dutch mechanical engineer R. J. Legger has questioned in correspondence the mathematics in Ives' papers of 1945 and 1950.

More positively, see Parts 3, 4, and 5 of *The Einstein Myth*, and Part 1 up to p. 55. Part 3 is Ives' neglected experimental demolition of light *transmission* by photons, not its quantized emission or absorption (*American Academy of Arts and Sciences, Proceedings* 81 [1951]: 1-31), regarding which see D. G. Ashworth's inadvertent support (*Journal of Physics A* 11 [1978]: 1759-1763). Part 4 reprints valuable papers by C. W. Sherwin (*Physical Review* 120 [1960]: 17-21); J. Nelson (*Philosophia Mathematica* 12 [1975]: 66-75); and A. Lovejoy (*Journal of Philosophy* 27 [1930]: 617-632, 645-654). Likewise see G. Sagnac (translated from *Comptes Rendus* [Paris] 157 [1913]: 708-710, 1410-1413); and A. A. Michelson with H. G. Gale (*Astrophysical Journal* 61 [1925]: 137-145); these proofs of absolute space as to rotations are absent from about all recent freshman-level textbooks. Likewise absent for a generation is the beautifully simple pendulum of J. Foucault that illustrates the rotation of the earth in absolute space. Physicist Thomas G. Barnes affords further insights toward unified physics in his book *Space Medium* (El Paso: Geo/Space Research Foundation, 1986), and in his earlier books.

On the apparently instantaneous action of gravity see Thomas E. Phipps Jr. in *Speculations in Science and Technology* 1 (1978): 499-508.

**10:6:** Christopher Dawson, *Progress and Religion* (Garden City, New York: Doubleday & Co., 1960), p. 28 (first published 1929). See his *Dynamics of World History* [2:17], (New York: Sheed & Ward, 1956), Part 2, Chapter 2 (pp. 294-325). See also the writings of Stanley L. Jaki, especially *Science and Creation* [3:14].

**10:7:** David C. McClelland, *The Achieving Society* (Princeton, New Jersey: D. Van Nostrand Co., 1961), p. 322-335. McClelland and his colleagues have compared a related psychological need for achievement among a great variety of peoples and conditions.

**10:8:** Alfred North Whitehead, *Process and Reality* (New York: Macmillan Co., 1929), p. 517.

**10:9:** William Ernest Hocking, *Thoughts on Death and Life* (New York: Harper & Brothers, 1937), p. 98.

**10:10:** Étienne Gilson, *The Christian Philosophy of St. Augustine*, translated by L. E. M. Lynch (New York: Random House, 1937), pp. 4-9, notes 3, 11, 27; p. 115, note 1; pp. 132-133. Also see Augustine, *On the Morals of the Catholic Church*, Chapter 3.

**10:11:** Democritus, in John M. Robinson, *An Introduction to Early Greek Philosophy* (Boston: Houghton Mifflin Co., 1968), p. 222, no. 11.21; from H. Diels, *Die Fragmente der Vorsokratiker* (Berlin: Weidmann, 1912), Volume 2, p. 95, fragment 170. Thomas Aquinas, *Summa Theologica*, I-II (first part of second part), Question 2, Article 7. On Eudoxus see Aristotle, *Nicomachean Ethics*, 1172b (Book 10, Chapter 2).

**10:12:** Albert Schweitzer, *Philosophy of Civilization* [1:11], p. 118 (35-36). See Lewis [17:17], Chapter 16.

**10:13:** John Locke, from a notebook. Quoted in a booklet, *Locke*, by Maurice Cranston (London: Longmans, Green & Co., 1961), p. 28.

**10:14:** Thomas Aquinas, *Summa Theologica*, I-II, Question 31, especially Articles 3 and 4, but see also nearby. Aquinas deserves the attention of psychologists.

**10:15:** Augustine, *On the Morals of the Catholic Church*, Chapter 3; *The City of God*, Book 14, Chapter 6.

**10:16:** Wilmon Henry Sheldon, *Rational Religion* [11:8], pp. 31-32. The scholastic philosophers distinguish longing for an absent good from enjoyment of its possession (fruition).

**10:17:** Thomas Aquinas, *Summa Theologica*, I-II (first part of second part), Question 34.

**10:18:** On the almost prehistoric Chinese monotheism, see John Ross (1842-1915), *The Original Religion of China* (London: Oliphant, Anderson & Ferrier, 1909), e.g., pp. 122-123, 136-137; Herbert A. Giles, *Religions of Ancient China* (London: Archibald Constable & Co., 1905), Chapter 1; *Encyclopaedia of Religion and Ethics* [7:1], the article "China," by W. Gilbert Walshe. A caution: the early-starting chronology stated by Confucius and used by the above authors is no longer accepted. More recently, see Daniel L. Overmyer in *Encyclopedia of Religion* [7:20], the article "Chinese Religion: An Overview." See the ethical emphasis of Ronald M. Green, *Religion and Moral Reason: A New Method for Comparative Study* (New York: Oxford University Press, 1988), Chapter 3. By the time of Confucius around 500 B.C., critical thought and doubts had set in, and by 300 B.C. the sage Mencius is found challenging the authenticity of the documents that affirm the primal henotheism, such as *The Book of History* and *The Book of Odes*. If Mencius recorded reasons for his doubts, they have not reached us (Ross, *China*, pp. 26-33). In recent times, Shang-ti has come to include the spirits of deceased rulers. The comprehensive collection of *The Chinese Classics* was edited by James Legge, 5 volumes (Hong Kong: Hong Kong University, 1960).

**10:19:** Abraham is thought to have lived between 2000 and 1900 B.C., per W. F. Albright, referred to by Paul Johnson in *A History of the Jews* (New York: Harper & Row, 1987). On historical Judeo-Christian interaction, the book *Anti-Judaism in Christian Theology* by Charlotte Klein is excellent (Philadelphia: Fortress Press, 1975). Further, see the books of James William Parkes and of Samuel Sandmel—for instance, Parkes, *Jesus, Paul and the Jews* (London: Student Christian Movement Press, 1936), *The Conflict of the Church and the Synagogue* New York: Atheneum, 1969), *The Jew in the Medieval Community*, second edition (New York: Hermon Press, 1976). See Sandmel, *We Jews and Jesus* (New York: Oxford University Press, 1973); *A Jewish Understanding of the New Testament* (New York: Ktav Publishing House, 1956), especially "The Gospel According to Matthew"; *Judaism and Christian Beginnings* (New York: Oxford University Press, 1978), *The Several Israels* (New York: Ktav Publishing House, 1971). Sandmel was the general editor of the New English Bible. Arthur Lovejoy writes of "The Origins of Ethical Inwardness in Jewish Thought," in *American Journal of Theology* 11 (1907): 228-249. Other books show the influence of Judaism on Islam. In *Warrant for Genocide* Norman Cohn proves "The Protocols of the Elders of Zion" a forgery; these "Protocols" influentially alleged worldwide Jewish conspiracy and deceived Henry Ford (Harper & Row, 1967).

Historically, it has been common in Judaic culture to pursue much booklearning. However, sometimes they have read the wrong books and have done so before a lot of the rest of us have. One of the results of this has been the widespread loss of faith in the conservation of the human person beyond the grave. The reading of the right books would help to correct this. For example, see *Judaism and Immortality* by Rabbi Levi A. Olan (New York: Union of Hebrew Congregations, 1971), e.g., pp. 100-104. In Juadaism, little belief in survival beyond the grave now remains. Also, there has been a significant loss of faith in God.

**10:20:** Raymond Dawson, *Confucius* (New York: Hill and Wang, 1982).

**10:21:** Ancestor worship is not the worship of family gods but rather expresses gratitude toward parents and grandparents for the gift of life. Heaven is "recognized as ancestor of all ancestors, the source of all life. Man comes from Heaven through his parents. Filial piety is to return to the origins." This is from Father Chih [20:30], p. 358, who continues: "Filial piety is not the root of love but the start of its practice (88). Filial piety unites the past, present, and future (368). The duty of a filial son is to nourish reverently his parents while they are alive and to sacrifice to them reverently when they are dead. His chief thought is how

to conduct his life in such a way that his parents will not be disgraced. He mourns all of his life for his [deceased] parents to demonstrate his gratitude. He seems never to exhaust his love, sincerity, and reverence for his parents who gave him life" (354; see also 300-301). Chih finds the present elite to lean toward agnosticism (414-417, 353-359). Brief, perceptive views of Chinese religion and other Eastern religions appear in Christopher Dawson, *Christianity in East and West* [6:25], Chapter 11, and *Religion and World History* [6:25], Part 1.

**10:22:** H. L. Mencken, in *Dictionary of Humorous Quotations*, edited by Evan Esar (New York: Paperback Library, 1962), p. 127, no. 20 (first published 1949).

**10:23:** Edward Conze, *Buddhism: Its Essence and Development* (New York: Philosophical Library, 1951), p. 129. But there is more to Buddhism than this; see Dawson, *Christianity in East and West* [6:25]. *Areopagus* (Hong Kong) explores ongoing interfaces between oriental religions and Christianity.

**10:24:** For detailed discussion of "hoof-in-mouth" contradictions see the Annex.

**10:25:** Charles Sanders Peirce gives valuable suggestions on dealing with the problem of doubt vs. knowledge; see *Collected Papers* [1:2], 5.264 ff., 5.370-5.387. This reprinted selection is **"The Fixation of Belief"** from *Popular Science Monthly* 12 (1877): 1-15, which is reprinted in selections of Peirce's works. Also see *Collected Papers* [1:2], 5.397, 5.416-5.417, 5.512, 1.145. Sections 7.108-7.109 have value, tied though they are to Peirce's fallibilism as to knowledge in general. See also Rescher [5:7], Chapter 4.

**10:26:** See Walter Kaufmann, *Nietzsche: Philosopher, Psychologist, Antichrist*, fourth edition (Princeton University Press, 1974), "Nietzsche's Repudiation of Christ," at pp. 354-357.

**10:27:** W. K. Clifford, [2:7]. Compare Bertrand Russell, "Reply to Criticisms," in *The Philosophy of Bertrand Russell* (Evanston, Illinois: Northwestern University, 1944), pp. 725-727. Clifford was from his early years an eloquent humanist; see Stanley L. Jaki, *Angels, Apes, and Men*

[4:14], pp. 54-55.

**10:28:** See notably [Annex:19] herein; David Hume, *Enquiries Concerning the Human Understanding*, Section 4, Part 1; Section 12, Part 3; *A Treatise of Human Nature*, Book 2, Part 3, Section 10. See G. W. von Leibniz, *Monadology*, Sections 33-36. Hume's fork follows from erroneous premises and is a *reductio ad absurdum*.

**10:29:** Deuteronomy 30:19.

**10:30:** One might wish for the argument used herein to receive some corroboration from experience. The book *Life After Life*, by Raymond A. Moody, recounts the remarkably similar experiences of many people who seem to have stepped somewhat over the threshold of death and then returned. We do not wish to be drawn into the controversy over just what these experiences mean; still, the data and presentation are impressive (Atlanta: Mockingbird Books, 1975). See further Karlis Osis and Erlendur Haraldsson, *At the Hour of Death* (New York: Avon Books, 1977).

**10:31:** Søren Kierkegaard, *Sickness unto Death* (first published 1849).

**10:32:** Besides Turner's 1978 work *Commitment to Care* [5:23], see F. R. Tennant, *Philosophical Theology* [5:8], Volume 2, pp. 269-270. See William Ernest Hocking, *Living Religions and a World Faith* (New York: Macmillan Co., 1940), pp. 219-222; Harry Emerson Fosdick, *The Assurance of Immortality* (London: James Clarke & Co., 1918).

**10:33:** Quoted by Ananda K. Coomaraswamy, *Buddha and the Gospel of Buddhism* (New York: Harper & Row, 1964; first published 1916), p. 251.

**10:34:** Charles Hartshorne, *Divine Relativity* [7:19], pp. 132-134 *et passim;* "The Immortality of the Past," *Review of Metaphysics* 7 (1953): 98-112; *The Logic of Perfection* (La Salle, Illinois: Open Court

Publishing Co., 1962), Chapter 9, from *Journal of Religion* 32 (1952): 97-107; [16:16], p. 321. Whitehead refers to this memory in God as constituting a growth in His own nature, "a tender care that nothing be lost" [10:8], p. 525). George Allan finds that the word "nothing" in this context goes so far as to nullify the reality of tragedy; see the *Review of Metaphysics* 40 (1986): 271-304 toward the end; also *The Philosophy of Alfred North Whitehead*, edited by Paul Schilpp (Evanston, Illinois: Northwestern University, 1941), p. 698.

**10:35:** Isaiah 54:10.

**10:36:** See Nicholas Berdyaev, *Dostoyevsky* (Cleveland: World Publishing Co., 1957), pp. 127-130: Dean Turner, *Commitment to Care* [5:23], "Care in Jesus of Nazareth"; also see index there under "Immortality." See Hartshorne, *Whitehead's Philosophy* [21:8], pp. 105-109. See David Ray Griffin's full discussion in [16:11], Chapter 6. A conceivable mediate view is presented by Donald Wayne Viney in *Charles Hartshorne and the Existence of God* [16:19], pp. 116-117. Much of what Dawson writes in "The Future Life" may be of interest to many (*Religion and World History* [6:25], Epilogue, reprinted from the *Spectator* 151 [1933]: 889-890).

**10:37:** Friedrich Nietzsche, *Thus Spake Zarathrustra*, "The Intoxicated Song," Sections 11-12: "Alle lust will Ewigkeit." See Immanuel Kant, *Critique of Pure Reason*, B xxxii. An argument suggestive of the present chapter is put forth by Feodor Dostoyevsky; see Paul Ramsey, *Nine Modern Moralists* (Englewood Cliffs: Prentice-Hall, 1962), pp. 11-34, 257-258.

**10:38:** 1 Corinthians 15:32, New English Bible, partly after Lucretius, *De Rerum Natura*, Book 3, line 914. The bereaved may find comfort in *A German Requiem* by Johannes Brahms; it is of a gentler spirit than Roman Catholic requiem masses.

# 11. Appreciation and Self-Esteem

**Epigraph:** Abraham Lincoln, speech at New Salem, Illinois, March 9, 1832.

**11:1:** See James J. Lynch, *The Broken Heart: Medical Consequences of Loneliness* (New York: Basic Books, 1977). Also relevant is the book *Isolation* by Charles A. Brownfield (New York: Random House, 1965); see *From Learning to Love: The Selected Papers of H. F. Harlow* (New York: Praeger Publishers, 1986), especially the latter papers; also Harry F. Harlow and Clara Mears, *The Human Model: Primate Perspectives* (New York: John Wiley & Sons, 1979), notably Part 4.

Colonel Samuel L. A. Marshall writes, "It has happened too frequently in our Army that a line company was careless about the manner in which it received a new replacement. The stranger was not introduced to his superiors nor was there time for him to feel the friendly interest of his immediate associates before he was ordered forward with the attack. The result was the man's total failure in battle and his return to the rear as a mental case" (*Men Against Fire*, third printing [New York: William Morrow & Co., 1966, first published 1947], Chapter 3, pp. 41-43). Corroborating Marshall's observation, a high-school friend of Hazelett was caught alone in a bombing raid in Korea and was a psychiatric case the rest of his short life. Marshall's book is a valuable source on the psychology of battle.

**11:2:** Edwards, *True Virtue* [6:3], pp. 45-46. "To" has been changed to "of" in several places. See Arthur O. Lovejoy, *Reflections on Human Nature* (Baltimore: Johns Hopkins Press, 1961), Lecture 3. Lovejoy's entire book will repay reading. Some of it deals with political theory. F. F. Centore offers a perceptive and usually sympathetic critique of Lovejoy in *Philosophical Studies* (Ireland) 20 (1972): 319-325. See further Lovejoy, "Terminal and Adjectival Values," *Journal of Philosophy* 47 (1950): 593-608, e.g., at p. 605; William James, *Principles of Psycho-logy*, 2 volumes (New York: Henry Holt & Co., 1890), Volume 1, pp. 293-294.

**11:3:** Lovejoy, *Human Nature* [11:2], Lecture 3: also see Lectures 4 and 5. As to the last sentence in the present text, see William James, *Principles of Psychology* [11:2], Volume 1, pp. 293-294; John Locke, *An Essay Concerning Human Understanding* (revised 1706), Book 2, Part 28, Section 12. At a popular level, see Arthur Gordon, "How Wonderful You Are," *Woman's Day,* October 1956, pp. 43, 124, 125, reprinted in *Readers Digest,* October 1956, pp. 33-36; Janet Graham, "Profits of Praise," *Readers Digest,* May 1968, pp. 117-119; Fulton Oursler, "There Is Magic in a Word of Praise," *Readers Digest,* August 1952, pp. 1-3; I. A. R. Wylie, "Compassion," *Christian Herald,* December 1955, pp. 21, 70-72 ff.; Gelett Burgess, "Sympathy Is What You Make It," *Readers Digest,* May 1942, pp. 10-12. Biblically, see Proverbs 16:24; contrast Proverbs 25:27.

**11:4:** Lovejoy, *Human Nature* [11:2], Lecture 3.

**11:5:** Kurt Goldstein, **"The Smiling of the Infant and the Problem of Understanding the 'Other',"** *Journal of Psychology* 44 (1957): 175-191, at p. 191.

**11:6:** H. B. Acton, *Philosophy* (U.K.) 30 (1955): 62-66, at p. 66. See Henry Sidgwick, *The Methods of Ethics* [8:1], p. 49.

**11:7:** O. H. Mowrer and A. D. Ullman, *Psychological Review* 52 (1945): 61-90, especially pp. 85-88; Neal E. Miller and John Dollard, *Social Learning and Imitation* (New Haven: Yale University Press, 1941), p. 55. See E. L. Thorndike, *Psychological Review* 40 (1933): 434-439; 45 (1938): 204-205; O. H. Mowrer, *Psychological Review* 53 (1946): 321-334. For general theoretical treatment in terms of derived drive or secondary reward see Leo Postman, "The History and Present Status of the Law of Effect," *Psychological Bulletin* 44 (1947): 489-563, especially at pp. 544-548 and 497.

**11:8:** Wilmon Henry Sheldon, *Rational Religion* (New York: Philosophical Library, 1962), pp. 20, 40.

**11:9:** Henry Sidgwick, *The Methods of Ethics* [8:1], Book 1, Chapter 4.

**11:10:** Adam Smith, *The Theory of Moral Sentiments*, sixth edition (Edinburgh, 1790), Part 3, Chapter 1. Smith's book can still be read with profit for its gentle wisdom, indeed with amusement for its anecdotes. See also Albert Schweitzer, *Philosophy of Civilization* [1:11], p. 152 (71-72).

**11:11:** Smith, *Moral Sentiments* [11:10], Part 3, Chapter 2, also Chapter 3, where one reads of the reverse case: "[Thomas] Gray, to whom nothing is wanting to render him, perhaps, the first poet in the English language, but to have written a little more, is said to have been so much hurt by a foolish and impertinent parody of two of his finest odes, that he never afterwards attempted any considerable work."

**11:12:** Joseph Addison, *The Spectator* no. 15, March 17, 1711. Capitalization and word division have been modernized.

**11:13:** David Riesman, *The Lonely Crowd* (New Haven: Yale University Press, 1950), e.g., Chapter 1.

**11:14:** See Robert A. Nisbet, *The Quest for Community* (New York: Oxford University Press, 1953), e.g., p. 204, where Nisbet quotes Adolf Hitler on the importance of political mass meetings. See Karen Horney, *The Neurotic Personality of Our Time* (New York: W. W. Norton & Co., 1937), pp. 35-36, 105, 115.

**11:15:** Smith, *Moral Sentiments* [11:10], Part 3, Chapter 2.

**11:16:** Henri Bergson, *Mind-Energy*, translated by H. Wilden Carr (New York: Henry Holt & Co, 1920), p. 30. From *L'energie spirituelle* (Paris, 1919).

**11:17:** Lovejoy, "Terminal and Adjectival Values" [11:2], at pp. 597-598.

**11:18:** Lovejoy, *Human Nature* [11:2], pp. 80-81. See Virgil Aldrich, "An Ethics of Shame," *Ethics* 50 (1940): 57-77.

**11:19:** Sheldon, *Rational Religion* [11:8], p. 22.

**11:20:** John Stuart Mill, *Utilitarianism* (first published 1861), Chapter 2. Despite

its problems, the entire essay will repay reading.

**11:21:** Philip Blair Rice [18:17], at p. 315.

**11:22:** Smith, *Moral Sentiments* [11:10], Part 3, Chapter 2. See David Hume, "Of the Love of Praise," "Of the Dignity or Meanness of Human Nature," in *Essays and Treatises on Several Subjects*.

**11:23:** Walter Houston Clark, *Journal of Social Psychology* 41 (1955): 57-69, at p. 68.

**11:24:** Thomas Fuller (1654-1734), *Aphorisms of Wisdom* or *Celebrated Proverbs* (1732). Pigs need appreciation, too. At the Champlain Valley Fair in Essex, Vermont, they will hardly perform in races without cheers from the sidelines, not even for the prize of an Oreo cream cookie by itself (*New York Times*, September 14, 1986, Section 1, p. 31).

**11:25:** Irenäus Eibl-Eibesfeldt, *Love and Hate*, translated by Geoffrey Strachan (New York: Holt, Rinehart & Winston, 1972). See also George Coffin Taylor's readable rearranged snippets of Shakespeare: *Essays of Shakespeare* (New York: G. P. Putnam's Sons, 1947), pp. 89ff.

**11:26:** See Centore's devastating critique: "The 'Creative' Ethics of Nietzsche and Sartre," *Faith and Reason* 10 (1984): 222-241. Nietzsche's sister survived Nietzsche by many years and was editor of his literary remains, including major works. She has been accused of clumsy tampering which may explain much of Nietzsche's negative ethical reputation; see Walter Kaufmann, *Nietzsche* (Princeton, New Jersey: Princeton University Press, 1950), the Prologue. Doubt is cast on Kaufmann's interpretations by Walter K. Stewart, " 'My Sister and I': The Disputed Nietzsche," in *Thought* (Fordham) 61 (1986): 321-335.

One may wonder where in all this to classify the biologist George Gaylord Simpson when he writes: "Altruistic behavior, which may be good by any yardstick, even a strictly biological one, is not overtly pleasurable." Does the word "overtly" get him out of this bind? (*American Psychologist* 21 [1966]: 27-36, at p. 30). Consider likewise the psychologist B. F. Skinner, who believes, "Admiration is a social practice used to eke out a defective control" (*American Philosophical Society, Proceedings* 108 [1964]: 482-485, at p. 484).

**11:27:** M. F. Ashley Montagu, **"A Scientist Looks at Love,"** in *The Humanization of Man* (Cleveland: World Publishing Co., 1962), pp. 99-113; condensed as "The Awesome Power of Human Love," in *Readers Digest*, February 1963, pp. 80-83. See also John Bowlby, **Maternal Care and Mental Health** (New York: World Health Organization, 1952), and other books by Bowlby. Bowlby pioneered in this and is still worth reading. The people of the Pacific island of Alor are a case in point; see Abraham Kardiner, *The Psychological Frontiers of Society* (New York: Columbia University Press, 1945), pp. 234-238, 250-258. The Old-Order Amish, by contrast, are discussed by Joe Wittmer in *Journal of Cross-Cultural Psychology* 2 (1971): 87-94. Learn from Karl Zinsmeister "How Day-Care Harms Children," in *Policy Review*, Spring 1988, pp. 40-48. Curiously, a group of six children, orphaned at age 3, continuously served as successful attachment figures for each other in place of mothers; see Samuel P. and Pearl M. Oliner, *The Altruistic Personality* [20:13], p. 172.

**11:28:** On psychopaths or sociopaths generally see Hervey Cleckley, **The Mask of Sanity**, fifth edition (St. Louis: C. V. Mosby Co., 1976); David and Joan McCord, *Psychopathy and Delinquency* (New York: Grune & Stratton, 1956); Norman Mailer, *The White Negro* (San Francisco: City Lights Books, 1957), or the same in *Dissent* (New York) 4 (1957): 276-293; Michael Craft, *Psychopathic Disorders* (Oxford: Pergamon Press, 1966); Stanton E. Samenow, *Inside the Criminal*

*Mind* (New York: Times Books, 1984). Among many articles, one stands out: F. W. Warburton in *Behaviour Research and Therapy* 3 (1965): 129-134. On measurement see e.g. Harrison G. Gough, in *Journal of Consulting Psychology* 24 (1960): 23-30; Gough, *California Psychological Inventory* (Palo Alto: Consulting Psychologists Press, 1956). See further Perry London and Robert K. Bower, "Altruism, Extraversion and Mental Illness," *Journal of Social Psychology* 76 (1968): 19-30; Robert W. Friedrichs, "Alter versus Ego: An Exploratory Assessment of Altruism," *American Sociological Review* 25 (1960) 496-508.

Crime and social class are explored by Walter B. Miller in *Journal of Social Issues* 14 (1958): 5-77; Lucius F. Cervantes (Ann Arbor: University of Michigan Press, 1965), 152-174; August B. Hollingshead and Fredrick C. Redlich, *Social Class and Mental Illness* (New York: John Wiley & Sons, 1958), 194-249. A maverick statement of class values and achievement is that of Robert Sheaffer, *Resentment Against Achievement* (Buffalo: Prometheus Books, 1988), especially Chapter 2.

**11:29:** David C. McClelland, *Power: The Inner Experience* (New York: Irvington Publishers, 1975), e.g., Chapter 9. There are many worthwhile publications that develop McClelland's work, for instance, Richard deCharms and Gerald H. Moeller, "Values Expressed in American Readers: 1800-1950," *Journal of Abnormal and Social Psychology* 64 (1962): 136-142. See e.g. Eric Hoffer, "Money," in *Between the Devil and the Dragon* [1:epigraph], pp. 320-321; also pp. 387-388.

**Epigraph:** G. K. Chesterton [14:8], p. 234.

# 12. Pooled Egotism

**Second epigraph:** Alexis de Tocqueville, *Democracy in America*, [6:23], Volume 1, Part 2, Chapter 9.

**12:1:** Boyd C. Shafer, *Nationalism: Myth and Reality* (New York: Harcourt, Brace & World, 1955), pp. 83-84. See Phillip E.

Hammond on "civil religion" in *Law and Social Inquiry* 14 (1989): 377-391. The rule of law is basic to American polity in a way that seems not to occur in Europe; see William E. Carroll in *Crisis* (Notre Dame, Indiana), June 1987, pp. 24-29.

**12:2:** Shafer [12:1], p. 147.

**12:3:** Adam Weishaupt, quoted in Shafer [12:1], pp. 132, 271.

**12:4:** Shafer [12:1], pp. 102, 116-117.

**12:5:** H. Morse Stephens, quoted in [12:1], pp. 216, 288.

**12:6:** See Peter F. Drucker [2:27], especially Chapter 7. Also see Shafer [12:1], pp. 215-237. Mikhail S. Bernstam insightfully calls nationalism a modern reaction to capitalism, which destroyed feudal walls between classes and opened equal opportunities for every individual to compete in the market. Many individuals, especially intellectuals, would like to avoid much competition. Nationalism is the movement which switches arrangements from individual competition to competition between groups and communities. Nationalism sees the best opportunities not in the private sector but in the bureaucracy. To put it plainly, nationalism is a protection racket and insurance against market failure, insurance for which other groups pay the price of restrictions imposed on them (*Chronicles* [Rockford], October 1988, pp. 12-18).

**12:7:** Georg W. F. Hegel, *Lectures on the Philosophy of History* (London, 1878), pp. 40-41, 70, quoted in Hans Kohn, *Nationalism: Its Meaning and History*, revised edition (New York: Van Nostrand Reinhold Co., 1965), pp. 110-112. *Philosophy of Right*, translated by T. M. Knox (London: Oxford University Press, 1942), p. 285; quoted in Christopher Dawson, *Understanding Europe* (New York: Sheed & Ward, 1952), Chapter 10.

**12:8:** Benito Mussolini, *The Doctrine of Fascism* (Florence: Vallechi, 1935), e.g., pp. 37-39, quoted in Kohn [12:7], pp. 170-174.

12:9: Arnold Toynbee [2:17], Volume 7, "Churches as a Higher Species of Society," p. 478.

**12:10:** For early warning see C. Northcote Parkinson, *Parkinson's Law* (Boston: Houghton Mifflin Co., 1957) and *The Law and the Profits* (Boston: Houghton Mifflin Co., 1960).

**12:11:** Charles Murray, *Losing Ground* (New York: Basic Books, 1984).

**12:12:** Rudolph J. Rummel, *Wall Street Journal*, July 7, 1986, p. 12; *International Journal on World Peace* 1 (1984): 4-15; Robert Conquest, *Harvest of Sorrow: Soviet Collectivization and the Terror-Famine* (New York: Oxford University Press, 1986); Elizabeth Burke, *When the War Was Over: The Voices of Cambodia's Revolution and Its People* (New York: Simon & Schuster, 1986); Armando Valladares, *Against All Hope* (New York: Alfred A. Knopf, 1986). On the surprising recommendations of genocide made by socialists like Marx, Engels, H. G. Wells, and G. B. Shaw see George Watson in *Chronicles* (Rockford), June 1988, pp. 27-30. See Lenin's mad 1917 ravings in Robert Payne, *The Life and Death of Lenin* (New York: Simon & Schuster, 1964), pp. 418-420. Payne's readable, generally accurate books are nearly all out of print at this writing.

**12:13:** Herbert Schlossberg, in *Idols for Destruction* (Nashville: Thomas Nelson Publishers, 1983), p. 231 and Chapter 5 generally. See also John E. E. D. Acton (Lord Acton), *Essays on Freedom and Power* (Cleveland: World Publishing Co., 1955), "Nationality," pp. 141-170; quoted in Kohn, [12:7], pp. 121-125.

**12:14:** Arthur Clutton-Brock, **"Pooled Self-Esteem,"** *Atlantic Monthly* 128 (1921): 721-731. A sequel appears in the *New Republic*, March 1, 1922, pp. 17-19. See also Arthur Lovejoy, *Reflections on Human Nature* (Baltimore: Johns Hopkins Press, 1961), especially pp. 117 ff.

**12:15:** Plato, *The Republic*, 521b — Chapter 25 in the Francis Cornford edition (London: Oxford University Press, 1941), emphasis added. One muses that those who can't manage their own affairs make bold to manage everybody else's. Kenneth Boulding puts forth, with qualifications, what he calls the "dismal theorem of political science," namely, "that all the skills leading to the rise to power tend to unfit people to exercise it" (*The World as a Total System* [Beverly Hills: Sage Publications, 1985], p. 116).

Karl Popper cogently interprets *The Republic* as "purely totalitarian" and a "betrayal of Socrates"; see *The Open Society and Its Enemies* [2:22], Volume 1. On the methods of tyranny see Aristotle, *Politics*, e.g. 1313-1314 (in Book 5, Section 11; also Payne [18:8], e.g., pp. 380-391, 421-431, 492-493, 690-691.

The American psychologist David C. McClelland has investigated and written of three personal characteristics: the need for power, need for affiliation, and need for achievement. These needs are keys to explaining and directing much behavior at a practical level in management, economic development, war, and therapy. See his *Motives, Personality, and Society: Selected Papers* (New York: Praeger Publishers, 1984). Practical insights and cross-cultural experiences are included. "The mills of God grind slowly, but they grind exceeding fine." McClelland's grind faster.

**12:16:** See Albert Schweitzer, *Philosophy of Civilization* [1:11], p. 337 (269-270). Striking examples of renunciation of political power for the good of a polity are gathered in *Profiles in Courage* (New York: Harper & Brothers, 1955). The nominal author is John F. Kennedy, though it is claimed that the book is substantially the production of others; see Herbert S. Parmet, *Jack: The Struggle of John F. Kennedy* (New York: Dial Press, 1980), pp. 330-333.

There is much to be said against allowing a mass of less-than-perfect people too great an immediate influence in the day-to-day affairs of government. There is also much to be said in favor of a structure of government and of election whereby rulers can be made responsive to a multitude of public needs and not to just a few needs. A mechanism to achieve this would be "pyramidal government," which is an improvement over James Harrington's scheme in *Oceana* (London, 1656). Harrington proposes that the populace elect local representatives who would conduct the local government and who moreover would elect the representatives to the next higher level of government. These representatives would in turn conduct

that government and elect the next higher level, etc., right up to the top.

The improvement of C. W. Hazelett stems from the now feasible elimination of terms of office-holding as is normal in private employment, so that pressure at the highest levels of government could be felt before many days, despite the layers of government that would intervene. The feasibility results from each election being a more wieldy affair. The result should be that the advantages of parliamentary government and of the council-manager form of local government could be systematically attained. Moreover, a voter's genuine power to influence some chosen aspect of events would lead him to study the relevant facts. Conversely, the representatives would find reason to educate the layer of representatives below them and, through them, the populace, since the process would take place in manageable steps instead of through covertly filtered national mass media (see C. William Hazelett, *A Dynamic Capitalism* [New York: Harper & Brothers, 1943], Part 2: also his *Practical Answers* [Greenwich, Connecticut: Incentivist Publications, 1951], Part 6).

In C. W. Hazelett's proposal, only one point of view would be likely to filter to the top. To correct this, not one but two representatives could be elected at every level, thereby tending toward a two-party system. Each winner would be apportioned in voting power according to votes received (see George S. Blair in *National Municipal Review* 42 [1953]: 410-414; also Richard Hazelett, "Multiple Weighted Voting in Government," *American Journal of Economics and Sociology* 20 [1961]: 287-290). The populace should have the right of direct recall of executives; this would amount to something like the desirable separation of powers that inheres in American government. On council-manager local government see the books of Richard S. Childs, *Civic Victories* (New York: Harper & Brothers, 1952), and *The First 50 Years of the Council-Manager Plan of Government* (New York: National Municipal League, 1965). E. E. Schattschneider provides a realistic view of

American government in *Party Government* (New York: Farrar & Rinehart, 1960), and in *The Semisovereign People* (New York: Holt, Rinehart and Winston, 1960); see especially *Two Hundred Million Americans In Search of a Government* (New York: Holt, Rinehart & Winston, 1969). A contrasting view of electoral structure is that of Friedrich A. Hayek in *Law, Legislation and Liberty* [2:28], Volume 2, p. 113; his plan should be considered. *The Federalist* is an unjustly neglected work.

**Epigraph:** Leo Tolstoy, *War and Peace*, as heard at the end of the Russian screen play of 1968, co-authored by Sergei Bondarchuk and Vasily Solovyov.

# 13. Music and Romantic Love

**Second epigraph:** Joseph Addison, *Cato*, Act 3, Scene 1.

**13:1:** Donald N. Ferguson, *Music as Metaphor* (Minneapolis: University of Minnesota Press, 1960), pp. 184-187. Father Chih describes the traditional Chinese view of music as being joy, an integral part of religion and education: "Music has its origin from Heaven; ceremonies take their form from the appearances of Earth. Music is a response to the life-giving rhythm of the divine love of the universe. It enhances the exuberance of life, in a cosmic symphony of love" [20:30] (pp. 272, 275). Popular songs and dramas are an important form of education of the masses (pp. 311-315).

**13:2:** Christopher Dawson, e.g., "Medieval Science," in *Medieval Essays* (New York: Sheed & Ward, 1954).

**13:3:** Dawson, "The Romantic Tradition," in *Medieval Essays* [13:2]. From ancient India comes an eloquent tribute and exhortation to marriage by Dindimus (Dandemis) in *Wisdom of the Ages*, edited by Mark Gilbert (London: St. Catherine Press, 1934). More generally, see Robert H. Lowie, *Social Organization* (New York: Rinehart & Co., 1948), pp. 220-224.

**13:4:** Roland Bainton, *What Christianity Says about Sex, Love and Marriage* (New York: Association Press, 1957), e.g., Chapter 3.

**13:5:** Nicholas Berdyaev, *Dostoevsky* (i.e., Dostoyevsky) (Cleveland: World Publishing Co., 1957), Chapter 5, e.g., pp. 112-113. Additionally, the disintegration of the family was for many early years an objective of Communist leaders in the U.S.S.R. (Nicholas S. Timasheff, *The Great Retreat* [New York: E. P. Dutton & Co., 1946], pp. 192-203, at p. 197).

**13:6:** Tones and their patterned combinations are inherently pleasant; music as such is a good, whatever the style. Hard rock as one extreme, and baroque and classical music as another, are indeed pleasant to their respective devotees. These art forms are a basis for community respectively among both performers and listeners. Is one music style as good as another? Is hard rock as desirable as classical or baroque music?

Arguably, stirring music of any kind comprises a sensual component, if only because the music itself is a basis for a kind of psychic unity between persons. Hence, sensuality as such is not a distinguishing feature of musical styles, though the kind of sensuality may be. In most of Europe, classical and baroque music has been a main cultural currency. In suitably prepared minds, these styles somehow elicit and cultivate ideas and ideals of humane order, care, and affection. For example, as the American composer Roger Sessions said, "Bach and Mozart and Beethoven did not *reflect* Germany, they helped to create it" (*Composers on Music*, edited by Sam Morgenstern [New York: Pantheon Books, 1956], p. 502). Baroque and classical music had their roots in Christian influence. All the great Western composers down through Brahms were devout Christians, despite estrangement from a church as with Beethoven. The devout and musically sensitive do not need to be told that these composers were devout, for their religious music rings it out it clearly, even without the words, and their other music affirms it.

The displacement of classical styles in the early twentieth century coincided with the widespread decline of Judeo-Christian religious faith in Europe. Of the serious music composed at that time, one thinks of the iconoclastic styles of Schönberg, Stravinsky, and the later Richard Strauss. Rock is the common currency of the young now, the seemingly inescapable esthetic background of their relatedness. Yet, could it be that much modern popular music consists of the blaring of "loud, dissonant defiance at all who would question the genuineness of its hilarity"? So implied Walter Marshall Horton writing of jazz in *Theism and the Modern Mood* (New York: Harper & Bros., 1930), p. 7. Chesterton said of jazz that it is the "very reverse of an expression of liberty," for it is "the expression of the pessimistic idea that nature never gets beyond nature," and so "it is the song of the treadmill" ([2:epigraph], p. 21). A little jazz should be innocuous, but could it be that hard rock music or, more precisely, sass 'n' howl music, beats into the minds of its devotees the message that the world is essentially an absurd place, worthy only of anger and contempt? Some of the lyrics, though by no means all, confirm such a message.

For the role of organized crime in the spread of sass-'n'-howl music from the mid-1950s on, see Tom Garlock in *National Review,* December 13, 1985, pp. 17-18. The motive is said to have been that of selling whiskey and juke-box music, under Mafia control. Stuart Goldman adds: "Rock has become distinguishable from overt pornography mainly in degree" (*National Review,* February 24, 1989, pp. 28-31, 59). Our younger friends resist this generalization while admitting its partial truth.

Musical styles encountered early in life are likely to be preferred by one for a long time thereafter, perhaps to the exclusion of a broader understanding. When one finds real pleasure and community in a style of music, change to a sharply different style does not come readily. If there is truth in these remarks, the music encountered by the young should be a matter of parental concern.

An excellent intellectual history of music is *The Philosopher and Music* by Julius Portnoy (New York: Humanities Press, 1954). On the psychology of music see Felicie Peterson, "The Psychological Influence of Music," *Music of the West Magazine,* April 1959, pp. 9, 28; Plato, *The Republic,* 400c-402e (in Chapter 9); Leo Tolstoy, *What Is Art?* (first published 1896), Chapter 5. See Sir James George Frazer, *Adonis Attis Osiris* in *The Golden Bough,* third edition, Volume 5 (London: Macmillan & Co., 1914), or Volume I of *Adonis Attis Osiris,* Part 4—i.e., Volume 5, pp. 53-54. Further, see John Henry Newman, *(Fifteen) Sermons Preached Before the University of Oxford* (Westminster, Maryland: Christian Classics, 1966; first published 1872), No. 15, pp. 346ff.; Gerhard Albersheim, "Mind and Matter in Music," *Journal of Aesthetics and Art Criticism* 22 (1964): 289-294; compare Aristotle, *Problems,* 919-920.

For a penetrating statement of the esthetics of Gothic church architecture see Henry Adams (1838-1918), *Mont-St. Michel and Chartres* (Boston: Houghton, Mifflin Co., 1913), notably pp. 376-377; quoted in Christopher Dawson, *The Formation of Christendom* (New York: Sheed & Ward, 1967), pp. 272-273. To Schweitzer, Bach's music is "Gothic architecture transformed into sound" ([1:1], Chapter 7). On the power of literature to shape values see Victor M. Hamm, "Literature and Morality," *Thought* 15 (1940): 268-280. Hamm refers notably to H. W. Garrod, *Poetry and the Criticism of Life* (Cambridge: Harvard University Press, 1931), e.g., pp. 6-13.

**13:7:** Attributed to William Blake but not verified.

**13:8:** Paul does better in Ephesians 5:21 and in Galatians 3:28. The problem of the anomalies in 1 Timothy 2 seems insoluble except on the assumption, supported by stylistic considerations, that the book is not from Paul's hand. See the editorial introduction to 1 Timothy in the full-size New English Bible; also Robert Jewett, "Paul the Apostle" in *Encyclopedia of Religion* (New York: Macmillan Publishing Co., 1987). Gilbert Bilezikian in *Beyond Sex Roles* (second edition) does not deny Paul's authorship, finding other ways to attenuate the passage (Grand Rapids: Baker Book House, 1989).

**13:9:** Shirley Robin Letwin, **"Romantic Love and Christianity,"** *Philosophy* (U.K.) 52 (1977): 131-145. Letwin finds in the novels of Stendhal the *reductio ad absurdum* of the simple fusion view. Tolstoy knows better, notably in his novel *Anna Karenina*. Tolstoy sees that the subjection of a woman, even when not explicitly intended by anybody, may subtly lead to a backlash of covert resentment that spoils everything; see his novelette *The Kreutzer Sonata* (but with Anna Karenina the problem was not subtle). On relevant counseling see Harriet G. Lerner, *The Dance of Anger* (New York: Harper & Row, 1985). See Letwin in *American Spectator,* June 1986, pp. 45-47: Galatians 3:26-28; James Bissett Pratt, *Eternal Values in Religion* (New York: Macmillan Co., 1950), p. 98.

**13:10:** See Hervey Cleckley, *The Caricature of Love* (New York: Ronald Press Co. 1957), Chapter 27, "Eros."

**13:11:** Margaret Mead, *Coming of Age in Samoa* (first published 1928, several editions). For criticism see Derek Freeman, *Margaret Mead and Samoa* (Harvard University Press, 1983); E. Michael Jones in *Fidelity* (South Bend), February 1988, pp. 26-37. Mead evidently embraced Christianity shortly before she died (*Fidelity,* April 1988, pp. 7-8).

**13:12:** See e.g. as to Dora in 1905, in *The Standard Edition of the Complete Psychological Works of Sigmund Freud,* edited by James Strachey (London: Hogarth Press, 1960), Volume 7, pp. 3-122. See also Reuben Fine, *Freud: A Critical Re-evaluation of His Theories* (New York: David McKay Co., 1962), pp. 117-119; Freud, *The Future of an Illusion,* Chapter 3 at the beginning. See Melvin Anchell on "Psychoanalysis vs. Sex Education" in *National Review,* June

20, 1986, pp. 33, 38, 60-61; O. Hobart Mowrer, *Journal of Counseling Psychology* 7 (1960): 185-188. See Charles Hartshorne, *Beyond Humanism* [14:34], Chapter 6. As to Freud's drug problem and its relation to his theories see *The Freudian Fallacy* by Esther M. Thornton (New York: Dial Press, 1983). Finally, see the excellent critique by the American sociologist Richard LaPiere, *The Freudian Ethic* (New York: Duell, Sloan & Pearce, 1959). Hayek delivered a stinging summary in *Law, Legislation and Liberty* [2:28], Volume 3, Epilogue, pp. 173-176. A relatively unpassionate view of Freud is that of Bernard I. Murstein, *Love, Sex, and Marriage Through the Ages* (New York: Springer Publishing Co., 1974), pp. 288-298. On the positive side see in Volume 9 of the *Complete Psychological Works* Freud's linking of sublimation with civilization, which is a matter that appears also in Freud's *General Introduction to Psychoanalysis* (first published 1920, several editions), see index there. As to Karl Marx and the denial of right and wrong see H. B. Acton's report on *The Holy Family* in *What Marx Really Said* (New York: Schocken Books, 1967), pp. 121-129.

**13:13:** A 1975 *Redbook* religion survey of 65,000 American women "shows the religious woman to be optimistic, generous, forgiving and independent. The more religious a woman is, according to our survey, the happier she is. The very religious woman, for example, is least likely to report frequent feelings of anxiety, tension, or worthlessness." In the survey, sexual satisfaction is related significantly to religious belief. The more intense a woman's religious convictions, the likelier she is to be highly satisfied with the sexual pleasures of marriage (Robert J. and Amy Levin, *Redbook,* September 1975, pp. 51-58, at pp. 52-54; April 1977, pp. 126-127, 217-222). The *Redbook* survey has been faulted for possible volunteer error, since the questionnaire was presented to all of the magazine's already self-selected readership, while not nearly all the readers replied. The possibility was admitted by the Levins as a remote one. But the respondents were not selected from notably deviant populations, in contrast to many of the respondents in the notorious reports by Alfred Kinsey around 1950.

Behavioral scientists argue about the import of surveys on the relation of marital happiness to theistic religiosity. Surveys in the Western world generally yield positive correlations. But a counterassertion has been made, to the effect that the favorable statements of such obviously "conventional" people as married churchgoers are subject, by their very conventionality, to a systematic bias of self-misreporting. See Walter R. Schumm et al., "The 'Marital Conventionalization' Argument," *Journal of Psychology and Theology* 1 (1982): 236-241; Schumm et al. in *Journal of Psychology and Christianity,* 1 (1982): 16-21; Gary L. Hansen in *Journal of Marriage and the Family* 43 (1981): 855-863, and further references. The upshot seems to be a compromise.

**13:14:** Charles Hartshorne, "Redefining God," *New Humanist,* July-August 1934, pp. 8-15, at pp. 13-14.

**13:15:** Leo Tolstoy, as heard in the film play *War and Peace,* co-authored by King Vidor (a Ponti-DeLaurentiis production, distributed by Paramount, c. 1956), Pierre speaking to Natásha.

**13:16:** Leo Tolstoy, *Die sexuelle Frage* (Berlin: 1901), pp. 42, 75. Tolstoy, *My Confession,* Chapter 2.

**13:17:** Psalm 51 (Catholic 50).

**13:18:** On the negative side are the famous chapters 5 to 7 in 1 Corinthians, as well as 1 Timothy 2. But the negative view is even more explicit in 1 Corinthians 15:42, where it is stated that we are "sown in dishonor" or "sown in corruption."

**13:19:** Augustine, *The City of God,* Book 15: see also Book 14, especially Chapter 16 therein, and his *De nuptiis et concupisentia* (Marriage and Concupiscence, A.D. 420). Augustine's position was reiterated by the reformers Martin Luther and John Calvin (Johnson [13:22], p. 512). One wonders whether the influential anti-sex bias resulted largely from the fact that church builders have in the main been single men or men not primarily committed to family; they would have more time for something as unrewarding monetar-

ily as pioneer church-building is apt to be.

**13:20:** See Charles Finney, "The Excuses of Sinners," reprinted in *God's Love for a Sinning World* (Grand Rapids: Kregel Publications, 1966). See James Bissett Pratt in *International Journal of Ethics* 13 (1903): 222-235; Brand Blanshard, *Reason and Goodness* (London: George Allen & Unwin, 1966), pp. 359, 335. F. R. Tennant concludes in *The Sources of the Doctrines of the Fall and Original Sin* that the doctrine of original sin "was less the outcome of strict [scriptural] exegesis than due to the exercise of speculation" (Cambridge: At the University Press, 1903), p. 345. John Locke made an early attack; see Carl L. Becker, *The Heavenly City of the Eighteenth-Century Philosophers* (New Haven: Yale University Press, 1932), pp. 63-65.

**13:21:** Thomas Aquinas, *Summa Theologica,* I-II (first part of second part), Question 34, Article 1.

**13:22:** John Ferguson, *Pelagius* (Cambridge: W. Heffer & Sons, 1956), p. 160, also Chapter 10. See Harry Austryn Wolfson, *Religious Philosophy* (Cambridge: Harvard University Press, 1961), Chapter 6. See Paul Johnson, *A History of Christianity* (New York: Atheneum, 1976), pp. 117-122 and 511-512. For a moral critique of original sin see T. E. Jessop [6:24], Lecture 5. Blaise Pascal presents a balanced general view:

It is dangerous to make man see too clearly how nearly equal he is to the beasts, without showing him his greatness. It is also dangerous to make him see too clearly his greatness without his baseness. It is still more dangerous to leave him in ignorance of both. But it is very advantageous to represent to him both (*Pensées,* no. 418).

**13:23:** See Edmund S. Morgan, "The Puritans and Sex," *The New England Quarterly* 15 (1942): 591-607; or Morgan, *The Puritan Family* (Boston: The Trustees of the Public Library, 1944).

**13:24:** Edmund Leites, *The Puritan Conscience and Modern Sexuality* (New Haven: Yale University Press, 1986), e.g.,

p. 157. At greater length see Jean H. Hagstrum, *Sex and Sensibility: Ideal and Erotic Love from Milton to Mozart* (Chicago: University of Chicago Press, 1980).

**13:25:** Ralph Barton Perry, *Puritanism and Democracy* (New York: Vanguard Press, 1944), p. 627.

**13:26:** See almost any series of pronouncements by the general authorities of the Church of Jesus Christ of Latter-day Saints, in the *Ensign* (Salt Lake City). Christopher Dawson [2:17], pp. 156-166, "The Patriarchal Family in History." T. E. Jessop [6:24], pp. 98-113; W. M. Foley in *Encyclopaedia of Religion and Ethics* [7:1], Volume 7, p. 434, in article "Marriage (Christian)." See further the immense scholarship of Murstein [13:12], e.g., pp. 104-106. Murstein is as impartial as an outsider to theism can be. Contrast these writings with the misleading obtuseness of Bertrand Russell in his *Marriage and Morals* (New York: H. Liveright, 1929), notably at pp. 44-62, also at p. 161, where we are misadvised that the sexually free "are likely to prove less cruel, less brutal, and less violent than their seniors." In *Education and the Good Life,* Russell claims: "The main causes of unhappiness at present are: ill-health, poverty, and an unsatisfactory sex-life." As to the latter he goes on: "A generation of women brought up without irrational sex fears would soon make an end of this" (in the chapter "The Aims of Education" [New York: Albert & Charles Boni, 1926]). Even Russell might have been dismayed at the results of the present predominant acceptance of his half-truths. As C. William Hazelett once declared to a haughty politician, "The toast of today is the crumb of tomorrow."

**13:27:** Will and Ariel Durant, "Continue Dissent but Stay Civilized," in *Hangups from Way Back,* edited by F. Gentiles and M. Steinfield (San Francisco: Canfield Press, 1970), pp. 155-157, at p. 156.

**13:28:** *Enemies of Eros* by Maggie Gallagher, pp. 269-270. The book articulately defends the roles and mores of former days (Chicago: Bonus Books, 1989).

**13:29:** The Myers-Briggs Type Indicator (MBTI), based on Carl Jung's *Psychological Types* (1923), is said to enable the matching (or complementing) of important personality characteristics; see the psychologist Marvin Rytting in *Sunstone* (Salt Lake City), January 1984, pp. 45-46; Autumn 1984, pp. 45-47; no. 6, 1985, pp. 41-43. Again, normal people differ in their chemical makeup. Some important chemical parameters vary over ranges as much as 16 to 1.

Pharmaceutical houses naturally prefer to sell medicines that act much the same upon all people. Substances acting much differently upon most people are not marketed, but it is precisely these discarded substances that might help to distinguish different personality types, so far as personality differences have a basis in constitution. Such extra experimental data have usually been destroyed by the pharmaceutical companies as being of no value to them but potentially valuable to competitors seeking to cut their own experimental costs (Garrett Hardin, *Nature and Man's Fate* [New York: Rinehart & Co., 1959], pp. 195-197). On individual variations in general see Roger J. Williams, *Biochemical Individuality* (New York: John Wiley & Sons, 1956). Perhaps the most learned book on marital therapy is *Helping Couples Change,* by Richard B. Stuart (New York: Guilford Press, 1980). Psychologists nowadays are not apt to think of the churches as resources for counseling. They should read *A History of the Cure of Souls* by John Thomas McNeill (New York: Harper & Brothers, 1951).

**13:30:** It may have been Mark Twain who sounded off: "I aspire to be a leader of men and a follower of women."

**13:31:** On the depressing effect of rigid sex roles see Lee Rainwater in *Journal of Social Issues* 22 (1966): 96-108, also Andrew Greeley and Mary Greeley Durkin, *How to Save the Catholic Church* (New York: Viking Penguin, 1984). Mary Stewart Van Leeuwen points to evidences that, during times of church revival, arguments about gender role have been nearly absent (*Journal of Psychology and Theology* 16 [1988]: 168-182, at pp. 180 ff.)

The somewhat improving position of women in Christendom historically is discussed by A. Dorner in *Encyclopaedia of Religion and Ethics* [7:1], in the article "Emancipation," Volume 5, pp. 270-279, at p. 272, though the progress has not been consistent. Brand Blanshard's conclusion in *Reason and Belief* is equivocal (London: George Allen & Unwin, 1974), pp. 351-359; likewise, Crane Brinton in *A History of Western Morals* (New York: Harcourt, Brace & World, 1959), p. 167. Women did have problems in the primitive Church, starting with Paul; see James Donaldson, *Woman: Her Position and Influence* (London: Longmans, Green & Co., 1907), Book 3, Chapters 1 and 2. Alexis de Tocqueville thought that the singular "prosperity and growing power" of America was attributable to the "superiority of their women" (*Democracy in America* [6:23], Volume 2, Part 3, Chapter 12, "How the American Views the Equality of the Sexes").

In 1955, Hazelett checked fifty-seven societies in the *Human Relations Area Files* on the right of women to inherit tangible property and on equality of right to divorce. Two societies came out more equalitarian than ours, namely, the Zuni and the Woleai. Thirty-four of the societies were less equalitarian than ours; the other twenty-one were about on a par with us.

Women in Christendom have generally proved more apt than men to embrace theism. They seem to intuit the truth in it, whereas men may demand analytical proofs that have not always convinced even themselves. Perhaps women's intuition exemplifies an extended coherence theory of truth unconsciously applied. The evidence is mounting that women possess as much intrinsic capacity for leadership and productivity in general human roles and careers as men do, and in some areas, possibly even more. See (with some cautions) George W. Albee, "The Prevention of Sexism," *Professional Psychology* 12 (1981): 20-28.

In primeval China, it seems that society was matriarchal; that is, the woman's surname was transmitted to the children, not the man's. Andrew Chih presents other evidence that women's position was higher long ago than in recent centuries; see [20:30], pp. 344-345. Much the same is true of early Islam; see Barbara Freyer Stowasser in *Muslim Women*, edited by Freda Hussain (London: Croom Helm, 1984), pp. 11-43. Lowly status of women has more than one cause, but when a society loosens its hold on an ethically serviceable religion, marital ties loosen and crime naturally increases, including rape. Historically, a reaction to these dangers seems to have been the seclusion or confinement of women. One might attribute this reaction to the property right in women presumed by most men, though it would be as true to attribute it to the societal need of keeping family emotional bonds strong, so that children are more likely to be raised in two-parent homes with sufficient support.

Assuming that present conditions continue and assuming a 50 percent rate of recent reporting, something like three percent of American women who are now young will be forcibly raped at some time during their lives, probably while young. If attempted rapes are counted, as they seem to be in the U.S. "uniform" crime reports, the rate comes to four times this. During some invasions or riots, rates seem to have approached 100 percent, sparing only the very young. The American armed forces in 1944 and 1945 behaved better than most, certainly as contrasted with the forces of Germany, Japan, and Russia; the quality of American leadership doubtless had a lot to do with this. The war leaders of Germany and Japan even promoted general rape as a deliberate weapon of terrorism (Susan Brownmiller, *Against Our Will* [New York: Simon & Schuster, 1975], Chapter 3; also see index there under "Toynbee, Arnold.") Brownmiller's is the pioneering, monumental treatise.

The point in all this is that, in the long run of history, men (and perhaps even women) are apt to define women's roles restrictively because of vulnerability of women amidst general decay of morals. Neither women's liberation nor other current achievements in civil rights (nor much of anything else, not even science) seem likely to be secure until problems at a religious level are resolved.

**13:32:** Some reflections appear in Midge Decter [14:21]. See also Sheldon Vanauken in *The Intellectuals Speak Out about God*, edited by Roy Abraham Varghese (Chicago: Regnery Gateway, 1984), pp. 301-326; Mary Anne Dolan in *New York Times Magazine*, June 16, 1988, pp. 20-23, 66. See reference in [13:35] to George Gilder, and reference in [13:28] to Maggie Gallagher.

**13:33:** Marcus Dods, *An Exposition of the Bible*, Volume 1 (Hartford, Connecticut, 1903), p. 10.

**13:34:** Richard Wagner's music illustrates that the same music played the same way may convey different messages to different people. In the Berlin State Opera House in 1934, C. William Hazelett attended a performance of *Parsifal*. Adolf Hitler was present and stayed the whole four and a quarter hours; devotion to Wagner's works was typical of Hitler and his associates. *Parsifal* is essentially a Christian opera, but Hitler despised Christianity and planned to destroy it (William L. Shirer, *The Rise and Fall of the Third Reich* [New York: Simon & Schuster, 1960], pp. 234-240). Some Jewish musicians were temporarily spared the infamous gas chambers of World War II so that they could play Viennese waltzes for their Nazi executioners (Albert Terry, *Terroism from Robespierre to Arafat* [New York: Vanguard Press, 1976], p. 214. Rescuing by Christians is the subject of *When Light Pierced the Darkness* by Nechama Tec [New York: Oxford University Press, 1986]).

**13:35:** Sexuality means such opposite things to different people that the presentation of any one point of view is bound to offend some. However, a uniquely intelligent and subtle book on sexual ethics is that of Lewis B. Smedes: *Sex for Christians* (Grand Rapids, Michigan: William B. Eerdmans Publishing Co., 1976). The partial freedoms that Smedes cautiously recommends should be counterbalanced by a reading of some views that appear below. See Rusty and Linda Wright, *Dynamic Sex* (subtitled "Beyond Technique"). Its Chapter 5 is unique,

though individual readers must decide whether the fundamentalist Christian beliefs of the Wrights fit their own needs (San Bernardino, California: Here's Life Publishers, 1979). A caution: the Wrights refer at one point to J. D. Unwin's 1934 book *Sex and Culture;* in no way can Unwin's book be relied upon; see Ruth Benedict's accurate review in *American Anthropologist* n.s. 37 (1935): 691-692.

Of negative observations, Nathaniel Hawthorne may well be quoted, despite his gratuitous restriction of gender:

> A woman's chastity consists, like an onion, of a series of coats. You may strip off the outer ones without doing much mischief, perhaps none at all; but you keep taking off one after another, in expectation of coming to the inner nucleus, including the whole value of the matter. It proves, however, that there is no such nucleus, and that Chastity is diffused through the whole series of coats, is lessened with the removal of each, and vanishes with the final one, which you supposed would introduce you to the hidden pearl (*The Heart of Hawthorne's Journals*, edited by Newton Arvin [Boston: Houghton Mifflin Co., 1929], p. 165, entry of March 16, 1854).

Marion Hilliard, M.D., was a counselor to women. She quotes their regretful wail of prematurely lost virginity: "I'm not *that* kind of girl."

> This is nonsense [she responds]. Except for a handful who have abnormally low metabolisms, every female *is* that kind of girl. Each of these women has made the common mistake of underestimating her biology. Femaleness is savage. Woman is equipped with a reproductive system which dominates her fiber. It has vicious power that can leap out of control without the slightest warning, when a man and a woman share a companionable

chuckle or happen to touch hands. The mechanism can be triggered unexpectedly by the low moan of a crooner, by a summer sky full of stars, even by fog collecting around a street light. There can come a moment between a man and a woman when control and judgment are impossible. A woman's best defense is to have no confidence at all in her ability to say nay at the appropriate moment. The belief that any woman can cooly halt lovemaking at some point before she is wholly committed is a tiger trap devised by romantics. The freedom a modern girl allows herself is a delusion—it gives her no freedom of choice whatever (*A Woman Doctor Looks at Life and Love* [New York: Doubleday & Co., 1957], Chapter 6. Or see *Readers Digest,* May 1956, pp. 38-40.)

More positively, a most literate and sensitive statement of the psychology of sexual ethics and etiquette is Jessamyn West's readable little book *Love Is Not What You Think* (New York: Harcourt, Brace & Co., 1959). It is, in a sense, about pleasure and how to get it, but then so are all good works on sexual ethics; they answer the question, "How can anything so good be so bad?" More narrow but wise in its way is the famous book *The Pleasure Bond* by William H. Masters and Virginia E. Johnson (Boston: Little, Brown & Co., 1975). Then there is the old saying, useful for good or ill: "Idleness is the greatest aphrodisiac."

An entertaining and edifying work of fiction is Clive Staples Lewis, *The Screwtape Letters* (New York: Macmillan Co., 1958). A valuable book for teens is *Dialogue in Romantic Love* by Prentiss L. Pemberton (Valley Forge, Pennsylvania: Judson Press, 1961). For a literary dim view of the scene even thirty-some years ago see Robert Elliott Fitch, *The Decline and Fall of Sex* (New York: Harcourt Brace & Co., 1957). Vernard Eller preceptively discusses the play *Who's Afraid of Virginia Woolf?* in his review article in *Christian*

*Century* 84 (1967): 689-691, reprinted in Eller's book *The Promise: Ethics in the Kingdom of God* Garden City, New York: Doubleday & Co., 1970). See three articles by Harvey Cox and Reinhold Niebuhr in *Christianity and Crisis* 21 (1961): 56-60; ibid., 24 (1964): 73-75, 75-80.

One regrets that Scripture and most of the founders of denominations have so little positive comment on sexuality, though Proverbs 5 and the Song of Songs (Canticle of Canticles) redress this lacuna. Alan Bloom's book *The Closing of the American Mind* is insightful into the dynamics of sexuality in college students (New York: Simon & Schuster, 1987). On the 1960s see Suzanne Rini and E. M. Jones, *Fidelity,* April 1990, pp. 28-42. Finally, "He that hath clean hands shall wax stronger and stronger" (Job 17:9). For an eloquent plea for male faithfulness, see the Book of Mormon, Jacob 2. When the Mormon founder Joseph Smith disclosed his revelation on polygyny to Brigham Young, who was to become the Utah empire builder, Young said that that was the first day in his life that he had "desired the grave" (*Journal of Discourses* [Salt Lake] 6 [1859]: 39-47; quoted in Murstein, *Love, Sex, and Marriage,* [13:12], p. 355). Young appears to have adjusted later. For history of the ideal of dedicated and continent sexuality see Alexander Sutherland [8:14], Volume 1, Chapters 8 and 9. See also "Chastity," *Encyclopaedia of Religion and Ethics.* George Gilder studies the surprisingly perverse demography of the sexual revolution; this appears in Chapter 5 of his wider-ranging book *Men and Marriage* (New Orleans: Pelican Books, 1986), which book is recommended with some reservations.

For effects of adolescent sex on academic performance see John O. G. Billy et al. in *Social Psychology Quarterly* 51 (1988): 190-212. The psychologist Kenneth R. Hardy attacks the exclusively biological-behavioristic explanations of sexuality in his technical paper, "An Appetitional Theory of Sexual Motivation" in *Psychological Review* 71 (1964): 1-18. See discussion of it in *Psychological Reports* 16 (1965): 713-719; ibid., 17 (1965): 11-14.

*Contraception: A History of its Treatment by Catholic Theologians and Canonists* details a checkered history; it is by the American jurist John T. Noonan Jr. (Cambridge, Massachusetts: Harvard University Press, 1965). Negative information on a vexed problem is contained in *The Case Against Pornography*, by Donald E. Wildmon and contributors (Wheaton, Illinois: Victor Books, 1986). A thorough earlier treatment is edited by Victor L. Cline, *Where Do You Draw the Line?* (Provo, Utah: Brigham Young University Press, 1974). For the social psychology that occasionally results from the sequestered nature of male homosexual existence see E. M. Jones in *Fidelity* (South Bend), May 1988, pp. 18-31; July-August 1988, pp. 2-3; April 1989, pp. 22-35. See William Main discussing the therapy of Gerard van den Aardweg in *Crisis* (Notre Dame, Indiana), March 1990, pp. 32-37.

**13:36:** J. W. von Goethe, *Faust*, Part 1, line 3374.

**13:37:** Alexis de Tocqueville reported long ago:

I do not doubt for an instant that the great severity of mores which one notices in the United States has its primary origin in [religious] beliefs. Certainly of all countries in the world America is the one in which the marriage tie is most respected and where the highest and truest conception of conjugal happiness has been conceived. In Europe almost all the disorders of society are born around the domestic hearth and not far from the nuptial bed. It is there that men come to feel scorn for natural ties and legitimate pleasures and develop a taste for disorder, restlessness of spirit, and instability of desires. Shaken by the tumultuous passions which have often troubled his own house, the European finds it hard to submit to the authority of the state's legislators. When the American returns from the turmoil of politics to the bosom of the family, he im-

mediately finds a perfect picture of order and peace. There all his pleasures are simple and natural and his joys innocent and quiet, and as the regularity of life brings him happiness, he easily forms the habit of regulating his opinions as well as his tastes. Whereas the European tries to escape his sorrows at home by troubling society, the American derives from his home that love of order which he carries over into affairs of state.

Tocqueville goes on to muse: "I do not know what is to be done to give back to European Christianity the energy of youth" (*Democracy in America* [6:23], "The Main Causes Tending to Maintain a Democratic Republic in the United States").

**13:38:** Alfred Lord Tennyson's epic poem *Idylls of the King* remains a classic of Christian conscience and idealism; see e.g. "The Coming of Arthur," lines 74-93, and "Guinevere" stanza 27, which begins, "Liest thou here so low?" For one thing, Tennyson's is probably the best statement of how romantic feeling arises from sexual restraint. But see at greater length Victor Hugo, *Toilers of the Sea*, and Thomas Carlyle, *Sartor Resartus* (The Tailor Retailored). A recent echo of Tennyson is heard in Michael Novak, who writes that "the governance of passion among the young" is not solely a private good; it is "the groundwork, the texture even, of all later self-governance" (*National Review* 36 [1984]: 48). It has been claimed with much truth that reformers are apt to come from the ranks of the sexually unemployed.

**13:39:** Jonathan Edwards [6:4], "Miscellany" no. 198.

**13:40:** Henry N. Wieman, *The Source of Human Good* (Carbondale, Illinois: Southern Illinois University Press, 1946), pp. 235-242. Father Chih conveys the sense of traditional Chinese religion in [20:30]:

The union between husband and wife is the very image and imitation of the union of Heaven and

Earth. All human relations begin with marriage. Man's separateness is conquered by the sacred union of husband and wife. The relationship is the very foundation of the extension of love to the wide world. All principles of moral and social ethics have derived from the relationship of husband and wife. They find the fullness of being human in the world of love (pp. 338, 346).

The family is a fundamental biological and natural structure. The society at large is only an enlarged family of mankind. The Chinese family, besides being a home, is also a government, a school, a church, a place for recreation and entertainment, a social security agency, a medicare unit, and a concretized ideal to which an individual dedicates his life and energy. The family altar is the center of communication beyond time and space (p. 333).

## 14. Humanistic Love Is Not Enough

**Epigraph:** Clive Staples Lewis, *The Abolition of Man* (New York: Macmillan Co., 1947), end of Chapter 1.

**14:1:** Wilmon Henry Sheldon [11:8], p. 41.

**14:2:** H. Richard Niebuhr, *The Purpose of the Church and Its Ministry* (New York: Harper & Brothers, 1956), pp. 35-36. See T. E. Jessop [6:24], Lecture 4. See paraphrase of Pelagius by John Ferguson in his book *Pelagius* [13:22], pp. 122-128.

**14:3:** Friedrich Engels, *Herr Eugen Dühring's Revolution in Science* (Anti-Dühring); quoted from secondary source. Pierre Teilhard de Chardin [14:15], p. 266.

**14:4:** Confucius, in *Chinese Philosophy in Classical Times*, edited and translated by E. R. Hughes (New York: E. P. Dutton & Co., 1942).

**14:5:** H. H. Dubs, "The Development of Altruism in Confucianism," in *Radhakrishnan: Comparative Studies in Philosophy Presented in Honour of His Sixtieth Birthday* (London: George Allen & Unwin, 1951), pp. 267-275. See also Chih [20:30], pp. 91-98. See *Violence in China*, edited by Jonathan N. Lipman and Stevan Harrell (Albany: State University of New York Press, 1990).

**14:6:** Luke 10:25-37.

**14:7:** George Herbert Palmer, *Altruism: Its Nature and Varieties* (New York:

Charles Scribner's Sons, 1920), pp. 51-53. See Charles G. Finney [8:7], pp. 70-71.

**14:8:** Gilbert Keith Chesterton, *The Quotable Chesterton* (San Francisco: Ignatius Press, 1986), p. 202.

**14:9:** On Mill's non-belief see John Stuart Mill, *Theism* (1874), last paragraphs. For Mill's earlier covert but definite atheism see his letter of December 18, 1841, to Auguste Comte, quoted in Vincent P. Miceli, *The Gods of Atheism* [14:34], pp. 154-155.

**14:10:** George Eliot, *Romola* (London, 1863), epilogue.

**14:11:** Josiah Royce, *The Religious Aspect of Philosophy* (New York: Houghton Mifflin Co., 1885), 163-165. See Immanuel Kant, *Kritik der praktischen Vernunft* (Critique of Practical Reason), Part I, Book 1, Chapter 1, Section 1, Theorem 2, Remark 1 (23).

**14:12:** Palmer [14:7], pp. 58-59. See E. E. Constance Jones, "Rational Hedonism," *International Journal of Ethics* 5 (1894): 79-97, at pp. 95-96.

**14:13:** Edwards [6:4], p. 127 ("Miscellanies," tt).

**14:14:** Brand Blanshard [1:5], Chapter 3, around pp. 62-63.

**14:15:** Immanuel Kant, *Grundlegung zur Metaphysik der Sitten* (1785) (Groundwork of the Metaphysic of Morals), Chapter 1;

Pierre Teilhard de Chardin, *The Phenomenon of Man* (New York: Harper & Row, 1959), p. 267. See Alfred North Whitehead, *Adventures of Ideas* (New York: Macmillan Co., 1933), Chapter 3, Section 7. See Donald Wayne Viney, *Charles Hartshorne and the Existence of God* (Albany: State University of New York Press, 1985), pp. 113-116.

**14:16:** Albert Schweitzer [1:11], p. 305 (235). John Maynard Keynes, *Two Memoirs*, (New York: A. M. Kelley, 1949), "My Early Beliefs," pp. 73-106, at p. 96.

**14:17:** Charles Hartshorne, seminar, spring 1965, University of Texas at Austin. See Hartshorne [7:19], p. 132; [16:16], p. 289: [2:2], pp. 64-68; [14:34], pp. 32-33. See Thomas Hill Green, *Prolegomena to Ethics* (Oxford: At the Clarendon Press, 1890), pp. 400-402 (Sections 358-360).

**14:18:** Elie Halévy, *The Growth of Philosophic Radicalism*, translated by Mary Morris (New York: A. M. Kelley, 1949), p. 309.

**14:19:** See "Individualism," by E. Ehrhardt in *Encyclopaedia of Religion and Ethics* [7:1]. On the relation of individualism to majority vote see Neal Reimer in *Ethics* 62 (1951): 16-32.

**14:20:** William A. Donohue, "The Social Consequences of the Rights Revolution," *Intercollegiate Review*, Spring 1987, pp. 41-46 — to be a chapter in his book **The New Freedom: Individualism and Collectivism in the Lives of Americans** (New Brunswick, New Jersey: Transaction Publishers, 1989).

**14:21:** Midge Decter, **"Liberating Women: Who Benefits?"** *Commentary*, March 1984, pp. 31-36, at p. 35. See David C. McClelland, "Encouraging Excellence," *Daedalus* 90 (1961): 711-724, at p. 716.

*First Things* by Hadley Arkes [1:5] is an intensely reasoned book of jurisprudence and political theory which culminates its theoretical considerations in the treatment of abortion as both a legal and moral matter. See John T. Noonan Jr., *A Private Choice: Abortion in America in the Seventies* (New York: Free Press, 1979). The promotion of abortion in the U.S. was touted as a great step forward for women's rights. Surprisingly, it has often worked rather to hobble and degrade individual women in their own eyes, perhaps especially those without prior children; see *Aborted Women: Silent No More*, edited by David C. Reardon (Westchester, Illinois: Crossway Books, 1987). Maggie Gallagher is eloquent against abortion [13:28]. Charles Hartshorne presents contrary arguments in *Wisdom as Moderation* (Albany: State University of New York Press, 1987). An attempt at a mediating view is that of Marvin Rytting in *Sunstone* (Salt Lake City), July-August 1981, pp. 20-24. Dietrich Bonhoeffer perhaps comes nearest to the possibility of satisfying all parties in his *Ethics* (New York: Macmillan Co., 1955), Chapter 3.

**14:22:** Donohue [14:20]. Peter L. Berger discusses the limitations of moral-political monomania: "Moral purity is one of the cheapest human achievements." His examples are the political pressures exerted by those who aimed to bring peace to southeast Asia and racial equality to South Africa — both of them laudable objectives that were treated by "the politics of moral purity that disdains the calculus of means, costs, and consequences" (*This World*, Spring 1988, pp. 3-17, at pp. 13-15). A perfectionist mania is making the U.S. legal system unworkable; see Macklin Fleming, *The Price of Perfect Justice* (New York: Basic Books, 1974). On this matter among others see Roscoe Pound, *An Introduction to the Philosophy of Law* (New Haven: Yale University Press, 1954). Robert H. Bork deals with the rule of law — Constitutional law — with commanding cogency in **The Tempting of America** and shows how judges abuse it (New York: Free Press, 1989).

**14:23:** See *Economist*, July 2, 1988, pp. 70-71; Robert L. DuPont in *Policy Review*, Spring 1989, pp. 52-57.

**14:24:** Gabriel Marcel, *Man Against Mass Society* (Chicago: Henry Regnery Co., 1962), p. 165.

**14:25:** James Thomson, "The City of Dreadful Night," Part 4.

**14:26:** See George Will, *Newsweek*, October 12, 1987, p. 100.

**14:27:** Demodocus, in Aristotle,

*Nicomachean Ethics,* translated by Martin Oswald (Indianapolis: Bobbs-Merrill Co., 1962), 1151a (Book 7, Chapter 8).

**14:28:** R. J. Rummel, as reported in *Religion and Society Report,* November 1986. A careful consideration of a long controversy is that of Gary North: *Conspiracy: A Biblical View* (Fort Worth: Dominion Press, 1986), notably Chapter 3. See *Political Terror in Communist Systems,* by Alexander Dallin and George W. Breslauer (Stanford: Stanford University Press, 1970).

**14:29:** See for instance Cyril Ponnamperum, *The Origins of Life* (New York: E. P. Dutton & Co., 1972), pp. 113-119: Barrow and Tipler [2:1], pp. 545-546.

**14:30:** Augustine, *De civitate Dei* (The City of God), Book 14. For an excellent modern critique of humanism see Thomas Molnar, *Utopia: The Perennial Heresy* (New York: Sheed & Ward, 1967). see further James Hitchcock, *What Is Secular Humanism?* (Ann Arbor: Servant Books, 1982).

**14:31:** Karl Marx, "Toward the Critique of Hegel's *Philosophy of Right* [Philosophy of Law]; in Karl Marx and Friedrich Engels, *Basic Writings on Politics and Philosophy,* edited by Lewis S. Feuer (Garden City, New York: Doubleday & Co., 1959), pp. 262-263.

**14:32:** V. I. Lenin to Maxim Gorky, 13-14 November 1913, quoted by Robert Conquest [12:12], p. 199. Chapter 10, "The Churches and the People," recount the all but complete destruction of pre-existing religious organizations in the Soviet Union, a process evidently being reversed as this is written. The frequently absurd employments of psychiatrists in American courts are said to be tolerated by liberals because psychiatrists are the ultimate defense against conservatives and other opponents. That is, in a crisis, the psychiatrists could declare opponents crazy! But such has heretofore been normal practice in the Soviet Union.

**14:33:** Keynes [14:16], p. 97.

**14:34:** An excellent statement of "selfism" in its promotion by secular psychology is *Psychology as Religion* by Paul C. Vitz (Grand Rapids: Wm. B. Eerdmans Publishing Co., 1977). On secular humanism, see in general Charles Hartshorne, *Beyond Humanism* (Willett, Clark & Co, 1937). Some bad results of humanist policies in political life are discussed in Herbert Schlossberg's *Idols for Destruction* [12:13]. While one need not agree at every point with the orthodox doctrines of Father Vincent P. Miceli, the final chapter of his worthwhile book *The Gods of Atheism* is eloquent on secular humanism (New Rochelle, New York: Arlington House, 1971). The chapters which precede it deal similarly with "Christian atheism." See also Thomas Molnar, *Christian Humanism: A Critique of the Secular City and its Ideology* (Chicago: Franciscan Herald Press, 1978) — a largely historical book, with Roman Catholic emphasis.

If one wishes to test his ability to answer secular humanists, good books to use for target practice are certain erudite, yet basically mistaken works of the brilliant secular humanists Walter Kaufmann and Sterling M. McMurrin. See Kaufmann's *Critique of Religion and Philosophy* (New York: Harper & Row, 1958), and *Religion from Tolstoy to Camus,* of which Kaufmann is editor (New York: Harper & Row, 1961). Kaufmann's later book, *Without Guilt and Justice,* must be described as moral nihilism (New York: Dell Publishing Co., 1973), a terminus which should not surprise those who have read this far herein. See also McMurrin's learned *Religion, Reason, and Truth* (Salt Lake City: University of Utah Press, 1982). Further, see Norwood Russell Hanson's essay "What I Do Not Believe," in a posthumous collection of that name (Dordrecht, Holland: D. Reidel Publishing Co., 1971), Chapter 19.

**First epigraph:** Leo Tolstoy, *My Confession,* Chapter 9.

**Second epigraph:** Eric Hoffer, *Before the Sabbath* (New York: Harper & Row, 1979), p. 120.

# 15. Rules and Rights

**Epigraph:** John T. Noonan, Jr., quoted in *Newsweek*, April 1, 1985, p. 82.

**15:1:** This observation contradicts somewhat the opinion of Immanuel Kant to the effect that virtue is no guarantee of happiness. See *Kritik der praktischen Vernunft* (Critique of Practical Reason), Book 2, Chapter 2, Sections 1-2 (112-119). Shalom H. Schwartz discusses "Normative Explanations of Helping Behavior" in *Journal of Experimental Social Psychology* 9 (1973): 349-364.

**15:2:** Besides the aforementioned works of Jeremy Bentham and John Stuart Mill, see also Felix S. Cohen, *Ethical Systems and Legal Ideals* (Ithaca: Cornell University Press, 1959, first published 1933), especially Chapter 3 ("The Good"), Section D ("The Criteria of Goodness"): Anthony Quinn, *Utilitarian Ethics* (New York: St. Martin's, 1973).

**15:3:** See Sissela Bok, *Lying* (New York: Pantheon, 1979); Morris Raphael Cohen, *Reason and Nature* (Glencoe, Illinois: Free Press, 1953), p. 433. See also John T. Noonan Jr., *Bribes* (New York: Macmillan Publishing Co., 1984); also by Bok, *Secrets* (New York: Pantheon, 1983).

**15:4:** See Lance Morrow, **"I Spoke as a Brother,"** *Time*, January 9, 1984, pp. 27-33, on the occasion of the visit of Pope John Paul II to his near-assassin Mehmet Ali Agca. The book *Biblical Law* by H. B. Clark reminds us in detail how much our law owes to the Judeo-Christian tradition and how far we are recently departing from it (Portland, Oregon: Binfords & Mort, 1943).

Jay S. Bybee informs us, partly by way of quotation, that, in Jewish law, the focus was that of duties rather than rights. "Litigation in Jewish law was in the nature of a common request for clarification. The people making the request were perfectly willing to perform their duty once they understood it. 'The judge was not an umpire between adversaries; rather he was best qualified to tell the parties what behaviour the Law prescribed for them, so as to prevent the erring party from committing a sin' (Amihud Ben Porath). 'The concern of the court is not the creditor's debt, his damages, but the duty of the debtor' (Moshe Silberg)" (*Sunstone* [Salt Lake City], January-February 1984, p. 47). Crosslights and related matters appear in *The Christian Legal Advisor* by John Eidsmoe (Milford, Michigan: Mott Media, 1984), *passim*. See also C. K. Allen in *Hibbert Journal* 23 (1925): 709-717.

Lawyers especially may wish to read Thomas L. Shaffer, *On Being a Christian and a Lawyer* (Provo, Utah: Brigham Young University Press, 1981); Shaffer is a Roman Catholic. Hadley Arkes defends legislation on morals in the last chapter of his generally valuable and practical book, *The Philosopher in the City* (Princeton: Princeton University Press, 1981).

Besides our obligation to forgive, there is another difficult rule, which concerns evil-speaking; see John Wesley's *Sermons on Several Occasions*, First Series, Sermon 43; and Matthew 18:15 ff.

**15:5:** J. C. Friedrich von Schiller, *Wilhelm Tell*, especially Act 2, Scene 2; Act 4, Scene 3. See also Oscar Jászi and John D. Lewis, *Against the Tyrant* (Glencoe, Illinois: Free Press, 1957).

**15:6:** See William James, quoted in William Savery, *International Journal of Ethics* 45 (1934): 1-26, at pp. 19-20. Feodor Dostoyevsky sets forth this dilemma in *The Brothers Karamazov*, Book 5, Chapter 4, near end, Ivan's question to Alyosha.

**15:7:** Luke 15:4-7.

**15:8:** Joseph Fletcher, *Situation Ethics: The New Morality* (Philadelphia: Westminster Press, 1966). J. Charles King offers a closely reasoned antidote to Fletcher in the *Thomist* 34 (1970): 423-437. See *Storm over Ethics* by John C. Bennett, James M. Gustafson and others (Philadelphia: United Church Press/Bethany Press, 1967).

**15:9:** Immanuel Kant, *Grundlegung zur Metaphysik der Sitten* (1785), (Groundwork of the Metaphysics of Morals), Chapter 2; Don E. Marietta Jr., **"On Using People,"** *Ethics* 82 (1972): 232-238; Heinrich Gomperz, **"When Does the End Sanctify the Means?"** *Ethics* 53 (1943): 173-183, reprinted in his *Philosophical Studies* (Boston: Christopher Publishing House, 1953); and Romans 3:5-8.

**15:10:** See the book *Not Our America: The ACLU Exposed*, by Daniel Popeo (Washington: Washington Legal Foundation, 1989). Some mitigating (though not contradictory) information appears in William A. Donohue, *The Politics of the American Civil Liberties Union* (New Brunswick, New Jersey: Transaction Books, 1985). A friend working in the ranks of the ACLU has a better report of its activities.

An exceptionally knowledgeable and readable book on causes and cures for crime is *Vigilante*, by William Tucker (New York: Stein & Day, 1985). Don't be put off by the title. For a profound insight into the nature of justice and the justification of punishment, see his p. 209, also pp. 116-120. In a 2000-subject study by Dean G. Kilpatrick et al., 19.2 percent of women rape victims had attempted suicide, whereas only 2.2 percent of nonvictims had done so (*Journal of Consulting and Clinical Psychology* 53 [1985]: 866-873); see also James Kilpatrick, syndicated newspaper column of April 17, 1989.

The problem of capital punishment continues to vex our society. Of a vast literature, three references are offered: Kent S. Miller and Betty Davis Miller, *To Kill and Be Killed: Case Studies from Florida's Death Row* (Pasadena: Hope Publishing House, 1989); Jacques Barzun, "In Favor of Capital Punishment," *American Scholar* 31 (1962): 181-191 (reprinted in Harry K. Girvetz, *Contemporary Moral Issues*, 1968+); Steven Stack, "Publicized Executions and Homicide," *American Sociological Review* 52 (1987): 532-540. In penology, the West has much to learn from China. On war, specifically the Vietnam War, an article, "The Bull's Eye of Disaster" by James Bond Stockdale, stands out (*Chroni-*

*cles* [Rockford], August 1989, pp. 14-20).

**15:11:** John Rawls, **"Two Concepts of Rules,"** *Philosophical Review* 64 (1955): 3-32: widely reprinted, usually condensed.

**15:12:** J. L. Mackie, **"The Disutility of Act-Utilitarianism,"** *Philosophical Quarterly* (U.K.), 23 (1973): 289-300: some emphasis added. See D. H. Hodgson, *Consequences of Utilitarianism* (Oxford: Clarendon Press, 1967), Chapter 2, e.g., pp. 56-58.

**15:13:** Compare *The Federalist*, No. 62 (James Madison). On the appointment of Felix Frankfurter to the U.S. Supreme Court, Whitehead admonished his friend: "Remember, Felix, we need order. But not too much order!" (through Charles Hartshorne).

**15:14:** Ralph Linton, "Universal Ethical Principles: An Anthropological View," in Ruth Nanda Anshen, *Moral Principles of Action* (New York: Harper & Brothers, 1952), pp. 645-660. Linton's comprehension of religion and of sexuality is deficient. See Chapter 11 of Frank Chapman Sharp, *Ethics* (New York: Century Co., 1928). For a treatise, see E. A. Westermarck, *The Origin and Development of the Moral Ideas*, 2 volumes (New York: Macmillan Co., 1906-08)—mentioned only with numerous strictures.

**15:15:** A treatise is that of Robert F. Weir, *Abating Treatment with Critically Ill Patients* (New York: Oxford University Press, 1989).

Morris B. Abram speaks out, soundly as we believe: "I would be loath to see decisions to forgo treatment made by the book—statutory laws interpreted by reported cases and refined by rules and regulations. A complex society must have its statutes and rule-makers, but I hope we shall be spared batteries of lawyers in intensive-care units flipping through loose-leaf books in order to determine what is permissible. It is better to have the present system by which those most closely involved decide what seems to be right, despite all the shortcomings of such an approach" (*Wall Street Journal*, June 18, 1982, p. 24).

In other words, reverence for (earthly)

life is inappropriate as an *all*-embracing, ultimate ethic. Despite great respect for Albert Schweitzer and for the practical educative value of his ethic, he seems to have said too much when he writes, "Ethics are responsibility *without limit* towards all that lives" [1:11], p. 311 (241). Taken as ultimate and unqualified, such an ethic has problems similar to those of Humanism. He did recognize in practice that there must be limits. At his hospital settlement near Lambarené (now in Gabon), his pet pig Josephine acquired the bad habit of eating chickens, a staple food brought in by the patients. When Josephine matured into a good rooter, segregation from the chickens was no longer feasible. Schweitzer was up to his duty: he enticed Josephine into his operating room and for some time thereafter, the local menu included smoked bacon (*The Animal World of Albert Schweitzer*, translated and edited by Charles R. Joy [Boston: Beacon Press, 1950], Chapter 8).

Schweitzer can only by an uncommon use of the word be called a theist, for he avoids affirming that God is a person. In writing philosophy he would refer instead to "the universal will to live"; see a letter of Schweitzer to Oskar Kraus in Kraus' book *Albert Schweitzer: His Work and His Philosophy* (London: Adam and Charles Black, 1944), p. 42. See also [1:11], pp. 304-305.

**15:16:** See David Lyons, *Forms and Limits of Utilitarianism* (Oxford: Clarendon Press, 1965), pp. 187-189. Lyons was answered well in advance by Ernest Albee, *A History of English Utilitarianism* (London: Sonnenschein & Co., 1902), Chapter 9, second last paragraph. See Brand Blanshard, "The Impasse in Ethics — and a Way Out," *Philosophical Forum* (U.S.A.) 17 (1960): 3-24, reprinted from *University of California Publications in Philosophy* 28 (1955): 93-112.

A dilemma of conflicting military rules is presented by Lieut. Commander Thaddeus V. Tulija in "An Error of Judgment" (*A Treasury of True* [the magazine], edited by Charles N. Barnard [New York: A. S. Barnes & Co., 1956], pp. 248-254).

**15:17:** Schweitzer [1:11], pp. 317-318 (248-249).

**15:18:** Kant [15:9], Chapter 2.

**15:19:** It is too simple to say that Kant is a consistent exponent of formalism in ethics. Kant himself often writes favorably of goal-oriented ethics and is even in favor of the goal of general happiness. He writes: "God wants mankind to be happy. He wants men to be made happy by men, and if only all men united to promote their own happiness, we could make a paradise of Novaya Zemlya" (some ice-bound islands north of Russia). This is from *Lectures on Ethics*, a book based on a student's lecture notes (New York: Harper & Row, 1963; from the third edition published at Königsberg, 1803), the chapter entitled "Universal Practical Philosophy." Similarly, see Kant, *Lectures on Philosophical Theology*, Ithaca: Cornell University Press, 1978), "Moral Theism," p. 41.

In the last sentence of his recondite *Kritik der reinen Vernunft* (Critique of Pure Reason), Kant writes of "the supreme end, the happiness (Glückseligkeit) of all mankind" (A 851 = B 879). See further Kant, *Kritik der praktischen Vernunft* (Critique of Practical Reason, revised 1797), First Part, Book 1, Chapter 1, Subsection 3, Theorem 2 (22-24). Kant's inconsistencies about all this are commented on by H. J. Paton in *The Categorical Imperative* (London: Hutchinson & Co., 1958), p. 105. For a brief critique of Kant's ethics see V. J. McGill, *The Idea of Happiness* (New York: Frederick A. Praeger, 1967), Chapter 8. On the subject of happiness, see notably the section of that name in *Great Treasury of Western Thought*, edited by Mortimer J. Adler and Charles Van Doren (New York: R. R. Bowker Co., 1977). Our only negative comment on this bargain: some recent pundits therein may not bear up well.

**15:20:** Frank Chapman Sharp, *Good Will and Ill Will*, Chicago: University of Chicago Press, 1950), p. 39, and Chapter 1 generally.

**15:21:** Sheldon [11:8], pp. 20-21. See Thomas Aquinas, *2 Corinthios*, Lecture 5, on verse 13:11.

**15:22:** Exodus 20: Deuteronomy 5.

**15:23:** See J. D. Mabbott, *Proceedings of the British Academy* 39 (1953?): 97-118, at pp. 113-114. As to Oates see Robert Falcon Scott, *Scott's Last Expedition*, 2 volumes (New York: Dodd, Mead & Co., 1913), Volume 1, p. 408. On Sartre as libertine see Simone de Beauvoir, *Adieux: A Farewell to Sartre* (New York: Pantheon Books, 1984). Dean Turner has treated of the philosophies of Sartre and Camus in the forthcoming book, *Escape from God: The Use of Religion and Philosophy to Evade Responsibility* (Pasadena: Hope Publishing House, 1991).

**15:24:** See Thomas Molnar, "Simple Goethe," *Chronicles* (Rockford), February 1986, pp. 26-27.

**15:25:** Paul Johnson [2:10], pp. 654-657, 687, etc. Johnson refers to John Barron and Anthony Paul, *Peace with Horror* (London: Hodder & Stoughton, 1977), pp. 10-31 — issued, apparently revised, in the United States as *Murder of a Gentle Land* (New York: Readers Digest Press, 1977). The quotation is Johnson's from the *Wall Street Journal*, January 5, 1987, p. 16. Johnson affirmed his report in *Intellectuals* (New York: Harper & Row, 1989), pp. 246, 340-341. Albert Camus' short novel *The Stranger* is perversely relevant (New York: Alfred A. Knopf, 1946).

Have we not heard enough of this baboon ethics? An exception to this stricture is theistic existentialism which, while beridden with contradictions, retains a spirit of love and care and would never condone any of the evils perpetrated by the followers of Sartre's atheistic existentialism.

**15:26:** See Paul Ramsey in "Dostoevski: On Living Atheism," which is Chapter 1 of Ramsey's book *Nine Modern Moralists* (Englewood Cliffs, New Jersey: Prentice Hall, 1962). Marvin Rytting suggests that there is a balance to be sought between the blame one inflicts and the blame one takes. That is, one can take too much blame and incur inappropriate guilt, or one can take too little on the ground — following Sartre — that he and everyone else is totally "responsible" even for the self-righteousness of blaming others for their unkindness. In this way, unkind behavior is released, since the victim is not to blame the persecutor. More sanely, one's decision to share responsibility "lets us get on with living" (*Sunstone*, April 1985, pp. 41-42).

**15:27:** Matthew 7:20.

**15:28:** Harold Willis Milnes, "Factors Involved in the Development of Civilization," *Toth-Maatian Review* 1 (1982): 92-120, notably pp. 98-102, approximately from *The Book of the Dead: The Chapters of Coming Forth by Day*, translated by E. A. Wallis Budge (London: Kegan Paul, Trench, Trübner & Co., 1898), pp. 192-196. For discussion of the early date of the compositions, see the historical introduction to the book.

Personal norms appear to predict behavior better than attitudes, according to psychologist Shalom H. Schwartz in *Journal of Experimental Social Psychology* 9 (1973): 349-364.

**15:29:** Jonathan Edwards, "God Makes Men Sensible," quoted in Clyde A. Holbrook, *The Ethics of Jonathan Edwards* (Ann Arbor, Michigan: University of Michigan Press, 1973), p. 25. Such an appeal is not characteristic of Edwards, though he often does use words like "rejoice." Compare John Stuart Mill, *Utilitarianism*, Chapter 2.

**15:30:** Augustine, *In Epistolam Joannis ad Parthos* (On St. John's Epistle), 7:4:8; quoted and discussed in Vernon J. Bourke, *Wisdom from St. Augustine* (Houston: University of St. Thomas, 1984), Chapter 9, at pp. 129-130. See also the discussion by Étienne Gilson in *The Christian Philosophy of St. Augustine* (New York: Random House, 1960), p. 140.

**15:31:** F. R. Tennant, [5:8], Volume 2, e.g., pp. 100-102, 204.

**First epigraph:** Frank McKinney (Kin) Hubbard, *Abe Martin's Broadcast* (Indianapolis: Bobbs-Merrill Co., 1930), p. 191.

# 16. Freedom of the Will

**First epigraph:** Voltaire, *Dictionnaire philosophique*, "Religion."

**Second epigraph:** Loren Eiseley, *Darwin's Century* (Garden City, New York: Doubleday & Co., 1961), Chapter 12, Section 5.

**16:1:** Arthur Lovejoy draws attention to what he finds to be a touchstone of the thought of the American philosopher William James around the turn of the century:

> Those who have followed Professor James's writings from the beginning must have long since seen what aspect of human experience, what sort of moment in life, has presented itself to him always as the central and illuminating fact, the fixed datum to which any philosophy that could be considered sound must be required to do justice, the point at which we have most reason to suppose that the inner and ineffable nature of reality is directly revealed to us. This is the moment of voluntary choice — the moment in which, in the presence of alternative real possibilities, and with the consciousness that some actual content of the future now truly hangs trembling in the balances of volition, the mind somehow reaches its fiat and, by "the dumb turning of the will," performs the daily miracle of excluding one of those real possibilities thereafter and eternally *from* reality ("Pragmatism and Theology" [9:29], Section 4).

**16:2:** From "The Late Papers of C. I. Lewis," by John Lange, *Journal of the History of Philosophy* 4 (1966): 235-245. See C. S. Peirce [1:2], 5.130.

**16:3:** See Joseph M. Boyle Jr., Germain Grisez, and Olaf Tollefsen, *Free Choice* [Annex:15]. See Thomas Aquinas, *Summa*

*Theologica*, I-II (first part of second part), Question 79. See William James, "**The Dilemma of Determinism**," in *The Will to Believe* [2:2]. More adventurously, see the Compton Memorial Lecture of Karl Popper, *Of Clouds and Clocks* (St. Louis: Washington University, 1966), reprinted in his *Objective Knowledge* (Oxford: At the Clarendon Press, 1972), pp. 206-255. Popper's earlier-written treatment, in various respects more thorough, appears in *The Open Universe* (Totowa, New Jersey: Rowman and Littlefield, 1982). See Barrow and Tipler [2:1], pp. 138-143. See Alfred North Whitehead, *The Function of Reason* (Princeton: Princeton University Press, 1929), Chapter 1. Most recently and strikingly, read e.g. the scientist Doyne Parker, quoted in *Chaos: A New Science* [5:12], pp. 248-252. See Dean Turner [5:23]; consult index under "Freedom of choice."

**16:4:** For instance see Elmer E. Anderson, *Modern Physics and Quantum Mechanics* (Philadelphia: W. B. Saunders Co., 1971), p. 99, or Kenneth W. Ford, *The World of Elementary Particles* (Waltham, Massachusetts: Blaisdell Publishing Co., 1963), p. 209. See also Turner [5:23], "Hume and Contemporary Physicists." A ray consisting of from 5 to 14 quanta can in fact be seen (Maurice H. Pirenne, *Vision and the Eye* [London: Pilot Press, 1948], p. 82). See *Chaos* [5:12] the index under "Butterfly Effect."

Objections have been made to the theory of physical indeterminacy as lacking any explanation of free will. A. O. Gomes answers: "What can be expected of micro-uncertainty in the physiological control of action is only the establishment and the maintenance of conditions different from those which would impose a completely deterministic work for the nervous system, which can thus become, in principle, favorable for the occurrence of free action — never the whole key to this action" ("**The Brain-Consciousness Prob-**

lem" in *Brain and Conscious Experience*, edited by John C. Eccles [New York: Springer-Verlag, 1966], pp. 446-469, at p. 450). Karl Popper adds: "A choice process may be a selection process, and the *selection* may be *from* some repertoire of random events, *without being random in its turn*" (*Popper Selections*, edited by David Miller [Princeton: Princeton University Press, 1985], p. 246). See further Holmes Rolston III, *Environmental Ethics* (Philadelphia: Temple University Press), p. 207.

**16:5:** See Charles Hartshorne's article "Freedom Requires Indeterminism and Universal Causality," which is Chapter 6 of *Logic of Perfection* [10:34], from *Journal of Philosophy* 55 (1958): 793-811.

**16:6:** Psalms 139:16, Revised Standard Version (Catholic 138).

**16:7:** Adolph Harnack, *History of Dogma*, translated from the third German edition by Neil Buchanan (New York: Russell & Russell, 1958), Volume 5, p. 174. See Hartshorne, "The Reality of the Past, the Unreality of the Future," in *Hibbert Journal* 37 (1939): 246-257; Hartshorne, "The Meaning of 'Is Going To Be,'" *Mind* 74 (1965): 46-58.

**16:8:** On omnipotence see Charles Hartshorne and William L. Reese, *Philosophers Speak of God* [7:25], especially Chapter 3. See Boyle et al. [15:3], pp. 97-103; Tennant [5:8], Volume 2, Chapter 7. In Turner [4:40] see the index under "God—omnipotence."

The word "almighty" is often applied to God in the Bible. But in the Old Testament, "almighty" translates the Hebrew word *shaddai*, which has merely the meanings of "sufficient" or "mighty." In the New Testament, the word "almighty" appears in only two books: in 2 Corinthians once, but several times in Revelations, where it translates the Greek word *pantokrator*, meaning the "all-powerful" or "ruler of all."

**16:9:** William Pepperell Montague, *Great Visions of Philosophy* (La Salle, Illinois: Open Court Publishing Co., 1950), p. 23.

**16:10:** Contrast Aristotle, *Magna Moralia*, 1200b.

**16:11:** Besides the listed writings of Hartshorne, see Edgar Sheffield Brightman, *The Problem of God* (New York: Abingdon Press, 1930), also his article "Finite God," in *Encyclopedia of Religion* (New York: Philosophical Library, 1945). See Arthur Lovejoy, "The Obsolescence of the Eternal," *Philosophical Review* 18 (1909): 479-502: "Pragmatism and Theology" [9:29], especially Section 4; Tennant [5:8], Volume 2, Chapters 5 and 6; David Ray Griffin, *God and Religion in the Postmodern World* (Albany: State University of New York Press, 1989). Griffin's views on defense and military motivations are at least controversial. So is the Whiteheadian view of God as not creating voluntarily (pp. 138-142). In general see John H. Lavely, "Personalism," in *Encyclopedia of Philosophy*, edited by Paul Edwards (New York: Macmillan Publishing Co., 1967). Tennant discusses the concepts of eternity and immortality in [5:8], Volume 2, Chapter 5, also Note E of Appendix.

E. LaBonne Cherbonnier presents spirited argument for distinctively human attributes in God, notably "the capacity for discriminating judgment, the exercise of responsible decision and choice, the ability to carry out long-range purposes." For God, "To be perfect means to be alive, to be alive is to be active, and to be active is to be temporal" ("The Logic of Biblical Anthropomorphism," *Harvard Theological Review* 55 [1962]: 187-206). See Turner's forthcoming book [15:23]; see Turner [5:23] in the index under "Hartshorne," "Brightman," "Lovejoy," and under "God—omnipotence and omniscience."

Jonathan Edwards, as a follower of John Calvin, adheres in his writings to the form of determinism known as predestination—the view that God determines in advance which of us are the elect and which of us are not. This doctrine stems from Paul, with anticipations in the Old Testament (Romans 8:28-34, 9:11-23; Ephesians 1:4-11, 2:8-10; 2 Timothy 1:9; 2 Thessalonians 2:13-14; Proverbs 16:4; Exodus 7:3-4; Malachi 1:2-4). Moreover Edwards, like many others attempting to universalize Newton's thought, misapplies the laws of dynamics in universalizing them to bar free will. Thus he asserts God's absolute and total power of determination. Spinoza concludes similarly.

**16:12:** Alfred North Whitehead, *Science and the Modern World* (New York: Macmillan Co., 1925), p. 250.

**16:13:** Charles Hartshorne, *Creative Synthesis* [16:16], p. 151.

**16:14:** Harry Austryn Wolfson in Chapter 6 of his *Religious Philosophy* finds that Augustine's truncated view of human freedom had no precedent among the fathers of the Church and that Pelagius represents the original Christian belief (Cambridge: Harvard University Press, 1961). See [13:22].

**16:15:** Whitehead, *Adventures of Ideas* (first published 1933), Chapter 10, last paragraph. V. I. Lenin argued in 1894 against freedom of the will and was fully aware of the undercutting entailed for "philistine morality" (*Collected Works* [2:8], Volume 1, p. 159).

**16:16:** Hartshorne, "Six Theistic Proofs," in *Creative Synthesis and Philosophic Method* (La Salle, Illinois: Open Court Publishing Co., 1970), Chapter 14, quoted at p. 290; this appeared also in *Mind* 54 (1970): 159-180.

**16:17:** See Gustav T. Fechner, in *Philosophers Speak of God* [7:25], p. 254, Section 341.

**16:18:** Hartshorne, *Man's Vision of God* (New York: Willett, Clark & Co., 1941), pp. 163-164.

**16:19:** Hartshorne names his *Creative Synthesis* [16:16] as his definitive technical work. His paper "Metaphysics and the Dual Transcendence of God" supplements this (*Tulane Studies in Philosophy* 34 [1986]: 65-72). The volume is devoted to Hartshorne's thought. George Allan presents a concise summary of Hartshorne's thought in **"The Metaphysical Axioms and Ethics of Charles Hartshorne,"** *Review of Metaphysics* 40 (1986): 271-304, the earlier sections. Hartshorne's thought is deeply and helpfully discussed in Donald Wayne Viney's book *Charles Hartshorne and the Existence of God* (Albany: State University of New York Press, 1985). For historical perspective see *Anselm's Discovery* (La Salle, Illinois: Open

Court Publishing Co., 1965).

This distinguished philosopher has incontestably contributed many invaluable insights toward further understanding of the nature of God. Hartshorne has brought clarity into many issues in epistemology, metaphysics, logic, and theory of relations in areas where previously philosophers had failed to do so. Hartshorne was awarded an honorary doctorate from the Université Catholique de Louvain, in Belgium.

As Hartshorne turns 93 years of age, we pay homage to him as the subject of a forthcoming festschrift of the Library of Living Philosophers, a series in which a distinguished philosopher receives and answers questions about his thought while he is alive to answer. This honor is considered by many philosophers to be the equivalent of the Nobel Prize in their discipline (Open Court Publishing Co., 1991?). Hartshorne's introduction to the replies therein is evidently of importance as a discipline for metaphysical method. The volume will offset the near total neglect of Hartshorne in Paul Edwards' *Encyclopedia of Philosophy* [16:11], a neglect that Hartshorne shares with other luminaries such as Albert Schweitzer and Henry Margenau. A primary bibliography up to 1976 by Dorothy C. Hartshorne appears in *Process Studies* 6 (1976): 73-93 (to be augmented in the Library of Living Philosophers volume).

The Gifford Lectures on natural theology are delivered in Scottish universities under the patronage of the respective academic senates. Under the terms of Lord Gifford's will, the lectures are to be "public and popular" and to treat of the subject by "able, reverent men" as "a strictly natural science without reference to or reliance upon miraculous revelation" (see Stanley L. Jaki, *Lord Gifford and His Lectures* [Macon, Georgia: Mercer University Press, 1986], p. 74). Unfortunately, F. R. Tennant died without having participated. It is to be hoped that the senates of the universities of Edinburgh, Aberdeen, Glasgow, or St. Andrews will make amends for this lapse of fifty years ago by inviting Hartshorne, but the time is late.

Hartshorne resists the idea of motivation as arising simply from personal happiness-pursuit. He denies the continuing reality of any person as an abiding spiritual agent. He finds in Buddhism and process philosophy alike proper affirmation that persons or souls are not permanently unchangeable entities. In the language of Whitehead, process philosophy teaches that a person is not a permanent entity but a series of momentary successive "actual entities" or "actual occasions." Process philosophy denies that there is any enduring substance. In this way, Whitehead and Hartshorne believe that they leave room for ethical choices which are sympathetic or altruistic and hence socially rational, even though they deny the existence of an agent (an ongoing spiritual entity).

Hartshorne has replied as follows: "Of course I grant important continuity in a personal sequence of experience. A lot of my old self is in the present self. And I think the word 'soul' can be used to refer to this continuous or persistent core. The mass of memories is only slowly added to and nothing of it is wholly lost" (per-

sonal communication, February 10, 1978).

In any event, we find the notion of ethical choice inconceivable without an abiding spiritual agent who is the chooser, to whom responsibility for a choice can be assigned. The American philosopher W. T. Stace once commented that "An engine is only propelled into motion by its own steam, and not by the steam in another engine." We see this as an apt analogy of the difficulty that process philosophers have in explaining human acts after denying the existence of the agent who commits those acts (Stace, *The Destiny of Western Man* [New York: Reynal & Hitchcock, 1942], p. 115). See Hartshorne, *Creative Synthesis* [16:16], pp. 198-202, also his article "Ethics and the Assumption of Purely Private Pleasures," *International Journal of Ethics* 40 (1930): 496-515. Hartshorne has a draft of an improved version of this article. His entire ethical project appears in brief in **"Ethics and The New Theology,"** *International Journal of Ethics* 45 (1934): 90-101. Buddhism is treated in a chapter of Turner [15:23].

**Epigraph:** Hartshorne [2:2], p. 163.

# 17. The Stuff of Motivation

**Epigraph:** Charles Hartshorne, *The Philosophy and Psychology of Sensation* (Chicago: University of Chicago Press, 1934), p. 168; *Texas Quarterly,* Spring 1964, pp. 131-140, at p. 139; [14:34], p. 190; [16:16], "The Aesthetic Matrix of Value," pp. 303-321, at p. 305, showing the Dessoir-Davis Circle. See Rice [18:3], p. 201; [17:20] p. 277; [18:17], at p. 315; Sidgwick [8:1], "Ultimate Good"; Book of Mormon, 2 Nephi 2:25.

We cannot say that Hartshorne would quite agree with the conclusion of this chapter and the next; see note 19 to Chapter 16 herein.

**17:1:** H. J. Campbell, *New York Times,* April 14, 1971, p. E29. See also Campbell's

book *The Pleasure Areas* (New York: Delacorte Press, 1973), largely recommendable in spite of his grossly uncomprehending view of religion. See his technical article in *Physiology and Behavior* 8 (1972): 637-640. See also D. O. Hebb, "The Problem of Consciousness and Introspection," in *Brain Mechanisms and Consciousness,* edited by J. F. Delafresnaye (Springfield, Illinois: C. C. Thomas, 1955), pp. 402-421, e.g., at p. 419.

**17:2:** Thomas Aquinas, *Summa Theologica,* II-II, Question 35, Article 4, Reply to Objection 2.

**17:3:** Aristotle, *Nicomachean Ethics* 1172b. See 1101b, 1104b, 1119b, 1151b, 1153b, but contrast his *Rhetoric* 1360b and *Politics*

1324a. See Socrates, in Plato, *Symposium*, 204-205; Thomas Aquinas, *Summa contra Gentiles*, Book 3, Chapter 26.

**17:4:** Thomas Aquinas, *Summa Theologica*, I-II (first part of second part), Question 5: *The Trinity*, 13:5: Joseph Butler, *(Fifteen) Sermons Preached at the Rolls Chapel*, Sermon 11.

**17:5:** Plato, *Philebus*, 21-23.

**17:6:** Peirce, [1:2], 1.310, 1.580, 5.243-5.249. See W. B. Gallie, *Peirce and Pragmatism* (Harmondsworth, England: Penguin Books, 1952), pp. 79-83; William McDougall, *Psychology* (New York: Henry Holt & Co., 1912), p. 32; J. B. Watson, *Behavior* (New York: Henry Holt & Co., 1914), p. 257; Edwin G. Boring, *The Physical Dimensions of Consciousness* (New York: Century Co., 1933). Consciousness of one's happiness entails introspection, a method in dubious repute. For defense see David C. McClelland in *Psychological Review* 62 (1955): 297-302; reprinted in McClelland [12:15], pp. 111-118; David Bakan, *On Method* (San Francisco: Jossey-Bass, 1967), Chapter 9.

**17:7:** James Olds in *Scientific American*, October 1956, pp. 105-116, 34, 36, 170; *Science* 127 (1958): 315-324; *Physiological Reviews* 42 (1962): 554-604; James and Marianne Olds in *New Directions in Psychology II* (New York: Holt, Rinehart & Winston, 1965), pp. 327-410; and other articles back to 1954. On the remarkable effects of nonvoluntary stimulation on monkeys see John C. Lilly in *Electrical Studies on the Unanesthetized Brain*, edited by E. R. Ramey and D. S. O'Doherty (New York: Paul B. Hoebner, 1960), Chapter 4, pp. 78-96; Chapter 2 is an article by Olds. Robert G. Heath has been central in work on humans; one may search for his name in *Cumulated Index Medicus* and predecessors back about 40 years—for instance, *Journal of Nervous and Mental Disease* 160 (1975): 159-175. Heath is founder of the journal *Biological Psychiatry*. For another kind of philosophically interesting psychophysical link see Robert Efron, "The Measurement of Perceptual Durations," *Studium Generale* 23 (1970): 550-561.

**17:8:** Some little-known neurology

makes it easier to take mind seriously and as something more interesting than an accumulation of telephone switches connected by wires. Our nervous system does not consist solely of "machine-like neural nets" that are merely pathways for digital electrochemical pulses to race to and fro in patterns describable in terms of something like Boolean algebra. True, the all-or-nothing scheme of "spike" transmission applies through most of the body and brain. Some investigators have thought that any one part of this all-or-none transmission of impulses is presumed to be as relevant to consciousness and mind as any other.

In a little-known body of work, the neurophysiologists Alfred E. Fessard, Madge E. Scheibel, and Arnold B. Scheibel describe clusters of unique kinds of neurons characterized by "graded potentials" or voltages—that is, by transmission of electrical effects between neurons in gently rising and falling "analog" electrical potentials, without the usual all-or-nothing voltage "spike." Such transmission occurs with endless variations in the reticular formation of the mid-brain, brain stem and beyond, the reticular formation being the evident locus of choice and consciousness. Numerous neural fibers known as dendrites transmit signals from each neuron, with each dendrite touching upon one further neuron. Many electrical touchings seem normally to contribute to the making of any one decision. See Alfred E. Fessard, "Mechanisms of Nervous Integration and Conscious Experience," in *Brain Mechanisms and Consciousness* [17:1], pp. 200-236, especially pp. 215 ff.; Madge E. Scheibel and Arnold B. Scheibel, "On Circuit Patterns of the Brain Stem Reticular Core," *Annals of the New York Academy of Sciences* 89 (1961): 857-865. For graded, non-spike potentials and other activities in the glia cells of the brain see Robert Galambos in *National Academy of Sciences, Proceedings* 47 (1961): 129-136; also *Neurones without Impulses*, edited by A. Roberts and B. M. H. Bush (New York: Cambridge University Press, 1981). One can learn something from these writings without knowing all the technical language. "Brain Death and Brainstem Death" by David Lamb is relevant, in *Moral Philosophy and Contemporary Problems*, edited by J. D. G. Evans (Cambridge: Cambridge University Press, 1987), pp. 231-249.

Affective processes are conceptualized as needful *intervening variables* by the American psychologist Paul Thomas Young in *Psychological Review* 66 (1959): 104-125. See Jan Smedslund, "The Epistemological Foundations of Behaviorism," *Acta Psychologica* 11 (1955): 412-431. Also see the debate between Brand Blanshard and B. F. Skinner, *Philosophy and Phenomenological Research* 27 (1967): 317-337.

One may speculate about the biological usefulness of the pleasure-pain continuum. Conscious motivation enables a creature to act in a unified way, if only for survival. To this end, the creature can make good use of a running affective criterion of all of its experience into a single dimension, in which some *one* quality of all experiences renders them commensurable and hence comparable. The objective is to guide decision-making, through comparison of the expected experienced value of the various alternatives. This criterion has only a single dimension and is objectified as a single linear memory-bank of ranked values of various potential actions within the mind of each person, since a creature can exert its will toward only one thing at a time.

Suppose the feelings of pleasure and pain were somehow reversed in us. Remember the cartoonist Al Capp and his race of little "kygmies," who just loved to be kicked. Suppose that banging our heads against hard objects felt good, that bitter substances tasted good to us but not sweet ones, that soft things were unpleasant but that scalding water or flame felt good, that we liked insults, etc. The rankings in one's ranked-value memory-bank or rank-bank would thereby be inverted in position. There seems to be no logical impossibility about this. Indeed, partial reversals of this sort are reported in medical practice. Neurologically, it might be a matter of transposing certain nerves. But practical considerations would be decisive. The victim of fully reversed affective circuitry would be dead in a minute. Maybe such infants are born now and then but do not survive long enough to be diagnosed.

**17:9:** "The good news of the heart is written in the face." True, and yet the news can readily be falsified, a phenomenon that occurs much of the time in some cultures; see Lafcadio Hearn, *Glimpses of Unfamiliar Japan*, 2 volumes (Boston: Houghton Mifflin Co., 1894), Volume 2, Chapter 26, "The Japanese Smile," pp. 656-683. Yet the method of observing faces should not be ruled out as a statistical method on sizeable populations. Some works of Charles Darwin and Paul Ekman on facial expression suggest its usefulness. See Darwin, *The Expression of the Emotions in Man and Animals* (London, 1872); Paul Ekman et al., *Emotion in the Human Face* (New York: Pergamon Press, 1972); Ekman and Wallace V. Friesen, *Unmasking the Face* (Englewood Cliffs, New Jersey: Prentice-Hall, 1975); Ekman, *Telling Lies* (New York: W. W. Norton & Co., 1985). As to some other objectives, see Harold Schlossberg in *Journal of Experimental Psychology* 29 (1941): 497-510. Most of the candid pictures in *The People of Moscow* by the photographer Henri Cartier-Bresson with his classic Leica are clearly not appropriate for a Russian tour advertisement (New York: Simon & Schuster, 1955). There has been opinion that, the farther one travels from Moscow, the happier the people appear to be. See further *Cartier-Bresson in India* (London: Thames & Hudson, 1987). Orientals, except the Japanese, habitually do not smile much, but bitterness and hopelessness are hard to conceal.

Hazelett photographed faces to compare average happiness in various locales. He used an 8 mm Beaulieu motion-picture camera (16 mm should do nicely) having single-frame, adjustable-shutter capability, with reflex groundglass focusing, in combination with C-mounted mirror lenses of 1000 or 500 mm focal length, enabling work at considerable distances from the subjects. A reflex-focusing video camera with the C-mounted lens should also serve. A camera support is essential, such as the convenient friction-swivel-base monopod or "Platterpod"™ developed by Hazelett and the subject of a U.S. patent application. With such equipment, it was easy to demonstrate that, as of 1970, the walks of University of Northern Colorado (Greeley) bore a far less proportion of frowns than those of Boston University. One important variable is whether the people are walking singly or in pairs; this explains many of the individual differences observed. But friends make for happiness, so why partial out this factor when measuring happiness?

Some Asians get upset over candid photography, though not only Asians; it is said to be illegal in some countries. A preliminary, more subjective method is to walk about while carrying a hand tally mechanical counter in each hand, depressing one key for a smile and the other key for a frown. The neutral faces, or the total, can be added in one's head meanwhile; buy from Veeder-Root, Hartford, Connecticut 06102.

Facial studies may be better for estimating average hardness or self-centeredness than for estimating either happiness or unhappiness. On the other hand, there appears to be a high correlation between these negative characteristics. Common experience suggests that rigidity or repetitiveness of facial expressions may mean falsification of one's psychical state; see Paul Ekman, Telling Lies, summarized in Time, April 22, 1985, p. 59. Among the very few Americans we have known who had a persistent smile, three of them turned out to be crooks who were covertly working against our interests.

A better book on psychological measurement than most is Unobtrusive Measures: Nonreactive Research in the Social Sciences, by Eugene J. Webb et al. (Chicago: Rand McNally & Co., 1966). A substantial work from the academic establishment is that of Alden Wessman and David Ricks, entitled Mood and Personality (New York: Holt, Rinehart & Winston, 1966). The sociologist Hornell Hart used a questionnaire method for measuring happiness, by which he sig-

nificantly correlated the results of his measurements with events in the lives of the responders, reported in Chart for Happiness (New York: Macmillan Co., 1940), Chapter 10: Autoconditioning (Englewood Cliffs, New Jersey: Prentice-Hall, 1956), Chapters 1 and 17. See further Joel R. Davitz, The Language of Emotion (New York: Academic Press, 1969). The happiness of an eight-month-old infant was carefully estimated continuously during a week and reported by Arthur E. Morgan in International Journal of Ethics 44 (1934): 236-243.

A pitfall of measurement by questionnaire is that high degrees of happiness may not receive their proper weight, since it is easier to formulate questions probing unhappiness than its opposite. Attempts at quantifying go back for decades. In searching the literature, one should use, for instance, Depress(ion) and Anxi(ety).

There has been much medical work on the measurement of pain; see Henry K. Beecher, Measurement of Subjective Responses (New York: Oxford University Press, 1959), e.g., pp. 188-190, 321-341; B. Berthold Wolff, "Behavioral Measurement of Pain," in The Psychology of Pain, edited by Richard A. Sternbach (New York: Raven Press, 1978), pp. 129-168. Attempts to find chemical correlates of happiness or its opposite have been made. Certainly, known chemicals affect one's decisions, whether carried into the brain from outside or manufactured in situ. Neurological methods of measurement are conceivable but obviously difficult.

**17:10:** On logical fertility of scientific concepts through multiple connections in the chart, see Henry Margenau, The Nature of Physical Reality (New York: McGraw-Hill, 1950), pp. 84-88; Margenau, Journal of the Operations Research Society of America 3 (1955): 135-146; Open Vistas (New Haven: Yale University Press, 1961), Chapter 1.

Clarence Irving Lewis observes in Mind and the World Order that "A large part of the scientific search is for things worth naming" (New York: Charles Scribner's Sons, 1929), p. 258.

**17:11:** Charles Hartshorne, *The Philosophy and Psychology of Sensation* (Chicago: University of Chicago Press, 1934), p. 259.

**17:12:** Hermann Lotze, *Microcosmus,* translated by Elizabeth Hamilton and E. E. Constance Jones (Edinburgh: T. & T. Clark, 1885), III:iv:2, pp. 349-352. See also Hartshorne [2:2], Chapter 1 and pp. 104-105.

The metaphysical theory of psychicalism denies that, at bottom, the world has real material aspects. Deriving mainly from Hartshorne, Whitehead, and Leibniz, the theory aims at a solution to the problem of the mind-and-brain dualism by denying the seemingly categorical difference in their ultimate micro-nature. The geneticist Sewall Wright remarks sympathetically: "Emergence of mind from no mind makes no sense" ("Biology and the Philosophy of Science," in *Process and Divinity,* edited by William L. Reese and Eugene Freeman [La Salle, Illinois: Open Court Publishing Co., 1964], pp. 101-125).

Hartshorne suggests that our brain comprises our nearest neighbors; see his Postscript herein and his book *The Logic of Perfection* (La Salle, Illinois: Open Court Publishing Co., 1962), Chapter 7, from *Philosophy and Phenomenological Research* 3 (1942): 127-136; *Philosophy* (U.K.) 36 (1961): 97-111. See also Alfred North Whitehead, *Modes of Thought* (New York: Macmillan Co., 1957), Lecture 8. Hazelett's master's thesis (University of Texas at Austin, 1969) has around a hundred relevant references; one is G. W. von Leibniz, *Monadology,* Sections 17 and 64.

A. A. Cochran relates quantum mechanical concepts to biological systems and to mind in *Main Currents in Modern Thought* 22 (1966): 79-88; also *Foundations of Physics* 1 (1971): 235-250; *Dialectica* 19 (1965): 290-312. See Bernard and Alberte Pullman, "Electronic Delocalization and Biochemical Evolution," *Nature* (London) 196 (1962): 1137-1142. Further, see Henry P. Stapp in *Foundations of Physics* 12 (1982): 363-399, ibid., 15 (1985): 35-47.

Turner finds any philosophy unconvincing which would collapse matter into mind. He agrees that "Emergence of mind from no mind makes no sense." But, he asks, Why cannot our minds, which were created by God, be housed in real material brains that God has formed out of the primordial material aspects of His own being? Turner contends that it is not necessary for present purposes that we be able to *explain* how mind and matter can interact and influence each other. He deems it a practical necessity, however, to recognize *that* we live in a world which has both material and spiritual aspects since, while we adhere to our common sense, it cannot be plausibly denied. Turner has found that, no matter how imaginative and sophisticated a case for psychicalism is put to his students, they laugh. This is not stated to ridicule the position but to state a pedagogical fact.

The neurologically trained philosopher Roland Puccetti is concerned to discredit the identity theory, which holds oddly that mind and brain are identical. He prefers the double-aspect theory but does not find it satisfactory; see his article in (*Philosophy* [U.K.] 50 [1975]: 259-269); **"The Sensation of Pleasure,"** *British Journal for the Philosophy of Science* 20 (1969): 239-245. Puccetti's articles listed in *Philosopher's Index* from about 1969 contain many dealing with topics of neurological interest, such as "On Thinking Machines and Feeling Machines," *British Journal for the Philosophy of Science* 18 (1967): 39-51, and the entertaining piece, "Can Humans Think?" *Analysis* 26 (1966): 198-202. The discussion *Brains, Minds and Computers,* by Stanley L. Jaki, is illuminating (South Bend: Gateway Editions, 1969).

**17:13:** Compare Matthew 6:24.

**17:14:** Donald Shepard and Richard J. Zeckhauser have systematically explored people's own opinions of the balancing of the desirability of money in their pockets vs. added life span in *Management Review* 30 (1984): 423-439. Also see "The Taxes of Sin," by Willard G. Manning et al., *JAMA* (formerly *Journal of the American Medical Association*) 261 (1989): 1604-1609.

**17:15:** The words "impartial spectator" are Adam Smith's. He seems to have left open the question whether the impartial spectator was to be identified with God;

see [11:10], Part 3, Chapter 3.

**17:16:** John von Neumann and Oskar Morgenstern, *Theory of Games and Economic Behavior* (Princeton, New Jersey: Princeton University Press, 1944), p. 11. Compare Thomas Aquinas, *Summa Theologica*, I-II (first part of second part), Question 1, Article 5; Georg Henrik von Wright, *The Logic of Preference* (Edinburgh: Edinburgh University Press, 1963), pp. 30, 34. Lewis has discussed ways in which to combine social goods into a manageable sum; see [17:17], pp. 533 ff.

There appears to be a neurological analogy to the fact that any animal or human suffers the inherent limitation that it can consciously perform only one action at a time. As a matter of neurology as well as of universal experience, a person can attend to only one conscious decision — indeed, only one basis for decision — at one time; see Madge E. Scheibel and Arnold B. Scheibel, "On Circuit Patterns of the Brain Stem Reticular Core," *Annals of the New York Academy of Sciences* 89 (1961): 857-865, who say on p. 861, "We are left to assume that ability to manipulate a number of inputs simultaneously is not a high-priority item for the reticular core."

**17:17:** Clarence Irving Lewis, *An Analysis of Knowledge and Valuation* (La Salle, Illinois: Open Court Publishing Co., 1946), p. 400.

**17:18:** Lewis [17:17], p. 401 — in general, Chapters 13 and 16. See John Locke, *An Essay Concerning Human Understanding* (revised 1706), Book 2, Part 7, Section 2; see Leslie Stephen, *The Science of Ethics* (London, 1882), p. 44; Bruce Buchenholz, *Journal of Nervous and Mental Diseases* 123 (1956): 351-355; ibid., 124 (1956) 569-577; ibid., 125 (1957): 396-402; Marghanita Laski, *Ecstasy* (Bloomington, Indiana: Indiana University Press, 1962). The following excerpt from Lewis is relevant:

> Immediate or directly findable value is not so much one quality as a dimensionlike mode which is pervasive of all experience. There is not one goodness and one badness to be found in living but uncount-

ably many variants of good and bad, each [being] like every other most notably in being a basis for choosing and preferring. Value or disvalue is not like the pitch of middle C or the seen color of median red or the felt hardness of steel. It is not one specific quale [i.e., independent quality] of experience but a gamut of such; more like color in general or pitch or hardness in general. It is like seen bigness or apparent littleness of things ([17:17], p. 401).

We may follow Lewis' thorough discussion of pleasure, pain, and displeasure, in which he notes that

> their significations in common speech are too narrow; they are unsatisfactory by preponderant connotation of the pallid and sentimental. Also "pleasant" as well as "pleasure" suggests too exclusively such felt goodnesses as are unsubtle, incomplex, and too exclusively associated with the organic sensations, and such as characterize passivity rather than the goodness of serious activity.

The philosophical hedonists, Lewis continues,

> have not — one presumes — intended such an unduly narrow meaning. They have stretched "pleasure" and "pain" beyond an original and plainer application to include all sorts of complex and subtler satisfactions and dissatisfactions, with the unfortunate result of making their doctrine misleading to the unwary and unsophisticated. An Epicurus may be clear that no more trustworthy pleasure can be found than that which is secure with a sufficiency of barley and water and the communion of friends; and a Bentham may understand that life holds no better pleasure than that which may come from devoted and

successful public service. But those who read them may fail to recognize such goods under the name of "pleasure" and pass these by in favor of more obvious but less genuinely satisfactory ones ([17:17], pp. 404-405).

Thomas Aquinas affords suggestive distinctions and insights about goals and happiness in *Summa Theologica*, I-II, Questions 1 through 5, even though not all of this is apposite to present purposes. See E. E. Constance Jones in *International Journal of Ethics* 5 (1918): 79-97, at pp. 80-81. Hartshorne finds that pleasure is one kind of harmony and that happiness is a harmony among aims, activities, memory, and perceptions. He finds beauty to be a better clue to happiness than is pleasure; in this he follows Whitehead.

**17:19:** See Ward Edwards, Harold Lindman, and Lawrence D. Phillips, **''The Concept of Rationality,''** which is a section of "Emerging Technologies for Making Decisions," in *New Directions in Psychology II* (New York: Holt, Rinehart

& Winston, 1965), pp. 259-325, at pp. 269.

**17:20:** Karl Duncker [18:21], at p. 400. Even though its conclusion is mistaken, the insights are brilliant. See Philip Blair Rice, "Science, Humanism and the Good," in *Value: A Cooperative Inquiry,* edited by Ray Lepley (New York: Columbia University Press, 1949), pp. 261-290, at 281-282, 288.

**17:21:** Peirce [1:2], 1.594-1.599, 1.606-1.607. See Aristotle, *Nicomachean Ethics,* 1099a. Similarly, John Stuart Mill observes that "Instead of willing the thing because we desire it, we often desire it because we will it" (*Utilitarianism,* Chapter 4). See Lewis [17:17], p. 500.

**17:22:** Nathaniel Branden, "Rational Egoism," *Personalist* 51 (1970): 196-211, at p. 209. We salute Branden for this insight, even though we cannot agree with him on some other points in his philosophy.

**First epigraph:** Abraham Tucker, *The Light of Nature Pursued,* abridged by William Hazlitt (London, 1807), pp. 332-333. This was originally one long sentence, here split.

# 18. The Benign Quality of Pleasure

**Epigraph:** Henry Veatch, *Rational Man* (Bloomington: Indiana University Press, 1962), p. 198.

**18:1:** Boris Pasternak, *Doctor Zhivago.* As heard in the film play produced by Carlo Ponti (distributed by Metro-Goldwyn-Mayer, 1965).

**18:2:** Eric Hoffer's book *The True Believer* is recommendable except that his view of Christianity is that of an uninformed and biased outsider (New York: Harper & Brothers, 1951); reprinted in [1:epigraph]. See David Rosenhan, "The Natural Socialization of Altruistic Autonomy," in *Altruism and Helping Behavior,* edited by Jacqueline Macaulay and Leonard Berkowitz (New York: Academic Press, 1970), pp. 251-268.

**18:3:** Philip Blair Rice, *On the Knowledge of Good and Evil* (New York: Random House, 1955), p. 212.

**18:4:** Ibid., pp. 199, 203, 209-210, 212; also [17:20], p. 282. Augustine would have approved: see Vernon J. Bourke, *Joy in Augustine's Ethics* (Villanova, Pennsylvania: Villanova University Press, 1979), pp. 36-38.

**18:5:** G. E. Moore, *Principia Ethica* (Cambridge: Cambridge University Press, 1903), p. 41, also pp. 16-17. See Plato, *Philebus,* 12-13.

**18:6:** Moore [18:5], pp. 188-189.

**18:7:** That is, Moore retracted his notorious "two worlds" argument, which was stated in *Principia Ethica* [18:5] at pp. 82-85 and retracted in "A Reply to My

Critics," in *The Philosophy of G. E. Moore*, edited by P. A. Schilpp, second edition (New York: Tudor Publishing Co., 1952), pp. 617-618. Compare Aristotle, *Nicomachean Ethics*, 1172b; E. E. Constance Jones, *International Journal of Ethics* 5 (1906): 429-464, at pp. 435-437; Edward F. Mettrick, *International Journal of Ethics* 38 (1928): 389-400; W. H. Roberts, *Journal of Philosophy* 38 (1941): 623-627.

**18:8:** Josef Stalin in 1923, quoted in Robert Payne, *The Rise and Fall of Stalin* (New York: Simon & Schuster, 1965), p. 369.

**18:9:** See Sheldon [11:8], pp. 25, 30; Jeremy Bentham, *Introduction to the Principles of Morals and Legislation*, Chapter 10, item 10 with footnote. Contrast Aristotle, *Nicomachean Ethics*, 1175b.

**18:10:** See Thomas Aquinas, *Summa Theologica*, I-II, Question 34.

**18:11:** Jonathan Edwards, *True Virtue* [6:3], p. 8.

**18:12:** Robert G. Heath expresses his misgivings about the overall effects of his own work in "The Human Brain: Instrument of Progress or Disaster?" *Biological Psychiatry* 20 (1985): 931-932.

**18:13:** William Alexander, *Darius*, chorus, quoted in *The Home Book of Quotations*, edited by Burton Stevenson (New York: Dodd, Mead & Co.), under "Happiness: Its Dangers."

**18:14:** See Aldous Huxley's *Brave New World* (New York: Harper & Brothers, 1946).

**18:15:** Eric Hoffer [1:epigraph], p. 71. See O. Hobart Mowrer, "Some Constructive Features of the Concept of Sin," *Journal of Counseling Psychology* 7 (1960): 185-188, with succeeding pages by others. David Belgum writes helpfully of "Hypocrisy and Mental Health" in *Morality and Mental Health*, edited by Mowrer (Chicago: Rand McNally & Co., 1967). Belgum's article is Chapter 1 of his book *Guilt: Where Religion and Psychology Meet* (Englewood Cliffs, New Jersey: Prentice-Hall, 1963). Generally, see Mike W. Martin, *Self-Deception and Morality* (Lawrence: University Press of Kansas, 1986).

Charles Finney is the author of a still relevant piece on "False Comforts for Sinners," Chapter 17 of his *Lectures on Revivals of Religion* (Cambridge: Harvard University Press, 1960).

**18:16:** Leo Tolstoy, *The Christian Teaching* (London, 1898), Part 3. We recite Tolstoy's lines here because we recognize their critical validity in principle. Unfortunately, a study of the biographies of Tolstoy — indeed, even of his own autobiographical writings — reveals that his love for human beings was hardly more than a verbal attention to the needs and ideals of humanity in the abstract. The fact is, he wrote passionately about the need to emancipate the serfs and poor peasants, but he literally looked down upon them with contempt when he saw them face to face as concrete individuals. He was often petty, selfish, uncaring, and cruel, even to his own wife and family. He had little capacity for a lasting love relationship with anyone. We lament that Tolstoy, like so many other idealistic reformers, seldom lived by his ideals in his daily human relationships.

**18:17:** See Dewitt H. Parker, *The Philosophy of Value* (Ann Arbor: University of Michigan Press, 1957), pp. 162-165. An act closely followed by a valued state of mind, say, by a pleasant feeling, will tend to be chosen repeatedly, habitually — that is to say, be learned. This is roughly the psychologists' "law of effect," which is "a law of retention of interests or dispositions." See Philip Blair Rice, **"The Ego and the Law of Effect,"** *Psychological Review* 53 (1946): 307-320, for the serious student. Also see O. H. Mowrer and A. D. Ullman, **"Time as a Determinant in Integrative Learning,"** in *Psychological Review* 52 (1945): 61-90.

**18:18:** Failure to distinguish present motivation from prospective pleasure has been a source of confusion as pointed out by W. K. McAllister in *Philosophy and Phenomenological Research* 13 (1953): 499-505. For example see C. (Charlie) D. Broad, *Five Types of Ethical Theory* (London: Routledge & Kegan Paul, 1930), pp. 179-192. Broad is mostly expounding Henry Sidgwick [8:1] but does not improve on him here. Compare Peirce [1:11], 7.361.

**18:19:** Hartshorne [2:2], pp. 209, 104-105; Lovejoy [11:2], Lecture 3, p. 79; L. T. Troland, *Fundamentals of Human Motivation* (New York: D. Van Nostrand Co., 1930), pp. 273-280.

**18:20:** Philip Blair Rice, [18:3], pp. 207n-208n. See Henry Sidgwick, *Practical Ethics* (London: Swan Sonnenschein & Co., 1898), Chapter 9: "Unreasonable Action."

**18:21** Karl Duncker, **"On Pleasure, Emotion and Striving,"** *Philosophy and Phenomenological Research* 1 (1941): 391-430, at p. 402, also pp. 398-405, 412, 425-430. Siding with Duncker is Nicholas Rescher [5:7], Chapter 13. But see C. I. Lewis [17:17], pp. 500-502.

**18:22:** Jonathan Edwards [6:3], p. 45.

**18:23:** Benjamin Franklin, after John Heywood. Leslie Stephen, *The Science of Ethics* (London, 1882), quoted in Alexander Bain's review in *Mind* o.s.v. 8 (1883): 48-68, at p. 67.

**18:24:** Sheldon [11:8], pp. 303, 291. See Thomas Aquinas, *Summa Theologica*, I-II (first part of second part), Question 1, Article 6. For disagreement see Broad [18:18].

**18:25:** Sidgwick [8:1], p. 51. See C. I. Lewis [17:17], p. 498.

**18:26:** A still influential school of English-speaking philosophers tend to confine their professional interests to what can be stated in, or analyzed from, the ordinary, everyday language of humankind. Many of them in their linguistic analyses would have us believe that, when people choose, they choose only something objective—say chocolate—and that therefore they do not choose the pleasure associated with the chocolate. The matter is important here because, if such statements are correct, the whole idea of ranking according to hedonic tone could not be maintained.

But as observed herein, our minds have a peculiar efficiency: we can think of two things at almost the same time, both the object pursued and the pleasure to be attained, interlaced in some alternating rhythm. This is a bit of psychology that is worth knowing. In contrast, "ordinary-language" philosophers or linguistic analysts are not, as such, interested in prying much beneath the surface of things. From personal observation, some of them oppose interest in science insofar as science requires acquaintance with concepts unknown or unthought by the mass of people, or by themselves. Their critic Ernest Gellner says, such philosophy "provides a powerful rationale for anyone wishing to have nothing or as little as possible to do with any one or more of the following three things: (1) science and technicality, (2) power and responsibility [and] (3) ideas."[13] It has been said with much truth that "ordinary-language" philosophy is not about language, but about whatever ordinary language is about. Generally, such philosophy has ignored genuine ethical or religious questions. See Ernest Gellner, *Words and Things* (London: Victor Gollancz, 1959); reviewed by P. L. Heath in *Philosophy* (U.K.) 37 (1962): 176-177; Bertrand Russell, *British Journal for the Philosophy of Science* 3 (1953): 303-307; Brand Blanshard [9:20]. See also Clarence Irving Lewis, *Mind and the World Order* (New York: Charles Scribner's Sons, 1929), pp. 54, 258; Jaki [3:33], pp. 203-204; Karl Popper [5:20]—notably the preface added in 1959. Whitehead writes, "If men cannot live by bread alone, still less can they do so on disinfectants" [20:16], Chapter 4. Thomas Hobbes is more blunt: "Words are wise men's counters; they are the money of fools." Of course, a thing or two can be learned from ordinary-language philosophers, but they should not be allowed to expel other ways of doing philosophy, as they did in one prominent midwest department about 1966.

**18:27:** R. S. Peters, *The Concept of Motivation*, second edition (London: Routledge & Kegan Paul, 1960), pp. 143-144. See Gilbert Ryle, *The Concept of Mind* (New York: Barnes & Noble, 1949), pp. 107-110. For critique of Ryle's book see C. A. Campbell in *Philosophical Quarterly* (U.K.) 3 (1953): 115-138. Similar questions are raised by G. E. M. Anscombe and Anthony Kenny, as noted by John Rawls in *A Theory of Justice* (Cambridge: Harvard University Press, 1971), p. 559n; the answer to their questions is the same as the answer to Peters.

In Rawls' widely discussed book, he elaborates and extends the insights of his excellent article [6:10-11] which relates how one general kind of good comes to pass. His theory narrows the range of justifiable decision in important social matters. However, Rawls holds that hedonistic evaluation cannot serve as a "dominant end" for ethics. Neither can anything else, in his view; he insists on "the impossibility of defining an appropriate definite end to be maximized. Human good is heterogeneous because the aims of the self are heterogeneous." Nor can the service of God be a suitable definite end; Rawls finds that such an end is vague and ambiguous and entails that "The self is disfigured and put in the service of one of its ends for the sake of the system" (Sections 83 and 84 in Chapter 9). But Rawls admits that his own theory does not provide a foundation for "the higher-order moral sentiments," and he foresees a place for metaphysics in relation to ethics (pp. 192, 512).

Rawls' positive thought is worthwhile, provided that it is not applied in every case as definitive or as displacing higher and more comprehensive ideals. It seems evident from the pallor of his page 557 that Rawls never got inside a genuine religious position or that he forgot all about it if he did. Despite Rawls' strictures, which are worth considering, the service of God actually has worked better as a unifying ideal than anything else has. The reply to Rawls is the entire present book. His fine mind is hereby invited to a higher service.

**18:28:** David C. McClelland, *Personality* (New York: Dryden Press, 1951), pp. 466-467. Compare Peirce [1:2], 7.361.

**18:29:** See McClelland, *The Achievement Motive* New York: Appleton-Century-Crofts, 1953), p. 28; D. O. Hebb, *The Organization of Behavior* (New York: Wiley & Sons, 1949), p. 149; Alfred North Whitehead [10:8], p. 407; Donald W. Sherburne, *A Key to Whitehead's Process and Reality* (New York: Macmillan Co., 1966), pp. 67, 40, 207; Peirce [1:2], 1.334; Jean-Paul Sartre, *Being and Nothingness* (New

York: Philosophical Library, 1956), pp. 433-438. One early challenge to the clear possibility of decidability between options is answered by the American psychologist Paul Thomas Young in his study of "mixed feelings," in which he concludes that pleasantness and unpleasantness are not experienced simultaneously by the same person. A bittersweet taste, say, is not experienced as two separate tastes at the same instant. If it were, a determinate decision regarding such a taste might not be possible, as we have seen in the matter of maximizing two things at once ("An Experimental Study of Mixed Feelings," *American Journal of Psychology* 29 [1918]: pp. 237-271).

**18:30:** On the constitution of personal identity see Peirce [1:2], 1.411. On psychological hedonism see L. T. Troland, *The Fundamentals of Human Motivation* (London: Macmillan & Co., 1928), Chapter 16.

W. P. Alston, philosopher of ethics and religion, contends that pleasure, happiness, etc., are not the only kind of rational internal motivation. Thus, Alston divides theories of the nature of pleasure into two kinds: conscious-quality theories (say, the pursuit of the qualities of truth or beauty), and motivational theories. Similarly, the moral philosopher Richard Brandt avoids narrowing basic motivations down to just pleasure because, as he and Alston both believe, this amounts to psychological hedonism—the necessary "choosing" or unavoidable motivation of the most pleasurable alternative of action. But as we have found psychological hedonism to be acceptable in a highly qualified sense, there seems to be no need to split the concept of pleasure. Despite this difference with Alston, his discussion will repay careful reading for its usually acute analysis. Together with his useful bibliography, his article is found in the *Encyclopedia of Philosophy* [16:11], "Pleasure."

A related point may be made as to Albert Schweitzer, for whom we have the highest respect. In his attempt to trace where the utilitarianism of Socrates and of the eighteenth and nineteenth centuries went astray, Schweitzer distinguishes sharply between "material happiness" and "spiritual happiness," identifying the former with egoism and the latter or "the rationally pleasurable" with altruism. Schweitzer says that neither "can find its continuation in the other," claiming,

> The man who does earnestly try to guide himself by the light of spiritual as well as material happiness more and more exclusively experiences spiritual happiness as the condition in which he is at one with himself and therefore can justifiably accord himself a certain amount of self-approbation. Spiritual happiness is sufficient unto itself. The fact that [one] is a moral man is in itself his happiness, even though it land him in the most disadvantageous situations (*Philosophy of Civilization* [1:11], pp. 152-153 [71-73], 158 [78-79]).

There is much to agree with here.

"Spiritual happiness" is more reliable, and more productive of happiness for others. But on its face, Schweitzer seems to state a harsh asceticism. Are we to deny to ourselves that sensuous or material good which we would bring to others? If so, "What are the others here for?" Further, doesn't some "material happiness" make the earning of spiritual happiness more feasible? Even Schweitzer seems to acknowledge this much (*Philosophy of Civilization* [1:11], p. 157 [77]). Schweitzer, a great musician, liked music that has a spiritual component. Yet music is based on the inherent material or sensuous pleasure of sounds and their combinations. In sum, both spiritual and material happiness are equally happiness, though one is more productive of further happiness than the other.

The alleged moral dichotomy between body and soul was stated in Plato's *Phaedrus* and carried forward in Neoplatonism and indeed in the letters of Paul. It has resurfaced as heresies and sects up to the present.

## 19. Joy, Spark of the Infinite

**First epigraph:** Dindimus (Dandemis) of India, in *Wisdom of the Ages*, edited by Mark Gilbert (London: St. Catherine's Press, 1934).

**Second epigraph:** Augustine, *De civitate Dei* (The City of God), Book 19, Chapter 1, 3.

**Third epigraph:** Thomas Aquinas, Opusc. 35, *De Duobus Praeceptis*, in *St. Thomas Aquinas: Philosophical Texts*, selected and translated by Thomas Gilby (New York: Oxford University Press, 1960), p. 276.

**19:1:** See Blanshard [1:5], pp. 40-41. Holmes Rolston III writes: "What we learn from the Greeks is that the unexamined life is not worth living, but what we learn from the Hebrews is that the un-

committed life is not worth examining" (*Science and Religion* [4:14], p. 338).

**19:2:** "Reason is and ought only to be the slave of the passions"—David Hume, *A Treatise of Human Nature*, Book 2, Part 3, Section 3. Thomas Hill Green points out that neither rationality nor desire ever exist entirely independently of each other: "If the 'intellectual' act implies attention, it implies *desire* for the attainment of an intellectual result, though the result be attained as quickly as, for instance, the meaning of a sentence in a familiar language is arrived at upon attention being drawn to it. If the desire is consciously for an object, it implies an *intellectual apprehension* at least of the difference between the object as desired and its realisation" (*Prolegomena to Ethics*, fifth edition [Oxford, Clarendon Press, 1907], Section 136, p. 155).

**19:3:** Charles Finney, "Selfishness," a sermon reprinted in *True Submission* (Grand Rapids, Michigan: Kregel Publications, 1967), conclusion. Benjamin Franklin as Poor Richard states, "When you are good to others, you are best to yourself."

**19:4:** See notably J. S. Mill's essay *Theism*, the last paragraphs.

**19:5:** The American philosopher William Pepperell Montague defines virtue as "the permanent potentiality of happiness" and concludes that "Habits of character, such as courage and charity, will appear as the substantive rather than the transient causes of happiness. And the happiness of which a virtue is the permanent potentiality will be related to that virtue as a surface is related to the volume of which it is the cross-section. The tender and courageous character will be a potentially infinite producer of happiness. And in this infinity of the cause lies hidden the secret of its superiority to any and all of its effects" (*The Ways of Things* [New York: Prentice-Hall, 1940], pp. 594-595).

Extending such a line of thought, Arthur Lovejoy defends an ethics that emphasizes personal goodness as opposed to an ethics of the impersonal nature of the good. We may weigh what Lovejoy says when he declares: "We admire or despise *persons* as agents, not the ends which their acts accomplish; and we admire them because of what they *are*, what types of thoughts and feelings are present in them, and what motives prompt their acts" ([11:2], Lecture 8, p. 253).

**19:6:** Sidgwick [8:1], p. 382. See Bentham [19.8], Chapter 4.

**19:7:** See Mary P. Mack, *Jeremy Bentham: An Odyssey of Ideas* (New York: Columbia University Press, 1962). On legal philosophy, Joseph V. Dolan's chapter, **"Relocating Justice,"** is an excellent attack on legal positivism and the detachment of law from morals (in *The Value of Justice*, edited by Charles A. Kelbley (New York: Fordham University Press, 1979), Chapter 5.

**19:8:** Jeremy Bentham, *Introduction to the Principles of Morals and Legislation* (1823), Chapter 4; Chapter 14, Section 28.

**19:9:** Economic theory has already gone through a phase of development parallel to the previously discussed distinction between bare value and hedonic value. Economics and ethics have even shared the word "utility" in the senses of subjective or hedonic value (see H. Stanley Jevons, *Essays on Economics* London: Macmillan & Co., 1905], *passim*.) But the English economist Alfred Marshall, among others, is uneasy about this identification (*Principles of Economics*, ninth edition [London: Macmillan & Co., 1961, first edition was 1890], Volume 1, pp. 17n, 92n, 93n, etc.) Theoretical economists find that they need to free themselves from problems of psychology in order to get on with their work. Thus, they have parsimoniously come to replace hedonic value with scales of ranked choices, or "directions of indifference" on charts that show the economic choices to be preferred. In this way, no hedonic quality of various choices need be assumed (see J. R. Hicks and R. G. D. Allen, *Economica* n.s.v. 1 [1934]: 52-76, 196-219, especially pp. 52-55).

This purified meaning of value has become for economists what bare value has been in the present discussion. Though the only ultimate conceivable rational motivation for acquiring what money can buy is that someone enjoy what is bought, this is a matter for psychology etc., not for economics.

**19:10:** John Stuart Mill, *Utilitarianism* (first published 1861), Chapter 2.

**19:11:** Exodus 20:13: Deuteronomy 5:17.

**19:12:** Bernard Bosanquet, *Science and Philosophy and Other Essays* (London: George Allen & Unwin, 1927), "Hedonism among Idealists," at pp. 199-200. See Lewis [17:17], Chapter 16. Another interesting critique of utilitarianism is that of Bryan G. Norton, *Why Preserve Natural Variety?* (Princeton: Princeton University Press, 1987), pp. 6-14.

**19:13:** A. P. Brogan in *International Journal of Ethics* 41 (1931): 287-295. Adam Smith comments on the "never-failing certainty with which all men, sooner or later, accomodate themselves to whatever becomes their permanent situation" ([11:10], Part 3, Chapter 3; compare Part 1, Section 3).

**19:14:** Philip Brickman, Dan Coates, and Ronnie Janoff-Bulman, "Lottery Winners and Accident Victims: Is Happiness Relative?" *Journal of Personality and Social Psychology* 36 (1978): 917-927. The concept of happiness gains stature when its temporal variations can be correlated with repeatable happenings.

**19:15:** Moore [18:5], e.g., p. 13. See "Ethical Naturalism" by Jonathan Harrison in [16:11].

**19:16:** See W. C. Allee, *Cooperation Among Animals* (New York: Henry Schuman, 1951). On sociobiology and E. O. Wilson's book of that title, see criticism in *Sociobiology Examined*, edited by Ashley Montagu (New York: Oxford University Press, 1980). Wilson claims that it is time for the subject of ethics to be taken from philosophy and delivered over to biology, so far following Darwin in *The Descent of Man*, Chapter 4. Michael Ruse supports a view like Wilson's in *Taking Darwin Seriously* (Oxford: Basil Blackwell, 1986). Gunther S. Stent, though no friend of anti-evolutionists, criticizes the "hyperevolutionism" of his less astute colleagues for giving leave to sociobiology and other misapplications of Darwinism (Montagu [4:14], pp. 136-141). For a balanced general view see Holmes Rolston III, *Philosophy Gone Wild* [4:14], e.g., Chapter 2. Friedrich A. Hayek presents a profound critique, "The Three Sources of Human Values," in [2:28], Volume 3, pp. 153-176. Hayek, an agnostic, affirms his profound respect for the role of the main monotheisms in sustaining beneficial customs (*The Fatal Conceit: The Errors of Socialism* [Chicago: University of Chicago Press, 1988], Chapter 9).

**19:17:** F. F. Centore, "God Against God: Theism in a Scientific Age," unpublished book manuscript, 1990. Short of the bypass of the naturalistic fallacy put forth in the present work, one is left with P. B. Rice's attempt to live with it; see [18:3], pp. 180-181.

**19:18:** Schweitzer, [1:11], p. 225-226 (151), 161 (82), 158 (78-79). The word "Widerspruch," translated as "contradiction," is here rendered as "paradox," since it does not appear that Schweitzer meant to imply an absolute contradiction.

**19:19:** See any Biblical concordance, or see Nehemiah 8:10; Psalms 16:11, 37:4, 144:15 (Catholic 15:11), 36:4, 143:15); Isaiah 40:31; Matthew 5, 7:2, 10:28, 17:52, 26:29; Luke 6:38; John 10:10, 15:11, 17:13; Romans 14:17, 15:13; Galatians 5:22; Philippians 4:4-7.

**19:20:** Charles Hartshorne in a lecture, c. 1967.

**19:21:** Yancey [5:21].

**19:22:** Democritus, in John M. Robinson, *An Introduction to Early Greek Philosophy* (Boston: Houghton Mifflin Co., 1968), p. 234. See Plato (who lived later), *Gorgias*, 527-529, 478, 469 ff.; *Apology* 32, 30.

**19:23:** See Herbert Fingarette, *Self-Deception* (London: Routledge & Kegan Paul, 1969) and *Heavy Drinking* (Berkeley: University of California Press, 1988).

**19:24:** Augustine, *On Psalm 32*, Sermon 3, 15-16; from *The Essential Augustine*, second edition, edited by Vernon J. Bourke (Indianapolis: Hackett Publishing Co., 1974), Chapter 7, pp. 151-153, or from *Ancient Christian Writers*, edited by J. Quasten et al. (Westminster, Maryland: Newman Press, 1946-1961), Volume 30, pp. 130-133.

# 20. Cultivation of Morality

**First epigraph:** Glenn Tinder, "Can We Be Good Without God?" *Atlantic Monthly,* December 1989, pp. 69-85, at p. 82.

**Second epigraph:** (David) Elton Trueblood, *The Predicament of Modern Man* (New York: Harper & Brothers, 1944), pp. 59-60; reprinted in Trueblood's *While It Is Day* (New York: Harper & Row, 1974), p. 69.

**20:1:** George Will, "Learning from the Giants," *Newsweek,* September 14, 1987, p. 96. For evidence of moral moronity in a business school see Amitai Etzioni, *Newsweek,* September 18, 1989, p. 10.

**20:2:** Lawrence Kohlberg, *Journal of Philosophy* 70 (1973): 630-646, at p. 642.

**20:3:** Kohlberg, *The Philosophy of Moral Development* (San Francisco: Harper & Row, 1981), p. 100.

**20:4:** Ibid., p. 304. In a book about ethics, one may challenge the tired myth that the way the U.S.S.R. has heretofore been organized results in moral superiority. See Konstantin Simis, *U.S.S.R., The Corrupt Society: The Secret World of Soviet Capitalism* (New York: Simon & Schuster, 1982); Eric Hoffer, *In Our Time* (New York: Harper & Row, 1976), p. 93. In a light vein see Vladimir Voinovich, *The Anti-Soviet Soviet Union* (San Diego: Harcourt Brace Jovanovich, 1986). Yet the problem of truthfulness is not to be identified simply with Communism; Russia's long history of despotism is relevant — even collectivism since Peter the Great.

**20:5:** Ibid., p. 304. Kohlberg features the ethical thought of John Dewey, Spinoza, R. M. Hare, and S. Toulmin. In ethics, these men appear to be either hopelessly confused or else pale to the point of triviality. See the article "Moral Development" by Martin L. Hoffman, in *Carmichael's Manual of Child Psychology,* third edition, edited by Paul H. Mussen, 2 volumes (New York: John Wiley & Sons, 1970), Volume 2, pp. 261-359, notably at pp. 276-282. See Richard S. Peters in *Phi Delta Kappan* 56 (1975): 678.

**20:6:** Hugh Hartshorne and M.A. May, *Studies in the Nature of Character* (New York: Macmillan Co., 1928), Volume I: *Studies in Deceit,* e.g., Chapter 19, pp. 254-255; see index therein under "Religious affiliation"; "Sunday schools." See also Robert J. Ritzema in *Journal of Psychology and Theology* 7 (1979): 105-113.

**20:7:** See Thomas W. Laqueur, *Religion and Respectability: Sunday Schools and English Working-class Culture, 1780-1850* (New Haven: Yale University Press, 1976), e.g., the conclusions. See Alexis de Tocqueville, *Democracy in America* [6:23]. Those exposed to conventional American Sunday schools in the 1930s and early 1940s can vouch for some effective indoctrination in the early years but also for a gaping lack of intellectual content, which drove off much of the teenage population.

**20:8:** See Ronald Duska and Mariellen Whelan, *Moral Development: A Guide to Piaget and Kohlberg* (New York: Paulist Press, 1975), e.g., pp. 75 ff. This book is a valuable introduction, though at points too deferential to Kohlberg. More negatively, see Paul Vitz in **Whose Values?** edited by Carl Horn (Ann Arbor: Servant Books, 1985), pp. 113-138. See Donna Steichen in *Fidelity,* November 1987, pp. 32-42, where we learn of Kohlberg's suicide under circumstances of "horrifying isolation."

Carol Gilligan, in her book *In a Different Voice: Psychological Theory and Women's Development,* suggests that Kohlberg's categorization needs correction at his levels five and six. The problem is illustrated as a tendency of the responses of girls to moral dilemmas to be relatively subtle, searching, and responsible while being less legalistic and rights-oriented than those of boys. The girls' responses tend not to fit Kohlberg's criteria. Some psychological theory and testing is shown to be inherently biased, to the disadvantage of women (Cambridge: Harvard University Press, 1982). To us, some of the difference seems new in our culture and may be due to the decline of Judeo-Christian faith and education. In complex cases at law, the deepest reasoning of male judges has been broader than merely legalistic.

**20:9:** Kohlberg [20:3], p. 187.

**20:10:** See William P. Alston, in *Cognitive Development and Epistemology*, edited by T. Mischel (New York: Academic Press, 1971), pp. 269-284, especially 276-277.

**20:11:** For Judaic ethics see Meyer Waxman, *Judaism: Religion and Ethics* (New York: 1958), pp. 220 *et passim*.

**20:12.** Christopher Dawson, *Progress and Religion* [10:6], Chapter 8, "The Secularization of Western Culture," paragraph 24. Like other books of Dawson, this one belongs in every library.

**20:13.** Dawson, *The Historic Reality of Christian Culture* (New York: Harper & Brothers, 1960), pp. 70, 92, 97. As a confirmation of the "flywheel" or cultural inertia thesis, see Perry London, "The Rescuers: Motivational Hypotheses about Christians who Saved Jews from the Nazis," in Macaulay [18:2], pp. 241-250. London notes that the rescuers tended to have very strong identification with parents who, while not necessarily religious, "had firm opinions on moral issues and (most important) who served as active models of moral conduct." Corroboration (and much more) appears in the important work *The Altruistic Personality* by Samuel P. and Pearl M. Oliner (New York: Free Press, 1988), especially Chapters 10, 6, and 7.

**20:14:** Herbert Schlossberg in *American Spectator*, September 1987, pp. 44-45.

**20:15:** Popper [2:22], (Princeton: Princeton University Press, 1962), Chapter 16.

**20:16:** Alfred North Whitehead, *Science and the Modern World* (New York: Macmillan Co., 1925), Chapter 12.

**20:17:** On churches and theological method see Peirce [1:2], 6.435-6.451, 5.537-5.546. Some churches, some congregations are more receptive to new ideas than are others. Along this line, an interesting pamphlet is *The Evolutionary Potential of Quakerism*, by Kenneth Boulding (Wallingford, Pennsylvania: Pendle Hill Publications, 1964).

**20:18:** Your authors do not read Chinese but suspect that the ethically oriented books for young readers as still used in Taiwan or Korea will repay close attention, as will the readers of William Holmes McGuffey in America (1836+). As to ethics textbooks, the American philosopher John Hospers is at his best in discussing ethical dilemmas in *Human Conduct*, second edition (New York: Harcourt Brace Jovanovich, 1982). The book is superior in its way, but his treatments of hedonic motivation and utilitarianism are not pushed far enough to arrive at acceptable answers. Moreover, his understanding of religion is minimal.

Vernon J. Bourke in his *Ethics* codifies the ethics of Thomas Aquinas, which is still very much a part of live Western culture (New York: Macmillan Co., 1966). See also Thomas Aquinas *On Law, Morality, and Politics* (Indianapolis: Hackett Publishing Co., 1988); *Tour of the Summa*, by Paul J. Glenn (St. Louis: Herder Book Co., 1960). *The Principles of Moral and Political Philosophy* by the eighteenth-century English cleric William Paley is a practical textbook, inspired in large part by John Gay and Abraham Tucker. In places it is dated, but it was an important constructive book in shaping culture (Houston: St. Thomas Press, 1977).

*Shakespeare's Portrayal of the Moral Life* by Frank Chapman Sharp is rewarding reading (New York: C. Scribner's Sons, 1902), as well as Albert Schweitzer's early sermons, published posthumously: *A Place for Revelation* (New York: Macmillan Publishing Co., 1988, translated from *Was sollen wir tun?* [1986] — not well titled either time). Three of John Wesley's sermons, "The Cure of Evil-Speaking," "The Good Steward," and "The Use of Money" are worth agonizing over. Alasdair MacIntyre presents helpful historical insights in *A Short History of Ethics*, though after the seventeenth century, his interpretations diverge sharply from the present ones (New York: Macmillan Co., 1966). Like most philosophers, he misses the positive essence of Judeo-Christian motivation.

*America's Steadfast Dream* by E. Merrill Root presents a vision of the world which the author finds that humankind enjoyed in a nobler time. For its superb eloquence and for its sensitivity to the problems of youth, one may overlook its occasional shrillness (Boston: Western Islands, 1971). A fine book is *The Intellectuals Speak Out about God* [13:32]. The impassioned eloquence of George Roche in *A World Without Heroes: The Modern Tragedy* should be in every young person's library (Hillsdale, Michigan: Hillsdale College Press, 1987). Churches often publish books for the practical guidance of their youth. While the books of Paul H. Dunn are oriented to Mormons, their sensitivity and readability recommend them to a wider audience.

The French sociologist Emile Durkheim, though not a theist, writes helpfully of *Moral Education* with particular reference to practical psychology and discipline (New York: Free Press of Glencoe, 1961; the lectures were delivered at the Sorbonne in 1902-1903). For a review of psychological literature on altruism to 1969 see Dennis L. Krebs in *Psychological Bulletin* 73 (1970): 258-302. As an aside on the cultivation of young genius, see Harold G. McCurdy, "The Childhood Pattern of Genius," *Journal of the Elisha Mitchell Society* 73 (1957): 448-462. Whatever the value of peer association among youngsters, superior intellect appears to be cultivated by early and prolonged association with elders. A book by our esteemed cartoonist, Bob Thaves, must be mentioned as raising ethical points: *Are We There Yet? A Frank and Ernest History of the World* (New York: Topper Books, 1988).

Some of the best ethical poetry since Thomas Gray is in *Sonnets of the Interior Life* by Kenneth Boulding (Boulder: Colorado Associated Universities Press, 1975).

There is no purpose here to explore "love in trifles" — i.e., manners — in detail. Yet a classic for youngsters is *Goops and How to Be Them: A Manual of Manners for Polite Infants*, by Gelett Burgess (New York, 1900). The cartoons of Jimmy Hatlo, a daily series that appeared in American newspapers in mid-century under the title, "They'll Do It Every Time," is a light-hearted school of manners, depicting situations not mentioned in books of etiquette. For listing of his books, see the *National Union Catalog* for the years 1939 to 1962.

**20:19:** An important reason for the mentally agile to study the history of philosophy is to provide strengthening exercise, so long as the students know what is not to be expected therein and when they should leave. The instant efficiency of vision is denied to humans when they study philosophy. Since the human being is constrained to explore philosophy with only his hands, his ears, and his nose as it were, the exercise of searching is of importance. However, our acid remarks about some philosophers should be tempered by a reading of the commentaries of Hartshorne. He has the happy faculty of quickly empathizing with other philosophers and patiently obtaining the best from them, even those with whom he has profound disagreements. See his *Creativity in American Philosophy* (Albany: State University of New York Press, 1984) and *Insights and Oversights of Great Thinkers* (Albany: State University of New York Press, 1983).

**20:20:** Ethical nihilism takes many forms. Among others see Ludwig Wittgenstein, *Tractatus Logico-Philosophicus* (New York: Harcourt, Brace & Co., 1922), pp. 144-147 (6.41-6.43), 183-184 (6.422); Rudolf Carnap, *The Logical Syntax of Language* (London: Kegan Paul, Trench, Trübner & Co., 1937), p. 279; Albert Camus, *The Myth of Sisyphus* (New York: Alfred A. Knopf, 1955); Alfred J. Ayer, *Language, Truth and Logic*, second edition (London: Victor Gollancz, 1946), e.g., Introduction and Chapter 6; Charles Stevenson, *Ethics and Language* (New Haven: Yale University Press, 1944); Bertrand Russell, *What I Believe* (New York: E. P. Dutton & Co., 1925), p. 29; *The Scientific Outlook* (New York: W. W. Norton & Co., 1931), p. 266; *Religion and Science* (New York: Henry Holt & Co., 1935), pp. 235-243, especially p. 237. For an excellent critique of "emotivism" in ethics see Brand Blanshard, *Reason and Goodness* [1:5].

Hector Hawton, a humanist, discusses existentialism and other modern forms of irrationalism in *The Feast of Unreason* (London: Watts & Co., 1952). The existentialist enterprise of Martin Heidegger (and, by extension, the anti-philosophical deconstructionism of Jacques Derrida) is presented with uncommon clarity and brevity in *The New Gnosis* by Roberts Avens (Dallas: Spring Publications, 1984), e.g., pp. 1-9, 102-103: "The point is to persevere in emptiness, to live without Why." José Ferrater Mora finds some reason to call Wittgenstein the "Anti-Socrates," in *Philosophy and Phenomenological Research* 14 (1953): 89-96. Dean Turner in *The Autonomous Man* undercuts fashionable ethical nihilism (St. Louis: Bethany Press, 1970). Finally, see the philosopher Harry Frankfort, "Reflections on Bull——," *Harper's Magazine*, February 1987, pp. 14-17. One remembers a radio program of the 1950s, "Duffy's Tavern." One night Duffy announced ironically: "If ya got anything to say, shuddup."

It is more than possible that the voluminous texts of Nietzsche, Hegel, Hume, and even Kant are, on balance, a waste of precious time to read at length. Hume and Nietzsche are of course atheists. Kant and Hegel might as well be. Hegel is best described as a sophisticated poet of ideas. All are worse than amateurs in natural science. These points are developed by Father Jaki. The pedagogical value of Kant is defended by John Lavely in "Personalism's Debt to Kant," in [7:10], pp. 23-37. Kant was better at identifying problems than in devising solutions. On Hegel see Popper [2:22], Chapter 12.

See Russell Kirk, editor, *The Assault on Religion* (University Press of America and the Center for Judicial Studies, 1986). Most prominent American publishers will no longer publish books in which theistic religion is taken seriously, even by way of brief references.

For its ethically relevant content, psychology is best studied by searching *Psychological Abstracts* or its electronic equivalent *PsycInfo*. Typical course offerings miss too much. A little knowledge of statistics is required to understand the articles.

**20:21:** Jaki [3:33], p. 305. By and large, colleges at the present time teach more atheism than theism, more socialism than freedom of enterprise, and more moral relativism than useful ethics.

Compare G. K. Chesterton:

We deny the snobbish English assumption that the uneducated are the dangerous criminals. We say that the dangerous criminal is the educated criminal. We say that the most dangerous criminal now is the entirely lawless modern philosopher. Compared to him, burglars and bigamists are essentially moral men; my heart goes out to them. They accept the essential ideal of man; they merely seek it wrongly ([14:8], p. 78).

**20:22:** Colossians 2:8, also 1 Timothy 6:20. In the context, the Greek word *philosophias* means the same as "philosophy" does now.

**20:23:** William Hazlitt, in the introduction to the abridgment of *The Light of Nature Pursued*, by Abraham Tucker (London, 1807), p. xl.

**20:24:** Arthur O. Lovejoy, *Nation* 89 (1909): 298-301, at p. 300. See Plato, *Republic*, Book 6, 495. On the methods of tyranny see Aristotle, *Politics*, Book 5, Section 11, also Payne [18:8], e.g. pp. 380-391, 421-431, 492-493, 690-691. On philosophical education see Stephen C. Pepper in *Journal of Philosophy* 41 (1944): 722-724.

**20:25:** Limiting the basic insight of monotheism to Western civilization turns out to be too narrow. For evidence of the great spiritual and ethical importance of the traditional monothism of preliterate Africa see e.g. E. Bolaji Idowu, the Introduction and Chapter 1 in *Biblical Revelation and African Beliefs*, edited by Kwesi A. Dickson and Paul Ellingworth (London: Lutterworth Press, 1969); also John S. Mbiti, *African Religions and Philosophy* (New York: Frederick A. Praeger, 1969), e.g., Chapters 4, 5 and 6. Of course, there have been superstitions, but Africa has had no monopoly on those.

**20:26:** Bertrand Russell, *Why I Am Not a Christian* (New York: Simon & Schuster, 1957), p. 22 *et passim*. A devastating critique of Russell's philosophy of religion is that of Edgar Sheffield Brightman, in *The Philosophy of Bertrand Russell*, edited by Paul A. Schilpp (Evanston, Illinois: Library of Living Philosophers, 1951), pp. 539-556; see also pp. 719-727.

**20:27:** *The Autobiography of Bertrand Russell*, 3 volumes (New York: Simon & Schuster, 1969), Volume 3, pp. 84-85.

**20:28:** Bertrand Russell, in Stanley L. Jaki [3:3], p. 411.

**20:29:** Stanley L. Jaki, *Angels, Apes, and Men* [4:14], p. 57.

**20:30:** See Andrew Chih, *Chinese Humanism: A Religion Beyond Religion* (Taipei: Fu Jen Catholic University Press [Hsin-Chuang, Taipei Hsien 242, Taiwan], 1981). The bibliography is extensive. In *Christianity and Chinese Religions*, Hans Küng and Julia Ching hold that the existing Chinese religious system is equal in value to Christianity. This claim holds no water; nevertheless, the West has much to learn from the Chinese, and there is value in the book (New York: Doubleday, 1989). Devout Catholics in particular may be offended; Küng would be better placed in liberal Protestantism. Also see [10:18].

**20:31:** On the societal importance of symbols see *Emotion as the Basis of Civilization*, by John Hopkins Denison (New York: Charles Scribner's Sons, 1928), even though Denison's emphasis on emotion misses much. James Bissett Pratt helpfully discusses the role of symbols in religion

in *Eternal Values in Religion* (New York: Macmillan Co., 1950). The nineteenth-century English poet Alfred Lord Tennyson was concerned in *Idylls of the King* about why civilizations decay; for enlightening discussions see Clyde De L. Ryals in *ELH* 30 (1963): 53-69; Joseph Solimine Jr. in the *Personalist* 50 (1969): 105-116.

A relative has claimed to observe that the influential, visibly successful people of our time tend to be those who intensely pursue athletic activities or physical achievement. The reason for this situation, if it is true, may be that the more reflective persons have more sorely felt the lack of a viable worldview but have not found one they can accept and are thereby hobbled. The physically active ones put aside the nagging, time-consuming search for meaning by substituting vigorous outward activity. Hazelett notes that his friends from the 1930s and '40s who were most like him have not done well, if indeed they survived. The seeming predominance of physically achieving types, as opposed to reflective types, may be an artifact of the times.

**20:32:** William Graham Sumner, *Folkways* (Boston: Ginn & Co., 1906), p. 2.

**20:33:** Stephen C. Pepper, "Observations on Value from an Analysis of a Simple Appetition," in *Value: A Cooperative Inquiry*, p. 258. See Rice [17:20], pp. 286: [18:3], p. 208.

**20:34:** O. H. Mowrer, **"The Law of Effect and Ego Psychology,"** in *Psychological Review* 53 (1946): 321-334, at p. 324.

**Epigraph:** Albert Schweitzer, *Philosophy of Civilization* [1:11], p. 315 (46).

# 21. Homiletic Epilogue

**Epigraph:** Caleb T. Winchester (1847-1920), *The Methodist Hymnal* (Nashville: Methodist Publishing House, 1966), Hymn 346.

**21:1:** See Peirce [1:2], 5.520.

**21:2:** Colossians 1:17, Revised Standard Version, emphasis added. Compare Ecclesiasticus (Sirach or Ben Sira) 43:26 or :28.

**21:3:** William Ernest Hocking, *Living*

*Religions* [10:32], p. 237n (a valuable ecumenical book). See also Hocking, *The Meaning of God in Human Experience* (New Haven: Yale University Press, 1912), Chapter 23.

**21:4:** Andrew Martin Fairbairn, *The Philosophy of the Christian Religion* (New York: Macmillan Co., 1902); *The Place of Christ in Modern Theology*—a superior Christology (New York: Charles Scribner's Sons, 1893). Fairbairn was a Gifford lecturer in 1891-1893. Attention may have been taken from Fairbairn by Schweitzer, whose first book on the historical Jesus appeared in 1906. Fairbairn writes as an Anglican.

**21:5:** Charles Finney, "The Excuses of Sinners," reprinted in *God's Love for a Sinning World* (Grand Rapids: Kregel Publications, 1966). See 1 Corinthians 10:31. Finney insists on strict ethical accountability. He avoids Jonathan Edwards' error of denial of freedom of the will. Finney denies the popular doctrine of personal predestination to heaven or hell, as well as the doctrine of God's granting in His own good time the "grace" to stop sinning. Finney, a disciple of Edwards, is said to have been the most successful evangelist ever, in terms of the numbers of people directly influenced. He became president of Oberlin College. One of your authors graduated from Oberlin without ever being told who Finney was. Though Finney is now all but forgotten, we must regard him and Edwards as among the great contributors to Western civilization.

**21:6:** This passage is in the Gloria recital of the Eucharist service. This work of Bach, a Lutheran, is his contribution to the reuniting of Christendom. To hear it is to believe.

On ritual hear Tocqueville: "I believe firmly in the need for external ceremonies. I know that they fix the human spirit in the contemplation of abstract truths and help it to grasp them firmly and believe ardently in them" [6:23].

**21:7:** Compare Romans 16:27. See *J. S. Bach*, by Albert Schweitzer, 2 volumes (London: A. & C. Black, 1923), Volume 1, pp. 166-167. Chapter 19 (Volume 2) and some following chapters afford superior

insight into musical esthetics. Bach's consistent dedication to the organizing and reforming of church music for Christendom is discussed by Jaroslav Pelikan in *Bach Among the Theologians* (Philadelphia: Fortress Press, 1986) and by Leo Schrade in *Journal of the History of Ideas* 7 (1946): 151-194. Bach has been well called "the fifth Evangelist" (Pelikan, *Jesus through the Centuries* [New Haven: Yale University Press, 1985], p. 163). A good brief story on Bach, by Alan Rich with Katrine Ames, appears in *Newsweek*, December 24, 1984, pp. 54-60. The potential of this sort of music as a binding force in civilization is generally underestimated. The taste for fine music is undoubtedly best implanted in the very young or, for all we know, before birth.

**21:8:** Finney [19:3]; Hartshorne [16:16], p. 310; Hartshorne, *Whitehead's Philosophy: Selected Essays* (Lincoln: University of Nebraska Press, 1972), pp. 106-108; Jonathan Edwards, *Concerning the End for Which God Created the World*, Chapter 1, Section 4.

**21:9:** See Paul C. Vitz in his article "The Psychology of Atheism: The Theory of the Defective Father," *Truth* (Dallas), reprinted in *Fidelity* (South Bend), March 1986, pp. 29-36.

**21:10:** Schweitzer [1:11], "The Ethic of Reverence for Life," p. 321 (253). The word "glücklich" was translated therein as "happy" but is here rendered as "fortunate."

**21:11:** 1 Corinthians 15:33.

**21:12:** Varied motives of modern liberals are delineated by Paul Hollander in the concluding chapter of *Political Pilgrims* (London: Oxford University Press, 1981).

*At a minimum*, the person who would be informed should read *AIM*, the economical, twice-monthly Accuracy in Media newsletter of Reed Irvine; it brings to light breath-taking American media distortions (Suite 1150, 1275 K St. N.W., Washington D.C. 20005). There are many books on the American news media including those of Irvine, Edith Efron, Ben H. Bagdikian, and S. Robert Lichter et al.

The *Wall Street Journal* is probably the most ethically oriented source of commentary among the standard daily media, even with its natural preponderance of business and financial news. From here, there are several ways to go. A left-leaning, religious-oriented journal that strives for balance is *The Other Side* (Philadelphia).

The following journals tend mostly rightward. The *National Review, American Spectator, Imprimis, Chronicles* (Rockford), *Fidelity* (South Bend), *Crisis* (Notre Dame), *St. Croix Review* (a good family publication), *Insight* (Washington), *Policy Review,* and *Reason* all have worthwhile articles. Those who can bear a seemingly endless deluge of neglected but important bad news may read the *Daily News Digest,* a weekly newsletter edited by W. A. Johnson (Phoenix: Research Publications). Most right-wing publications are better at reporting problems than in finding much hope of their proposed solutions coming to pass. The right wing of the general public seems to err mainly toward complacency and narrowness.

In general, one may well keep track of, or search back to, such names as Raymond Aron, Arnold Beichman, Raoul Berger, Tom Bethell, Richard Brookhiser, William F. Buckley Jr., James Burnham, John Chamberlain, Robert Conquest, Brian Crozier, Dinesh D'Souza, Thomas Fleming, Milton Friedman, Benjamin Hart, Jeffrey Hart, Hans-Hermann Hoppe, Russell Kirk, Ludwig von Mises, Malcolm Muggeridge, Gary North, Michael Novak, George Roche, Momcilo Silic, Joseph Sobran, Alan Stang, R. Emmett Tyrrell Jr., Jude Wanniski, Walter Williams, and Karl A. Wittfogel. This list adds to authors mentioned elsewhere herein and *many* unmentioned worthies. One must select from large libraries, since scholarly books are hardly to be found in bookstores and only partially in book clubs. Yet the Conservative Book Club is worth looking into (15 Oakland Drive, Harrison, New York 10528), as well as the Cato Institute (224 Second St. S.E., Washington, D.C. 20003). Further, contact the Ethics and Public Policy Center (1030 Fifteenth St. N.W., Washington, D.C. 20005). The reader may well consider "adopting"

a school library and stocking it.

The way we as a society are going has been trod before; see Thucydides, *The Peloponnesian Wars.* This is long, so first one may wish to see selections in *Greek Literature in Translation,* edited by Whitney J. Oates (New York: Longmans, Green & Co., 1944). Thucydides' rendition of the "Funeral Oration of Pericles" should be part of everyone's education (pp. 757-762 or 2:35-46).

One's sleep will not be aided by *America the Vulnerable: The Threat of Chemical/ Biological Warfare,* by Joseph D. Douglass Jr. and Neil C. Livingstone (Lexington, Massachusetts: D. C. Heath & Co., 1987).

**21:13:** Israel W. Durham, quoted in *The Autobiography of Lincoln Steffens* (New York: Harcourt, Brace & Co., 1931), p. 412. See the important book of Jean-François Revel, *How Democracies Perish* (Garden City, New York: Doubleday, 1984).

**21:14:** Albert Schweitzer, *On the Edge of the Primeval Forest* (London: A. & C. Black, 1922, pp. 167, 155. Reprinted (New York: Macmillan Publishing Co., 1956), pp. 112, 104.

**21:15:** Schweitzer, *Christianity and the Religions of the World* (London: George Allen & Unwin, 1923), p. 53. Of many spiritually oriented commentaries on the life of Jesus, two come to mind: *The Humor of Christ,* by D. Elton Trueblood (New York: Harper & Row, 1964), and the monumental *Life and Times of Jesus the Messiah,* by Alfred Edersheim (London, 1883; reprinted at Grand Rapids, Michigan: Wm. B. Eerdmans Publishing Co., 1971).

**21:16:** Frank C. Laubach: *Wake Up or Blow Up* (Westwood, New Jersey: Fleming H. Revell Co., 1951); Laubach, *Thirty Years with the Silent Billion* (Westwood, New Jersey, Fleming H. Revell Co., 1960). The book *Motivating Economic Achievement,* by David C. McClelland and David G. Winter, while not specifically religious, is of interest regarding the Third World (New York: Free Press, 1971).

On the dignity of lowly labor see Vermont Royster in *Wall Street Journal,* April 18, 1979, p. 24; T. (Thomas) V. Smith, *The Democratic Way of Life* (Chicago: University of Chicago Press, 1926), Chapter 5; Douglas V. Steere, *Work and Contemplation* (New York: Harper & Brothers, 1957). A "philosophic illumination of pride in craftsmanship" is a good description of the book *The Existential Pleasures of Engineering,* by Samuel C. Florman (New York: St. Martin's Press, 1976). Most recently is the book of Charles Murray, *In Pursuit of Happiness* (New York: Simon & Schuster, 1988). Murray relates happiness to self-esteem and to pride in one's work, showing why some well-intended governmental programs actually decrease the happiness and wealth of those ostensibly helped.

**21:17:** Laubach, *Silent Billion* [21:16], p. 16.

**21:18:** Matthew 6:33.

**21:19:** The oft-alleged relation of crime to high intelligence is reversed in an article by Abbie F. Salny in *Mensa Journal,* June 1988, pp. 10-11.

**21:20:** Amos 8:11-13, Isaiah 40:31, New English Bible.

**21:21:** Libretto by Adelheid Wette, in the opera *Hänsel und Gretel* by Engelbert Humperdinck (1854-1921).

**21:22:** Katharine Lee Bates, "America the Beautiful," a hymn written right after a trip up Pikes Peak in Colorado. She describes well the view from the top.

**21:23:** Jonathan Edwards, *A History of the Work of Redemption,* Period 3, Part 8, Sections 5 and 6, in any edition of Edwards' *Works.*

**21:24:** Jonathan Edwards, *A Humble Attempt to Promote Explicit Agreement and Visible Union of God's People in Extraordinary Prayer,* Part 2, Section 2, in any edition of Edwards' *Works.* This quotation and the previous one were found in Roland André Delattre's *Beauty and Sensibility in the Thought of Jonathan Edwards* (New Haven: Yale University Press, 1968), p. 210. Compare Habakkuk 2:14: "The earth shall be filled with the knowledge of the glory of the Lord, as the waters cover the sea."

To Edwards, beauty is pre-eminent among the divine perfections. This crowning aspect of God's being as seen by Edwards — His beauty — is presented by Sang Hyun Lee in *The Philosophical Theology of Jonathan Edwards* (Princeton: Princeton University Press, 1988). A short description of this aspect of Edwards' thought is "Beauty and Theology," by Roland André Delattre in *Soundings* 51 (1968): 60-79, reprinted in *Critical Essays on Jonathan Edwards,* edited by William J. Scheick (Boston: G. K. Hall & Co., 1980), pp. 136-150.

God is beautiful in His "awful greatness," as "the infinite Fountain of Good," as "the foundation and fountain of all being and all beauty," and in His "divine, transcendent, supreme glory." To speak as Edwards does of beauty in connection with theology puts one in mind of William James' footnote on the hypothetical "automatic sweetheart." This "soulless body" should be "absolutely indistinguishable from a spiritually animated maiden, laughing, talking, blushing, nursing us, and performing all feminine offices as tactfully and sweetly as if a soul were in her." James implies that a man knowing that this body was soulless would not respond to it with any more dedication or affection than might an atheist respond to a universe taken to be soulless ("The Pragmatist Account of Truth and Its Misunderstanders," second footnote, in *The Meaning of Truth* [New York: Longmans, Green & Co., 1909], pp. 189-190).

**21:25:** "Kids Can't Take Another Decade Like the '80s," by Joan Beck, *Denver Post,* January 14, 1990, editorial page.

**21:26:** Calvin Coolidge as president of the Massachusetts Senate pleaded to the senators, "Be brief. Above all, be brief" (Paul Johnson, *Modern Times* [2:10], p. 220). John Silber proposes a Constitutional amendment forbidding anyone admitted to the bar to serve as legislators (except as existing incumbents) or as directors of regulatory departments (*Straight Shooting* [New York: Harper & Row, 1989], p. 241).

**21:27:** Malcolm Muggeridge, *Jesus: The Man Who Lives* (New York: Harper & Row, 1975), p. 71.

**21:28:** Pitirim A. Sorokin tells further how widespread calamities "split up the bulk of the population — which in normal times is neither very sinful nor very saintly — into three different groups: first, the moral heroes and intensely religious persons; second, the morally debased and irreligious; third, the remnants of the previous more or less balanced majority" (*Man and Society in Calamity* [New York: W. W. Norton Co., 1942], pp. 226, 161). Sorokin shows in his *Social and Cultural Dynamics* that historical periods of "ideational" emphasis as opposed to "sensate" emphasis are clearly distinguishable by several objective measures; see e.g. the revised and abridged edition (Boston: Peter Sargent, 1957). Many Westerners now alive know something of both modes of civilization.

Whether or not one regards the Book of Mormon as a history of pre-Columbian North America, it may be regarded as an essentially truthful literary depiction of cycles of civilization, strongly echoing the ethical cause-and-effect messages of the Old Testament or Judaic scriptures. The historian Hugh Nibley argues persuasively for its cogence in "Last Call" (*Sunstone* [Salt Lake City], January 1988, pp. 14-25). Much of the relevant material is in Alma, a book of the Book of Mormon.

To get some idea of what the nadir of human group existence is, see Colin Turnbull, *The Mountain People* (New York: Simon & Schuster, 1973).

**21:29:** Peter F. Drucker, *The End of Economic Man: The Origins of Totalitarianism* (New York: John Day Co., 1939), pp. 109, 236, 237. Chapter 4, "The Failure of the Christian Churches," and the latter third of Chapter 7 are profoundly important.

# *Annex. The Answer to David Hume*

**Ann:1.** David Hume, *A Treatise of Human Nature*, Book 3, Section 1, Part 1. R. M. Hare, *Language of Morals*, pp. 28, 91-93 *et passim* [Annex:17]; P. H. Nowell-Smith, *Ethics* (Harmondsworth, England: Penguin Books, 1954), pp. 180-182.

**Ann:2.** Lewis [17:17], p. 481.

**Ann:3.** Ibid., pp. 479-484. Lewis [9:35], p. 86. In place of the term "hoof-in-mouth contradiction" herein, Lewis speaks of "pragmatic contradiction."

**Ann:4.** Jaako Hintikka, **"Cogito, Ergo Sum: Inference or Performance?"** *Philosophical Review* 71 (1962): 3-32, reprinted in *Descartes: A Collection of Critical Essays*, edited by Willis Doney (Garden City, New York: Doubleday & Co., 1967), pp. 108-139. Where the term "hoof-in-mouth contradiction" is used herein, Hintikka uses "performatory contradiction." Descartes' statements appear in *Discourse on Method*, Part 4, first three paragraphs, and in *Meditations*, Second Meditation, paragraph 3.

**Ann:5.** Challenges to the logical device of proving something by means of a hoof-in-mouth contradiction have come from various directions. Some scholars point out that the act of asserting something is not, as such, a part of formal logic, since acts are not themselves logic. Thus, as some hold, a hoof-in-mouth contradiction is not a logical contradiction. This challenge is well answered by the logician Arthur Pap. In Pap's language, an act that implicitly asserts a statement, such as that something exists, is called an *ostensive* assertion. Pap is able to show that any supposedly purely logical statement inevitably is lowered in a scale of purity by implicit psychological elements — lowered, indeed, to the same level as the ostensive statement implied by a performance or act. His presentation is readable (*Semantics and Necessary Truth* [New Haven: Yale University Press, 1958], Chapter 9. See Peirce [1:2], 5.340.)

Another attack comes from those who

hold to the "theory of types," wherein the contradictoriness of a hoof-in-mouth contradiction is supposedly removed by separating classes of statements into hierarchical groups and then claiming that statements in a higher group which are about the lower-class statements are therefore privileged and not to be set against conflicting statements in the lower group. But the proponent of the theory of types falls into the same trap against which he warns. See especially Paul Weiss, "The Theory of Types," in *Mind* 37 (1928): 338-348. See also Frederic B. Fitch, "Self-Reference in Philosophy," *Mind* 55 (1946): 64-73. Some remarks of J. L. Mackie are directly to the present point; see his *Truth, Probability and Paradox* (Oxford: At the Clarendon Press, 1973), especially pp. 250-254. Appreciation of Alfred Tarski's defense of hierarchical language appears in Karl Popper's charming "Socratic" dialog in Chapter 14 of *Conjectures and Refutations* [9:21]. Dean Turner presents contrary argument in [5:23]; see index there under "Tarski" and "Gödel." The *reductio ad absurdum* argument form of hoof-in-mouth contradiction should appeal to those who value facts above words as such.

A far-reaching attack is the denial of the principle of noncontradiction itself [Annex:12].

**Ann:6.** Arthur O. Lovejoy, **"The Paradox of the Thinking Behaviorist,"** *Philosophical Review* 31 (1922): 135-147. Rudolf Carnap and Otto Neurath hold to extreme metaphysical behaviorism, which is the theory that mind, thought, consciousness and feeling do not exist except in terms of mere mechanics. See Carnap, "Psychology in Physical Language," Neurath, "Sociology and Physicalism," both in *Logical Positivism*, edited by A. J. Ayer (New York: Free Press, 1959), Chapters 8 and 13 respectively. Both are translated from *Erkenntnis* 2 (1931-32).

**Ann:7.** Brand Blanshard [1:5], pp. 238-241; [9:20], e.g., pp. 146-149 on Wittgenstein, and p. 424 on challenge to laws of logic.

**Ann:8.** See Titus (The Letter of Paul to Titus) 1:12, emphasis added; also Psalms

116:1 in the King James Bible (Catholic 115).

**Ann:9.** Chuang Tzu. Quoted by Christopher Dawson in his *Religion and Culture* [6:25], p. 169n.

**Ann:10.** See Hartshorne [16:18], p. 285.

**Ann: 11.** As to indirect proof of a necessity resulting from the denial of a contradiction, see for instance Irving M. Copi, *Symbolic Logic*, fourth edition (New York: Macmillan Co., 1973), pp. 55-58. In an analysis by truth tables, the pair (i) and (ii) as combined is always false, since either (i) is false or (ii) is false under any condition. That is, the combined statement is false, period—i.e., necessarily false. There is no condition under which the combined statement could be true.

**Ann:12.** The principle of noncontradiction may be stated: "No proposition can be both true and false." The original statement is that of Aristotle, in *Metaphysics* at 1005b-1009a (Book 4, Chapter 4). A selection is reprinted in Ernest Nagel and Richard B. Brandt, *Meaning and Knowledge* (New York: Harcourt, Brace and World, 1965), pp. 184-186. Also see Plato, *Cratylus*, the latter part—an important and neglected work of rock-bottom logic, anticipating Aristotle. Aristotle extends the principle of noncontradiction to include noncontradiction in nature.

Bodhidharma's challenge is quoted in Edward Conze, *Buddhism: Its Essence and Development* (Oxford: Bruno Cassirer, 1951), p. 129. Conze attempts unsuccessfully to justify the ignoring of the principle of noncontradiction; see *Philosophy* (U.K.) 10 (1935): 205-218. Naturally, the principle is presumed in any attempt to refute it, or to refute anything else. See Dale Riepe's critiques of Zen in two articles: *Philosophy of Science* 31 (1964): 71-74 and in *Philosophy and Phenomenological Research* 26 (1966): 434-437. For more denial see Arthur Schopenhauer, *The World as Will and Idea*, Sections 69, 48, 68. Alfred Korzybski has also denied the principle in his *Science and Sanity*, third edition (Lakeville, Connecticut: International Non-Aristotelian Publishing Co., 1948), e.g., pp. xxiv-xxvii. The recent *est* movement of Werner Erhard had roots in

Zen. Positive points of Buddhism and Hinduism are discussed by William Ernest Hocking in *Living Religions and a World Faith* (New York: Macmillan Co., 1940), e.g., pp. 255-259.

For a defense of the principle of non-contradiction see Brand Blanshard, *The Nature of Thought*, [9:9], Volume 2, pp. 252-259 (Sections 35-39) and pp. 411-414, 422-423. See further his *Reason and Analysis* [9:20], Chapter 6, pp. 271-283. See also Blanshard in *Idealistic Studies* 4 (1974): 107-130, at 108-111 and the preceding article by Herbert Garelick at pp. 50-63; see [10:8]. For refutation of the contradiction of considering the world as essentially dialectical, see Karl R. Popper, "What Is Dialectic?", which is Chapter 15 of his *Conjectures and Refutations* [9:21]. Even the mathematical logicians who would render the law of noncontradiction less than fundamental cannot escape its use in their own supposed proofs; see V. J. McGill, "Concerning the Laws of Contradiction and Excluded Middle," *Philosophy of Science* 6 (1939): 196-211. In another connection see Martha Hurst, "Can the Law of Excluded Middle Be Stated without Reference to Time?" *Journal of Philosophy* 31 (1934): 518-525. For a brief treatment see Morris R. Cohen and Ernest Nagel, *An Introduction to Logic and Scientific Method* (New York: Harcourt, Brace & Co., 1934), pp. 181-185.

**Ann:13.** Schweitzer [1:11], p. 280 (208). See generally Schweitzer, *Indian Thought and Its Development* (London: Hodder & Stoughton, 1936), though this work has not pleased some scholars of India such as S. Radhakrishnan.

**Ann:14.** G. K. Chesterton, *St. Thomas Aquinas* (Garden City, New York: Doubleday & Co., 1956), p. 185.

**Ann:15.** When this annex was written, we were not aware of the thorough treatment of performatory contradiction as a source of knowledge presented in *Free Choice: A Self-Referential Argument* by Joseph M. Boyle Jr., Germain Grisez, and Olaf Tollefsen (Notre Dame, Indiana: University of Notre Dame, 1976). Their painstaking arguments come together in their last two chapters. The definitions on

their p. 4 are keys for reading.

**Ann:16.** Herbert Bohnert, "The Semiotic Status of Commands," *Philosophy of Science* 12 (1945): 302-315. Bohnert was neither the first nor the last to think independently of the translatability between imperative and indicative sentences; others have touched on the idea. Compare Ludwig Wittgenstein in his *Tractatus Logico-Philosophicus:* "The first thought in setting up an ethical law of the form 'Thou shalt' is: And what if I do not do it?" [20:20], at 6.422. Morris Cohen and Ernest Nagel were similarly brief in *An Introduction to Logic and Scientific Method* (New York: Harcourt, Brace & Co., 1934), at p. 28. Again, there was Karl Menger in *Reports of a Mathematical Colloquium* (Notre Dame), second series, issue 1, (1939): 53-64. B. F. Skinner later made the same discovery as Bohnert et al.; see *Science and Human Behavior* (New York: Free Press, 1953), pp. 429-430. For a near miss see Charles L. Stevenson, *Ethics and Language* (New Haven: Yale University Press, 1944), p. 24.

The major credit should go to Bohnert for his clear, lengthy exploration in 1945. The others did not pursue the matter. In any event, here are four scholars who, having tangentially anticipated Bohnert, obviously believe a translation such as his to be valid, a belief shared by us. Bohnert notes: "Living organisms are motivated ultimately by situations, and situations are designated by declarative sentences" (p. 303).

Nicholas Rescher objects, in effect, that certain normally permissible logical manipulations (as with the propositional calculus) result, in Bohnert's work of translation between moods, in various inferences which are counterintuitive and therefore suspect (*The Logic of Commands* [New York: Dover Publications, 1966], 41-42; also see pp. 8-10, 72-75). One need not here tarry to deal with Rescher's objections except to note that at one point he does not see in his formulation a problem that involves modal logic. That is, the usually proper translation of an imperative is to the future indicative, not to the present indicative. Rescher's objections may be left to the serious student as an exercise in seeing how the ranked-choice imperative slips through Rescher's net.

**Ann:17.** Bohnert's translation of imperatives into alternate choices in the indicative mood, as to foundations of ethics, has been challenged by the British moral philosopher Richard Merwyn Hare, who points out that the unattractive alternatives require an evaluative idea in order to be seen as unattractive. That is, the introduction of an evaluative idea is circular when one is talking about evaluation in general. This is true, but the entire present book, setting forth as it does a viable basis of evaluation, should take care of this objection. Hare further states that imperative statements in general are not intended as statements of fact—this despite the plain fact (which he sort of acknowledges) that translation of them brings to light the facts that such sentences imply. We find the argument unintelligible. See *The Language of Morals* (Oxford: Clarendon Press, 1952), pp. 7-9 ff. In a 1973 essay, Hare claims that philosophy of religion is "a subject which fastidious philosophers do not like to touch," lest presumably they soil their fingers.

**Ann:18.** Matthew 7:1: Luke 6:37.

**Ann:19.** The result of this chapter is an example of a synthetic *a priori* statement. We have here avoided working with this abstruse concept of Immanuel Kant which, however, might have been used instead. For most students and most purposes, hoof-in-mouth contradictions are pedagogically preferable to handling the Kantian terminology, which requires the juggling and untangling of several abstractions at once, a feat which the great majority of the human race cannot or will not perform.

On the reality of the synthetic *a priori* in general see Blanshard [9:20], notably Chapters 6 and 10. On the fact of the blurring of the synthetic-analytic distinction see Blanshard, *The Nature of Thought*

[9:9], Chapter 30; Arthur Pap, *An Introduction to the Philosophy of Science* (New York: Free Press, 1962), Chapter 5; Willard Van Orman Quine, "Two Dogmas of Empiricism," *Philosophical Review* 60 (1951): 20-43, which is reprinted in his book *From a Logical Point of View* (Harvard University Press, 1953), Chapter 2; Morton G. White, "The Analytic and the Synthetic: An Untenable Dualism," in *John Dewey: Philosopher of Science and Freedom*, edited by Sidney Hook (New York: Dial Press, 1950), pp. 316-330, which is reprinted in *Semantics and the Philosophy of Language*, edited by Leonard Linsky (Urbana: University of Illinois Press, 1953), pp. 272-286; Arthur Pap [Annex:5], Chapter 5.

For statement of Kant's position see Kant and Johann Schulz, *Rezension des zweiten Bandes von Eberhards Philosophischen Magazin* (*Jenaische Allgemeine Literatur-Zeitung*, September 1790, No. 281-284), in *Immanuel Kants Werke* (Berlin: Bruno Cassirer, 1923), Volume 6, pp. 73-117, at p. 106; see also pp. 525-527. Translated by Lewis White Beck in "Can Kant's Synthetic Judgments Be Made Analytic?" *Kant-Studien* (Cologne) 47 (1955/1956): 168-181, at p. 175; reprinted in Robert Paul Wolff, editor, *Kant: A Collection of Critical Essays* (Garden City, New York: Doubleday & Co., 1967), pp. 3-22, at p. 13. See also Kant's *Critique of Pure Reason*, A xv to A xvii, B xviii, B 1 to B 4, A 7 = B 11 ff., A 598 = B 626.

For exposition see "Kant's Theory of Definition," *Philosophical Review* 65 (1956): 179-191, at p. 182; reprinted in Wolff, editor, *Kant: Essays*, pp. 23-36, at p. 26; "On the Meta-Semantics of the Problem of the Synthetic A Priori," *Mind* 66 (1957): 228-232.

When Hazelett was 16, he projected that he might write something significant in ethics during a couple of weeks. His estimate of the elapsed time required to complete his contribution was off by a thousand to one.

# Acknowledgments

WITH DEEP THANKS, the authors acknowledge the searching and careful criticisms of John H. Lavely (Boston University), Rev. Nancy Turner, Joseph V. Dolan, S.J. (Fordham University), Nancy Frankenberry (Dartmouth College), James G. Villa, Randall Jones, Rev. Joseph H. Albrecht, Kenneth Boulding (University of Colorado at Boulder), our publisher Faith Annette Sand, and Charles Hartshorne (University of Texas at Austin). Early versions of portions were helpfully criticized by Ward Edwards (University of Southern California), Kenneth R. Hardy (Brigham Young University), and Michael T. Walton. Hazelett acknowledges a manifold debt to Hartshorne, in whose philosophy class Turner and Hazelett met in 1964. All responsibility for the content remains with the authors.

Hazelett attributes to others whatever literary grace the book may show. He acknowledges with gratitude the contribution that R. William Hazelett has made to the family financial security, thereby affording the personal freedom and time to participate in the present work. He is grateful for the help and inspiration of William Rowland Hopkins, Gabrielle Fischer Baldner, Thomas Billings, Blair Stewart, Paul Dunn, Albert G. Hart, David C. Colander, Truman G. Madsen, Ellis T. Rasmussen, Victor B. Cline, Floyd Centore, and many others.

Special thanks are due to the staffs and benefactors of the following libraries visited personally and repeatedly by the authors: Bailey-Howe Library of the University of Vermont, Michener Library of the University of Northern Colorado, Oberlin College Library, the libraries of the University of Colorado, Penrose Library of the University of Denver, Taylor Library of the Iliff School of Theology, Mugar Library of Boston University, the libraries of the University of Texas at Austin, Lee Library of Brigham Young University, Marriott Library of the University of Utah, Freiberger and Sears Libraries of Case Western Reserve University, Cleveland State University Library, Sterling Memorial Library of Yale University, University of Iowa Libraries, Regenstein Library of the University of Chicago, Baker Memorial Library of Dartmouth University, Pius XII Memorial Library of St. Louis University, Cleveland Public Library, Boston Public Library, New York Public Library, Library of Congress, Durick Library of St. Michael's College and Burnham Memorial Library, both of Colchester, Vermont.

Our thanks go to the following publishers, authors, and syndicates for their generously granted permissions to reprint copyrighted material in this volume. The copyright notices are listed below, arranged alphabetically by authors' names.

**Darrow, Whitney**
Drawing in *The New Yorker.* Copyright © 1980 by The New Yorker Magazine, Inc. Reprinted by permission of the New Yorker Magazine, Inc.

**Dawson, Christopher**
*The Historic Reality of Christian Culture.* Copyright © 1960 by Christopher Dawson. Reprinted by permission of Mrs. Christina Scott.
*Religion and Culture.* Copyright © 1948 by Sheed & Ward Inc. Reprinted by permission of Sheed & Ward Inc.
*Religion and the Rise of Western Culture.* Copyright © 1950 by Sheed & Ward Inc. Reprinted by permission of Sheed & Ward Inc.
*Understanding Europe.* Copyright © 1952 by Sheed & Ward Inc. Reprinted by permission of Sheed & Ward Inc.

**Denton, Michael**
*Evolution: A Theory in Crisis.* Copyright © 1985 by Michael Denton. Reprinted by permission of Burnett Books.

**Donohue, William A.**
"The Social Consequences of the Rights Revolution," *The Intercollegiate Review.* Copyright © 1987 by The Intercollegiate Studies Institute Inc. Reprinted by permission of the Intercollegiate Studies Institute Inc.

**Duncker, Karl**
"On Pleasure, Emotion and Striving. Copyright © 1941 by The University of Buffalo. Reprinted by permission of *Philosophy and Phenomenological Research* and Brown University.

**Forman, Templeton G.**
Cartoon, *Motley's Crew.* Copyright © 1989 by Tribune Media Services. Reprinted by permission of Tribune Media Services.

**Gallagher, John**
Cartoon in *Liberty* (Hagerstown, Maryland), September-October 1979, p. 15. Copyright © 1979 by John Gallagher.

**Harris, Errol**
*Hypothesis and Perception.* Copyright © by George Allen & Unwin Ltd., 1970. Reprinted by permission of Unwin Hyman Ltd.

**Hartshorne, Charles**
*Creative Synthesis and Philosophic Method.* Copyright © 1970 by SCM Press Ltd. Reprinted by permission of SCM Press Ltd., The Open Court Publishing Co., and Charles Hartshorne.
*The Divine Relativity.* Copyright © 1948 by Yale University Press. Reprinted by permission of Yale University Press, and Charles Hartshorne.
*Reality as Social Process.* Copyright © 1953 by The Free Press. Copright © renewed 1981 by Charles Hartshorne. Reprinted by permission of the Free Press (a division of Macmillan Publishing Co. Inc.) and Charles Hartshorne.

**Hayek, Friedrich A.**
*Law, Legislation and Liberty.* Copyright © 1973, 1976, 1979 by F. A. Hayek. *Studies in Philosophy, Politics and Economics.* Copyright © 1967 by F. A. Hayek. Reprinted by permission of International Thomson Publishing Services Ltd. (Routledge), and University of Chicago Press.

**Hilliard, Marion**
*A Woman Doctor Looks at Life and Love.* Copyright © 1957 by Marion Hilliard. An earlier version appeared in *Chatelaine* (Toronto), February 1956. Reprinted by permission of Bantam, Doubleday, Dell Publishing Group Inc.

**Hocking, William Ernest**
*Living Religions and a World Faith* by William Ernest Hocking. Copyright © 1940 by the Macmillan Co.; copyright renewed 1968. Reprinted by permission of the Macmillan Publishing Co., Inc.

**Hoffer, Eric**
*Between the Devil and the Dragon* by Eric Hoffer. Copyright © 1982 by Eric Hoffer. Reprinted by permission of Harper & Row, Publishers, Inc.

**Hoyt, Elizabeth**
"Tiquisate: A Call for a Science of Human Affairs," *Scientific Monthly.* Copyright © 1951 by the American Association for the Advancement of Science. Reprinted by permission of the American Association of the Advancement of Science.

**Kepler, Johannes**
In "Johannes Kepler: A Case Study on the Interaction of Science, Metaphysics, and Theology," translated by Gerald Holton, The *Philosophical Forum.* Copyright © 1956 by The Philosophical Forum Inc.

**Jessop, T. E.**
*The Christian Morality.* Copyright © 1960 by Epworth Press. Reprinted by permission of Epworth Press.

**Larson, Gary**
Cartoon, *The Far Side.* Copyright © 1986 by Universal Press Syndicate. Reprinted by permission of Universal Press Syndicate.

**Laubach, Frank C.**
*Thirty Years with the Silent Billion.* Copyright © 1960 by Frank C. Laubach. Reprinted by permission of Fleming H. Revell Co.

**Lewis, Clarence Irving**
*An Analysis of Knowledge and Valuation.* Copyright © 1946 by Open Court Publishing Co. Reprinted

# Index

Ellipses in quotations have been omitted in the interest of smooth reading. Assurance is given that meanings have not been altered by selective quotation.

# About the Authors

Richard Hazelett has pursued philosophy as a 50-year avocation. He is a research engineer in Hazelett Strip-Casting Corporation, Colchester, Vermont. Hazelett has been granted ten U.S. patents and many foreign ones on machinery for the continuous casting of metals. He was project engineer for the prototype of modern high-speed zipper manufacturing machines. He was co-developer of the first molybdenum-disulfide lubricating pastes, now made by Dow Corning. He has published in economic stability, political representation, mechanical engineering, and the foundations of geometry. He was born in Cleveland, Ohio, and graduated from Oberlin College. He received master's degrees from the University of Texas and Boston University.

**FRANK and ERNEST®**     by Bob Thaves     September 10, 1986

Dean Turner was born in Tyrone, Oklahoma, and was raised in Stratford, Texas. He now teaches in the University of Northern Colorado at Greeley and is a minister in the Disciples of Christ Church, as is also his wife Nancy. He received a B.A. degree from the Centro de Estudios Universitarios in Mexico, and the Ph.D. degree from the University of Texas. He served in the U.S. Army in the Korean War and was director of ocean traffic for Otaru Port, Hokkaido, Japan. The author or co-author of seven books, he has given over three hundred television, radio, and after-dinner addresses. His writings have been mostly in the fields of ethics, religion, education, and philosophy of science. He taught in Mexico, the University of Maryland, the Azores, Labrador, Newfoundland, Greenland, and Bermuda. He also taught in Sullins Women's College. He has received numerous Outstanding Teacher awards. He has a son, Taos, and a daughter, Summer.

If you would like to network with other readers of this book, send your name and address to

Malletts Bay Associates
Box 8
Colchester, Vermont 05446, U.S.A.

Please enclose a self-addressed, stamped envelope. Readers in foreign countries should include a postal international reply coupon instead of the stamp.

Contacts are at the risk solely of the contacting persons. No warranty of the quality of the persons listed is, or can be, made. Precautions that are normal in meeting or dealing with strangers are advisable. The publisher includes this invitation as a service to Malletts Bay Associates and can assume no responsibility.

Typography in Palatino by Susan Ball, Burlington, Vermont
Printed by Thomson-Shore, Dexter, Michigan

*In one way or another all people need and seek happiness.*

*Throughout the ages philosophers have attempted to define happiness, to distinguish between wise and unwise ways of pursuing it, and to determine what the conditions are that make it possible and enduring.*

*Both empirically and creatively, **Benevolent Living** examines every major aspect of the problem of happiness — the economics, politics, sociology, psychology, esthetics and ethics of the sense of well-being and joy in being alive.*

*This work not only talks of achieving a comprehensive philosophy of happiness and responsibility but actually develops one that can be represented as solid and of distinct value in the face of sophisticated criticism.*

*The authors uniquely incorporate clever cartoons in their study of mirth, hedonism, and morality. They address the most basic, relevant questions about the kind of life we should live in a world that seems bent upon self-destruction. Eric Hoffer declared, "We are warned not to waste our time, but we are brought up to waste our lives." Seeing this as a challenge, the authors respond by establishing ethical principles and attitudes that can create the motivation for widespread benevolent behavior.*